Baraka Books

ober 2, 2009

Marjorie and Maxwell Ward,
69 Westbrook Drive,
Edmonton AB T6J 2C8

Re: *Joseph-Elzéar Bernier, Champion of Canadian Arctic Sovereignty*

Dear Mr. and Mrs. Ward:

On behalf of Baraka Books, I would like to thank you very much for financially supporting the publication of the enclosed book on Joseph-Elzéar Bernier by Marjolaine Saint-Pierre and translated by William Barr of the Arctic Institute of North America. Without your generous support and that of the others in the late Doug Matheson's "team," this book might never have appeared.

Warmest regards,

Robin Philpot

Baraka Books
6977, rue Lacroix
Montréal, Québec
H4E 2V4

answered Nov. 16/09

JOSEPH-ELZÉAR BERNIER

Marjolaine Saint-Pierre

JOSEPH-ELZÉAR BERNIER
CHAMPION OF CANADIAN ARCTIC SOVEREIGNTY

1852-1934

Best regards,
Marjolaine
Saint-Pierre

Translated by
William Barr

To Max & Marjorie,
With sincere thanks.
Bill Barr

Baraka
Books

Arctic Institute of North America
1945

Baraka Books is grateful for the generous support of the Arctic Institute of North America in the publication of this book.

Cover: Joseph-Elzéar Bernier, collection Musée maritime du Québec à l'Islet

Legal Deposit—3rd quarter 2009
Bibliothèque et Archives nationales du Québec
Library and Archives Canada

ISBN 978-0-9812405-1-0 (Paperback)
ISBN 978-0-9812405-4-1 (Hardcover)

Translation and Foreword by William Barr
Design: Folio infographie
Editing: Robin Philpot

Originally published as *Joseph-Elzéar Bernier, Capitaine et coureur des mers* by Éditions du Septentrion, Québec, 2005

6977, rue Lacroix
Montréal, Québec
H4E 2V4
Telephone: 514-808-8504
info@barakabooks.com
www.barakabooks.com

Trade Distribution & Returns
LitDistCo orders@litdistco.ca

C/o 100 Armstrong Ave.
Georgetown, ON
L7G 5S4
Ph: 1-800-591-6250
Fax: 1-800-591-6251

Dedicated to the memory of
Douglas (Doug) Matheson,
whose passion for the North was surpassed
only by his passion for flying.

Table of contents

List of maps

List of illustrations

Acknowledgements

I wish very much to thank the many people who have believed in this book and who have given me a helping hand. Their enthusiasm and generosity have nurtured my years of work:

- my husband, Lynn Ernest Fournier, television producer, who collaborated in the research and who produced the maps, the illustrations and the photos;
- my mother, Rita Nadeau, who never ceases to demonstrate that her three daughters are the apple of her eye;
- Gaston Deschênes, historian who agreed to sponsor my project;
- Jeanne Coudé and Simone Dion of Lévis;
- Angèle Gagnon, Martin Caron and the staff of the Musée maritime du Québec (Musée Bernier) in L'Islet-sur-Mer;
- Magdeleine Bourget, Michelle Audet, Suzanne and Andrée Normandeau, descendants of Captain Bernier's adopted daughter, Elmina Caron;
- Louis Terrien, the nephew of Alma Lemieux, and his wife, Carol;
- Benoît Robitaille, Québec geographer;
- Cyril Bernier, genealogist and historian, and also the *Association des Bernier d'Amérique*;
- Suzanne Boucher, library technician at the Municipal Library in Saint-Laurent;
- and the personnel of the Archives nationales du Québec, the Library and Archives of Canada and the Archives du Séminaire de Trois-Rivières.

A solitary archival centre refused me access to documents pertaining to Captain Bernier, namely that of the Collège de Lévis. Its curator repeatedly refused my requests to study the important Bernier collection located there. I owe it to myself to point this out. Captain Bernier's manuscripts, photos and possessions are a testimony to the man himself and to his times. They are part of our heritage and should be accessible to all.

Baraka Books and William Barr also join me in thanking the following people for their generous financial contributions towards publication of this English edition: the late Douglas and Margaret Matheson, Stanley and Loraine Milner, Max and Marjorie Ward, Samuel and Nancy Lieberman, Howard Irving, Donald and Marion Wheaton, Ross and Linda McBain, Sandy and Cécile Mactaggart, and J. Douglas and Katherine Matheson, all of Edmonton, Alberta, and John Parker of North Saanich, British Columbia.

Baraka Books wishes to thank William Barr, Senior Research Associate at the Arctic Institute of North America, for taking the initiative to translate Marjolaine Saint-Pierre's biography of Joseph-Elzéar Bernier. We are also very grateful for the unwavering support of the Arctic Institute of North America. Without the combined efforts of William Barr and the Arctic Institute, this book might never have been published in English.

Foreword

by William Barr, translator and Senior Research Associate at the Arctic Institute of North America, University of Calgary

On 31 July 1880, after considerable debate in both Ottawa and Westminster, the British government issued an Order-in-Council, the intent of which (far from clear from its wording) was that the Arctic Islands lying north of the Canadian mainland should be transferred from Britain to Canada. The arctic mainland, as part of Rupert's Land and the Northwestern Territories, had already been acquired by Canada from the Hudson's Bay Company on 15 July 1870. The true intent of the 1880 Order-in-Council was made clear only on 2 October 1895 when the Canadian government issued an Order-in-Council to constitute the Districts of Ungava, Mackenzie, Franklin, and Yukon, the District of Franklin comprising the Arctic Islands, plus Melville and Boothia peninsulas.

Prior to that date (and after the 1880 transfer) there had been several incursions by foreign expeditions into the Arctic Islands, without Canadian permission having been requested. Thus during the first International Polar Year the Germans established a station at Kingua Fiord in Baffin Island (1882-83) while the United States occupied a station at Lady Franklin Bay, Baffin Island (1881-83). But more serious infringements on Canadian arctic sovereignty were to follow. In 1898-1902 the American Robert E. Peary, in an attempt to reach the North Pole, operated from a base at Fort Conger on Ellesmere Island, and his Inughuit assistants (from Northwest Greenland) made serious inroads into the muskox population of Ellesmere Island to supply Peary's dog-teams with meat. But an even more serious challenge to Canadian sovereignty came from the Norwegian, Otto Sverdrup. From wintering bases in Rice Strait, Harbour Fiord, and Goose Fiord (all on Ellesmere Island) he and his men explored much of southern and western Ellesmere Island, Axel Heiberg Island, and Amund and Ellef Rignes islands, raising the Norwegian flag and claiming the islands they had discovered for Norway. And even as the Canadian government was contemplating taking steps to counter such incursions, a further Norwegian expedition, that of Roald Amundsen, had established itself at Gjoa Haven on King William Island, during its successful transit (1903-1906) of the Northwest Passage, although Amundsen would not make any overt claims on behalf of Norway.

The Canadian government was also concerned about the activities of whalers, especially those from Britain, who had been pursuing whales in Lancaster Sound and in the fiords of eastern Baffin Island since as early as

1820. Scottish whalers had also been operating from shore-stations such as Kekerten and Blacklead Island in Cumberland Sound since as early as 1857.

The steps taken by the Canadian Government to reinforce Canadian sovereignty over the Arctic Islands will always be linked to the name of a remarkable Québecois ship captain, Joseph-Elzéar Bernier. Through his persistent badgering he had elicited from Sir Wilfrid Laurier's government the promise of a ship and support (to be matched from public subscription) for an attempt at reaching the North Pole. He even thought that this was still to be his objective when he was dispatched to Germany in 1904 to take delivery of the ice-strengthened ship, the *Gauss* (quickly renamed *Arctic*). But in fact he was then directed by the Canadian government to proceed in the *Arctic* to Cape Fullerton, in northwestern Hudson Bay, where he was to winter as second-in-command to Inspector J.D. Moodie, R.N.W.M.P., to reprovision the police post there, and in 1905 to search for further suitable locations for police posts in Hudson Strait and the Eastern Arctic. But in 1906-07 he redirected his considerable energies from his quest for the North Pole to buttressing Canadian sovereignty over the Arctic Islands, this time in sole of command of an expedition on board the *Arctic*. He wintered at Albert Harbour in Pond Inlet, Baffin Island and raised the Canadian flag at various locations, including on Bylot Island, Baffin Island, and Melville Island. He also obliged the few whalers whom he encountered to purchase licences. Bernier repeated the process in 1908-09 when he wintered at Winter Harbour, Melville Island and took possession of Banks and Victoria islands and in 1910-1911 when the *Arctic* wintered at Arctic Bay, Baffin Island, and his men completed the mapping of the northwestern coasts of that island.

Marjolaine Saint-Pierre's excellent biography covers in detail these, the best-known expeditions of Bernier's career, but it embraces vastly more of the remarkable career of this truly unique Canadian. She traces his deep roots in L'Islet-sur-Mer, and his eventful sea-going career. In command of his own ship at the age of 17, he made his name as a particularly competent "delivery captain," delivering over 44 newly-built sailing ships from Québec to Britain, usually in record times. Nor did his arctic career end with his expeditions aimed at establishing Canadian arctic sovereignty. In 1912-13 he was back in Pond Inlet on board the schooner the *Minnie Maud*, trading with the Inuit. In 1914-15 and 1916-17, he was again in Pond Inlet trading from the trading post that he named Berniera, which was supplied by his steamer, the *Guide*. And for four seasons (1922-25) he commanded his old ship, the *Arctic*, on the government's Eastern Arctic Patrol, aimed at providing basic medical services for the Inuit, establishing and resupplying RCMP detachments, transporting scientists to their field areas, and generally reinforcing a Canadian presence in the Arctic Islands.

Publication of this English translation of Marjolaine Saint-Pierre's book on this the centennial of the return of Bernier from what was in many ways the most important expedition of his career, is very appropriate. In view of the present official concerns over Canadian arctic sovereignty (although these are directed more to marine areas, rather than the land), it is very important that the role played by this immensely patriotic, and larger-than-life Canadian, in safeguarding Canada's claim to the Arctic Islands, should become better known in English-speaking Canada.

William Barr

Introduction

"The fact of coming into the world gives rise to a question to which one must reply."

ERICH FROMM[1]

IF I LOVE HEROES it is because they experience the full urgent need to respond to that terrifying question: How can I give meaning to my life?

Their journeys inspire me profoundly. They speak to me of passions, dreams, determination, love, failures, challenges to be met and missions to be accomplished.

This certainly applies to the life of the youngest captain in our history, Joseph-Elzéar Bernier, a "p'tit gars" from Québec, who succeeded in finding his right course and in making his mark on his time.

This inquisitive, independent spirit, raised in the coastal village of L'Islet-sur-Mer, inherited his devouring passion for the sea and ships from the men in his family, all sea-going adventurers who possessed a remarkable knowledge of the currents, the channels, the topography and the reefs of the mighty St. Lawrence as well as of navigation on the high seas.

Bernier understood at a very early age that he was meant to follow in their footsteps and that his strong personality and considerable physical energy were his driving forces. Nothing could or would keep him from achieving his goal of becoming a great master mariner.

With the decline of the era of the large sailing vessels, captain Bernier's passion for the sea extended to the Far North. This man of action contrived for himself a fabulous dream: to conquer the North Pole in the name of Canada. Along the way he discovered instead a most important political mission: that of giving his country an arctic frontier.

I have devoted more than four years to the research, interviews and preparation of this biography. To tell the truth, the years count for little when one is passionately motivated and is ensnared by a personality as fascinating as Bernier. I was determined to discover Joseph-Elzéar, the man behind the Bernier phenomenon, the sometimes controversial individual, one certainly "larger than life." My quest proved to be a true personal mission to restore to us this hero whom our collective memory has unfortunately forgotten.

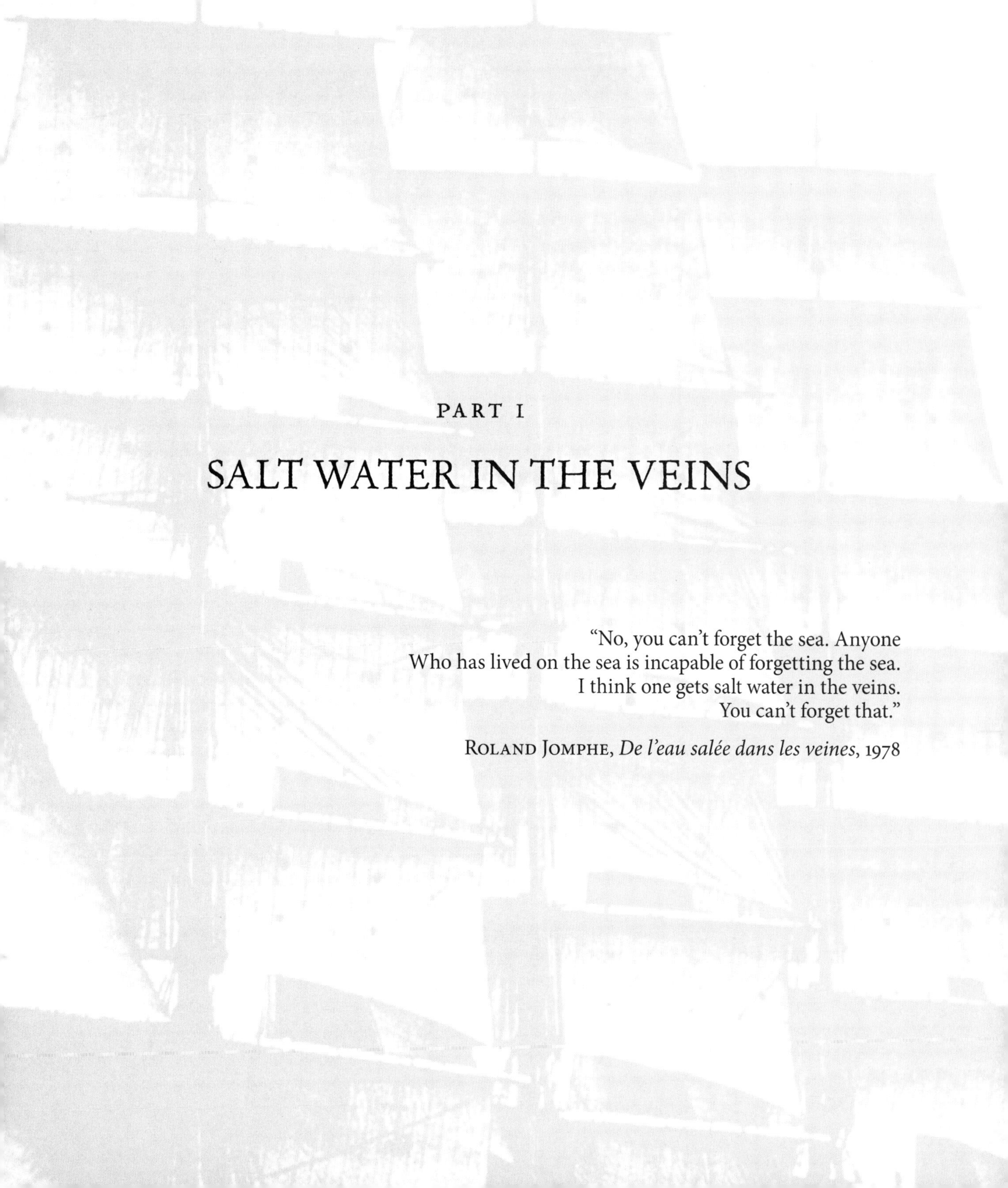

PART I

SALT WATER IN THE VEINS

"No, you can't forget the sea. Anyone
Who has lived on the sea is incapable of forgetting the sea.
I think one gets salt water in the veins.
You can't forget that."

ROLAND JOMPHE, *De l'eau salée dans les veines*, 1978

CHAPTER I

His ancestors

"To know the origins and the individuals who comprise a family tree constitutes a powerful stimulus and an innate desire to investigate our human and spiritual potential."

Cyril Bernier, October 2001.

JOSEPH-ELZÉAR BERNIER took an interest in his own genealogy at quite an early age, not only because he was a curious, intelligent person who was keen on defining his heritage, but also because he realized that he had an obligation to ensure the continuity of those who had built his country by transmitting their story of courage and endurance to future generations.

In the prologue to his memoirs[1] he stresses the motto *Je me souviens* featured on Québec's coat-of-arms in order to emphasize that French Canadians of that period should remember since "their present is solidly anchored in the past, and the traditions passed down by their ancestors are a source of inspiration for their future dreams."

Guided by the oral traditions of his family, Joseph-Elzéar therefore undertook genealogical searches which disclosed his origins. He thus discovered that the first person in his paternal line to make the difficult crossing from the old continent to the New World was Jacques Bernier (1633-1713), also known as Jean de Paris. What surprised him initially was that the man who was to become the ancestor of a remarkable line of seafarers had neither the passion for the sea nor the sea-legs of the first colonists who came from French provinces oriented towards the Atlantic such as Normandy, Brittany, Aunis or Poitou. Jacques Bernier was perhaps not a sailor "by blood," Joseph-Elzéar noted, but "he certainly possessed a leaning to adventure and sufficient courage to face migrating to New France."[2]

Jacques, the son of Yves Bernier, barrister or judge in the High Court in Paris, and of Michelle Trevilet or Treuillet, was born on 16 November 1633 in the parish of Saint-Germain-l'Auxerrois.[3] Being born into a privileged environment probably gave him access to some schooling, since he knew how to count and to sign his name.

The 28-year-old Parisian entered the harbour of Québec on 13 October 1651 on board the *Saint-Joseph*, a ship of 300 tons, in the company of his patron Jean de Lauson.[4] This was indeed a beneficial relationship since after 1635 the Sieur de Lauson was also director of the Compagnie des Cent-Associés, and a firm friend of the Jesuits.

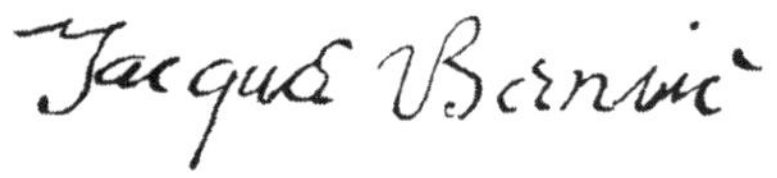

Archival documents reveal that the ancestor, Jacques Bernier, alias Jean de Paris, was a resourceful fellow with a good business sense.

A few years later:

> On 23 July 1656, all the banns having been read and all legitimate requirements having been met, I, Jérôme Lalemant, as curate of this parish, solemnly married Jacques Bernier, son of Yves Bernier and Michelle Treuillet of the parish of Saint-Germain de l'Auxerrois in Paris, and Antoinette Grenier, daughter of Claude Grenier and Catherine (?) of the parish of Saint-Laurent in Paris, this in the home of the Governor and in the presence of Messire Jean de Lauzon, Governor, and of the Sieur d'Auteuil.[5]

The fact that this marriage was celebrated in the home of the Governor, rather than in the church, as was then customary, proves that the first Bernier to establish himself in the French colony was a cut above the other poor colonists seeking a better life.

Little is known about his wife, Antoinette Grenier (1635-1713), who also came from Paris.[6] It is impossible to attest that she was betrothed to Jacques Bernier before she left France. She had probably arrived in New France only shortly before her marriage, in the summer of 1656. She lacked her husband's education. She could neither read nor write, and signed the notarized marriage deeds with an "X".

Captain Bernier took pride in associating her with the *filles du roi*, orphans, widows or daughters of impoverished parents, who were under the protection of the King of France. Even though Antoinette's mother's name does not appear on her marriage certificate, this does not mean that she was a *fille du roi* or an orphan. Did Joseph-Elzéar possess private documents confirming that his ancestor's chosen one was one of those courageous young girls selected by the Church or the State to populate Nouvelle-France? He does not mention any such proof in his memoirs, but he appears so certain of this fact that he dwells at length on the subject. Among other things, he states:

> They (the *filles du roi*) were sent out to Quebec, under the care of the Ursuline nuns. On arrival they were distributed among the bachelor colonists [... to whom thereby] many privileges became available, and their brides were dowered by the King. The bride of Jacques Bernier brought him 25 *écus* (about $12.50 or two and a half guineas face value, but much more in purchasing value of the day), and this sum was presented to the couple by Governor de Lauzon.[7]

However, Antoinette Grenier's name is not to be found among those of the 770 women listed in Yves

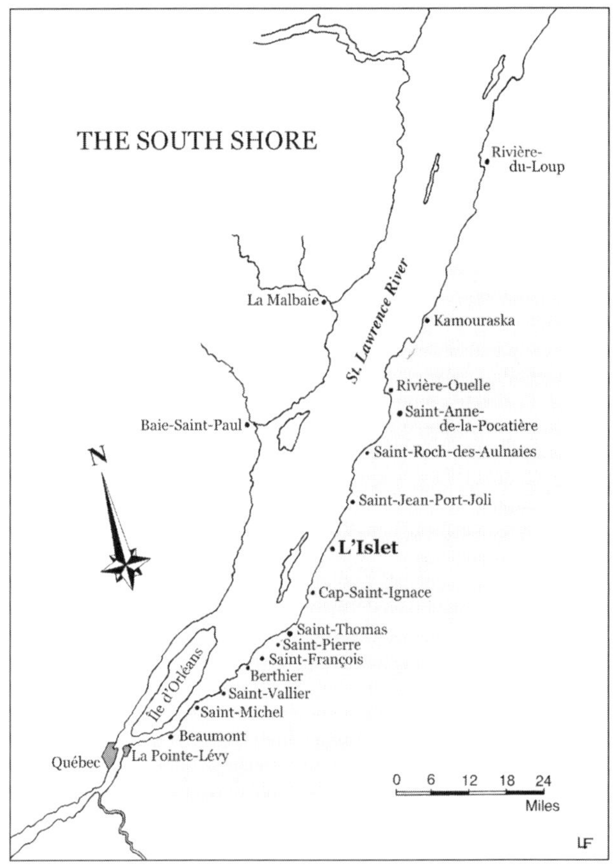

Regional map listing the parishes of the South Shore around the middle of the 18th century.

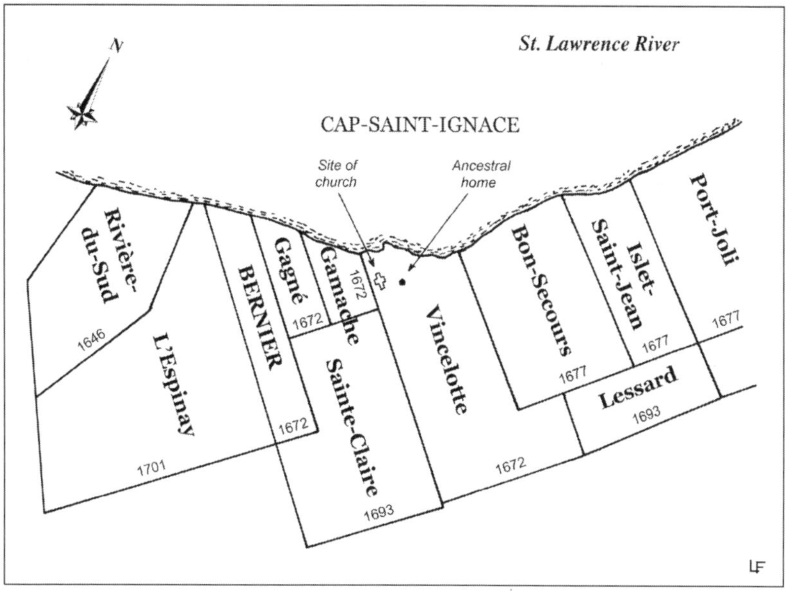

Some seigneuries on the South Shore with their dates of concession.
Note the location of the Bernier ancestral home at Cap-Saint-Ignace.

Landry's important demographic study. The latter defines the *filles du roi* as "immigrant girls or widows who came to Canada between 1663 and 1673 inclusive and who had presumably benefited by royal assistance, either in terms of their travel or of becoming established, or both."[8] Antoinette was already in the country by 1656, seven years before the first contingent of these "selected" women arrived.

In October 1656 Jacques Bernier installed his new bride on the Île d'Orléans on a farm he had leased, located at Saint-Pierre (in the present parish of Sainte-Pétronille) on the fief of the seigneuresse de Beaulieu, Éléonore de Grandmaison (1622-1692). Île d'Orléans is the long delta-like island located just downstream from Québec City where the St. Lawrence widens and becomes the estuary. Over the years the enterprising farmer from Paris became a landed proprietor and considerably increased his holdings. According to the 1666 census he owned 25 arpents of land, eight head of cattle and had three employees: Gilles Gaudreau, a nephew and Guillaume Ferté.

With the passage of time Jacques realized that Île d'Orléans, only 19.5 miles long and 5.5 miles wide, was really too restricted to support all the new arrivals as well as his own family, which was growing rapidly, and sought to establish elsewhere in New France. Everything pointed to the fact that he should not plunge deep into the interior, but rather establish himself along the St. Lawrence River, the vital artery of the small French colony in America.

On 1 April 1673 Jacques Bernier became the first colonist at Cap-Saint-Ignace, officially taking possession of a property measuring nine arpents (540 metres) along the river front and 40 arpents deep (2400 metres); it had been granted to him by Geneviève Chavigny de Berchereau, Seigneuresse de Vincelotte[9] two months before.

His first house at Cap-Saint-Ignace was located on the banks of the St. Lawrence. It undoubtedly resembled all

The monument erected by the Association of Berniers in America to celebrate the tricentennial of the Berniers' arrival in Canada. It is located on the ancestral lot at Cap-Saint-Ignace. [Courtesy Cyril Bernier]

the other log cabins that the colonists built as a temporary solution while they cleared their land. Then of necessity and over the years this temporary residence was replaced by a more imposing, permanent abode.

The Berniers' ancestral home at Cap-Saint-Ignace was spacious enough to accommodate about 30 people and it served as chapel and presbytery for the Catholic population until 1683, at which time Monseigneur de Laval decided to elevate the seigneurie of Vincelotte into a parish. This dwelling no longer exists. But Captain Bernier used to say that he had seen the stones of its massive foundations at low tide. It was probably in this house that Jacques and Antoinette died in 1713, five months apart, after living together for 57 years.

In thus turning to the past Joseph-Elzéar Bernier undoubtedly realized that his love for the sea, inherited from his own parents, had its roots in the view his ancestors had enjoyed of the great river, the sole major communications route in New France.

Life ebbed and flowed to the rhythm of the tides. The entire lives of these pioneers, homesteaders and farmers derived from the advantages offered by this "living" route. Without it, and without the possibility of using a boat for transport and for buying merchandise, Joseph-Elzéar's ancestor Jacques Bernier might perhaps have not become a prosperous merchant, a well-to-do landowner (in 1703 he owned 12 properties between Montmagny and L'Islet), and the Seigneur of the fief of Saint-Joseph, known as Pointe-aux-Foins, in 1683.

For Jacques Bernier and Antoine Grenier the gamble had paid off. Emigrating to New France had been worthwhile. They left an impressive inheritance to their eleven children:

1. Noëlle (1657-1666)
2. Pierre (1659-1741)—the eldest son, inheriting half the seigneurie of Pointe-aux-Foins (his brothers Jean-Baptiste and Philippe inherited the other half); married Françoise Boulé; progenitor of Berniers with surnames Basile and Rigaud.
3. Marie-Michelle (1660- ?)
4. Charles (1662-1731)—husband of Marie-Anne Lemieux and ancestor of Berniers with surnames Clément, Polite, Lafeuille, Charlotte and Belone, i.e. 56% of the Berniers now in North America.
5. Jacques (1664-1702)
6. Jean-Baptiste (1666-1717)—married Geneviève Caron; the first Bernier to embrace the career of seaman and navigator.
7. Élisabeth (1668-1744)
8. Geneviève (1670- ?)
9. Philippe (1673-1750)—husband of Ursule Caron and progenitor of the Berniers with surnames Verbois, Desilets, and Mimi-Lambert.
10. Ignace (1675-1678).
11. Antoinette (1678- ?)[10]

Genealogical table of Captain Joseph-Elzéar Brenier (paternal line)[11]

Yves Bernier and Michèle Treuillet
m. Saint-Germain-l'Auxerrois, Paris, 1631

Jaques Bernier, alias Jean de Paris and Antoinette Grenier
(Claude and Marie-Catherine?)
m. at the home of the Governor of Québec, 23 July 1656

Charles Bernier and Marie-Anne Lemieux
(Guillaume and Élisabeth Langlois)
m. at Cap-Saint-Ignace, 25 October 1694

Charles-Alexandre Bernier and Marie-Geneviève Bélanger
(Pierre-Paul and Geneviève Lessard)
m. at L'Islet-sur-Mer, 2 May 1740

Charles Bernier and Marie-Josephte Tondreau
(François and Josèphe Caron)
m. at L'Islet-sur-Mer, 17 February 1770

Jean-Baptiste Bernier and Marie-Geneviève LeBourdais,
alias Lapierre
(Jean-Baptiste and Geneviève-Victoire Panet)
m. at L'Islet-sur-Mer, 8 January 1811

Thomas Bernier and Henriette-Célina Paradis
(Étienne and Olivette Chamberland)
m. at Saint-Roch de Québec, 19 November 1850

Joseph-Elzéar (1852-1934), Joseph-Alfred (1853 ?),
Marie-Henriette Émilie (1859 - ?), Thomas-Delphis-Marie
(also known as Thomas-Philippe (1861-1863), Augustina (1864 -?),
Marie-Léda Justine (1865-1872) and an unnamed child (1870).

CHAPTER 2

L'Islet-sur-Mer

JOSEPH-ELZÉAR BERNIER's family tree reveals that the Christian name of the first of his paternal line to settle in the parish of L'Islet-sur-Mer, formed by the seigneuries of Bon-Secours and Islet-Saint-Jean, was Charles-Alexandre (1712-1770) and that he married Marie-Geneviève Bélanger (1726 - ?) on 2 May 1740. He chose this small town, named after the islet (l'îlette) formerly surrounded by water at high spring tides, because he received a plot of 10 arpents of land as a wedding gift the year before his marriage from his father-in-law, Pierre-Paul Bélanger, seigneur of part of the fief of Bon-Secours. Indeed documents reveal that three other Berniers were already copyholders in the seigneurie of Bon-Secours by 1739 and that their lands were located along the shores of the St. Lawrence in the first *rang*, west of the village of L'Islet.

Their early years were certainly difficult for the young married couple. Clearing and cultivating their land demanded considerable, slow, toilsome manual labour. Despite everything Charles-Alexandre and Marie-Geneviève persevered and accepted their daily life, which was no different from that of their parents or their friends in L'Islet. Since they knew nothing else but this existence, revolving around work, prayer, family and the subsistence of their six children, they were no doubt, quite happy with their fate… at least until 1759… "the year of the British!"

Their house, their stocks of grain, their harvest and the few possessions that they had amassed by the sweat of their brows were probably looted and burned with the arrival of the British.[1] Few families between Kamouraska and Québec were spared by the campaign of terror then systematically waged by the red-uniformed enemy under Wolfe's command!

Under the British régime the Bernier household did the same as the other inhabitants of this agricultural Côte-du-Sud who decided not to emigrate to France: they rolled up their sleeves and started again.

Charles-Alexandre's and Marie-Geneviève's second home was built on the former foundations of their first house, as was then the custom. The latter is recognized as being the "ancestral home" of the Berniers in L'Islet-sur-Mer. This building has disappeared but two images of it exist. Geographer Yolande Dorion-Robitaille[2] has reproduced a photograph of the rear of an old house, identifying it simply as "the first house of the Bernier family in L'Islet, built in 1748." This date seems too early for a building that probably postdates the ravages of the British. A photo also exists in the *Archives nationales du Québec*, dating from the 1920s and commemorating the visit by Captain Bernier and his second wife, Alma Lemieux, to his native village. This photo reveals little of its actual appearance. However, judging by the architectural style that then predominated in the region, it may

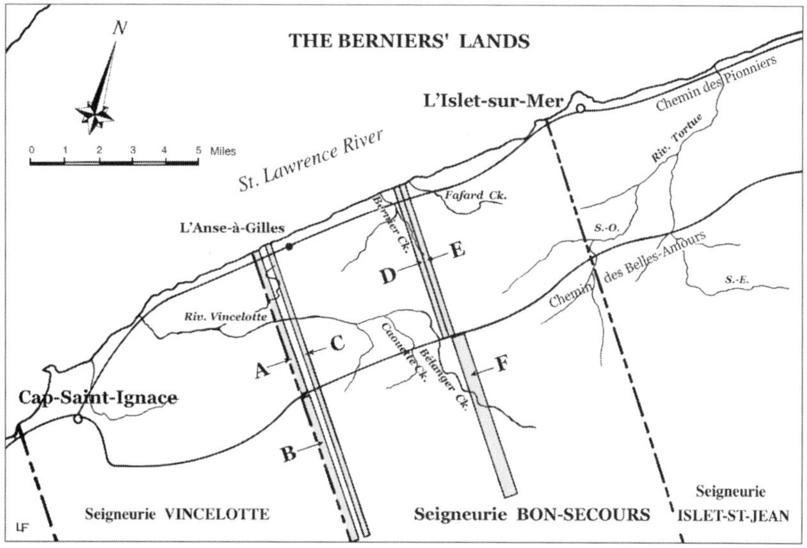

A: Jean Bernier	(3 X 42)	**D**: Louis Bernier	(2 X 42)
B: Jean Bernier	(3 X 42) [*in arpents*]	**E**: Joseph Bernier	(2 X 42) [*in arpents*]
C: Charles Bernier	(3 X 84)	F: Joseph Bernier	(3 X 42)

Locations and subdivisions of the lands of the first Berniers at L'Islet-sur-Mer in the seigneurie of Bon-Secours, around 1739.

possibly resemble the stone house built by François Guyon in 1681. The Berniers may have copied the domestic architecture with which they were already familiar.

With the passage of time life in the Catholic parishes of the Côte-du-Sud resumed the rhythm of the seasons and the harvests. For the Berniers and their fellow-countrymen, the political or military affairs of their country must have seemed very remote and certainly less concrete than their land, their home, their family, their church, and the sea.

Over the years the inhabitants of the county of Devon learned to adapt to their status which was no longer that of a Frenchman. Their eyes turned more frequently to the river, curious to observe the numerous ships plying between the British Isles and their colony. With the increase in sea-going traffic, matters of the sea increasingly occupied this rural community. The L'Isletains built their own boats and used them for fishing, or to go to the big city of Québec to sell the produce of their harvests and to bring back all they needed. "The father at the helm, the mother in the galley, and the children working as sailors, they would make sail and set a course for Québec."[3]

It was only a matter of time before the passing British sailing ships seduced some of the young men into turning their backs on the occupation of farmer and into risking adventuring on the open sea. Moreover Captain Joseph-Elzéar Bernier was convinced that the wide expanses of the sea necessarily widen the vision of a man who is bold, curious and enterprising and that they inspire in him "that divine restlessness" as he was wont to say, a divine restlessness that leads to great explorations and that ensures the evolution of the world and man's progress.

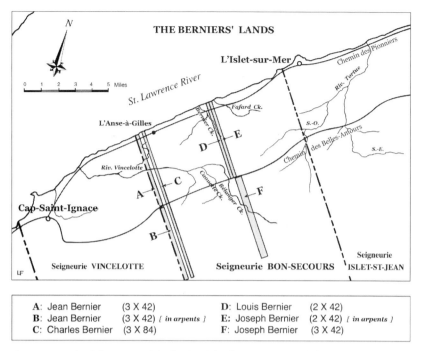

The ancestral home of the Berniers at L'Islet-sur-Mer.
[Robitaille Collection, *North/Nord,* 1978]

Thus it was for his paternal grandfather, Jean-Baptiste (1786-1868), the ninth child in a family of 10, who is remembered as a fearless seaman and an intrepid master mariner, in love with the sea. Perhaps he was inspired by Charles Bénoni,[4] 10 years his elder, who was a pilot on the river. This was the assumption of his grandson, who always had great admiration for these ancestral sea-going adventurers, who possessed a remarkable knowledge of the currents, the channels, the topography and the reefs of the St. Lawrence, as well as of navigation on the high seas. "They were fit to go foreign," he would say of them. They were qualified to command the large sailing vessels and to sail them in any seas in the world:

> My grandfather, Jean-Baptiste Bernier, became a shipmaster, a *capitaine au long cours,* and voyaged much to Europe, to New England and other Atlantic ports, and to the Gulf of Mexico; but most of his voyages were to the West Indies. This was the heyday of the sailing-ship trade between Quebec and the West Indies, a day to which many of the wealthiest families of Canada owe the foundation of their wealth.[5]

In 1828, while returning from one of his numerous voyages to Barbados or Jamaica, the ship which Jean-Baptiste then commanded, *La Capricieuse,* a brigantine of 120 tons, built in the naval shipyards in Québec, encountered a severe storm and was wrecked on the eastern tip of Anticosti Island. The ship and her cargo of molasses and rum were a total loss, whereas Providence spared the captain and his eight men who managed to make it ashore. These fine men, left to their own devices on an uninhabited island right in the middle of the St. Lawrence, managed to survive the six long months of winter, until a schooner rescued them and took them to Gaspé. It took them a further month to get back home.

> This harrowing experience led my grandfather to reduce the length and frequency of his voyages and, a few years later, when he was offered the Pointe-Platon light at Lotbinière, on the St. Lawrence forty miles above Quebec, he accepted. But in 1833 when the cholera epidemic was at

Captain Bernier and friends in front of what was said to be the "ancestral home" of the Berniers at L'Islet-sur-Mer. His second wife, Alma Lemieux, is standing in front of him.
[Photographer unknown, ANQ, P188-D1-P44]

François Guyon's house, now located at 176 chemin des Pionniers Est in L'Islet-sur-Mer. [Photo: Lynn Fournier]

> its worst among the Irish immigrants landed at Grosse-Isle, thirty miles below Quebec, he left his light to become master of a Government ship plying between Quebec and Grosse-Isle. After some years of Government river service, he returned to the open sea and sailed many vessels. His final retirement was in 1866, at the age of eighty.[6]

This man, who had commanded the first light-ship on the river, had married Marie-Geneviève LeBourdais, alias Lapierre (1788-1873) on 8 January 1811, in the parish church at L'Islet.

Captain Bernier contacted his cousin, Mother Saint-Alexis[7] for details concerning this grandmother. She replied on 6 June:

> Dear Elzéar,
>
> I hasten to respond to your request for the genealogy of our dear family. Our paternal grandmother was the daughter of Dr. Jean-Baptiste LeBourdais of Paris and Dame Geneviève Panet, sister of Mgr. Bernard-Claude Panet, Archbishop of Québec, of Abbé Jacques Panet, parish-priest of L'Islet, and of the Reverend Mothers Saint-Bernard and Saint-Jacques of the Ursuline nuns of Québec, and the aunt of His Eminence Cardinal Taschereau, Archbishop of Québec.[8]

Marie-Geneviève lost her mother, Geneviève-Victoire, while still an infant. Dr. LeBourdais then entrusted the upbringing of his only daughter to his unmarried sister-in-law, Rose, and to Mgr. Panet, 12th bishop of Québec, until she entered the convent of the Ursuline Sisters. When Geneviève had completed her studies she came home to keep house for her father at L'Islet. And that was how, shortly afterwards, she made the acquaintance of the young master mariner, Jean-Baptiste Bernier, who had come home to the village between two overseas voyages. Geneviève refused to contemplate marriage while her father was still alive.

The future spouses signed their marriage contract on 5 January, before Maître Simon Fraser "notary public in the Province of Lower Canada, residing in the parish of Saint-Jean-Port-Joli in the county of Devon"[9] and before several witnesses. This notarized contract is important since, apart from listing the property of each of the engaged parties, it indicates that Marie-Geneviève had two brothers, Joseph and François LeBourdais. This 23-year-old young woman brought to the marriage sums of money inherited from her deceased parents and from her uncle the parish-priest Jacques Panet, as well as her trousseau, household linen, jewellery, etc.[10]

Jean-Baptiste Bernier, master mariner, was co-owner of the schooner, *Belle Feuille*; he was also owed a sum of money by the merchant James Ballentyne. He owned a fifth share in a property with a frontage of three perches and running back for 40 arpents (2400 metres), located between the first *rang* in the parish of L'Islet and the land of Louis Fournier. Moreover he had bought from his future brother-in-law, Joseph LeBourdais and his wife, Dame Marie-Marthe Couillard,

> a property located in the first *rang*, measuring eleven perches and four and a half feet of frontage and extending the full distance south from the Chemin du roi at the top, and running down to high-water mark on the sea-shore, bounded by the land of Joseph Fortin to the southwest and that of Jean-Baptiste Poitras to the northeast.[11]

The seller had acquired this land as a gift from his father, Joseph (Jean-Baptiste) LeBourdais, alias Lapierre, on 7 August.

Jean-Baptiste Bernier, Captain J.-E. Bernier's paternal grandfather. [Archives of Carol and Louis Terrien]

Captain Bernier and his cousin, Mother Saint-Alexis, in front of the Convent of the Sisters of Jesus-Mary in Sillery, shortly before the latter's death. [Archives of Carol and Louis Terrien]

Does this transaction between Jean-Baptiste Bernier and Joseph LeBourdais imply that after their marriage Captain Bernier's grandparents settled on the LeBourdais's land, rather than on a property "known as Bernier's" as popular tradition would have it? It is possible that the couple was waiting to become more settled before building a home at L'Islet. The death certificate of their son Marc, dated 1817, reveals that the funeral service took place in the parish of Notre-Dame in Québec and that his parents were "of that city." Jean-Baptiste and Geneviève were thus listed in the 1818 census of the city of Québec, as also were their children Jean-Baptiste and Marie-Rosalie.

In 1848 Jean-Baptiste added to his "LeBourdais" property by acquiring a property from Damasse Kyrouack:

> with a frontage of three perches, and a depth of forty-two arpents, located in the First concession of the parish of Notre-Dame de Bonsecours de L'Islet. It extends from the southwest side of the purchaser's land and runs northeast to the seller's land; to the St. Lawrence River to the northwest and to the lands of the second *rang* to the southeast; it thus forms part of a larger property located in the first concession [...] adjoining the lands of Jean-Baptiste Bernier to the southwest and those of Joseph LeBourdais to the northeast.[12]

Other notarized documents state that in 1836 and 1837 Jean-Baptiste was still keeper of the Richelieu light house, and that he was then living at Lotbinière. Moreover, already by 1850 he was also identified as a "former sea-captain," and by 1851 as a "man of means," and that he could no longer sign his name or write because he had a crippled right hand. This handicap would certainly have prevented him from pursuing his passion, that of going to sea up to the age of 80, as his grandson has assumed in his memoirs.

There is no doubt that from their ancestor Jean-Baptiste onwards, the quest for adventure drew Bernier men[13] to the sea, and that the occupation of sailor was definitely an integral part of their daily lives and perhaps even programmed in their genes. At the same time, several other bold L'Isletains were leaving the family lands to learn to master the sea, thus conferring on their village the title of "the sailors' home-land."

Marie-Geneviève LeBourdais, alias Lapierre, wife of Jean-Baptiste Bernier and Captain Bernier's paternal grandmother. [Bernier Collection, *Master Mariner*]

Marble plaque presented by Captain Bernier to the church of Notre-Dame-de-Bonsecours in L'Islet on 2 December 1929, in homage to his relative, parish priest Jacques Panet. [Photo: Lynn Fournier]

From the 18th century onwards shipping and shipbuilding became important economic levers for the coastal villages, over the course of time shaping a maritime culture peculiar to the French-Canadian people who increasingly learned and profited from the savoir-faire and trade of British sea-farers.

⚓

During their 57 years of married life Marie-Geneviève and Jean-Baptiste Bernier had 13 children. Five of their sons became captains or pilots and two of the daughters married sailors.

1) Marie-Geneviève or Javotte (1811- ?)
2) Jean-Baptiste (1812-1891) m. Marie-Émilie-Marguerite Paradis (or Huguette-Émilie, 1818-1869), daughter of Étienne and Olivette Chamberland, on 19 November 1839 at Québec; he would marry his second wife, Marie-Elmire-Émélie Lucas, daughter of Jean-Baptiste and Anastasie Bouchard, on 22 November 1876 at Rimouski.
3) Ludger/Eucher (1813-1853) m. Marie-Azéline Bélanger, daughter of Charles and Marie-Marthe Couillard, on 10 February 1852 at L'Islet.
4) Jacques-Philippe (1814-1817 or 1818)
5) Marie-Rosalie (1815-1885) m. Jean-Baptiste Boucher, son of Pierre-Guillaume and Marie-Madeleine Blais, on 10 January 1832 at L'Islet.
6) Marc (1817)
7) Louis-Bruno (1820-1866 or 1868) m. Appoline Cloutier, daughter of Louis Romain and Marguerite Martin, on 7 January 1846 at L'Islet.
8) Eugène (1821 - ?)
9) Joseph (1822-1896) m. Geneviève Fortin, daughter of Joseph-Ignace and Angélique Moreau, 27 October 1846 at L'Islet.
10) *Thomas* (1823-1893) m. Henriette-Célina Paradis, daughter of Étienne and Olivette Chamberland, on 19 November 1850 at Québec.
11) Marie-Julienne (1824 - ?)
12) Marie-Louise (1829- ?) m. Cyriac Fortin, son of Charles and Anastasie Langelier, on 1 May 1848 at L'Islet.
13) Geneviève or Henriette (?) m. Joseph Caron, son of Joseph and Geneviève Lamy on 27 February 1832 at Louiseville.

CHAPTER 3

Thomas and Célina

SEAFARERS already occupied a special place in the coastal community that welcomed home Thomas Bernier (1832-1893), Captain Bernier's father. Sailors perhaps then represented the only true professional body on the Côte-du-Sud, since they were united in the same struggle against the elements and not in competition with each other.

Grandfather Jean-Baptiste had been able to initiate his sons into the secrets of the seaman's trade and to transmit to them the unconditional love for, and the appeal of, the open sea that had been the driving forces during his career as master mariner.

Thomas, the youngest son, realized in his soul very early on that the sea was the only school that he wanted to attend. Already by the age of seven or eight he was assisting his father in maintaining the lighthouse at Pointe Platon. One day, as he was taking a walk along a cliff-top overlooking the St. Lawrence "the edge of the cliff gave way and he tumbled down several hundred feet to the beach below. He was believed dead when picked up, but revived and eventually recovered, to the great surprise of everyone."[1]

At age 11 he was serving as "boy" on the government schooner commanded by his father and running between Québec and Grosse Île. Then, determined to discover the world beyond the St. Lawrence and to pursue his sea-going apprenticeship, he signed on as "boy" on ocean-going vessels carrying cargoes to Britain.

He was no more than 14 when he joined Queen Victoria's Royal Navy to taste other great adventures and to serve aboard a man o' war; in other words to "take the Queen's shilling" and to receive a rigorous training with a view to serving the interests of the sovereign of the provinces of Lower and Upper Canada. What an honour for this adolescent, brought up in a British colony, to be accepted in the prestigious ranks of the Royal Navy!

The five or six years that he spent in the British Navy were critical in the moulding of Thomas Bernier.

When he returned to Québec Thomas did service with his brother, Captain Louis Bernier, who was building his own sailing ships and was delivering them to Britain to sell them to British owners. He also worked for some years on board other large sailing vessels before attaining the rank of First Officer and, later master mariner. The remarkable aspect of his father, as stated by the son, was that he won the respect of his men by his talents, his ability, and his generosity. He was always ready to share his knowledge with those who showed interest. "He had the Navy habit of keeping everything shipshape and his vessels were always models of neatness and orderliness."[2]

Thomas Bernier, Captain Bernier's father, at age 40. [Archives of Carol and Louis Terrien]

Louis-Bruno Bernier, Captain Bernier's uncle. [Bernier Collection, *Master Mariner*]

Joseph-Elzéar was clearly very proud of his paternal ancestry. He would say that the men in his family displayed five very well defined characteristics: a true devotion to sea life, a passion for hunting, unusual height, great physical strength, and also unusual longevity. His grandfather, his uncles and the majority of his Bernier cousins were over six feet tall. His father was the sole exception to the rule. "And those members of the family who were not quite so tall, made up in sturdiness of build the inches they lacked in height,"[3] he liked to add, to justify the small stature that he had inherited from his father.

Thomas and his brothers were all intensely fond of hunting and fishing. In his memoirs Joseph-Elzéar took real pleasure in recalling their hunting trips:

> Each of the brothers had a home at L'Islet, and every year by common understanding each one made every effort to be free of his ship and home [to go hunting] by the middle or at least the end of November. Often one of them was thousands of miles away on a long trip, or perhaps tempting Providence in running the gauntlet of late autumn storms in the Gulf.[4]

There then followed a frenzy of hunting that lasted until Christmas!

The brothers would return on snowshoes from the backwoods with a sled loaded with caribou, deer, moose, partridge, and hares. Their return signalled the start of joyous holiday celebrations, whereby each member of the family acted host to all the other families in turn, serving dishes based on the fruits of the hunt. Among the Berniers these meals were the occasion of prolonging the pleasure of seeing each other again and of the annual holidays.

As soon as they could take advantage of a short break between voyages the Bernier brothers would go duck-hunting on the sand-banks or trout-fishing in the nearby rivers. Sometimes they would leave their ships to mark the birth of a little Bernier, or the engagement and wedding of a close cousin. These celebrations gave rise to important meetings between the boys and girls of the surrounding area.

This is what happened in the case of Joseph-Elzéar's parents. Thomas probably encountered Henriette-Célina Paradis (1832-1906), daughter of the carpenter Étienne Paradis (1787-1870) and Olivetti Chamberland (1795-1839) of the parish of Saint-Roch de Québec during the festivities associated with the marriage of the eldest Bernier. On 19 November 1839 Jean-Baptiste[5] was marrying Célina's elder sister, Marie-Émilie-Marguerite Paradis, in the church at St. Roch. Given the difference in age between Thomas and Célina, one can easily imagine that their first contacts were rather casual. The idea that he would some day marry this 7-year-old child certainly would not have crossed the mind of the young man of 16!

Célina became an accomplished young lady, well trained by the Québec nuns in the area that was to

Henriette-Célina Paradis, Captain Bernier's mother. [Bernier Collection , *Master Mariner*]

Étienne Paradis, Captain Bernier's maternal grandfather. [Bernier Collection, *Master Mariner*]

become her own—home economics. At the convent she had been taught all that a wife should master in order to carry out her duties to God, her spouse, and her children. She had developed a taste for singing and for embroidery. She was gentle and likable by nature, and loved to tell stories that she recalled from her extensive reading.

Joseph-Elzéar gives the impression that he knew little about his mother, since he says little about her in his writings and makes no mention of genealogical research on his maternal side.[6] It must be said that this line did not possess the prestige of that of his grandmother Panet-LeBourdais. In any case at that time women rarely developed a life outside the home. They had no legal rights except through the intervention or under the guardianship of their husbands. If they left their mark it was because they had contributed to society by producing sons who pursued brilliant careers or experienced great adventures in their place!

The marriage contract of Uncle Jean-Baptiste and Aunt Émilie-Marguerite reveals that the Paradis children had already lost their mother by 1839. It is possible perhaps that Émilie took the place of her mother for young Henriette-Célina? From 1845 or 1846 Célina was in the habit of visiting the older woman, and of staying in the new house that the couple had just built east of the village.[7] She may perhaps have had occasion to meet Thomas there.

Joseph-Elzéar's parents were married at Saint-Roch de Québec on 19 November 1850. Thomas was 27 years old and had not yet reached the rank of Captain. Célina was only 18.

A few years after this marriage Thomas Bernier's name began to appear fairly frequently in the documents of the notary Germain-Alexandre Verreau. The majority of the recorded transactions represented loans to his fellow-citizens. Since there were not yet any bank branches in the region, more well-to-do individuals would lend sums of money to those in need, who sometimes mortgaged their land to secure the loan. Between 1858 and 1875 documents indicate that Thomas Bernier, "seafarer" (18 December 1858) or "master mariner" (17 April 1860), was extending loans to farmers, blacksmiths and even to the parish shoemaker, Zéphirin Bernier, who, on 6 November 1875, borrowed $100 from him at 8 per cent interest. Between 1864 and 1869 Thomas purchased several wood lots with timber-cutting rights.

Everything seemed to be going well for the Berniers, in terms of profession, business and family … but not entirely. Only three of their seven children lived to adulthood.[8] 1863, 1864, 1868, 1869, 1870, 1872 and 1873 were years of mourning for Célina and Thomas! And then, as if these losses did not represent enough suffering, a further tragedy appeared on the horizon. Joseph-Elzéar described it in his memoirs:

Jean-Baptiste Bernier, Captain Bernier's uncle. [Bernier Collection, *Master Mariner*]

The Caron house opposite the Mailloux monument; this lodging house was the first home of Joseph-Elzéar Bernier's parents in L'Islet-sur-Mer. [Photo: Lynn Fournier]

> Early in April 1873, he [Thomas] and his cousin Joseph Chalifour had gone over to Batture-à-Loup-Marin (Seal Bank) on the north shore opposite Saint-Jean-Port-Joli. As they were stepping out of their boat, my father told his cousin to turn his gun the other way as it was pointing at my father. As Chalifour went to lift the gun the trigger caught in one of the thwarts and the full charge of goose-shot was discharged into my father's arm, practically severing it at the elbow. This was at 5 o'clock in the morning and the two were ten miles from the nearest village. Despite the intense pain my father did not lose his courage or presence of mind. He directed the application of a tourniquet, and then sat down in the stern-sheets of the boat to be rowed back. Port-Joli was reached at noon and a carriage was hired to take him to L'Islet for medical aid. But the jolting of the vehicle on the rough country road was too painful, so he went back to the boat and was rowed up 12 miles against the tide, reaching home after 6 o'clock, when the arm was amputated.[9]

This accident did not prevent his father from resuming his profession of captain, or continuing to hunt, since he learned to fire with remarkably good aim with just one hand. However, his son admitted sadly that he suffered from pain from this amputation until his death, which occurred at Lauzon in 1893.

Thomas and Célina lived in the village of L'Islet-sur-Mer for 28 years, in three different houses.

On 8 August 1856, as recorded by the public notary, Maître G.-A. Verreau, Thomas made the following purchase:

> A house built of wood measuring 30 feet by 28 feet, French measure, in a "bouclave [?]", ready for occupation and well-panelled and shingled, with door-frames and doors and various rooms and various appurtenances [...] the location or lot located to the northwest of the Public Road in the first concession in the aforesaid Parish of Notre-Dame Bonsecours de L'Islet [...] consisting of a frontage of three perches and 25 feet, or approximately, more or less, for the entire depth starting from the southeast side of the said Public Road and running down to the northwest to the St. Lawrence River, and abutting on the land of Barthélémy Pouliot to the northeast and that of Sieur Joseph Moreau to the southwest [...].

This was the "Caron house" today located at 390 chemin des Pionniers Est. Joseph-Elzéar may have lived there for some time as a child, because he could recall the Temperance Cross on the Mailloux monument which he could see from his bedroom window.

His parents sold this home to Charles Frédéric de Koënig, master pilot for the port of Québec, on 17 October 1859 for £53. The Koënigs took possession on 15 April 1860.

Twenty days after acquiring this first house Thomas signed another sales contract, witnessed by Maître Verreau:

> On 28 August 1856 Isaac Gamache and his wife Dame Marie-Émérence Lacroix sold Thomas Bernier, master mariner, of the same parish [...] a property located northwest of the Public Road in the first concession in the parish of Notre-Dame de Bonsecours de L'Islet, on the shores

This house in the centre of the village was the second residence of Joseph-Elzéar Bernier's parents in L'Islet. It faces the Auberge de La Marguerite. [Photo: Lynn Fournier]

> of the St. Lawrence, […] with a frontage of three perches and a depth of one arpent […] with dock, house, sheds and other buildings […] for the sum of $1125.

This is the present home of Alice Walsh at 91 chemin des Pionniers Est.

Two properties acquired at the same time? It would appear that Thomas was renting out the house "with various rooms" to obtain a steady income, while living with his family in the centre of town? Moreover Captain Bernier always identified this second house as "my father's house." It was sold at a loss to Onésime Ménard on 3 April 1873 for the sum of $925.

Finally, on 27 October 1873 Thomas bought a further property in the heart of the village of L'Islet. This is the fine stone house of Nicole and Martin Toussaint, known today as the "Doctor's lodging."

> Dame Émilie Pouliot, wife of Collin McCallum, Esquire, merchant […] has sold to Thomas Bernier […] a certain plot of land or building site located northeast of the public road in the first concession of the parish […] with a frontage of about 95 feet, and extending for the entire maximum distance from the said road down towards the northwest as far as the river […] the said plot is bounded by the land of Germain Giasson to the southwest […] and that of François Lemieux to the northeast […] with buildings […] The seller acquired this property from Vincent Martin, doctor, on 12 July 1858 for the sum of 200 louis.

The contract stipulated that Captain Thomas Bernier had paid "150 louis" in cash and that he owed the rest. It is interesting to note that in 1878, when they moved to Québec, the Berniers sold their house back to the widow Émilie Pouliot who had remarried to a doctor. The present owner is also a doctor.

There can be no doubt that Thomas Bernier was a shrewd businessman; this allowed him to build his own ships and to devote himself to the lucrative trade in timber derived from his lands. It would appear that this flair for trading and his love for money were communicated to his eldest son, Joseph-Elzéar, but not to his two other children.

The Doctor's bed-and-breakfast place located at 81 chemin des Pionniers Est, was the third residence of Joseph-Elzéar Bernier's parents in L'Islet.[Photo: Lynn Fournier]

Alfred Bernier, younger brother of Joseph-Elzéar. [Bernier Collection, *Master Mariner*]

Henriette-Émilie Bernier-Boisjoly, Joseph-Elzéar's only sister. [ANQ, P188 D1 P33]

Alfred (1853 - ?), who had married Philomène Alvine Roy, daughter of Majoric and Philomène Bacquet on 21 April 1884 at Beaumont, became a widower quite early. He had no children and lived rather modestly in Montréal until his death, which probably occurred in the late 1930s or early 1940s. Captain Bernier remained very attached to this brother, who had sailed with him, and he assisted him financially throughout his life.

Henriette-Émilie (1859- ?) married Georges Boisjoly, widowed husband of Marie-Cynodine Fournier and son of Moïse and Marie-des-Anges Pruneau, on 11 May 1881 at the church of Saint-Sauveur in Québec. Twelve years later, documents relating to the estate of her father, Thomas, would indicate that she was already separated from her husband, "carpenter and contractor." In the Lovell Directory for 1900 she reappears, reunited with her husband, who had now become a "painter," and was living at 150 rue Ontario in Montréal. In 1905 the couple was living at 317 rue LaSalle in the parish of Maisonneuve. Henriette's situation with Georges Boisjoly was probably quite precarious, and her existence with four children rather difficult; these were Alice (1882-1956), who married Georges Corriveau in 1900, Albert (1883 - ?), Alfred, a day-labourer who married Luce Tremblay in 1906, and Eugène who married Albina LaPlante in 1908.[10]

Their mother, Célina Paradis, Thomas Bernier's widow, died at the Hôpital Maisonneuve in Montréal in 1906.

CHAPTER 4

The house where Bernier was born?

Where was Captain Bernier born? Some older residents of the village of L'Islet can remember that, shortly before he died, and with a special dispensation from the Archbishop of Québec, the octogenarian captain was invited to give a speech from the pulpit in the church of Notre-Dame-de-Bonsecours. In 1934 only officers of the church were granted this "sacred" privilege. This is a measure of the degree to which Captain Joseph-Élzéar Bernier had attained a level of importance in the eyes of the men of the Church and of the State. It was a living legend, a Chevalier de l'Ordre équestre du Saint-Sépulcre, who ascended the pulpit steps to address an awe-struck public. In his speech, the greatest of Canadian explorers announced that he was "born in the shadow of the Temperance Cross." With this the cat was out of the bag!

In 1977 Abbé Léon Bélanger added the following on this subject:

> He is considered to have been born at the top of the village of L'Islet in one of the houses now owned by Messrs. Harry Walsh and Pierre-Simon Paré. Captain Bernier refuted these claims in a speech that he gave at a banquet thrown in his honour by the Société St-Jean-Baptiste of Lauzon: "I was born by the Mailloux Monument.[1]

Since then several people have claimed that the home of florist Henri Caron and his wife Lucienne opposite the Temperance Cross is definitely the house where the famous captain was born. Joseph-Elzéar's parents became owners of this lodging house four years after his birth, i.e. between 1856 and 1859. However it is possible that they lived there for some time, as tenants, before buying it.

Until their first baby arrived Célina and Thomas probably did as most young couples do in their situation. They took advantage of the situation to travel together. Perhaps they were staying with their parents between two voyages.

Joseph-Elzéar Bernier saw the light of day on 1 January at L'Islet. In his memoirs he omitted to specify where he was born. He simply stated that his father was "on shore for the winter."

Réal Laberge has defended another theory:

> One old residence, among others, has caught the attention and been the object of overtures by the association [of sailors of the Côte-du-Sud] as the future site of the Maritime Museum.
>
> The house in question, more than 200 years old, is located in the centre of the village, right on Route 2, and belonging at present to Mr. and Mrs. Charles Caron; it in all probability is the house where the illustrious arctic explorer, Captain Joseph-Elzéar Bernier, was born [...]
>
> One cannot be absolutely certain at present, says the President of the Société historique de la Côte-du-Sud, Mgr. Léon Bélanger, recently appointed parish priest of L'Islet-sur-Mer, but it appears more than likely that the historic house of Mr. and Mrs. Caron is the authentic birth-place of this great captain and explorer of the North Pole.[2]

The interior of the Notre-Dame-de-Bonsecours church in L'Islet. [Photo: Lynn Fournier]

Temperance Cross on the Mailloux monument in L'Islet. [Photo: Lynn Fournier]

Mr. Laberge also published a photograph of this "house where Captain Bernier was born," but without any proof in support of his claim.[3]

Geographer Yolande Dorion-Robitaille repeated the same stereotype, with no other annotation than "The house where Bernier was born."[4]

Would Célina have wanted to give birth to her first baby in this house that belonged to her elder sister? The fact that Émilie and Jean-Baptiste already had 11 children makes this theory improbable. The young married couple would certainly have avoided this household occupied by a mob of children!

Another hypothesis has been advanced by author Gilberte Tremblay:

> Captain Bernier was born in L'Islet on 1 January 1852. His cousin Narcisse Paradis, then 10 years old, has described the events for us:
>
> The red sleighs went jolting along the road, crossing each other's tracks in the drifts of powdery snow. There was a lot of coming and going, in the midst of a fine storm!
>
> My father and mother were really making light of the snow flurries! They were taking us to grandfather Bernier's place, the family home. My uncle Thomas, who had been married for one year [actually two years], was also living there.
>
> [...] an hour later the team stopped in front of grandfather's fine house with its dormer windows, facing the river.
>
> Drowsy from this three-mile trip, I felt a powerful pair of arms hoist me out of the sleigh and right into the middle of the fine, warm kitchen[5].

According to Gilberte Tremblay the captain was born in his paternal grandfather's house, three miles by sleigh from their starting point. Unfortunately she did not specify the starting point.

Residence said to be the birthplace of Captain J.-E. Bernier. It is located at 276 chemin des Pionniers Est in L'Islet-sur-Mer, and was built by Jean-Baptiste Bernier (uncle) and Émilie Paradis (aunt) in 1845 or 1846. Since 1973 it has been owned by Jovette Rousseau and Simon-Pierre Paré. [Photo: Lynn Fournier]

Old Jean-Baptiste had built his home on the land he had bought from his brother-in-law Joseph LeBourdais, located at the west end of the village, probably between the Route Morin and the Route l'Anse-à-Gilles. If Narcisse Paradis had been visiting his aunt Émilie in the middle of the village, he might have taken more than an hour to cover this distance. His testimony seems credible, and, in the absence of any proof to the contrary, it vindicates the novelist's conclusion.

In reality did the house in which he was born have any significance for Joseph-Elzéar? It is doubtful, since he does not talk about it in his memoirs. On the contrary, he liked to recall his father's second home where he spent a good part of his youth.

In 1852 grandfather Bernier was 66 years old and his wife, Geneviève 64. It is easy to imagine that they were beginning to find their responsibilities as home-owners more and more onerous and that they wanted one of their sons to relieve them of them. Moreover, on their LeBourdais property, west of L'Islet, they must have found themselves very far from the village activities and from their parish church. Notarized documents permit us to confirm this supposition and to discover what became of the LeBourdais-Bernier property.

A month after the birth of Joseph-Elzéar on 3 February, Jean-Baptiste, "former seafarer," and his wife Dame Geneviève LeBourdais made a gift of their property to their second son, Eucher (or Ludger), a Québec port and harbour pilot, who was to marry Azéline Bélanger on the following 10 February.[6] In exchange for this gift their son promised "to provide food, clothing, heat, light, laundry and care for the donor and the lady his wife as long as they lived and survived" and to provide them with a room measuring 15 feet "in the house built on the above-deeded land." Jean-Baptiste declared that he was able to sign the document although for several years he had been unaccustomed "to signing due to an infirmity."

A year later when the schooner *Sutherland* was wrecked in the St. Lawrence, Eucher was drowned along with his crew. On 28 February 1853 his young widow surrendered all rights to the gift of her parents-in-law.

On 24 December 1857 Jean-Baptiste and Geneviève made the same offer, with "house, barn, shed and other buildings erected on the said plot of land" to their eldest son, Jean-Baptiste, a Québec port and harbour pilot.[7] The son had the choice of moving to the piece of land he was being offered and of accommodating his parents in

Old photo of what is said to be Captain Bernier's father's house in L'Islet-sur-Mer. [Bernier Collection, *Master Mariner*]

"the attic rooms of the said house, where they at present have a bedroom" or of installing them on the ground-floor of the house where he had been living for several years with his wife and children. Jean-Baptiste and Émilie agreed to take care of his old parents, but refused to leave the house they had had built 12 years earlier, in the middle of the village. The grandfather, Jean-Baptiste, would live there for 11 years, scanning the sea through his telescope, while Geneviève, his faithful companion, would outlive him by five years.

On the same day the son, Jean-Baptiste sold his inheritance to his younger brother, Joseph, captain and seafarer.[8] The latter was able to intimate that the descendants of Joseph Bernier and his wife Geneviève Fortin, would still live on the LeBourdais-Bernier land and in the house which saw the birth of the courageous explorer of the Arctic.

CHAPTER 5

The *Zillah*

YOUNG NARCISSE PARADIS has described the celebrations surrounding the arrival of his cousin, Joseph-Elzéar, at 6 p.m. on 1 January 1852 as follows:[1]

> "He is a strapping lad… a true Bernier!" pronounced my grandfather.
>
> Hot toddy was served, and when everyone had a glass in hand, my grandfather rose, very solemnly, and declared gravely:
>
> "Here's to the health of your first-born, Thomas."
>
> "He will be a captain!" the latter replied. "To his health!"
>
> "A captain! Yes! Like his father and grandfather," my Aunt Célina added her support proudly, from the depths of the big bed.
>
> And this wish was echoed from every corner, in tones full of conviction and enthusiasm:
>
> "He will be a captain!"…
>
> "Like father like son!" my uncles agreed.
>
> "Even when we're little, we're gripped by the call of the sea," said one of them. "There's nothing else for it!" added another.
>
> "As soon as we draw breath we need a schooner!"
>
> "That's what we're born to do!"
>
> "That's what they're born to do," my grandmother said nobly.
>
> "Now let's eat!"
>
> The dining room looked like a small museum with its boats, schooners, its old-copper gong and its portraits of ancestors hanging on the walls. The Berniers, my uncles, moustached, their eyes closed to slits from the sun on the sea, exuded strength and health. Four fine captains sat around the table and I contemplated them with pride!

A fine New Year's gift weighing 12 pounds!

This desire of his parents to make a child of the sea of him, surfaced at an early age since, at the age of two years and 11 months, he was taken aboard the *Zillah* for his first ocean voyage. Thomas had bought this American brigantine in Montréal the previous summer, and he owned the 100-foot ship that had a displacement of 120 tonnes in partnership with the firm of Torrance and Stearns. The *Zillah* had a good turn of speed despite being 10 years old. "She was a trim little two-masted vessel, and could do 10 knots or more under full sail and a fair wind."[2]

On 17 November 1854 Thomas moored her to the jetty built on the rock off L'Islet to embark his wife, his son, and his niece, Rosalie Boucher.[3] The child was still too young to realize that his father, the ship's master, was

> a vigorous man, shaped by the Royal Navy. He took discipline seriously and would not hesitate to settle arguments with his fists when things deteriorated on deck. It must be said that at that time the task of a captain in the merchant navy was not one of total relaxation. At Québec, as in any port of some importance, the seamen were often recruited from among the strange clientele of the taverns and seedy hotels of the Lower Town and the captain's main concern when it was time to sail, was to make the rounds of the

Joseph-Elzéar Bernier, aged three, with his young mother, Célina Paradis. [Archives of Carol and Louis Terrien]

> bars to round-up his men and then to put to sea with the help of those who were the least inebriated…[4]

Joseph-Elzéar would understand all this much later, when he was serving his own apprenticeship in the difficult profession of seaman. He would always respect his strict father, concerned about maintaining order and discipline on board his ships. He would always have a deep love for this man who could be gay and playful towards his own family and could joke with his officers when off watch.

Carefree, the three-year-old infant would prattle beside his mother and his cousin who would protect him from the sailing ship's rolling or pitching, and would teach him to hold himself erect like a "true, little man" despite the ship's movement. Captain Thomas Bernier's son was already developing differently from other children brought up on shore. His first toys and his first words assumed a maritime flavour.

Each stop in this voyage on board the *Zillah* and, subsequently, every important moment in Joseph-Elzéar's childhood were recorded patiently and tenderly in Célina's personal diary. At a period when cameras were still not available, writing remained for this young woman an excellent means of preserving memories and vivid images for her son. She would bequeath to him this desire to record everything, and from the moment he was old enough to keep his own diary, the future captain would daily note all the events that would form the web of his remarkable life.

⚓

Their destination on that voyage late in 1854 was Cardenas on the north coast of Cuba.

Apart from the foul weather that immobilized the brigantine for three days in the Gut of Canso, the voyage south to the warm, luminous waters of the Florida Strait and Cardenas Bay, was without incident.

Reaching port safely the L'Isletains had leisure to explore its tropical surroundings with perfumed air and extravagant colours which made them forget the grey of the icy St. Lawrence and the white of its snowbound shores. The group was under the spell of the exotic.

Célina was realizing, perhaps for the first time, what attracted her husband to these distant horizons. His sons would follow in his footsteps. This is how it was with the Berniers. The call of the sea was so deeply ingrained in them that they had to return to it again and again, despite the greatest dangers. This loving woman was powerless in the face of the ascendancy of this redoubtable rival.

From his mother's diary Joseph-Elzéar learned that he was almost asphyxiated during a violent tropical storm. The torrential rain was beating so hard on his little body that it prevented him from catching his breath and only his father's muscular arms managed to save his life. There, too, he read that his birthday on 1 January was marked by another terrible storm and that, on the following day, he was able to visit the sugar cane plantations where hundreds of black slaves were at work. Célina's diary entries depicted the contrast she perceived between the reality of life as experienced by the Whites and that of the Blacks, between the privileged existence of the plantation owners who rode around their vast estates, groomed to perfection, in elegant carriages, and who lived in their own delightful mansions, and the more precarious existence of their slaves who worked very hard, who lived on bananas, rice and sweet potatoes, and who had almost no clothes on their backs.

Possibly the reason that Joseph-Elzéar found it important to record these memories in his memoirs, was that he perhaps wanted to pay homage to the intelligence of his mother, who had taught him to look at the world around him, and who had watched over his childhood and youth. For this seafarer who could talk more easily about his ships than about his feelings, this was perhaps his way of expressing the affection he had always held for the first woman in his life.

It is evident that Joseph-Elzéar was proud of having experienced the sea at the age of three, and that he took a certain pleasure in describing the difficulties of that first great sea-going adventure.

> Our return cargo consisted of sugar for Boston. We made a swift run, reaching sight of land off Martha's Vineyard on the seventh day out of Cardenas. But here we met heavy north-west winds and were forced to anchor in Tarpaulin Cove. The ship was covered with a heavy sheet of ice and while waiting for the winds to abate this ice was removed from the rigging, deck, and deck-houses. The sixth day we proceeded to Boston, where my mother was delighted to see so many fine buildings. It was a very severe winter, however, and the water about the vessel froze while she was at anchor, and when she was ready to go in to her wharf it was necessary to cut the ice in front of the ship with long saws.[5]

A month later Thomas Bernier's vessel was leaving the thriving port of Boston, with a cargo of rum and tobacco destined for the British fleet engaged in the Crimean War (1853-1856). The *Zillah* was under charter to the British government to supply units stationed at Valetta, Malta. Great Britain had agreed to become involved in this conflict, aligning herself with France, Turkey and Sardinia, especially to protect her interests in the Middle East and to contain Russian ambitions in the region. This war, which ended with the Treaty of Paris in 1856, put an end to Russian aggression and succeeded in maintaining the balance of power in the Balkans.

And the *Zillah*, under the command of her skilled captain and driven by fair winds, headed for Valetta swiftly and resolutely, despite having women and a child on board!

Joseph-Elzéar has written that his mother was greatly impressed by the 22 frigates and ships lined up in the Maltese harbour, in the shadow of the palace of the Knights of Malta. The largest ships of the British fleet bristled with guns, in some cases in three tiers.

One day the *Zillah*'s passengers were witness to a strange sight:

> One of the stewards of a man-o'-war anchored beside the *Zillah* came out to shake a large table-cloth from the ward-room. Leaning over the rail he caught sight of an enormous shark swimming about near the surface. He began teasing the shark by waving the table-cloth a few inches above the water. With a lunge the shark caught the cloth. The poor steward lost his balance and fell overboard with a pitiful shriek. My father immediately ordered a boat lowered but when our men reached the spot all that was left was a great patch of blood-stained water where the poor man had disappeared.[6]

After a certain delay the *Zillah* joined a convoy of merchant ships that were to resupply the Royal Navy ships patrolling in the Black Sea. Escorted by British frigates the convoy ran through the Dardanelles, linking the Aegean Sea with the Sea of Marmora, and then through the Bosporus into the Black Sea. This resupply mission and the return trip to the Maltese capital certainly did not represent a pleasure trip. The situation was explosive and the danger for Thomas and his seamen, bold, hardened men, was very real. In recognition of this, the *Zillah*'s brave captain was decorated with the Crimean War medal.[7]

The port of Valetta also held perils for Célina:

> He (Captain Bernier) relates that on one occasion when the sailors were walking through the streets, his father went into a shop to make some purchases, while Mrs. Bernier waited for him at the door. A sailor grabbed her, threw her over his shoulder and was running off with his victim, when Mr. Bernier raced after the rapist and struck him with his stick right in the face. At the sight of the blood flowing from the wound, Mrs. Bernier lost consciousness.[8]

In May 1855 the *Zillah* sailed in ballast for Leghorn [Livorno], then on 16 June for Boston with a cargo of Italian marble bound for the rich merchants of New England. The enormous blocks had been stowed on rags to prevent them from slipping and crashing into each other during the voyage. What nobody had foreseen was that the rags were infested with hungry insects that immediately began to take great delight in tormenting the passengers, day and night, from the Mediterranean via the important route of the Strait of Gibraltar, into the Atlantic, without respite and without anyone being able to counter them!

Of course, one misfortune always gives rise to another…

A week later, off Cape St. Vincent and the Spanish coast, the shadow of a tragedy surprised the vessel as she prepared to celebrate Saint-Jean-Baptiste's day. Bérubé, the first officer, was suddenly pitched into the sea while taking a reef in the mainsail. Captain Thomas, who was suffering from an infected right hand, immediately forgot that his arm was in a sling, and lowered a boat.

Joseph-Elzéar did not need to have recourse to his mother's diary to recall the incident: "One of the earliest scenes I can remember is that of my father pacing the deck in anxiety over Bérubé's fate, and my mother and cousin trying to learn what was happening astern by means of a spy-glass, tears streaming down their cheeks."[9]

The strong emotions and the vivid images associated with this rescue operation remained in his young mind, especially when the sailors hoisted the rescued man on deck and pumped his chest to make him expel the water he had swallowed.

This was not the last of the misfortunes that awaited the *Zillah*'s crew.

The great weight of the marble blocks in the hold seriously threatened the vessel by destabilizing the way she rolled and, as Elzéar recalled:

> In a bad sea she was rolling heavily with an occasional "fourth sea" (or big wave) causing a sharp jerking roll. On one of these sharp rolls her main-topmast head snapped off, carrying the gaff-topsail and part of the upper rigging overboard with it. We proceeded under reduced sail but met unfavourable winds and bad seas all the way, arriving in Boston forty-five days out of Leghorn; a voyage that compares unfavourably with our outward journey to Valetta of twenty-three days.[10]

To crown all, as the *Zillah* was entering Boston harbour a brig with a cargo of ice ran so close across her bow that Captain Bernier was unable to avoid a collision. The *Zillah*'s bow carried away part of her stern, while her jib-boom ripped through her mainsail.

Thomas's son, who still could not grasp the concept of danger, was not greatly upset by the incident. He was surprised by the resultant gaping hole in the other vessel's stern, and amused to see the blocks of ice in her hold.

Bad luck continued to dog them, however. Once she had moored to the quay to unload the marble the *Zillah* was the target of a thief who set fire to the cabin while he fled with some money and the captain's watch. Almost all the Bernier family's clothing and personal effects went up in flames before the fire could be extinguished.

This was too much for Célina's nerves. She decided to return to L'Islet with Joseph-Elzéar and Rosalie

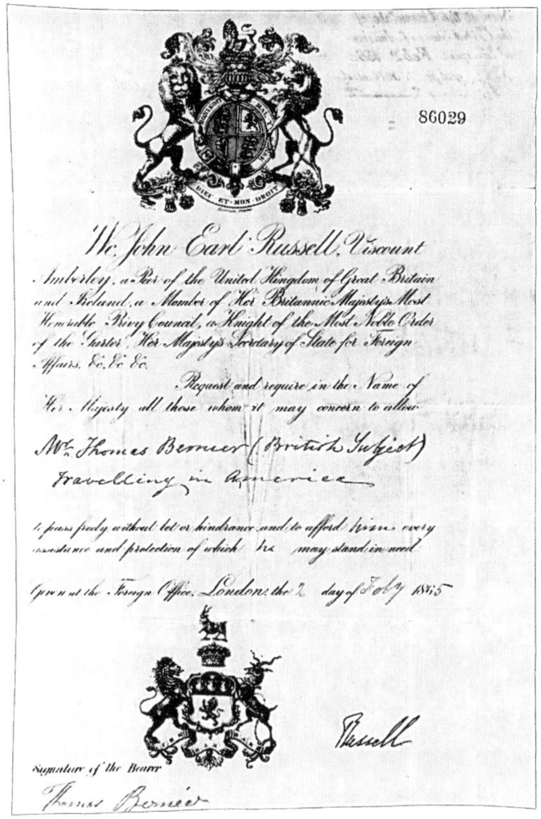
86029

DIEU ET MON DROIT

We John Earl Russell, Viscount Amberley, a Peer of the United Kingdom of Great Britain and Ireland, a Member of Her Britannic Majesty's Most Honorable Privy Council, a Knight of the Most Noble Order of the Garter, Her Majesty's Secretary of State for Foreign Affairs, &c. &c. &c.

Request and require in the Name of Her Majesty all those whom it may concern to allow Mr. Thomas Bernier (British Subject) travelling in America to pass freely without let or hindrance and to afford him every assistance and protection of which he may stand in need.

Given at the Foreign Office, London the 2 day of Feby 1855

Russell

Signature of the Bearer

Thomas Bernier

Joseph-Elzéar carefully looked after this official document, which permitted his father, a British subject, to travel in the United States. [Archives of Carol and Louis Terrien]

overland, taking the train to Lévis and then a horse-drawn carriage to L'Islet.

⚓

> Two winters and the intervening summer were passed at home while my father sailed alone. But on March 10th 1857, my mother and I set out from L'Islet in a sleigh for Levis, and there entrained for Boston. Since we had last seen her, my father had become sole owner of the *Zillah*. She was now loading a general cargo for Trinidad.[11]

The five-year-old already gave the impression of sensing the joy of putting to sea.

His father's vessel was carrying soap, candles, herring, ham, cane-bottomed chairs, and even washing machines for the inhabitants of Trinidad, located off the coast of South America.

> We had an uneventful voyage to Port-of-Spain, the heat being excessive. I still remember the pilot we took on off Port-of-Spain. He was a Spaniard, tall and handsome, very dark and wild-looking. He wore no shoes and looked as if he had never worn any; his feet were enormous with the toes wide apart. But what struck me most was the fact that he wore his shirt outside his trousers.[12]

The *Zillah* next called at Turks Islands, near Haiti. It was there that he saw flying fish for the first time. The little lad marvelled at these creatures that shot out of the water in groups of ten or a dozen and could reach spectacular heights, sometimes even 40 feet.

There were so many things to explore. At L'Islet there was really nothing to compare with all the colours, sounds and smells. What a remarkable way to initiate a young lad into the pleasures of travelling, to excite his curiosity and to inculcate in him a love of learning!

Did all the eldest sons of master mariners of that era experience such a training or was little Elzéar a privileged child? It is difficult to say. On the other hand, from reading his memories of childhood it is clear that the future seafarer realized that his parents matched his personality.

While the *Zillah* was loading tons of salt, Thomas took advantage of this time to show his son the origin of this natural resource. He took him to the saltpans of the Turks Islands; these were large basins where the sea water was impounded until it evaporated and formed a salt crust which could then be shovelled up.

Before they returned to Boston Thomas gave his son a tiny pet monkey; the captain came to regret this gift, however, since the animal had the bad habit of stealing everything it saw. While this trick amused the five-year-old boy, the crew found it a real nuisance!

In Boston Thomas decided to take back his gift and sold it to an Italian, owner of a barrel organ.

> But this [my grief] was soon forgotten in the excitement of my first sight of the "Glorious Fourth" of July, as celebrated in Boston. There were great festivities, including the launching of three balloons, one of them with two men in the basket… And throughout the day and night firecrackers crackled constantly. My mother's journal records the fact that I returned to the ship that night *very* tired.[13]

In late July he returned with his parents to the shores of the St. Lawrence, far from the exotic smells, the unusual sights, the shades and hues that were now part of his imagination. He had enjoyed the good fortune of a free childhood on board his father's sailing ship. The time had come for him to enter another school, that of the Brothers of the Christian Schools.

CHAPTER 6

Geography to the rescue

WHEN ONE READS THE BIOGRAPHICAL accounts of the childhood of great explorers and seafarers one realizes that they have several points in common with Joseph-Elzéar Bernier. Firstly there is a passionate, unconditional love for the sea that they ply day after day. Henry Larsen (1900-1964), the captain of the Canadian vessel, the *St. Roch*, which made successful traverses of the Northwest Passage in 1940 and again in 1944, said that the sea became his greatest love, from the moment he was able to go aboard the pilot boats in the bay off his Norwegian village during his summer holidays. Influenced by their environment all marine adventurers necessarily began their sea-going apprenticeship when they were small.

Gustave Vallat, biographer of the Norwegian explorer, Fridtjof Nansen (1861-1930) has also written:

> His parents considered correctly that a child had to live in the open air to enjoy the best of health, allowing him to amuse himself in perfect freedom out of doors the whole time. For it is only over the long run and by habituating oneself from an early age that one manages to achieve a truly strong constitution that will allow one to endure every type of foul weather, something that is of prime importance.[1]

All the great explorers developed an inordinate taste for freedom, a strong personality and considerable physical energy at a very early age.

The same applied to Joseph-Elzéar. By the age of six or seven it already appeared that his entire personality was strongly influenced by his small, but muscular, solid and broad-shouldered build, that his instinct as an alert hunter gave him an extraordinary élan and a dynamism, and that willpower was already well represented in him. His independent spirit bubbled with curiosity. He knew what he liked and did not hesitate to yield to his natural impulses. His intensity could not have been very restful for his parents or for those around him.

Célina and Thomas Bernier's eldest son shared another feature in common with all embryonic seafarers, and that was a taste for studying geography and the natural sciences. These subjects stimulated him and satisfied his desire to traverse all the seas of the world and to discover new horizons.

Many children dream of unknown lands, of islands filled with emerald birds, where they would be kings or queens, or of heroic exploits driven by the multicoloured sails of a magnificent caravel. For the majority of them, the explorer of these dreams remains a fine fairy-story. But for a few rare individuals, every aspect of their lives prepares them for the day when they set out to the ends of the earth to realize their mission.

What is certain is that one will never manage to penetrate the mystery of these chosen beings who manage from childhood to set themselves apart from others

The former Collège de L'Islet around 1890. This building, built in 1853, consisted of two components, one built of stone, the other of wood. [Courtesy of Angèle Gagnon]

by their energy, their willpower, their competitive spirit, or simply by the intensity of their character. One can but envy their assurance and their magnificent obsessions.

On 1 September Joseph-Elzéar entered the L'Islet college run by the Brothers of the Christian Schools. Believing that he would find there only materials and theories that would be a waste of his time in that they would divorce him from the "real life" and the school of the sea, this seven-year-old school-boy embraced this new stage in his life without any great motivation, being obliged to "undergo the torture of the school-desk!" Fortunately Célina had informed the institution's director, Brother Jean Chrysostôme,[2] about her son's desire to be a seaman, so that the stress would be laid especially on the practical side of things.

> This good man, to whose memory the families of L'Islet County owe a vast debt of gratitude, took his task earnestly, for during the few years I spent under his guidance he instilled in me a real love of geography and furnished me the only education I have had, except what I have managed to acquire by reading.[3]

In order to nurture this growing interest in geography on the part of his eldest son Thomas had developed the habit of writing to him from the various sea ports that he visited, without ever making reference to the name of the place. His letters contained scientific details, demographic data, degrees of latitude and longitude to encourage the boy to make his own discoveries. Thanks to his intelligent father the future sailor came to know the countries of the globe by heart and to be able to plot their capitals on a world map and to describe their climates, their populations, and their commercial activities.

By comparison with these imaginary voyages, the little country school seemed like a limited and mediocre

The Collège de L'Islet and the Notre-Dame-de-Bonsecours church. Joseph-Elzéar would not have known this College building, which dates from 1920. [Photo: Lynn Fournier]

world. Joseph-Elzéar admitted that initially he was not very studious, and that the idea of hanging about the beach with his brother Alfred seemed much more profitable to him.

He recalled that one morning during the holidays he had slipped outside when the household was still asleep, dragging with him his mischievous little brother, who was ready to follow him to the ends of the earth. They then had the idea of launching an old hay cart and of removing its wheels, thus converting it into a magic raft that could take them to great adventures. Of course the two crew members had not foreseen the effect of the falling tide which carried them towards the open sea before they could react in time or manoeuvre their strange vessel. They were rescued two hours later and received a severe punishment.

This bad experience did not have the effect anticipated by their parents since during their next holidays, the two accomplices decided to row across the river. Bad weather set in, forcing the adventurers to row until nightfall. They were less than proud of themselves when they got home, sheepish and soaked to the skin.

Despite the punishments that always followed this type of bravado, the Bernier brothers never hesitated to begin plotting other unforgotten escapades.

But one punishment had the desired effect, since Joseph-Elzéar never forgot it. This was the punishment administered by Brother Chrysostôme to cure him of his desire to chew tobacco. One day somebody brought a tobacco pouch to school and quietly passed it around to all the boys who were keen to try this miraculous product that gave so much pleasure to men of that period. Elzéar tried chewing some and became violently sick. This reaction immediately marked him as one of the tobacco chewers in school. The headmaster did not hesitate to send him home with a notice around his neck, identifying him as an "apprentice chewer." Seeing how humiliated he was Célina gave him a second spanking and sent him to bed without supper. This memorable experience explains why the future seafarer never touched tobacco in any form.

His childhood world thus evolved with the rhythm of the seasons, between the walls of the boarding school and the classrooms, between the freshness of the waters of the St. Lawrence and the warmth of home, where his family made him feel that he belonged.

His daily existence also revolved around the holidays in the village or the religious ceremonies celebrated in the church of Notre-Dame-de-Bonsecours.

> There were months consecrated to St. Joseph, to Mary, to the Sacred Heart, the month of the rosary and the month of the dead. The fast days marked the seasons, as well as Lent and Advent. The first Friday of the month was celebrated; abstinence was observed on Fridays and holy-day vigils, not to mention the Forty-hour exercises, parochial retreats, the triduums, the rogation days and the angelus… People's lives followed the Church calendar in large part.[4]

The parish church, which is now over 235 years old, has perhaps lost the enclosure that Joseph-Elzéar would have found as he walked by, but it still retains its appearance of yester-year and its slender belfries. Despite his long sojourns abroad Captain Bernier remained attached to the church of his childhood, where he developed a profound faith and a taste for the Catholic form of worship that were to sustain him in his more difficult moments. Moreover in 1885 he accepted the invitation of his former teacher, Brother Jean Chrysostôme, to sponsor the new church bell in L'Islet.

As a child Joseph-Elzéar also liked to take refuge with his grandfather, Jean-Baptiste, who spent his time scanning the sea through his telescope, lying in wait for a sailing vessel to pass by, and never taking his eyes off it until he had identified it. This old seafarer was delighted by the sea-going bent that was taking shape in the case of his grandson. He spent hours describing for him the far-away places that he had visited, and the various cargoes that he had transported from one port to another, and in inculcating a sense of duty to be accomplished and of the responsibilities he himself would assume towards the men he would command and, especially, to instill in him the profound respect he had always had for the nature that had given him life. Elzéar would remember his grandfather's words and advice. He would repeat them, over 65 years later:

> One must remain in balance with Nature in everything. Only Nature is sovereign in all things. With all his intelligence, all his courage, with all the data of modern science, man is nothing compared to the natural environment and if he tries to defy it, it is he who will be mercilessly broken by it. Always let yourself be guided by Nature. This is the key to success.[5]

Notre-Dame-de-Bonsecours church in L'Islet as it appears today. [Photo: Lynn Fournier]

CHAPTER 7

The *Saint-Joseph*

HISTORIAN EILEEN REID MARCIL began her remarkable work on the building of the great sailing ships at Québec as follows:

> The launching of the little barquentine *White Wings* from a Lauzon shipyard in 1893 brought an end to the construction of square-rigged sailing ships at Québec, an industry which at times had provided work for several thousand of her artisans and labourers. With its passing, it was soon forgotten, and of some 1600 stately ships that were built there, not one was conserved as a reminder of sailing ship days. No maritime museum was created at Québec to keep its history alive and serve as custodian to things that are now lost or scattered. Today, few Quebeckers can name even one of the vessels built by their ancestors. Yet, there were times when as many as 28 shipyards were in operation. There were shipyards where four or five vessels waited side by side for their launching at the first spring tides. And there were years when as many a 50 or 60 vessels sailed from Québec on their maiden voyage laden with timber and masts from Canada's heartland.[1]

With the start of the new régime in 1759, private enterprise progressively took charge of the colony's commercial activities and its shipyards, which had been controlled by the King of France. During the following century British businessmen, who had settled there in large numbers, as well as the British companies that they represented, maintained a tight monopoly on this business sector and transformed Québec, the heart of the colony in the 19th century, into an important British maritime and commercial centre.

The ships that the largely French-Canadian workforce[2] built in the Québec shipyards were sold to British owners, and the goods they transported were in response to the steadily growing demands of the British Empire. Of course the Québec "lumber lords" had their share of the market and profited amply from the scarcity of woodlands in Great Britain. For 1811 alone "Québec had shipped 19,925 masts, 1,223,450 cubic feet of oak and 2,644,400 cubic feet of pine."[3]

Thomas Bernier had long wanted to become an entrepreneur and earn his living on board his own vessel. He was very much aware that the challenge was an enormous one and that few French Canadians dared to compete with the British businessmen because they did not have the financial support of the important British companies.

But gradually some craftsmen attempted to match their ability against those of the British and the names of French Canadian shipbuilders began to appear on the registration certificates of new vessels: the Valin, Charland, Trahan, Gingras, alongside the Ross, Davie, Gilmour, Baldwin, Blakiston, and Sewell. Moreover the early 1860s saw a spectacular rise in shipbuilding in Québec, a boom that allowed anyone who could borrow enough money to risk taking the plunge.

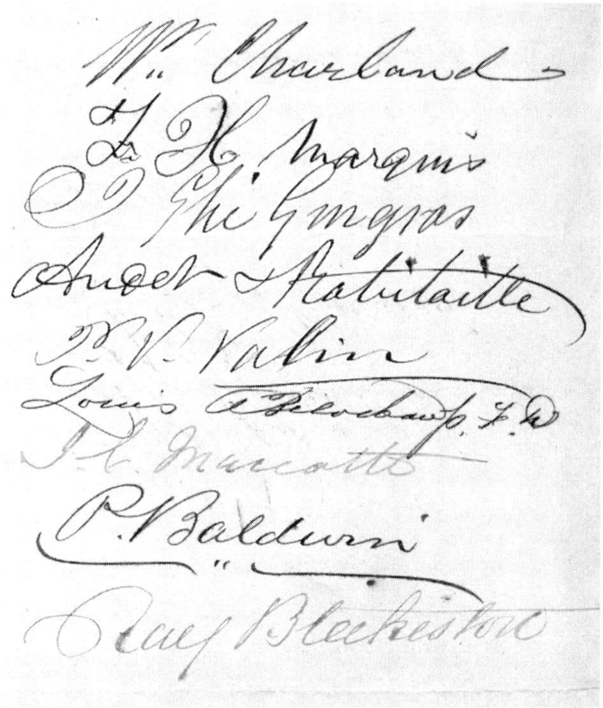

Signatures of several major Québec shipbuilders on a document that belonged to Captain J.-E. Bernier. [Archives of Carol and Louis Terrien]

This shipbuilding sector really represents the first major manufacturing industry in the history of the colony. In 1863[4] 55 large sailing vessels were built within the limits of the port of Québec, and 10 large sailing vessels outside those limits. French Canadians like the Saint-Jeans, the Laroches, the de Portneufs, the Beaudets, the de Lotbinières, the Houdes, and the de Grondines fell into step and a year later 55 large sailing ships were completed within the limits of the port of Québec, as against 18 in coastal shipyards elsewhere in the Province.

The time was propitious for Thomas Bernier. In the spring of 1864 he finally made the decision to become a shipbuilder.

While he was delivering the square-rigged three-masted 956-tonne *Angélique* to her purchasers W. Ross and Alexander Cassell in Liverpool, Thomas made the acquaintance of Pierre Labbé, the ship's designer and main overseer at Pierre Valin's shipyard.[5] The naval architect helped him to refine his plans and give a style to the sailing vessel he wanted, one as elegant, responsive and manoeuvrable as the *Angélique.*

Thomas was very familiar with the craftsmen who lived in L'Islet and area. He therefore chose to build his first ship among his own folk.

To finance part of his timber requirements he took out a loan with a rich Québec merchant, Nicolas Allard, a native of Jersey, whose name appears on the original registration certificate for the port of Québec alongside his own. Since he owned several woodlots he could provide the remainder of his timber requirements himself and, moreover, could count on the support of his father and brothers who were also woodlot owners with timber-cutting rights.

> [...] Captain Thomas Bernier had joined forces with the firm of Stearn for transporting Powell's timber to the seaports of Ireland. He owned his own shipyard on the site now occupied by the houses of Alphonse and Amédée Saint-Pierre, opposite the home of Simon-Pierre and Jovette Paré.[6]

This yard was therefore located opposite his brother Jean-Baptiste's house, between the beach and the public road.

> The fundamental requirement for a shipyard was a gently sloping beach where a slip could be built that was long enough for a vessel to gain enough momentum on launching so as not to get stuck on the ways.[7]

There also had to be enough room around the ship being built to erect scaffolding and to allow the men to move around freely with building materials. The bed of the slipway had to be solid enough and level enough to take the weight of the beams and tree-trunks that supported the ship's keel. As with any other shipyard, Thomas certainly had all rocks and debris cleared away

The *Saint-Joseph* was built in Thomas and Jean-Baptiste Bernier's shipyard in L'Islet. Alphonse and Amédée Saint-Pierre's garage is located on the site of the former shipyard. [Photo: Lynn Fournier]

from the river bed at the foot of the slipway so as to ensure an adequate depth of water and prevent the vessel from running aground when it was launched.

There was just as much effort invested in preparing and equipping the site as in the rest of the operations. Of course, such an enterprise involved the entire community of L'Islet: the shipwrights, drillers, caulkers and the other workmen who made their contribution, including the owner's sons.

Joseph-Elzéar was delighted at his father's initiative. On leaving school, the 12-year-old, supported by his brother Alfred, who stuck to him like glue, could finally become involved in the world of men.

Throughout the summer of 1864 the two buddies scoured all the sheds in the neighbourhood for old cordage. It was their responsibility to convert these ropes into oakum, what was then called "étoupe noire," since it derived especially from tarred ropes. To encourage them Thomas would certainly have made them understand that this material was indispensable in building wooden ships, since it ensured that they were watertight when it was rammed firmly between the planks. Elzéar and Alfred could thus tell themselves that they were contributing seriously to the building of their father's ship during the interminable hours they spent collecting, cutting, soaking, and teasing-out the rope-ends to produce fine fibres which they laid out in the sun to dry before laying them aside till the stage of caulking the ship was reached.

That autumn Elzéar attended school only intermittently. There still remained some oakum to be produced and Thomas considered that his eldest son was responsible and strong enough to lead the horse hauling the timber sled.

> By this time the upper storey of a wheel-wright's shop near my uncle's house in the village had been converted into a mould loft. And in this loft had been made the moulds for the various members of the ship. These moulds are frames representing the shape of each member. They are made of thin boards of "white-wood," a soft, pliable wood, and nailed to planks to preserve the angles and bends.
>
> When the moulds were all complete my father and his brother Jean-Baptiste set off for the woods to choose the timber for the ship. With them went a load of moulds so that they could measure the timber and only bring back

the pieces required. It was at this point that I became useful for I would drive down the timber and bring back a fresh lot of moulds.[8]

Joseph-Elzéar was privileged. While hauling the timber and the moulds he learned from these "men of many skills," foresters, surveyors, and loggers who were familiar with all the trees in the forest.

> Various kinds of woods were used [in building a ship]: birch for the "floors" (which are not flooring as the name implies but the members that are placed across the keel and on which the keelson rests); birch also for the first foothooks (members which continue the frame up the side of the ship above the "floors"), tamarack or spruce for the second foothooks, for the tops (members which complete the frame above the foothooks), for the knees (members which brace the beams on which the deck rests); spruce for most of the beams, for the inner topside planking, and for spars such as main boom, jib-boom, gaffs, gallant and royal mast, main topmast and yards. All of these woods had to be cut in the last quarter of the moon when the sap is close to the bark. This insured a lighter wood slower to rot.
>
> [...] oak for the keelsons, for the main beams, and for the stem and stern-post; pitch pine for the mainmast, foremast, and bowsprit, and for the outer planking above the waterline; white pine for the decking; birch and elm for the outside planking below the water-line; and elm for the inner bottom planking.[9]

A wooden ship being built in a Lévis shipyard at the end of the 19th century. [J.-Ernest Livernois Collection, ANQ, CM 154 11531]

The future shipbuilder absorbed everything, instinctively and with a passion.

The timber-cutting began in the fall, just before the first snowfalls. After High Mass on Sundays, on the square in front of the church, the village crier would inform the people that Captain Bernier was undertaking the building of his ship, and that he was interested in buying timber from the owners of woodlots.

Imagine the pride of Bernier Junior! He was participating in an enterprise that was the talk of the whole of L'Islet. His father was the man of the hour!

With the arrival of winter Elzéar increasingly abandoned his classes and instead headed for the shipyard. The blocks were in place on the beach, behind the sheds and the workshops. On them rested the keel, shaped from two pieces of Michigan oak, bought in Québec, and each 35 feet in length.

While the ship's frame was being erected, the young man continued making oakum, as well as whittling treenails made from dry elm. These pegs, about 30 inches in length, fastened together the components of the ship, as our metal nails do nowadays.

At the large shipyards in Québec it generally took five to seven months to build a ship.[10] In the Berniers' shipyard at L'Islet, that possessed neither the conveniences nor the organization and finances of Gilmour,

The *Saint-Joseph,* Captain Thomas Bernier's first brigantine. [Archives of Carol and Louis Terrien]

Sharples, Black or Munn, who sometimes engaged 100 workmen for one ship, the work proceeded at a steady rhythm and without respite until the winter of 1865-66. Thus this single-decked, three-masted brigantine took almost 18 months of work.

In April 1866 Thomas Bernier and his family and friends finally saw the results of their labours. The *Saint-Joseph* had a proud look about her. She smelled of fresh wood, paint and tar. She smelled good. What a success! She was 98 feet in length; beam 28 feet, and she drew 13 feet. Her masts were exceptionally tall, more than 100 feet in height. Thanks to her vast sail area, she would have a good turn of speed, even in light winds. In normal weather she would average 10 knots, and in heavy seas she would roll very little and would handle easily. These predictions were accurate. The finished product exceeded Thomas Bernier's dreams.

She was given the name *Saint-Joseph*, just like the ship that had brought Jacques Bernier, alias Jean de Paris, the first of their ancestors to settle in the New World. *Joseph,* just like the owner's eldest son, who would himself command her one day, and *Joseph,* because Thomas harboured a particular soft spot for that saint inspired by the following incident:

> A score of years before the launch of the *Saint-Joseph,* while strolling on the beach of Miquelon Island, he stopped to examine the wreck of a very old Breton ship half-buried in the sand. In the bow he noticed a patch of wood that had been fitted in, apparently to stop a hole. His curiosity aroused, he found a stick and poked at the block of wood until it came free. Into the sand at his feet fell a porcelain statue of St. Joseph, about nine inches tall. This statue he carried with him always at sea. When he retired he gave it to me and I have carried it ever since. It is of white unglazed porcelain and is a real work of art [...] In the *Saint-Joseph* the statue was given a place of honour in the cabin.[11]

In April 1866 a launching way, borrowed from Valin's yard in Québec, was placed ahead of the waiting ship. Then, early in May the parish priest of L'Islet blessed the ship, sprinkling her bow generously with holy water. The proud workmen and their families waited impatiently for her launch. The entire village was living in expectation. Of course there had been the launch of Basile Deroy's brigantine two years previously; it too had exhilarated the population, but that was quite a long time ago, and the *Saint-Joseph* was a different matter. Her 216 tonnes easily eclipsed the 120 tonnes of M. Deroy's *B.L. George!*

Early on the morning of the first high tide in May the villagers, dressed in their best, flocked to the shipyard. Célina smashed a bottle of port against the ship's bows to baptize her, and to give the long-awaited signal. Men hurriedly knocked away the supports with vigorous blows of their sledge-hammers and the elegant vessel slid easily into the river, encouraged by loud and prolonged cheering.

After being launched at L'Islet the *Saint-Joseph* was towed to Palais Beach on the St. Charles River, to be rigged. This meant setting up the topmasts and spars, that had been finished by Joseph-Elzéar's uncle, Narcisse

The port of Québec in 1864. [Archives historiques de la ville de Québec, Collection documents iconographiques, No. 04887]

Paradis[12] at L'Islet, and had been stowed on deck for the trip upriver, and fitting her with a suit of hemp canvas sails, so that she could pass inspection by the colony's Customs House. But before the masts were stepped, Thomas Bernier made sure that the critical custom of placing a coin of that year under each of the masts, to identify the ship's age, was not forgotten. Maritime tradition had to be honoured.

On 28 July 1866 the *Saint-Joseph* passed all the obligatory inspections, and was registered with the port of Québec. On 8 August, with the wind in her sails and her bow in the foaming waves of the St. Lawrence that had seen her birth, the brigantine rounded Pointe-Lévy and set sail for Ireland with a cargo of deals. On board was her proud owner, who had realized his dream, accompanied by his 14-year-old son, who could finally embark on his amazing career as a *coureur des mers*.

CHAPTER 8

The ship's boy comes up to the mark

WHEN VERLAINE was publishing his "Poèmes saturniens" or Fiodor Dostoyevsky was publishing "Crime and Punishment," Joseph-Elzéar Bernier was leaving the shores of the St. Lawrence, bound for his future. He was not yet *Captain Bernier,* but the ship's boy, ready to follow his father to the ends of the earth.

At the same time as the *Saint-Joseph* was bowling along towards Ireland, the colonies of Lower and Upper Canada were preparing for their Canadian adventure.

> Within the framework of the British Empire, Canada, like all the other colonies fulfilled a specific function: to provide the motherland with raw materials and to represent a market for its manufactured products. Moreover this had been its role since the days of Nouvelle-France.[1]

Despite the enormous advantages connected with intercolonial trade, and even if Britain believed that she possessed industrial, social and governmental organizations superior to those of the rest of humanity and wanted to spread these benefits to the different parts of the globe, the reality was that the administration of the colonies was costing more and more. From the mid-nineteenth century onwards, London was compelled to adopt a more flexible policy by giving a certain degree of autonomy to the colonial governments. The British wanted to profit from their vast empire, but without paying the costs involved.

In parallel with this initiative of opening-up on the part of capital from Britain, her North American colony found itself seriously threatened by the expansionist policy of her neighbour to the south. She feared a military invasion and annexation by the United States. The united provinces of Lower and Upper Canada, as well as New Brunswick and Nova Scotia were obliged to wonder about their future. And that future, according to the politicians of the period, lay in Confederation, i.e. a federal union governed by a constitution modelled on that of Great Britain.

While the colony was preparing to reconstitute itself into a single Canada under the terms of the British North America Act,[2] young Elzéar Bernier was being initiated into the harsh reality of the seaman's profession.

In contrast to three-masters that required a crew of 30 to 40 men to handle them, Thomas Bernier's two-master needed a more modest crew, consisting of a captain, two officers, a cook, three seamen, and a boy. The captain and the first officer each had his own cabin, while the second officer and the cook shared another. These three cabins were located aft of the mainmast. The seamen slept in the fo'c'sle, forward of the foremast. The boy usually lived with the seamen, but for this first voyage Thomas had decided to keep an eye on his lad (moreover he had promised Célina to do so) and to install a rudimentary bunk off the main cabin. "But this

Joseph-Elzéar Bernier at age 13-14 when he shipped as cabin-boy on board the *Saint-Joseph*. He is wearing the suit made by his mother. [Archives of Carol and Louis Terrien]

was the only concession made to the captain's son," as Joseph-Elzéar stated in his memoirs.

The ship's boy was the ship's drudge who had to handle all the domestic chores, secondary tasks and minor jobs with a good grace, and was at the mercy of everybody's wishes and moods, at any hour of the day. Thomas was aware of this, since he had gone through the same initiation himself, but he could not make any further concessions. If his son wanted to become a sailor, he had to undergo this test and cope with this initiation. Sailors would not tolerate weaklings.

> From the galley to the deck; from the hold to the crow's nest, from the pilot to the mate, and from one sailor to another, Joseph would be climbing the mast, coming down again, filling buckets of water at the pump, climbing aloft again, polishing, and would then start all over again: "Here boy!" To port, to starboard; everyone was looking for him and he was overwhelmed! They hustled him around with this terrifying "Here boy!"[3]

The boy was obliged to clean the cabins, carry wood to the galley, distribute food to the men, swab the deck, launder clothes and follow orders, day and night. To prove that he was already a man Elzéar had to answer "Aye!" and to react immediately. What was his remuneration for this slave-labour? Eight dollars per month, payable to his mother!

In return Célina made his clothes, his straw-mattress, and his catalogne (rag-coverlet). Despite his mother's good intentions and love, the clothes made of hemp canvas that she gave him added to his afflictions, since they were not waterproof and, in rainy weather they became so saturated, heavy and stiff that they chafed his skin like emery paper.

It goes without saying that a 14-year-old lad, constantly working in the open air, develops a rather voracious, even gargantuan, appetite. Since the boy was at the bottom of the heap in the shipboard hierarchy, Elzéar was obliged to serve everyone else first and to content himself with the crumbs that remained. "Goodbye, soup, meat, biscuits!" the lad would lament, his mouth watering at dishes that smelled so tantalizing but which were disappearing as he watched! Did he have to die of hunger to prove that he was a man? No, but he had to understand the importance of mastering his urges. Later he would assert that he had learned that lesson well:

> If a man does not discover his faults and does not correct them, he will die from them. If a man wants to succeed he must first triumph over himself, take control of his mind, his eye-sight, his hearing, of all parts of himself as an individual. In a word, he must take control of himself before he can control others. One weak trait in him might result in his death.[4]

It was indeed an initiation: he must succeed in developing never-failing personal discipline, despite hunger, difficulties and dreadful sea-sickness that assailed one's guts.

Yes, the notorious *mal-de-mer* struck, with the first symptoms appearing at the mouth of the Gulf of St. Lawrence when the *Saint-Joseph* was encountering heavy seas. The ship's boy had never experienced such dizziness, with repeated vomiting and violent intestinal cramps. Incapable of continuing his work he sought refuge in his bunk.

But the captain, his father, evidently saw things differently. In his view the only way to cure sea-sickness was to go to the extremes of torment. The boy was lashed to the windlass on the fo'c'sle head, for his protection and to prove a theory that appears quite ridiculous nowadays. His poor body, hurting and weakened from sea-sickness was forced to endure the ship's rolling and pitching. Each time she dove into the trough of the wave the boy would feel his heart in his mouth, as if he were on a roller-coaster.

This martyrdom lasted for two hours. When he was freed, he was ordered to finish his watch before returning to his bunk.

This radical antidote was totally ineffective since:

> A few days later I was sent aloft at dawn to take a reef in the topsail. The wind was on the increase and the sea was rough. As I scurried up the ratlines of the shrouds I felt the old illness coming over me, and as I stood on the middle of the footrope, one arm clutching the yard, the other hand reaching blindly for the slack of the sail, I did not care whether I fell out of the rigging or not. And when I finally reached the deck, I made for the cabin. But the men were merciless. They laughed heartily at my pallor and sent me aloft again to fasten an earring that had worked loose. However, I survived all this harsh treatment and after this voyage rarely suffered from seasickness.[5]

These misfortunes did not prevent him from studying the rudiments of navigation, and from taking the helm in fine weather. His father kept an eye on him, guided him, and taught him how to tie knots, to box the compass, how to read the stars, how to execute a manoeuvre or to determine the ship's position from the sun. These moments of happiness were some compensation in that they made him almost forget the kicks up the backside, the boredom, the hunger and the exhausting work. Joseph-Elzéar told himself, that despite everything, he was really lucky to see the world, to learn navigation and to be able to lead an active life in the open air.

Two weeks after leaving the Gulf of St. Lawrence, the *Saint-Joseph* reached the Irish coast and headed for Killala Bay in the north-western part of this, the most westerly of the British Isles, formerly known as Eire. The fisherman who acted as their pilot, as well as the other Irish people that the ship's boy saw around him, looked like beggars. Their village, located at the mouth of the River Moy was a collection of poor thatched cottages sullied by the peat that they burned in their fireplaces. Even the church, with its thatched roof, was in harmony with this lugubrious décor.

The *Saint-Joseph* had to wait for a week for the high spring tide that allowed her to make her way up the shallow river, and to drop anchor at Ballina, 10 miles upriver. The villagers greeted her arrival with great excitement, since they had never seen such a large vessel penetrate so far up the River Moy.

Before putting to sea again the captain and his crew went to mass at Ballina cathedral. Elzéar has made no comment on the architecture of the place, and even less on the importance of this gesture towards the religious crew members, who were left to their own devices for a part of the year. On the other hand he was astonished to see that there were few men in the church. Around him he could see only women on their knees, sobbing as they listened to the preacher's words and groaning as they wrung their hands. Unaccustomed to this type of immoderate behaviour in a sacred place, and having understood not a single word of the sermon, he concluded that the priest must be very gifted and particularly eloquent.

These rare breaks in the voyage, marked by strange discoveries as to people's manners, could only gladden the ship's boy, who could temporarily forget the thankless tasks and the ill-treatment that was imposed on him.

The troubles had not ended for the young fellow since the return voyage, in mid-September, was made in foul weather. First of all a persistent series of severe squalls lashed the *Saint-Joseph,* followed by a terrifying storm that drove her to within 60 miles of Greenland, where the ship was surrounded by ice.

Joseph-Elzéar has not revealed the fear he experienced faced by the violence of nature or by the real possibility of a premature death. He stated simply that it was a great comfort for the crew when they reached the more clement waters of the Gulf of St. Lawrence. He learned later that several ships had been lost during this ferocious autumnal gale, including the Canadian government steamer *Queen Victoria*.

On his way upriver to Québec, Captain Bernier took the time to drop anchor off L'Islet to briefly greet his family and to get news of everyone. Then he sailed up to Québec to discharge his cargo.

For the young Bernier this voyage had been a tough initiation into the realities of his father's profession. Unfortunately a further trial, just as painful, awaited him at Québec:

> While at anchor at the Pointe-à-Carcy in Quebec late in the forenoon of October 14th, I noticed a great cloud rising above the Faubourg Saint-Roch, a suburb of the Lower Town of Quebec. As my uncle, Narcisse Paradis, lived there, I was immediately interested, and I set off to see where the fire was. As I approached the Faubourg the clouds of smoke increased in volume and angry flames were leaping skyward through the smoke. It was the Great Fire of '66, in which 2,129 houses were destroyed. When I reached my uncle's house I found his family in great distress, hurriedly transferring all their possessions to Jacques Cartier Square, facing the church. I stripped off my coat and vest and set in to help them. But on my return from the square for another load of goods I was stopped by a policeman and forbidden to return to the house, as were also the rest of the family. The flames were dangerously close and within a short time had consumed not only the entire street in which my uncle's house stood but the great accumulation of household effects in the church square. My own loss was serious to a ship's boy of fifteen, my Sunday coat and vest.[6]

Elzéar was badly shaken by this horrible tragedy and by the painful feeling of impotence that he observed among the victims, people he had known and loved since childhood.

The Saint-Roch and Saint-Sauveur districts after the fire of 1870 only four years after the terrible fire of 1866 that had totally razed them. The building at top-right is the Naval Hospital. [Photo: Augustin Leggo, ANQ, P600-6/GH273-41]

This disaster forced the Québec authorities to reorganize their system of fire protection. The fire, which had originated at a grocer's on Saint-Joseph Street near the Jacques-Cartier market, had quickly spread to the western sector of the Saint-Roch neighbourhood, and had then consumed almost the entire village of Saint-Sauveur. Present-day assessments place the number of homes that went up in flames at 1,837 and the number of people affected at 20,000.

By 17 November the *Saint-Joseph* was securely moored in the winter harbour at Boucherville. Thomas Bernier's wooden two-master and his ship's boy had come up to the mark and had surmounted all the obstacles on this voyage of initiation. They were both fully seasoned.

Joseph-Elzéar had indeed behaved well throughout the voyage and had demonstrated that he was a true Bernier. But, at the bottom of his heart, had he had enough of the blows he had received, the hunger, the sea-sickness, the storms, the wet clothes? Did he have some doubts? Was the life of a sailor really for him?

CHAPTER 9

A promotion

After the Treaty of Paris in 1763 and the annexation of the French colony to the British Empire, all the constitutional documents imposed by London, including the British North America Act, were published in English, without an official French version. Right from the start Britain had made an effort to transform Nouvelle-France into New England. The British "face" of the institutions of power had been duplicated in the place names given to towns and streets: Hull, Sherbrooke, Dorchester, Wolfe, Durham, Waterloo, Wellington … and gradually the English language had become dominant, powerful, and overbearing because it was the language of technology and big-business, and hence that of prestige and economic control.

> Besides the convenience that it ensured for English speakers, this situation made economic life appear as an English reality, an impression reinforced by the fact that those who spoke French, in response to the impact of English, ended up by losing, or more accurately, never learning, the French vocabulary of technology and business […]The French-speaking people drew the lesson from this and attempted to access the prestige of English by operating their businesses under English names […].[1]

This was the reality for the Berniers of L'Islet in the County of Devon. Captain Thomas Bernier, his brothers, as well as their father, Jean-Baptiste and several of their cousins, had made a good living by trading with the British. The same would apply to Joseph-Elzéar who, at the age of 15, was increasingly determined to pursue a sea-going career. He learned English unquestioningly, since that was the way it had been for a long time. It was the language at work, but at home French would remain the normal language. His bilingualism and his lack of schooling meant that his spelling and his syntax showed the effects throughout his life. Elzéar had only a poor command of the language of Shakespeare, which he spoke with a Liverpool accent and "which he also wrote very badly, and which he mixed ruthlessly with that of Molière."[2]

On 1 April 1867 Captain Thomas Bernier broke some good news to his son. He would promote him to seaman, and he could come with him on his next voyage, if that was what he wanted. Not only did he want to go, but the idea overjoyed him and he had absolutely no doubts. He really had salt water in his veins!

On April 12th the *Saint-Joseph* left her winter berth at Boucherville and set sail for Montréal.

Right from the start of her second season at sea, fate dogged the *Saint-Joseph*. She ran aground on a wooden dock, submerged by the flood that then occurred every spring in Montréal harbour. One must realize that at that time that port did not yet have the revetment walls, nor modern concrete quays. Only wooden wharves,

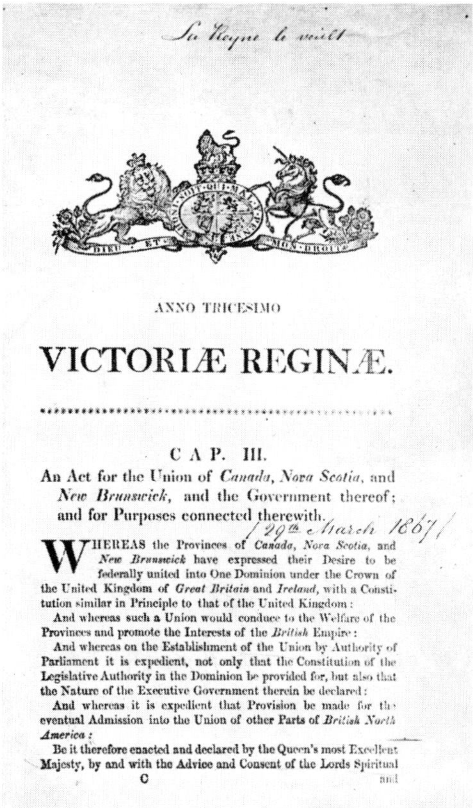

La Reyne le veult

ANNO TRICESIMO

VICTORIÆ REGINÆ.

C A P. III.

An Act for the Union of *Canada*, *Nova Scotia*, and *New Brunswick*, and the Government thereof; and for Purposes connected therewith. [29th March 1867]

WHEREAS the Provinces of *Canada*, *Nova Scotia*, and *New Brunswick* have expressed their Desire to be federally united into One Dominion under the Crown of the United Kingdom of *Great Britain* and *Ireland*, with a Constitution similar in Principle to that of the United Kingdom:

And whereas such a Union would conduce to the Welfare of the Provinces and promote the Interests of the *British* Empire:

And whereas on the Establishment of the Union by Authority of Parliament it is expedient, not only that the Constitution of the Legislative Authority in the Dominion be provided for, but also that the Nature of the Executive Government therein be declared:

And whereas it is expedient that Provision be made for the eventual Admission into the Union of other Parts of *British North America*:

Be it therefore enacted and declared by the Queen's most Excellent Majesty, by and with the Advice and Consent of the Lords Spiritual

C and

First page of the British North America Act, 1867.

built at water-level, were provided for the loading or unloading of cargoes. Captain Bernier had to call upon the aid of a steam tug to rescue his ship from this awkward situation.

While the ship was loading flour, barrels of pork, leather, bags of biscuits, and other products bound for Barbados, the new seaman took advantage of this sojourn to visit the city of Montréal, which he was really seeing only for the first time. He behaved like any other tourist: he climbed one of the towers of Notre-Dame Church, which was taller than the masts of his father's ship, and carved his initials on a beam to ensure his immortality, then he strolled around Mount Royal to admire the view of a city in ferment.

The *Saint-Joseph* topped off her cargo at Repentigny with a deck-load of deals, before running down the river to the open sea and heading for warmer waters.

Elzéar was astonished by the change of climate as the ship ran through the Gulf Stream, the warm current also known as the North Atlantic Drift, and the way in which it led him to modify his behaviour and work habits:

> Day and night I walked about bare-foot, and wore only a light shirt, trousers rolled to the knee, and a straw hat. But there were drawbacks: for one thing, the decks had to be washed down twice a day to prevent shrinking or warping in the scorching rays of the tropical sun. And then the weather was changeable, and often we were called out of bed in the middle of our watch below with the command "All hands aloft; reef in the fore-topsail." For a boy of fifteen, called out of his sleep after a hard day's work, forced to climb the ratlines with sleep still in is eyes, then stand on a footrope 60 feet above the deck, clutching the yard with one hand, and working with the other, life at sea seems particularly hard. But afterwards, more often than not, the cook was ready with a cup of hot coffee for each man, and life seemed happier again.[3]

During this voyage Captain Thomas continued with his eldest son's apprenticeship. He hoped to make a real man of him, aware of the risks of his trade, respectful towards his superiors and his colleagues, keen to work and proud of his profession. Discipline, cleanliness and energy were the order of the day, as in the Royal Navy. There was no unfair favouritism for the boss's son, who was expected to earn his wages and to contribute to the success of the voyage. Incompetence, poorly handled work, insolence, alcohol, and insubordination were unacceptable faults, causes for severe punishment.

Thomas wanted to impart to him all his knowledge.

> My father literally pounded mathematics into me, for the maxim of instruction at sea in those days was that intelligence is prompted by hard knocks. I was taught to take longitude and latitude, to calculate the ship's position, to measure the ship's run, to keep the log, and how to handle the ship under various conditions.[4]

Towards the end of the 19th century large sailing ships from the four corners of the world were moored to the quays bordering the Rue de la Commune, in the port of Montréal. [Photo: Alexander Henderson, Canadian Pacific Railway Archives, Image No. NS 709]

Before leaving Québec he had even given him a quadrant that he had picked up in a pawn-shop for the modest price of five dollars, to help him observe the sun's position with respect to the horizon.

When there was no sun we had to depend on the ship's run to calculate our position. On a sailing ship, the ship's run was taken every two hours when the wheelsmen changed watch. Today the ship's run is simply read off a gauge attached to a patent log that floats behind the ship. But in those days things were not so simple. It required three men to take the ship's run. One held a sand glass in his hand, usually a fourteen-second glass. The other hove the "log," which was a triangular piece of flat board weighted with lead so that it would float with the apex pointing skyward. An ingenious arrangement of cords, a wooden plug, and knots, made sure the triangle would float in this position even against the pull of the ship. The man would heave the log overboard from the lee quarter near the stern, paying out the rope for 45 feet. This distance was marked by a tiny piece of rag worked into the rope. After that every knot and half knot was spliced into the rope, a knot being represented by 46 feet six inches of rope. At the 45 feet mark, the glass was turned. The moment the sand was all run out, the glass man sang out "Stop." The knots were then counted. The answer was the speed of the boat.[5]

Soundings were taken when land was approached, in fog, in unfamiliar waters or near shoals. A sailing vessel would then be "hove-to," which meant that it was brought up into the wind so that it lost way, and the lead was heaved. This was a lead cone, weighing about 28 pounds, at the end of several fathoms of line. Standing amidship a crew member would drop a bight of the line into the sea, while another seaman on the stern would count aloud every 10 fathoms that ran out, until the line went slack, to indicate that the lead had reached bottom.

Since it was sometimes important to know the nature of the sea-bed below the ship, the captain would "arm" the lead with a piece of soft soap that would take the impression of a rocky bottom, or would incorporate samples of a sandy or muddy bottom.

Under his father's vigilant gaze Joseph-Elzéar thus had the good fortune to learn the first rules of ship-handling by observation, namely the three "l's", log, lead and look-out.

The *Saint-Joseph* took 34 days to reach the port of Bridgetown, capital of Barbados, located in the south-west of that island:

> [...] at the Point outside Bridgetown harbour we took on a pilot [...] this man was a negro, tall, handsome and well-formed.
>
> The small harbour was impressive to me, being crowded with more than one hundred vessels, most of them small. It made a beautiful sight, the deep blue of the bay, studded with ships, framed in the golden rim of the sandy beach, with a background of graceful coco-nut palms like a fringe about the bay.[6]

The *Saint-Joseph* dropped anchor at the mouth of the river that flows into Bridgetown Bay, to begin unloading the cargo.

Joseph-Elzéar seemed delighted at his promotion that made him an integral part of the crew. He slept with the other sailors on the poop beneath a vast awning made from the topgallant and royal sails. He bathed daily in a barrel of sea water for fear of encountering the numerous sharks in the blue waters of the bay. He tasted flying fish for the first time, and found that their flesh, fried in butter since it was a little dry, could not be compared with the salmon trout and the cold-water fishes of home. Like Ali Baba, the hero of the "*Thousand and one nights,*" faced with the treasures of the 40 thieves, he marvelled at each new discovery. But it was especially the modern technology of the only steam vessel, moored among the wooden hulls, that held his attention. That was progress. He was quite sure of it and it heralded the day when steam would overtake sail.

Shortly before putting to sea again, Joseph-Elzéar had the pleasure of meeting one of his cousins, Samuel Bernier, captain of the *Annette* that had arrived from Halifax. This led him to say, not without some pride, that there were "so many members of our family at sea that within a few years it ceased to be a surprise to me to meet a relative in some distant port."[7]

On 14 July they sailed for Montréal.

Barely 17 days later the elegant brigantine, loaded with barrels of molasses and hogsheads of sugar, was running at a good speed past Sable Island, east of Nova Scotia. Thomas Bernier was in a hurry to reach the Gulf of St. Lawrence, to make port safely and to moor in front of the Bonsecours Market in Montréal since, for this captain-cum-owner, time was money.

CHAPTER 10

The crimps

> During the summer months there are so many ships in Québec harbour that the upper masts with their yards give both shores of the river the appearance of a forest of leafless trees. The discipline observed on board the sailing ships while at sea encourages their crews to jump ship at every port whenever it was possible to get ashore. Once on shore, knowing that during the next voyage they will be condemned to a further period of fasting and to a succession of dangers, miseries, and privations, the sailors easily sink into every sort of excess.[1]

This is a good description of the situation in port that Captain Thomas Bernier had to contend with. In the summer of 1867 he had succeeded in repaying all his loans and had become the sole owner of the *Saint-Joseph*. Thomas had worked hard to attain this culminating point in his career. To add to the responsibilities associated with the position of ship's master, he now had to shoulder all kinds of other responsibilities, including the need to find new freighting contracts and to hire the crew, something that was not a simple matter at that time.

In 1870 exports from the port of Québec exceeded $10 million. That year over 1091 ships called there, carrying 756,078 tonnes and 21,931 sailors.[2] This meant that competition among the various ship-owners was quite fierce. The power of the dollar could take precedence and could easily tip the balance. This predicament must have been doubly difficult for small ship-owners, such as Captain Thomas, who did not have the financial support of the big British firms but who, nevertheless, had to play in the same sand-box to win their share of the market and to recruit their crews. The majority of the latter, incidentally, were British since French-Canadian sailors, in general, were reluctant to leave the shores of the St. Lawrence. Coastwise voyages suited them better than deep-sea voyages.

This combination of circumstances favoured the work force.

> In 1856, ten pounds a month was paid for able seamen to man Quebec ships. In those days the mate of a large sailing ship only got seven pounds a month, and it often happened that men before the mast were receiving more than the masters themselves. In 1870, sailors were getting 12 pounds a month with six pounds advance. With such a demand for men, and with the sailor supply commanding such prices, crimping and its criminal practices flourished, and every house on Champlain Street became a sailors' boarding-house and a crimps' hang-out.[3]

Naturally seamen took full advantage of this situation. Some would flatly refuse to work, and would leave their ships without permission. Others would return from the taverns completely sozzled. Absenteeism, violence, insubordination, and alcoholism were prevalent. No captain was spared this plague.

This drastic situation clearly raised another serious problem: that of prostitution. In the harbour region

A discussion is underway just off the former Rue Champlain, in Québec. The building to the right is the Cap-Blanc school. [Photo: Valentine, ANQ, P547,DL431,Q1,P29]

hundreds of specialized houses sprouted like mushrooms alongside public buildings, religious institutions or schools. The city even obliged:

> the owners of brothels to cover their windows with iron or wooden shutters. A list of the "paying guests" had to be provided to the police and soliciting outside or from the windows or doors was forbidden. Contraveners had to pay a fine of $100 or go to jail for four months."[4]

The harbour area was a paradise for inn-keepers. After their enforced abstinence at sea, the sailors "let their hair down" once they got ashore. This habit was actively exploited by the tavern owners, who sent their touts to the ships to rout out new customers. An impressive number of thirsty sailors were quick to accept these invitations, while the rum flowed like water to encourage them to spend more of their pay.

The notorious crimps operated in the midst of all these transactions. The captains and these "agents" engaged in a severe type of competition: the former trying to keep their seamen, and the latter to steal them away. Knowing that there was no law effective enough to curb their activity, the crimps stopped at nothing to get their man, and even went to the extreme of boarding ships, revolver in hand, to corrupt the sailors or to force them to follow them. In most cases a bottle of whisky and the promise of high wages would succeed in persuading them to desert. Anyone who persisted in remaining loyal to his captain would be savagely beaten or kidnapped by force, or he would be brutally shot down.

Conversely, if one of these kidnappers was killed, there was never an investigation for lack of an effective police force.

During the American Civil War, Québec crimps would kidnap sailors and transport them to the border where they were forcibly recruited to fight for the Union Army. The crimps would receive $500 to $1000 per head, sometimes even from men who intended that the seamen would take their place at the front.

The Seamen's Act attempted to tackle the problem, by imposing prison terms of two to three years for any person boarding a ship without permission.

> Despite their reduced numbers the crimps were particularly effective in the summer of 1872. The English would blame their success on the new Chief of Harbour Police who, for the first time, was a French Canadian. In their view the increasing number of French in this police force was responsible for its ineffectiveness. On average, however, the small group of policemen laid about 500 charges against crimps and deserters.[5]

Only the decline in the timber trade, the shipyards, and the shipping industry would succeed in putting an end to this terrible situation.

How did Thomas Bernier cope in such an environment? Quite well, since nine days after reaching Montréal harbour the *Saint Joseph* had been discharged of her cargo

The former Rue Champlain below the cape at Québec. [Philippe Gingras Fonds, ANQ, P585, P238]

of sugar and molasses, thoroughly cleaned, reloaded with staves, her crew rehired, and all sails set, bound for Porto, capital of the northern region of Portugal.

As always, abeam of L'Islet the father/son duo would take the time to go ashore and say goodbye to family and friends, a ritual that Joseph-Elzéar would maintain throughout his numerous deep-sea voyages. He would always insist on this practice, as if the success of the voyage depended on the gestures of friendship and on the waving of those who had assembled on the quayside.

This crossing, that lasted 42 days and was marked by foul winds and heavy seas, seemed interminable to the young Bernier, who complained of the shortage of drinking water, the ship's constant rolling, and its rather boring routine, all of which made him miss the comforts of home and the company of his childhood pals. These were passing regrets, as he admitted,[6] immediately dismissed by the delightful sight of about 30 large sailing vessels, anchored in Porto harbour, on the shores of the Douro estuary.

The drawbacks of the long sea-voyage were soon dispelled by the unexpected effect of the sun on the multicoloured facades of the strange buildings that clung to the steep slopes of Portugal. All the tedium of the voyage faded away in the face of the gaiety of the washing lines that ran from one balcony to another, displaying long strings of unmatched clothes, as if the town overlooking the activity on its docks, was *en fête*. There were even orange, lemon and fig trees bearing fruit… in mid-October!!

But what could one say about the strange behaviour of the Portuguese? The woman did the bulk of the physical work around the docks. They loaded and unloaded ships, while their men took their ease in the shade of the trees, shouting orders to them. An upside-down world indeed!

The "Old Man," as ships' captains were always called then, brought his seaman-son back to more urgent preoccupations: an overhaul of the *Saint-Joseph*. Since Thomas did not manage to find another cargo, he decided to refurbish his ship. Apart from the usual cleaning of decks and hold, the masts and yards were greased, the deck reinforced and re-caulked, the rigging inspected, and the deck-houses repainted.

> But the most important work done was the cleaning of the ship's bottom. The long trip down through warm water had invited many barnacles to fix themselves to the ship. And there was danger of worms attacking the planking. My father knew of a special preparation used by Portuguese and Spanish shipbuilders to protect the bottoms of their ships and he was glad of the opportunity to have it applied.[7]

Thomas thus initiated his son in the celebrated secret of the Iberian shipbuilders that would permit the future master mariner to improve the performance of all his ships, to hold 22 records for the fastest transatlantic crossings, and to earn him the prestigious Atlantic Blue Ribbon. The process was really very ingenious. At high tide the *Saint-Joseph* was towed over a sand shoal just deep enough to support her when the tide dropped, forcing her to careen to one side. With the hull thus exposed members of the crew and some local workers were able to scrape away the barnacles that had fastened themselves to the hull with their powerful peduncles. The strakes were then dried, one by one with burning bunches of weeds so that the special preparation would adhere better to the hull. The same process was repeated on the other side of the ship on the next low tide.

But what was the actual secret of this mysterious coating that repelled parasites and enhanced the performance of the vessel? It was a mixture, in equal parts of two solids—sulphur and beef tallow—to which a little arsenic was added. This mixture produced a protective layer with the appearance of enamel, as smooth and hard as our modern varnishes.

The *Saint-Joseph's* captain had to wait about three weeks to obtain a further contract that would get his ship and his crew moving again.

These were tedious days for Elzéar, who found himself handicapped by his youth and his small size. He was working as much as the others, but he did not feel that he was the equal of the other mature sailors. "My father was away practically all of the time…," he wrote. "On Sundays and at night, the rest of the officers and the crew would go ashore, leaving me as watchman of the ship.[…] So I was left alone aboard, and remained alone until the first drunken sailor came staggering aboard to curse me."[8] The word "drunken" is fired off like a complaint.

At sea Thomas maintained an iron discipline but in harbour, during these waiting periods he obviously could not impose conditions on his seamen, who had finished their work. And the men enjoyed themselves to the full.

In his memoirs Elzéar recounted how, on their arrival in Porto, his father had paid off the cook and one of his officers for drinking at sea, and had replaced them with a French mate and a Scandinavian cook. One evening the latter and three other sailors came back aboard after a particularly drunken foray ashore and decided to provoke the "Old Man" in his cabin. Although he was the only officer on board Thomas refused to let himself be intimidated by the vehemence of these drunks and ordered them out of his cabin. They refused to budge.

> My father was a very strong and very resolute man. He was not tall but a blow from his fist was something to be remembered. He was not one to be intimidated by four drunken sailors. A struggle began in the cabin and continued on deck, lasting nearly fifteen minutes. Two men were knocked senseless within the first few minutes. The other two were hungry for punishment, and came back and back, but finally they were glad to slink away to the fo'c'stle.[9]

Joseph-Elzéar was a witness to this unequal fight. He would always remember being riveted to the spot, held back by his youth and his small size. Although he was well aware of the power behind his father's formidable fist and was never in doubt as to the outcome, he was annoyed with himself at not being able to help him. He would always abhor the depraved effects of alcohol and would always be disgusted by men who indulged in it shamelessly, getting intoxicated in order to escape reality. "This scene, and hundreds of other ones," he concluded, "[...] taught me early in life the dangers of indulgence in strong liquor. All my life I have been a teetotaller."[10]

Thomas finally succeeded in finding a cargo of cork and lead bars bound for New York. It looked as if they would soon be putting to sea. The sailors set to work again, whistling the melodies of home.

Elzéar, too, was quite excited, a new departure, new horizons, new adventures, the challenge of facing the sea and the elements, the freedom of the open sea, and his apprenticeship as a sailor: these were what he liked above all. Other aspects—the dangers, the fear of dying, the uncertainty, the physical hardships, the boredom, the loneliness—he would learn to accept and overcome with age and experience. The young lad was not a fool; the call of the sea that had had an intestinal hold on him since childhood represented good fortune tinged with risk.

His account of this first voyage to Portugal seems to be that of a young man in a hurry to grow and mature in order to be accepted and to take his place in the world of adults. One gains the impression of somebody who is too serious and too responsible before his time. Of course, he was probably somewhat like all the adolescent of that period who had to work to earn a living, but his photograph at the age of 14 would suggest hat he was perhaps more intense, more obstinate, more serious and more conscientious than the average.

By contrast, his last memory of Porto clearly reflects the child he still was, despite himself... Joseph-Elzéar was sitting in a boat alongside the quay waiting for his father to return with the documents they needed to put to sea. He was not looking at anyone. He was not talking to anyone. He was being patient, gazing at the pastel-coloured building that housed the port authorities. The warm rays of the sun caressed him pleasantly. Suddenly a projectile grazed his face, then another, splattering his jacket with an orange, sticky substance. Before he could react he was bombarded with oranges by a group of local urchins who had chosen him as their target. This time Elzéar responded vigorously and delightedly and a battle royal ensued, until his father arrived!

This represented a rare moment of playfulness, a last momentary lapse into childhood before he tackled the rigours of the homeward voyage and of the transition into adulthood.

CHAPTER II

Accordant with his character

The *Saint-Joseph* sailed from Porto in the fall of 1867 and coasted south along the Iberian coast. Before she reached the mouth of the Tagus a monumental storm took a hand,

> [...] with a hard gale blowing from the north-west, rain coming down in sheets, and the sea running high. A north-west wind was an inshore wind, which meant grave danger unless we could tack out from the shore. We shortened sail and tried to tack, but with half a cargo and little ballast the ship simply drifted broadside to the wind, refusing to answer the helm.[1]

As night fell the ship was still drifting and still in danger. Thomas knew that he was not far from the estuary of the Tagus, and he calculated that he could negotiate the entrance to the estuary and take refuge there. As a precaution he had continual soundings taken, and he prepared the anchors.

Joseph-Elzéar, who was posted as lookout on the stern, was the first to spot the Lisbon lighthouse and to alert the crew, but the lighthouse disappeared again in an instant behind a heavy curtain of rain, so that the ship was again sailing blindly.

> On the poop deck I was again first to report, this time breakers to starboard astern. Immediately the port anchor was dropped. Then the starboard anchor was started, but jammed in the windlass. A two-minute struggle freed it, and it was followed by the kedge, a small anchor carried on deck. For a dreadful few minutes, with the breakers pounding astern, the anchors dragged. Then they found holding ground, the ship hove to with a sickening jar, and we were safe—or comparatively so, for the surf was breaking close to our stern.[2]

If the anchors had not held, there would have been few survivors to tell the tale.

By daybreak the storm still showed no sign of slackening. Her crew fully realized that they were still vulnerable since they were only four ship's lengths off the breakers and the shore. They had overshot the entrance to Lisbon Bay by over half-a-mile.

During the morning a steam tug appeared out of nowhere to offer its services in exchange for £100. Thomas offered £25, and a deal was struck.

The manoeuvre attempted by the tug was unsuccessful. The cable with which it tried to tow the ship was so rusted and rotten that it broke just as the *Saint-Joseph* was rounding the end of the reef. There was only one option to save the situation: to set all sail and to attempt the impossible by storming into the mouth of the river.

Captain Thomas had assessed the situation correctly in risking all or nothing. His guiding star led the *Saint-Joseph* into calm waters, inside Lisbon harbour. She had suffered only one ripped sail and the loss of a bell.

After 48 stressful hours her crew had only one aim, to head for their bunks.

Elzéar did not seem too impressed by the Arab and mediaeval character of the Portuguese capital, neither by the Belem Tower at the harbour entrance, nor by the hieronymite monastery, founded by Manuel I in the 16th century. He noted 13 frigates and over 100 merchant vessels moored off the city. But nothing further. In fact the Portuguese bureaucracy was so unwieldy and corrupt that it tainted his view of Lisbon:

> We found the port regulations even more trying than the Oporto rules. As in Oporto, we were required to drop two anchors at the bow and a kedge astern. Customs inspectors came aboard on our arrival, intimated they were hungry, proved to have voracious appetites, and afterwards an unbounded curiosity. Not content with this first inspection, they returned several times, turning every corner of the ship topsy-turvy. They were insolent and high-handed, and had the reputation of being thievish.
>
> No one was allowed to land without a written permission from the port authorities, countersigned by the customs clerk, for which a fee was required. Under no conditions was anyone allowed ashore after 8 o'clock. When our party went ashore to take on water, the men were not allowed to fill the cask because the permit secured did not mention that the landing was to secure water.[3]

Thomas quickly arranged the consignment of other cargoes to fill his ship and to clear out as quickly as possible ... marble blocks, each weighing 3 or 4 tonnes, nuts in sacks, gum in barrels, coffee, almonds, and raisins in bags, figs in boxes, and more cork.

Early in December he put to sea from Lisbon harbour without a backward glance at these unpleasant officials who had done nothing but delay his departure and harass him.

They soon encountered very favourable winds and unexpectedly mild weather. It was so warm that the captain's eldest son spent his first Christmas at sea barefooted and lightly dressed, something he found very strange, accustomed as he was only to Canada's white Christmases and below-zero temperatures. Of course the *Saint-Joseph*'s youngest seaman could not anticipate that after this fair weather he would face trials that would make the last leg of the voyage an initiation into the adult world. The weather conditions changed as they entered the Gulf Stream. Despite variable and fitful winds, the ship managed to maintain her course until about 80 miles out of New York. But then came a fateful moment when the weather broke with a vengeance:

> [...] the wind veered to the north-west, stiffened to a gale, and before it abated we were driven many hundred miles from our destination. Winds then varied from north-west to north-east, with rain, hail, and snow. As days passed and we could make no headway north-eastward, our provisions ran low. Our meat first ran out. Then our cook, who proved as negligent as the one we had paid off in Lisbon, upset a pailful of kerosene in the store-room, spoiling our provision of rice, peas, and coffee and part of our store of biscuits. We were then reduced to a ration of one biscuit a day per man, helped out with almonds, figs and raisins from the cargo. The seventh day of our fast we spoke a barque which consented to supply us with 15 pounds of biscuits.[4]

In addition the members of the crew were very ill-assorted. They did not get on well together, and, for the most part, were lazy, coarse and vindictive. The bad weather and the second mate, an Acadian by the name of Briand, combined to poison the atmosphere on board. Although a fine seaman, Briand was incapable of controlling his bad temper, his virulent attacks, and his vulgar remarks in his relations with the others. He bore ill-will towards the "Old Man" for having engaged a first mate at Lisbon, rather than promoting him, and since he was of the type to bear a grudge, he was just as odious and detestable towards his skipper as he was towards the others. His resentment was redirected towards the captain's son. One day, during his watch, Elzéar was leaning on the capstan on the fo'c'sle head and whistling nonchalantly as he usually did when he was alone. The second mate came on deck and caught him in this posture.

> He took off his boots and came up quietly in stocking feet and struck me sharply on the side of the head. He followed the blow with an accusation that I had been sleeping on look-out duty and said that he was going to report me to the captain for punishment. His accusation was accompanied by a volley of abuse.[5]

Stunned by the blow and furious at the insults Elzéar grabbed a capstan bar and knocked the man senseless. He immediately went to his fellow crew-members and told them about the incident. They all rushed to the bow, just in time to see Briand regain consciousness. He got up without a word and without picking up his boots headed for his cabin.

> In a few minutes the "Old Man" appeared, very angry. The second mate had told him I had struck him from behind without notice. My father was ready to thrash me for what he thought I had done. He had had so much trouble with the men, and now his own son was contributing to make the situation worse! But I hotly explained what had happened, and my story was borne out by the stockinged feet of the second mate, and his boots on the deck. Despite this I received a sound tongue-lashing, as did also the second mate.[6]

He justified his reaction by saying that the memory of the blows and injustices inflicted on him while the ship's boy, combined with this last attack, had convinced him that he should no longer submit to iniquities caused him by others. Henceforth Joseph-Elzéar Bernier would give blow for blow. In refusing to submit to the violence of others he was becoming an adult, taking charge of his destiny.

Much later he would admit that a man, "for whom all goes well in life, will never count for much; some storms, some set-backs are necessary to bring out his character."[7]

CHAPTER 12

A confrontation

As soon as unloading was complete Thomas Bernier was quite relieved to pay off his cantankerous crew. The 45-year-old captain had found this last voyage much too difficult, exhausting, and stressful.

As soon as they were back in New York he decided to undertake the building of a second ship, offering the command of the *Saint-Joseph* to his elder brother, Captain Joseph Bernier (1822-1896). And he would reward his son's resolve, talents and boldness by promoting him to second mate.

Thus on 18 February 1868 Joseph-Elzéar reached an important milestone in his youthful career as a sailor. Alongside his Uncle Joseph he would learn to adapt to another captain, to assume more responsibility, and to operate with a new crew. For the first time he would be heading into the Atlantic Ocean and into the unknown, without his father.

... Cadiz, Lisbon ...

The young second mate lived by the rhythm of the watches, of storms and calms, of loading and unloading of cargo, of arrivals and departures, of ship's maintenance, of moments of great loneliness, of surprising discoveries, of highs and lows ...

...New York, Québec, Montréal, Newfoundland, Cape Breton Island, Boston ...

All in all, 1868 was a critical year for Thomas Bernier's son, since in October he was promoted to first mate on board the *Saint-Joseph*. This promotion provided him not only with a modest increase in salary and greater freedom of action, but also the possibility of proving what he could do. The main drawback was his youth and his small stature. At 16 Joseph-Elzéar felt that he possessed the gravity, the pugnacity, the will power, and the knowledge of a man of 25, and a body muscular and robust enough to withstand the worst tests. But this officer with the piercing blue eyes realized that his height of 5 feet 4 inches and his schoolboy appearance represented serious handicaps that would encourage sailors to defy his authority

The problem came to the fore early in 1869, in Boston harbour, when he had ordered the unloading of a cargo of wood from Jamaica, and the cleaning of the entire ship that was infested with lizards and scorpions that had stowed away among the tropical logs.

> Many ships have hoodoos that seem to pursue them throughout their careers. The *Saint-Joseph*'s misfortune seemed to centre in the galley. We had had much trouble with cooks, and when we had shipped our crew at Quebec the fall before and the cook had turned out to be a good one, we had re-engaged him for a year. He was a Swede and a good cook, but exceedingly surly, stubborn, and insolent, and if it had not been for the year's contract we would have discharged him long before our voyage to Boston.[1]

Joseph-Elzéar ordered the cook to do the same as the rest of the crew, and to clean the galley. The Swede

Captain Joseph Bernier, Joseph-Elzéar's uncle. He had married Geneviève Fortin at L'Islet on 27 October 1846. They are known to have had two children: Philomène, who married Adolphe Morin, and Joséphine, who married Zéphirin Bernier. [Bernier Collection, *Master Mariner*]

refused to take him seriously, and stupidly replied that he would clean his galley when he felt like it, and that it would take more than some young puppy to make him change his mind!

> I told the cook that I gave him fifteen minutes to clean his galley, and that if it was not cleaned by then that I would have the men clean it for him. He broke into a torrent of abuse, grasped a carving knife, and brandishing it in front of my face and chest told me to get out of his galley. The man seemed dangerous, so I kicked the knife out of his hand, grabbed him by the scruff of the neck, hauled him on deck, and gave him a good thrashing. When I was through with him, two men carried him aft. The other two were set to clean the galley.[2]

Despite his youthful appearance Joseph-Elzéar had demonstrated his composure and had proven to the hard cases in his crew that he was up to the rank that had been entrusted to him. He followed proper procedure in such cases, and reported the incident to the captain. His uncle approved of his conduct, but neglected to record the incident in the log or to get the testimony of two witnesses.

After receiving first-aid, the cook was confined to his cabin for an enforced rest. Determined not to be outdone by this smooth-chinned upstart, as soon as he could walk, the grudge-bearing cook left the ship without permission, which, at that time, was considered to be desertion. "But he returned to the ship with a policeman, who questioned me and the captain. Two hours later the cook came back with two policemen and a warrant, and I was taken into custody under a charge of assault and battery."[3]

This incident with the cook seems to have left its mark on the young man, less for this defiance from a coarse, violent seaman, than for the fact that his Uncle Joseph had been wanting in his duties as captain. He had always seen the role of ship's master through the example and the behaviour of his father, an authoritarian, disciplined man of integrity, ready to defend his sailors under any circumstances. His uncle had disappointed him since, by forgetting to record the Swede's behaviour in the log, he had weakened his nephew's defence and credibility.

The magistrate charged with the investigation ruled that the first mate's actions would have been permissible at sea but, since the ship was alongside, he ought to have contented himself with taking the knife from the cook and with having him arrested for insubordination. He sentenced Joseph-Elzéar to paying a fine of $50 before he could be freed.

The latter had every reason to be disillusioned at his Uncle Joseph's attitude. The captain did not even take the trouble to attend court to support his officer and he took four hours before replying to his message asking that he be released!

> When he arrived, the "Old Man" tried to make me sign a discharge for the sum against my wages. But I felt that the charge should be against the ship, and refused to sign the paper. Finally, I signed an ordinary receipt for the money, and by agreement the dispute was referred to the shipping-master at Quebec.[4]

Replacement of the cook before the ship sailed from Boston did not mean that the first mate's troubles were over, however.

Throughout the voyage to Pictou, Nova Scotia, certain members of the crew, who had managed to smuggle

Joseph-Elzéar Bernier, aged 15-16.
[Archives of Carol and Louis Terrien]

some alcohol on board, started drinking it overtly, trying to test the young officer's authority. They showed themselves to be arrogant, lazy and so brazen that Joseph-Elzéar had to react to put an end to the situation. The first seaman to display insolence was thrashed and severely punished.

> This method of enforcing discipline at sea may seem rather brutal to the casual reader. But the sea life of the day was rough and turbulent, and a good proportion of the sailors were hard cases, not far removed from a certain class that today, while not exactly criminal, give much trouble to police magistrates. Discipline aboard ship had to be maintained at all costs as the officers were so few compared to the men that only discipline could ensure obedience of orders and proper operation of a ship. A master or mate, noted for fearlessness and a strong arm, rarely experienced trouble, except in port, where the men were almost constantly inebriated, or shortly after leaving port, when the men were recovering from their carousals or still imbibing from small stores of liquor smuggled aboard.[5]

Elzéar had to shift for himself. His survival depended solely on himself, his instincts, and his physical strength. If he did not assert himself, one of these evenings he might find himself hanging from a rope, or tossed overboard with his throat cut from ear to ear!

Could he not count on the captain's support? Relations between uncle and nephew had been rather strained since they had left Boston; on the one hand because the nephew was probably unable to respect the man who had left him in the lurch in a cowardly fashion, and on the other hand because the uncle felt perhaps somewhat embarrassed or ashamed at his own ineptitude. The confrontation that erupted at the entrance to Pictou harbour would confirm that hypothesis.

It was night-time; the ship was in unfamiliar shoal waters and Joseph-Elzéar, who had the watch, decided that it would be prudent to call all hands and to wake the captain before tackling the difficult manoeuvre of tacking ship.

The "Old Man" came on deck in a bad temper, took the wheel and ordered the gaff-topsail set before tacking. Elzéar, who was standing on the poop deck, superintending the setting of the sail, noticed that one of the sailors handling the topsail was slow and awkward. While he was showing him how to pass the line so that it would not foul other rigging, his uncle, who could not see what the man was doing, lost patience and shouted to him to hurry and hoist the sail. Elzéar explained the situation to the captain, and then told the sailor to pass the line properly.

> Angered by what I said, and forgetting for the moment that I was now a man and mate of the ship, my uncle left the wheel, jumped on to the poop, and administered a vigorous kick at me.[6]

Joseph Bernier was a strapping individual, 6 feet 2 inches in height, and this was no gentle kick. Elzéar saw red. He threw himself on the captain like a wild animal and knocked him down from the poop. Then, with the same ferocity, he took a dive down to the quarter-deck and landed on top of his recumbent uncle.

The "Old Man" got up, crestfallen, and refused to prolong the confrontation. He went back to his cabin without a word, leaving command of the ship to his nephew who immediately tacked ship and, with the help of a local pilot, took the ship into Pictou.

At Québec the crew was paid off as usual, in the presence of the harbour's shipping-master. This official was also responsible for inspecting logs, issuing service certificates or discharges, and arbitrating disputes between captains, officers or other crew members. It was he who settled the affair at Boston, siding with Elzéar.

What became of Joseph Bernier? On reaching Québec he learned that his wife Geneviève was seriously ill. He left immediately to join her, leaving the command of the *Saint-Joseph* to his nephew. In his memoirs Elzéar mentions that his aunt did not survive her illness, but he makes no further reference to his uncle. Joseph was never able to regain his nephew's respect and confidence. He retired after 40 years at sea and died in 1896 at the age of 74.

CHAPTER 13

Captain at 17!

> Ship's master at seventeen! The fact may seem incredible to some, particularly to mariners who have served in the British Merchant Service, the regulations of which strictly provide a minimum age of twenty-one for an aspirant to a shipmaster's certificate. Nevertheless the fact remains that in July 1869, I was appointed master of the *Saint-Joseph*, a sea-going brigantine, that in August I cleared the ship without difficulty for Teignmouth, that I cleared from Teignmouth and New York as well as from other ports in the same year. And on the first of July 1869, I was seventeen years and six months: as far as I know, the youngest skipper in the world.[1]

Several researchers confirm that he was the youngest skipper in the world. Frederick William Wallace accords him the title of the greatest Canadian seafarer,[2] but he also says that he was a man of iron who, at the time, was the youngest captain in the world to command a sea-going vessel. In 1901 R.H.C. Brown[3] added that Bernier was the youngest ship's master of all time, since a new law had forbidden anyone becoming a captain before the age of 21. Some Canadian authors believe that he could take the credit for being the youngest captain in the long history of our country.[4]

This precedent did not fail to make the headlines in the newspapers of the day:

> Nowadays taking a ship across the Atlantic would be proof of very great ability on the part of a young man of 17. In 1869, when transoceanic sailing involved major risks Captain Bernier, who was still only 17 years old, sailed a brigantine safely to the ports of Spain. By this achievement he was demonstrating his ability as master after a tough apprenticeship of five years on board the brigantines of his father and his uncles.
>
> In terms such as these the newspapers greeted the first deep-sea effort on the part of the future explorer of The Arctic regions.[5]

The good fortune of some may sometimes represent the ill fortune of others. In Elzéar's case his aunt's illness and the departure of his Uncle Joseph allowed him to realize his dream of becoming a deep-sea captain, and of commanding large sailing ships filled with merchandise bound for distant ports with exotic and evocative names.

Like one of Joseph Conrad's heroes[6] the 17-year-old became Captain Joseph-Elzéar Bernier, a man facing his destiny alone.

At the time that he took charge of the helm of the *Saint-Joseph* Canada had no regulations governing the issue of certificates of competence for ships' officers. The system of certificates was introduced only in 1870, and applied by the new federal Department of Marine two years later. In 1869 it was sufficient for a candidate to

The Québec Customs building seen from the river, as Captain J.-E. Bernier would have known it. [Photo: Louis-Prudent Vallée, ANQ, P1000,S4,D59,P14]

present his credentials before the master of the port and prove that he had the knowledge and the competence to assume the post of captain.

Hence Joseph-Elzéar presented himself to John Dunscombe, Collector of Customs and master of the port of Québec, accompanied by his father and by Nicolas Allard, newly co-owner of the ship. He was questioned at length about his experience, his apprenticeship, his capacity in making decisions and in commanding men.

> At this time I was as tall as I have ever been since. I had a well-knit, thickly-set frame, with broad shoulders and a deep chest. I was very dark and wore (*then-fashionable*) bushy *favoris* side-whiskers. I was deeply impressed with my responsibilities, and was stern and grave in appearance. I looked every bit of twenty-five years of age.[7]

In light of his physical appearance he had no difficulty in obtaining the necessary papers.

Thus, on 12 August 1869 Joseph-Elzéar Bernier, now the "Old Man" was in command of the *Saint-Joseph* as she sailed from the basin at Cap Brulé, opposite Montmagny. Standing beside him was his mate, John MacLeod, a seasoned Scotsman from Cape Breton Island, who had accepted the challenge. In the hold of his ship he was transporting a cargo of timber, bound for Teignmouth, in Lyme Bay in south-western England.

The new captain deemed this first voyage to be favourable since he had no confrontations with his sailors, no difficult trials such as gales, and since his ship achieved a crossing of only 27 days. However the captain of the tug that took charge of the ship at the entrance to the English port was not very skilful. He missed the channel and the *Saint-Joseph* struck repeatedly on the bar, losing pieces of her false keel.

While the ship was being towed, the pilot showed a keen interest in the L'Isletain and tried to engage him in conversation. This was a labour lost since, at that time, Elzéar's command of English was limited to certain terms appropriate to his profession. What surprised him, however, was that the day after they reached port the pilot renewed his attentions, inviting both Elzéar and MacLeod to dine at his home.

> There we found about a dozen guests, all of whom showed exceptional interest in me. After we left I learned from MacLeod that all these people had been invited to "see the Indian who commanded a British ship." It seems that the pilot had mistaken my heavily-tanned face for the natural skin of an American Indian, an impression that was greatly aided by my poor efforts to speak English.[8]

Joseph-Elzéar took delight in recounting this story about the Indian from Canada who was in command of a British ship. Indeed, when he had occasion he liked to candidly make fun of his own gaucheries:

One day when I was applying coal-tar to the side of the ship, I advanced too close to the end of the plank I was standing on. In a moment I was in the water, tar-pot and all. It was early October and the water was cold. When I rose to the surface my head was covered with coal-tar, which was floating all about me. I tried to reach for a rope I knew was hanging by the ship but the coal-tar in my eyes prevented my seeing it. I struck out for the shore, but the tide carried me up past other wharves. Suddenly I heard a voice say: "Look at the nigger deserting his ship." I looked in the direction of the voice and saw two men in a row-boat. I recognized one of them as the master of a vessel in harbour. "I am no nigger, sir," I said, "I am Captain Bernier's son."

So I was fished out of the water and taken aboard my own ship, where I stripped, set my clothes to dry, made my supper and went to bed.[9]

This penchant for laughter and jokes surfaced again when he was older, more experienced and confident in being the sole real master on board his ship. But initially, the 17-year-old captain had to display a serious demeanour and mature behaviour, matching the prestige of his position and the importance of his responsibilities.

Elzéar could be proud of his first transatlantic crossing as captain. The mistakes of the English tug and the fact that the cook (another one!) had decided to desert on the eve of sailing, obliging him to call on the local police to bring him back by force, did not diminish in the slightest the success of the enterprise, especially since he was able to achieve a record time for the return voyage to Sydney, Nova Scotia. A single grey cloud cast a shadow over this fine crossing of 19 days:

Stepping on a loose hatch, he [First Officer, MacLeod] had pitched into the hold, landing on the rock ballast. His back was badly wrenched. I tore up a sheet into three strips which I sewed end to end. I then rolled John very tightly in this improvised bandage. By the time we reached Sydney he was able to work.[10]

The young captain was particularly fond of this Scotsman, who had sailed with his father for many years and who had agreed to follow him to his first command. These two men, from different cultures, had hitched their destinies to that of the brigantine *Saint-Joseph*. On 12 October 1870 they parted from her for the last time at the Customs House at Québec.

Saying goodbye to his friend MacLeod and to his father's ship, Joseph-Elzéar was prepared to chart his own course towards the unknown and towards new challenges.

The *Saint-Joseph* put to sea again with a new cargo of timber, bound for Ireland. Despite the skilled hand of her master, Joseph Bernier, the ship encountered a terrible storm off County Cork that carried away her topmast, sails and yards. With difficulty she limped into Crook Haven harbour. "She was refitted and returned to Quebec where she was sold to a Quebec merchant. She made several trips abroad, and was finally wrecked and abandoned on some foreign strand."[11] The poor brigantine was condemned in 1872 then sold to Saint Thomas in the West Indies.

CHAPTER 14

A Rose from L'Islet

Awaiting the day when you will come to me
Your eyes full of love, modesty and trust,
I dream of all the future words from your lips
That will seem like a touching musical melody,
And whose charm I will taste at your knee [...]
And this dream is as dear to me as one of your kisses!

"Intimité," from *L'Âme solitaire* by ALBERT LOZEAU[1]

JOSEPH-ELZÉAR had long been dreaming of a young woman, Rose, a tall blonde, with a well-proportioned body, pale blue eyes and a fresh, rosy complexion.

Rose-de-Lima Caron (1855-1917) was the second daughter of Louis-Marie Caron,[2] known as Grand Louis, and of Marie-Priscilla Fournier who were married at Saint-Jean-Port-Joli on 5 July 1850. Louis-Marie's first wife, Marie-Appoline-Dessaint, known as Saint-Pierre, had died six months earlier, and he was the guardian of his two sons by her: Joseph-Enselme (or Eusèbe Isaïe) aged seven and Louis-Stanislas (or Arthur), aged four.[3]

The Caron-Fournier couple and their children lived on an "irregularly-shaped lot and house" in the corner known as "Carons'" on the first concession at the eastern end of the seigneurie of Islet-Saint-Jean, where the land was the finest and the most arable. Their neighbours on one side were the parents of Appoline Saint-Pierre and on the other, the Fortins.

> Their house was "one up and one down," of axe-squared logs. Furthermore there are still traces of the shed, the barn and the house foundation [...] This is where Rose was born. Here, far from the road [...] It was not until around 1870 that the house was moved bodily down to the High road, facing the river. Yes, Grand Louis was a man of wide-ranging interests. He also had a saw-mill on the stream that ran along his property.[4]

In the church of Notre-Dame-de-Bonsecours Louis-Marie Caron's pew was just beside that of Thomas Bernier, something that had facilitated their children getting to know each other. Elzéar and Rose would each sit at the ends of their respective family pews, to be sure of taking communion together. After the mass they would walk together, while their parents and the whole of L'Islet witnessed their friendship and affection. Elzéar maintained that he had loved her from the age of 10.

The Caron monument erected in 1986 to the memory of the first Carons to settle in the L'Islet region. [Photo: Lynn Fournier]

The Carons did not live near the Berniers, as Gilberte Tremblay has suggested,[5] to explain the fact that they were childhood friends. Thomas Bernier's house, in the centre of the village,[6] was located about three miles from the Carons' lands.

It has also been suggested that they fell in love at school. Rose did not attend the L'Islet college, opposite the parish church, since it was solely for the education of boys. Rather she would have attended elementary school at the country school serving the *rang* at Trois-Saumons. She would not have gone on to secondary school, even if rumour has it that she was a teacher in the village. Neither was she a boarder at the convent school run by the Soeurs du Bon-Pasteur, since it was not built until 1877-78.

From the age of 13 or 14, thoughts of Rose seem to have accompanied Joseph-Elzéar on all his voyages that took him so far from her corner of the country. A few passages in his memoirs reflect the poetic and romantic thoughts that she inspired in him:

> The city itself [Seville] proved to be the most beautiful city I had yet seen, with its great Cathedral, its fine buildings, its lovely parks and private grounds about its mansions. As we anchored in the early evening the peals of the *angelus* came floating over the water, and, closing my eyes, I could almost imagine myself on the banks of the St. Lawrence near one of those old parishes of the south shore where my early boyhood days were passed. And throughout the twilight and the early dark, the romantic music of guitars and of Spanish songs mingled with the river sounds to which we were more accustomed. My first impression of Seville was most enchanting, and was like an accompaniment to thoughts of my sweetheart waiting for me so many miles away.[7]

This intrepid seafarer rarely spoke of affairs of the heart. He never had the reputation of being sensitive or emotional. Hence these rare moments of tenderness allow us to see him other than as an adventurer impassioned by the sea and enamoured with his profession.[8]

Rose Caron's parents' house. It is located at 556 chemin des Pionniers Est in L'Islet-sur-Mer. [Photo: Lynn Fournier]

The former girls' convent in L'Islet, now the Musée maritime du Québec (Bernier Museum). It became the property of the Association des marins de la Côte-du-Sud in 1970, which converted it into a maritime museum. [Photo: Lynn Fournier]

Rose and Elzéar were deeply in love and wished to share a joint destiny.

Early in October 1870, when he was on his way to the port of Québec to hand over command of the *Saint-Joseph* to his uncle, Captain Joseph Bernier, Elzéar had stopped in L'Islet for a few days, with the aim of obtaining the necessary consents for their marriage.

It is easy to imagine Rose at the kitchen window, watching excitedly for her captain to arrive. Like all girls of that era, she had prepared herself for the role of the ideal wife. She could sew, embroider, and cook, and her mother had instructed her in running a household. Of course since her mother had married a man of the land, she could not forewarn her of the difficult realities facing the wives of sailors, constantly having to come to grips with their departures and forced to await their return. Gilberte Tremblay notes correctly that "her sweetheart would be leaving her like this throughout her life, responding to the call of a bewitching rival, the sea."[9]

Their engagement was of short duration.

> After I had docked the *Saint-Joseph* [at Québec] I drove down to L'Islet to prepare for the wedding, which was to be a big one, as both families were very large and well-known in the country-side. But economy was kept well in sight, for my total wealth amounted to little more than three hundred dollars. The only dower my wife brought me was the traditional feather bed, with bedstead and bedding. My mother furnished us most of the remaining essential household goods. And my bride had a fine trousseau.[10]

Their wedding took place on a week-day, 8 November 1870 in the parish church of L'Islet-sur-Mer.

One sign of the constraints of a sailor's life was the fact that the groom's father was not present at the happy event. Thomas was detained at Québec by the building of his new ship, in dry-dock. Uncle Jean-Baptiste[11] agreed to stand witness in his place, while his cousin,

Interior of the church of Notre-Dame-de-Bonsecours in L'Islet. Rose and Elzéar pronounced their marriage vows here in November 1870. In those days, the end of the fall and especially the month of November before Advent and the winter months before Lent constituted the popular times for weddings. The wedding ceremony was not celebrated on a Saturday, for fear that the wedding festivities might be prolonged until the following day, a Sunday. [Photo: Lynn Fournier]

the pilot Joseph Bernier and his brother-in-law, Louis-Stanislas Caron, acted as bridegrooms.

After the church ceremony a wedding breakfast at the home of Célina and Thomas Bernier set the tone to a series of festivities that were spread over several days. One could expect a profusion of dishes cooked in wood-burning ovens: golden loaves of home-baked bread, beans cooked in salt bacon fat, roast pork and lamb, perfectly seasoned game pies, maple-syrup crêpes, raisin pies, spice cakes …

The cheerful company then moved on to the home of Priscilla and Grand Louis Caron for a bountiful dinner, followed by a dance, and a wedding supper, and another dance to which the entire population was invited. A crowd of young boys and girls from the surrounding area known as the "drop-ins" took advantage of the opportunity to stay up late, sing, drink a little, and dance away a good part of the night!

Next day the festivities continued with renewed vigour. It was the turn of Célina and Thomas to host the revellers for supper and dancing. And the day after that everyone went dancing at the home of one of Rose's uncles.

Let Elzéar conclude this breathless round:

> After the festivities at L'Islet, my wife and I came up to Quebec where we stayed with a cousin of mine, Arthur Morin. Here there was another dance. By this time the *Saint-Michel* was ready for sea, and was loading timber and deals for Liverpool. It had been my intention to take my bride with me for our honeymoon, but she was so fatigued by the wedding festivities, and besides so young to go to sea, that I decided to leave her at L'Islet.[12]

It must be said that Joseph-Elzéar was privileged to be able to contemplate a honeymoon voyage, since this was an uncommon luxury in the 19th century. More often, once the festivities were over the new wife moved to the location where her husband was settled, and immediately became absorbed in the realities of married life.[13] This "law of husband's domicile" did not apply to Rose since she was a daughter of L'Islet. From all appearances, therefore, marriage had changed almost nothing in the life of this young wife of 15 years and 11 months. She would continue to live in her parents' house, sleep in her own bedroom, continue to see her pals, and continue to go through the same motions as before, while she waited for her spouse to return. But, in fact Rose was no longer the same. She was no longer her parents' daughter. In the eyes of the Church and the State, Rose Caron had assumed a new identity, that of Madame Joseph-Elzéar Bernier. Hence forth her destiny was linked to that of her husband.

This is the only known visual representation of the young married couple. It is a hand-coloured photo on a metal plate, probably taken in an American or European studio during their honeymoon trip. Their pose and their clothes suggest that they are ready for travelling. [Archives of Carol and Louis Terrien]

CHAPTER 15

The *Saint-Michel*

As a child, my mother would occasionally tell me about *Saint-Michel* being built, on the lot opposite Jean-Baptiste Bernier's house. She was young at the time, and having to walk under the ship's bowsprit to go to town or to mass, made a great impression on her. The brigantine was so long that she was longer than the shipyard and overhung the Chemin du Roy. Everyone had to walk under her.

Statement by MARTIN CARON, L'Islet-sur-Mer, June 2002.

THOMAS BERNIER'S SECOND SAILING SHIP, registered to the port of Québec on 10 June 1870, was certainly quite impressive. She was 132 feet long, with a beam of 32 feet. Laden, she had a draft of 16 feet and needed a crew of 13 men to handle her. When empty she weighed 460 tonnes, and with a full a cargo she displaced 700 tonnes.

Raymond Blakiston, merchant and sail maker in Québec city, had partially financed the building of the ship:

> Thomas Bernier has begun building a sailing ship, a brigantine, in a shipyard located in the parish of L'Islet, measuring about 150 feet in depth, bounded on the north by the St. Lawrence River, on the south by the chemin de la Reine, on the east by the property of one Francœur, and on the west by that of Eugène Talon. The said land belongs to Jean-Baptiste Bernier, a pilot from the parish of L'Islet, who certifies that the ship should be about 500 tons according to old carpenters' measure; and is to have the following dimensions: length of keel 116 feet 6 inches, English measure, beam 29 feet 6 inches, depth of hold 18 feet; the said Thomas Bernier intends to have completed the ship and to launch her in spring, around the month of May. The ship's keel was laid in the shipyard in question in November 1868, and Monsieur Thomas Bernier is seeking an advance of $3000 to build his brigantine, to rig her and make her seaworthy. Mr. Thomas Bernier is to deliver the builder's certificate to the said Raymond Blakiston on the day the ship is launched...[1]

In officially taking possession of the *Saint-Michel* on 20 November 1870, Joseph-Elzéar was accepting the challenge of commanding a ship that was more imposing, heavier, and slower than the *Saint Joseph*. And he

The *Saint-Michel,* Captain Thomas Bernier's second brigantine. [Photo Lynn Fournier, Permanent collection of the Musée maritime du Québec (Musée Bernier)]

very soon realized that his father had learned a great deal about building ships, and that he had succeeded in applying that knowledge to his new two-master. She was enormously strong. She rolled and pitched less than her predecessor and was distinctly more comfortable since her cabins were larger and were located below deck.

For her young captain there was another dimension to the challenge associated with the *Saint-Michel*, that of financial gain. Joseph-Elzéar had amassed sufficient capital to risk investing $100 in 7 per cent of the shares in the brigantine. Of course, his father was there to guide his first steps in the world of business, and the fact the impressive ship could carry twice as much freight as her predecessor reduced the risk and made her a sounder investment.

Four days later the *Saint-Michel* sailed from the Québec basin with a cargo of timber, bound for Liverpool, "with my father as passenger... and my brother Alfred ... as A.B. At L'Islet ... my mother and my sister Augustina, then six years old," came aboard.[2]

Right from the start the late season took a hand in slowing the ship's speed and, during the first night, abeam of Saint-Jean-Port Joli, her captain was forced to drop anchor, helpless in the face of the strong, persistent head-winds.

Next morning the wind had swung into the west. Under normal circumstances this wind would have been in their favour, but this one blew at gale force.

Joseph-Elzéar was anchored close enough to the three-master *Alfred,* under the command of Captain Cyrille Duquet, to notice that she was drifting dangerously, despite her two anchors, which ought to have held her securely. With just a single anchor the *Saint-Michel* really had no chance of avoiding Horseshoe Bank, a dangerous shoal. Fast action was required:

> All hands were ordered to the windlass in the bow, even the pilot and cook being pressed into service. There were forty-five fathoms of chain out. But it was late November and zero weather, and windlass and bow were smothered in ice from the spray. And even when this had been broken off the windlass, the wet chain froze as it came through the hawse-pipe, and the spray coated the windlass again as well as the workers. The cook was sent to the galley for a panful of hot ashes, and application of these on the windlass and chain allowed some fifteen fathoms to be drawn up. But the ashes had given out and the spray was as heavy. By this time the anchor had loosed its hold on the bottom and we were drifting toward the Bank. There was only one thing to do and that was to sacrifice the anchor and the thirty fathoms of chain. Men were sent aloft to set the fore-topsail and as the ship got under weigh, the chain was unshackled and cast off. We drove past the *Alfred* at nine knots under our fore-topsail. The unfortunate ship was pounding on the rocks of Horseshoe Bank. Later, in a lull and in the shelter of Brandy Pot Island, we dropped our pilot, landing him at the lighthouse from our small boat, as we knew there would be no chance to drop him at Bic.[3]

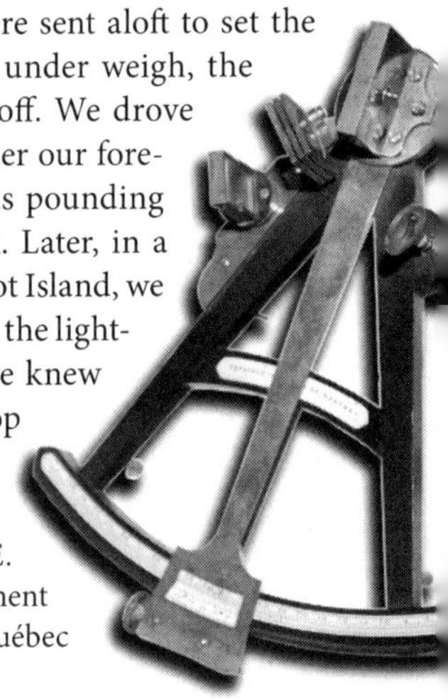

An octant that belonged to Captain J.-E. Bernier. [Photo: Lynn Fournier, Permanent collection of the Musée maritime du Québec (Musée Bernier)]

Foul weather pursued them throughout the voyage; this no doubt made the captain appreciate his father's enlightened choice in making the *Saint-Michel* a brigantine with twin-decks. On the lower deck there was the fo'c'sle, a space for cargo, and the cabin. Her upper deck was a hurricane deck, that is entirely flush, except for a very small galley, and sufficiently open that the water did not accumulate on deck when swept by waves during heavy weather. The *Saint-Joseph*'s single deck was enclosed by wooden bulwarks, pierced by scuppers, that were not very effective at draining the water; the result was that the ship was carrying tons of water in addition to her cargo. By contrast in the case of the *Saint-Michel* the bulwarks had been replaced by an ingenious arrangement of netting and steel cables, supported on posts.

Despite his lucky escape and the performance of his new vessel, young Elzéar felt very relieved when he reached port safely, 28 days later. This was the first time that he had sailed with women on board, and he had no doubt felt greater responsibility because of them, not to mention the presence of his father, the veteran seaman whom he admired more than anybody else, and whom he especially did not want to disappoint.

At that time the port of Liverpool, on the Mersey estuary, was the second most important port in the United Kingdom, after London. It was then experiencing its golden age, thanks to colonial traffic and the export of British manufactured goods. Since Canadian lumber was one of the most sought-after materials, the port authorities had built a special dock, the Canada Half-Tide, with a low sill to facilitate the discharge of this highly-valued product at low tide.

In December 1870 the *Saint-Michel* was moored in the Canadian dock, among other merchant vessels engaged in unloading their cargoes. Captain Bernier remains silent concerning the sights of this seaport that he was seeing for the first time, the fabulous Victorian houses that bore testimony to the success of the city's merchants, as well as the high percentage of Irish labourers in the Royal Docks, who would bequeath a Celtic flavour to the local dialect. In his memoirs that he wrote in his old-age, only one image has survived associated with that first visit to the port of Liverpool, and it is that of the *Wasp*, moored to the same quay. Théophile Deroy was in command of this 442-tonne brigantine, built the previous year at Québec by McKay and Warner. Since the Deroys were another great family of sailors from L'Islet, Elzéar was not surprised to run across one of them at Liverpool. The reason that this fortuitous meeting remained imprinted on his memory was because the *Wasp* was among the 22 ships wrecked or abandoned in the Gulf and the St. Lawrence River in the fall of 1871. Every one of these wrecks involved the death of a close friend or relative.

As he reported quite simply, without any great show of emotion: "This was the last time I was to see the *Wasp*, for the next year she was lost in the early winter on the dunes of the Magdalen Islands in the Gulf of St. Lawrence… Her mate then was my cousin, Auguste Le Bourdais, the only man to be saved from the *Wasp*."[4]

This cousin, the son of Jean-Baptiste LeBourdais and Pauline Bernier, born at L'Islet-sur-Mer on 28 August 1844, was a strapping lad, more than 6 feet tall and weighing almost 300 pounds. As far as Joseph-Elzéar was concerned, he was the typical sailor from that region, smitten with the sea, proud, brave, high-spirited, and determined to attain his goal of becoming a deep-sea captain. Furthermore, according to LeBourdais's biographer, Azade Harvey:

> The seamen of the lower river were among the toughest in the world at that time. They feared nothing. Their fame had spread to the European ports. At that time it was unwise to take a stroll along the quays in London, since thieves ruled supreme there. Sailors were often knocked unconscious, and then shanghaied to join the crews of big sailing vessels, leaving for the Orient. But the word had gone out among the major crooks: "Don't touch those French Canadian sailors! They are dynamite. Any one of them is worth ten Englishmen in a street-fight.[5]

Elzéar was definitely touched by the tragic fate of his cousin who had knocked around every sea on the globe, who had even rounded Cape Horn several times, and

Joseph-Elzéar Bernier, aged 18. [Archives of Carol and Louis Terrien]

The *Saint-Michel* during a gale in the North Atlantic. [Artist unknown, Archives of Carol and Louis Terrien]

who had survived the wreck of the *Wasp*. But at what price? Both legs were amputated, immobilizing this man of action and shattering all his dreams of life at sea.

Would the same fate be in store for him?

At the age of 18, the *Saint-Michel*'s captain was, above all, a realist, to whom the probability of such a tragedy, at some point in time, was almost a certainty. Being the practical man that he was, he hoped to get all the luck on his side, by disciplining himself, by improving himself, and by learning everything about ship-handling and about the elements that he faced on a daily basis.

⚓

The *Saint-Michel* put to sea on 28 January with a full cargo of salt; she was about to undertake a crossing that would go down as the longest crossing in Elzéar's entire record-breaking career. It should be mentioned that even nowadays the winter season on the North Atlantic is rarely accompanied by fine weather or fair winds.

The weather was atrocious right from the start!

From Liverpool, the brigantine took nine days to clear St. George's Channel, between Ireland and Wales, and to emerge into the Celtic Sea. And 60 interminable days later she was cruising north of Cape Hatteras, and was finally able to make out the mouth of magnificent Chesapeake Bay on the east coast of the United States. It took her a further four days to reach the port of Alexandria, Virginia. Hence a total of 73 days from port to port.

Part of the cargo of salt was unloaded at Alexandria to allow the *Saint-Michel* to run up the Potomac to Georgetown, a suburb of Washington D.C.

Fortunately for Elzéar the disappointment, anxiety and tensions associated with this miserable crossing were quickly eclipsed by the affairs of the heart, that would soon demand his full attention. Rose, his Rose, would shortly be joining him!

CHAPTER 16

An absinthe-flavoured honeymoon

ROSE ARRIVED IN WASHINGTON by train, in early May. For a young girl of 16, who was leaving her own country for the first time, the long trip by train, and this visit to the federal capital of the United States must have been thrilling, exciting, and representing a rather exceptional way of starting a honeymoon. In 1871, the administrative centre of the country, named in honour of the first American president George Washington (1732-1799), and built according to the plans of the Franco-American architect and engineer, Pierre Charles L'Enfant (1754-1824), was one of the most beautiful cities in the world, with its wide avenues, its magnificent buildings, its green spaces, its remarkable monument to Abraham Lincoln (1809-1865), and with its White House, so called in 1809 because of its polished white stone contrasting with the brick of the surrounding buildings. Undoubtedly, Rose had never seen anything like it.

In his memoirs Captain Bernier does not mention how long they stayed in Georgetown but does specify that on the first leg of the voyage his ship sailed in ballast to Philadelphia in Pennsylvania. This meant quite a long trip since it meant retracing her route as she descended the Potomac to Chesapeake Bay, rounding Cape Charles, running north along the Atlantic coast to Cape May and Delaware Bay, then ascending the Delaware River to the mouth of the Schuylkill River and the important port of Philadelphia, one of the most prosperous industrial towns of the United States and also considered a major intellectual centre.

The *Saint-Michel*'s log[1] indicates that she sailed from Philadelphia on 7 June with a load of coal oil, bound for the Mediterranean.

The Québec two-master achieved the fastest crossing of her short career, taking 30 days from Cape May to Cape St. Vincent in south-western Spain. A summer crossing, shorter, less rough, and less difficult than the previous one, in Rose's company. What more could Bernier ask for? True happiness! Or almost. The only thing marring this idyllic picture was an unpleasant incident provoked by a seaman who obstinately refused to carry out the task assigned to him by the mate. "Not only did he refuse to do his work, but he endeavoured to arouse the rest of the crew to mutiny."[2]

The "Old Man" had him brought to his cabin and, with the mate as witness, recorded the infraction, the punishment and the man's response, in the ship's log.

Rose-de-Lima Caron, aged 16. [Archives of Carol and Louis Terrien]

The seaman became mad with rage at the sentence that he would be imprisoned, placed in irons, and fed on bread and water until he agreed to go back to work. He managed to escape from the grasp of the man holding him and savagely attacked his captain.

Elzéar reacted immediately. He pinioned his adversary in a judo hold. The enraged man tried to bite his arm. The captain responded just as savagely, getting him in a powerful strangle-hold. Gasping for breath the insubordinate sailor calmed down. He was placed in irons and sequestered in a cabin.

> But this man was truly stubborn. He did not consider himself beaten by this punishment. During the night, whenever he heard one of the officers come down from his watch to rest, he would begin hammering and kicking the door, renewing the noise often enough to keep anyone from sleeping. So I had him taken out, had a hole bored in the deck in the centre of the room and a ring-bolt fitted into it, and the man chained to this ring.[3]

After two days on bread and water the prisoner let it be known that he was ready to return to work. His statement to this effect was recorded in the log, in front of witnesses, before his handcuffs were unlocked and, on releasing him, the captain gave him a stern warning that if he again attempted to rouse the other members of the crew to mutiny he would be clapped in irons for the rest of the voyage then handed over to the port police.

⚓

Initially the Italian port authorities prohibited the *Saint-Michel* from entering the Bay of Naples, since they were afraid that cinders from Vesuvius might ignite the cargo of coal oil. The ship was therefore obliged to continue her voyage to the island of Necita where Captain Bernier was forced to agree that convicts from the penitentiary should unload part of her cargo, and stow it in an enormous sea-cave, formerly the hide-out of a band of brigands who had terrorized Naples. Once the work was completed the couple were able to explore at leisure one of the most famous ports in Europe with its rich monuments, its lively neighbourhoods, its numerous Gothic churches, its museums, and its theatres.

> During our stay in Naples, my wife and I visited the city, under the courteous guidance of Dr. Cesare Pini, members of his family, and his friends. Dr. Pini was the port examining physician and had befriended us. Through arrangements made by him we had our portraits painted by a talented young artist some of whose work we had seen at the art gallery.[4]

There can be no doubt that the taste for works of art, high-quality furniture, and luxury objects that one can see in him later was starting to germinate and become focused during his tourist visits and his contacts with cultivated people. Did Rose share her husband's artistic leanings? If her liking for lace, embroideries, rich fabrics and elegant outfits is any indication one may suppose that she also took a certain pleasure in the quest for the beautiful.

The remainder of the cargo was discharged at Livorno (Leghorn), in Tuscany, and was immediately replaced by a large load of marble blocks, each weighing between three and 20 tonnes.

Here Elzéar had to make a difficult choice between his intuition and experience, which told him to be careful with this marble, and his father's recommendation that he should take all he could carry. He opted for complying with the owner's wishes and gave orders to load 700 tonnes of marble, going against the advice of others. "Other skippers," he wrote, "who were loading marble for Boston told me quite cheerfully that I would never reach the port, and I was not without misgivings myself."[5] And as if to tempt the gods, or to test his guiding star, the captain had the bad idea of weighing anchor on 13 October! The challenge had been thrown out.

> We left Leghorn at dawn on a strong north wind which increased steadily in strength through the day. By nightfall it was blowing a gale. By 10 o'clock the wind had shifted to the east and was blowing a hurricane. The ship

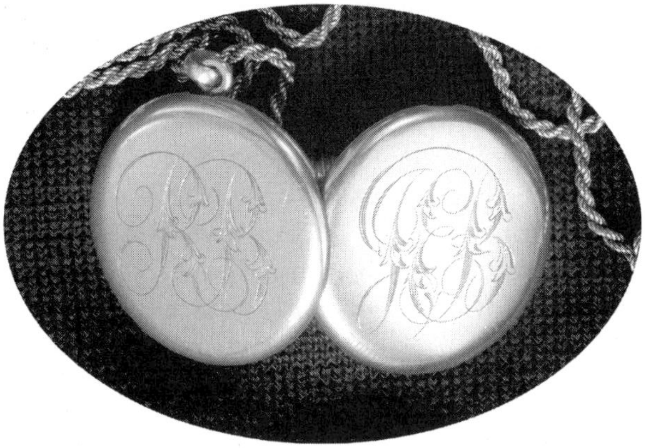

Gold locket with the initials R.B. and J.E.B. a gift from Joseph-Elzéar to Rose. [Suzanne Audet-Normandeau's Collection]

was very badly balanced by the marble in the hold and 'tween decks. She rolled and pitched with unusual force, and the strain caused her to make water to an unusual degree. The pitching was particularly bad just before the wind changed, for the direction of the waves always changes before the wind. For about two hours we were running on a cross sea. In a sudden squall that hit us as the ship rose from a deep dive, both our topmasts snapped and went by the board, carrying much of the rigging over the port side with them.[6]

The crew worked all night to repair the damage and to try to recover the cordage and gear hanging from the sails and masts.

Then there was a bit of a respite. During the following seven days less violent winds allowed the seamen to send up two replacement masts and to rig them. But in reality it was not much of a respite since the Tyrrhenian Sea remained rough and threatening. In every watch the men had to work the pumps to discharge the water that was flowing into the ship through the cracks caused by the pressure of the waves on the wooden hull. Every day the captain had to go down into the hold to stabilize the blocks of marble that had moved under the impacts that the poor ship was enduring.

Fatigue gradually took hold of the sailors who were constantly on the alert. To crown all, Rose was laid low by sea-sickness and became seriously ill, but Elzéar had neither the leisure to sleep nor the time to worry about his sweetheart, or even to regret his decision, for the gods had not had the last word:

On the eighth day we were travelling along on a strong breeze from the east, gradually rising. On the ninth day, at ten in the morning it veered to the northeast, and the sky grew black with heavy clouds. By four in the afternoon the wind was blowing a gale and the rain was falling in squalls. At six a furious gale was raging, and at eight-thirty it grew worse. At midnight we were running before the hurricane with only the lower topsail and the staysail set on the foremast. An hour later a terrific electric storm struck us, and the rain came down in torrential downpours with almost constant lightning and deafening thunder.[7]

Assuredly the Mediterranean was falling into step with its neighbour, the Tyrrhenian Sea, greeting their arrival with ferocity, indifferent to Rose's terror and the anxiety of the men on deck, as they listened to the marble blocks shifting beneath them, in the bowels of the ship.

Suddenly, right in the middle of a terrible squall, the wind dropped. Overwhelmed by the weight of her cargo of marble, the ship refused to answer the helm and turned broadside to the waves. Like a child's toy, a wooden model, she slid into the trough of a mountainous, powerful, voracious wave, then with a sickening jerk rose to a foam-fringed crest. This was too much for the ship, weakened in every member. The new masts snapped like matchsticks.

As the fore topmast tore through the rigging to port, I set out on the run from the wheel up the starboard side. But the sea that swept aboard as the main topmast toppled to starboard washed me under the fallen rigging where I lay unconscious and half-drowned, my foot jammed under a spare spar lashed to the deck. There I lay for about an hour and a half, unconscious. Then slowly regaining consciousness I found that I could not shout, possibly by reason of the water I had swallowed. My frantic efforts to release my foot were unavailing, and the frequent seas that swept over

> the deck made me lapse again into unconsciousness. The wheelsman had seen me washed away on the sea, and the crew had come to the conclusion that I had been swept overboard.[8]

In the meantime, stretched out on her bunk in the noise-filled darkness, Rose was enduring the ship's gyrations. Paralyzed by a fever, the vomiting, and her fear of the unknown, she waited, trembling, for her husband to deliver her from her anguish. If only she had known that he was lying somewhere between unconsciousness and lucidity.

Elzéar would regain consciousness from time to time and would try desperately to free his foot that was wedged beneath the weight of the spar and the sail that had crashed to the deck along with the mast. It was already daylight when he spotted the bare foot of a sailor, standing beside him. He grasped it as if it were a life-buoy.

Despite the fact that he was quite shaken by his ordeal, the "Old Man" quickly set to work again, since there was much to be done. Firstly the foremast had to be secured; even though it had snapped it was still hanging, swinging dangerously with its mass of rigging and spars, and threatening every minute to carry away the stays supporting the surviving masts.

And then he had to go below to check on Rose... especially to reassure her...

To his horror he found that the force of the waves had stove in the door and surged down the companion-way and that the cabin was flooded. He found Rose standing in the middle of a pool of salt water, her eyes wild, shivering with cold in her soaking clothes.

Elzéar picked up his feverish wife and quickly found her a dry bed and warm bedclothes. While he gently calmed her and wiped away her tears, he could hear the grinding noises of the cargo that had broken loose, combined with the splashing sounds of the water that had penetrated the compartments below. A quick glance confirmed that he had read the situation correctly: one third of the depth of the hold was already submerged.

Rather than alerting the crew to this situation, to put new heart into them, exhausted as they were by lack of sleep and the rolling of the ship, he had a good shot of rum served to the men. Then, in his powerful voice he ordered: "All hands to the pumps!"

They had to work fast to discharge the four feet of water that was weighing the *Saint-Michel* down and dragging her to her doom. Above all the captain had to get the situation under control without alarming the crew. If there were moments when Elzéar must have felt the enormous weight of his position, this would be one of them. He was solely in command, solely responsible for the failure or success of the enterprise, for the death or survival of his men, and for his Rose's well-being.

Everything was going badly. Even the shaft of the main pump had been bent when the topmast fell on it. The pump was inoperable.

> There was only one thing to do; that was to straighten the shaft of the pump. So the top of the stove in the galley was removed and a roaring wood fire built. Coal was then thrown on, and when the coals were red-hot the shaft was lashed over them. As the shaft reddened in the heat it was unlashed and taken for'ard where the crown of an anchor served as an anvil and a maul as a blacksmith's hammer. All this was no easy task with the ship rolling and pitching. But after three spells of heating and hammering and filing smooth, the shaft fitted and worked. The pumps were set in motion and kept going as long as the men could stand up.[9]

This hell lasted for an eternity. It took 14 days before the *Saint-Michel* came within sight of the mountain of Tariq, at Gibraltar.

While the port master recommended that the deck and topsides of the ship be caulked and that the topmasts be replaced and the rigging repaired, a Spanish doctor prescribed that Rose be taken to hospital immediately. It was thus inevitable that they be separated. She would return to New York by steamer, as soon as she was strong enough. Their honeymoon was turning into a nightmare.

Elzéar was obliged to replace the entire crew, who refused to continue the voyage on a cursed ship. It goes without saying that he experienced enormous difficulties in assembling another crew for the Atlantic crossing. Some of the men even had the nerve to decamp after pocketing an advance on their wages.

The sailing ship from L'Islet was perhaps cursed, since she took over 53 days to reach Boston, having encountered violent storms, snow, and hail, and having been handicapped by her heavy cargo that continued to shift dangerously in her hold.

The young captain realized that he had had a narrow escape. Never again would he allow a businessman or a ship-owner to dictate to him how he should behave. Henceforth he would be the true master on board.

> I was also anxious to obtain a master's certificate, as the Canadian law requiring certificates had come into force a month before, January 1st, 1872. My father came on from Quebec to take charge of the *Saint-Michel*. He wanted me to apply for a certificate of service, which would have taken a few days only to obtain, and then to take the *Saint-Michel* on a voyage to the West Indies. But I was determined to sit for the examinations and obtain a certificate of competency, which would take at least a month.
>
> So I said farewell to the *Saint-Michel*. She was the last ship I commanded for my father. After her trip to the West Indies she returned to Quebec, under my father's command. Here he sold her and for many years she was engaged in the West Indian trade.[10]

Elzéar knew that he was responsible for Rose becoming ill. Throughout that terrible Atlantic crossing he had never stopped thinking of her and worrying about her state of health. He had expected to find her in Boston, since the voyage by a steamer with auxiliary sail power, generally took between 12 and 15 days.

She was not at Boston to greet him when he arrived in late January 1872 and nobody in the family had had any news of her since she had left Gibraltar six weeks earlier. However, his friend Francis Lapointe, a former Québec sail-maker who had moved to New York, finally relieved his anguish. He reported "that my wife had just come in on the *Northumberland,* which had lost her propeller soon after leaving Gibraltar, being obliged to make for Bermuda under sail. She had encountered bad weather and been much delayed even after a new propeller had been fitted on at Bermuda. Francis had gone aboard on her arrival to inspect her sails for the owners, and the master had told him that there was a French Canadian lady on board. On seeing her he recognized my wife and wired me immediately. She came up from New York without delay; needless to say, we were overjoyed to see each other."[11]

Rose was still not recovered and, upon the recommendation of a doctor, her husband elected to take her back to L'Islet.

But there is another ending to this absinthe-flavoured honeymoon. The rumour still persists in the family that Rose had a miscarriage and that the accident prevented her from having more children. This possibility would explain the long convalescence, the mystery surrounding her illness, and the fact that the couple decided to adopt a little girl.

CHAPTER 17

A sought-after ship-deliverer

IN MARCH 1872, at the age of 20, Joseph-Elzéar began intensive studies at the Navigation School in Québec. An Englishman, William Seaton, had been recruited by the Canadian Government to coach the colony's captains and ships' officers in the British standards of seamanship and to teach them the new regulations imposed by the Department of Marine and Fisheries.

A month later Elzéar was among the group of 12 to pass the first exams in competence in seamanship in the history of Canada and to obtain the first official certificate of seamanship.

Armed with his certificate, bearing the number CCC93, duly signed by the Minister, Peter Mitchell and the Deputy-Minister, William Smith, the proud captain was henceforth qualified to command the largest ships.

Over the following 20 years he became unquestionably the most sought-after "deliverer" of Canadian ships as well as being the man on whom the most important ship-owner in Québec, Senator James Gibb Ross (1819-1888), relied.

> During that decade [1860s] Ross bought 124 ships and financed 24 others, representing 35 per cent of the ships. A total of 34 different shipyards in the port of Québec were involved, including the establishments of Charland & Marquis (13 ships) and Dunn & Samson (6 ships) of Lévis, for which he financed their entire output.
>
> The 1870s saw Ross consolidating his monopoly. During that period of decline in shipbuilding he acquired or financed 47 per cent of all ships built. On the south shore the entire production of Charland & Son (21 ships) and three quarters of that of François-Xavier Marquis (15 ships) and of Dunn & Samson (8 ships) were in the hands of James Gibb Ross.[1]

Ross earned the title of "king of the entire shipbuilding industry" that was bestowed on him.

> Without him shipbuilding might perhaps have disappeared from Québec at that time. He is credited with having saved it, not only in terms of the capital that he injected into it, but also in terms of the rigorous administrative methods that he inculcated to the shipbuilders with whom he placed his orders.[2]

As an experienced businessman Ross had studied the market around him. He knew the type of ships that were sought after and he encouraged the builders to respond to that demand. He financed the shipyards, ordered the rigging, imported the ships' gear and managed the sales. Under his influence the majority of the French-speaking shipbuilders, Labbé, Charland, Gingras, Valin, Rosa, Marquis, Samson, Dubord, etc. made fairly good profits.

Financing of shipbuilding in the Québec region was mainly accomplished by means of mortgages on the ships. Ross & Co. preferred this type of investment, or patronage, in order to be able to control not only the quality of the product, but also its sale and distribution.

The first captains to receive the Department of Marine and Fisheries' Master Mariner's Certificate in 1872. Joseph-Elzéar Bernier is the fifth from the left in the upper row. [Bernier Collection, *Master Mariner*]

Since numerous mortgages were not repaid during the days following the launch, as had been specified in the contracts, the ships were then registered in the company's name.

> While waiting to be sold, the vessels were skillfully managed by Ross and earned their way carrying cargoes of timber from Québec, coal from Newcastle, guano from Callao, cotton from Pensacola, and grain from Montréal.[3]

In practice the financier would issue a certificate, or a safe-conduct to the ship's captain, or to a European agent, who became responsible for the delivery and conditions of sale of the ship. In this manner Ross succeeded in establishing an impressive international network for the distribution of ships built in Québec yards.

The boom in that industry was directly linked to the trade in timber with Britain. In 1872 almost $12 million worth of timber was exported from the port of Québec alone.[4] High stakes, indeed, since the sailing vessels were built with the merchants' capital and timber, in addition to being used to transport their timber to markets in Great Britain. Some of these ships were even "built of squared timbers, to be disassembled and sold for the timber once they'd reached their destination."[5] Later the advent of iron ships built in English and Scottish yards, whose tonnage and speed greatly exceeded those of the wooden sailing ships, led to the decline in Québec shipbuilding that was almost entirely based on exploitation of the forests.

Captain Bernier was one of the rare witnesses of this evolution. Late in 1876, at Liverpool he:

> decided to remain there for part of the winter until I could sell the *Supreme* and the *Sterling*, which was also laid up awaiting sale. The competition of Clyde-built iron and steel vessels was beginning to tell on the market for wooden ships.[6]

Joseph-Elzéar was aware of what was in the wind around him but he always remained focused on the work at hand. When the new ship under his command was ready to load her cargo of timber, he would take her to one of the yards located around Québec. The banks of the St. Lawrence were ideal for storing and squaring the timber that arrived in rafts from the Great Lakes

Senator James Gibb Ross, originally from Scotland, was the principal owner of Ross and Co., which monopolized the shipping industry in Québec during the 1860s and 1870s. [Bernier Collection, *Master Mariner*]

The timber cove at Sillery around 1890. [ANQ, 516 470-68]

and the tributaries of the St. Lawrence, since they consisted of small bays sheltered from the prevailing winds and the strong tidal currents. Caissons, built at the ends of the jetties connecting the booms, allowed the ships to come alongside and be loaded. Moreover the use of a loading port beside the stem allowed long timbers to be man-handled right into the hold. The rectangular opening was then sealed up by a well-caulked hatch.

Once loading was completed Captain Bernier would go off in search of his crew in the lodging houses in the streets Champlain, Sault-au-Matelot or Sous-le-Cap. And in contrast to the general practice on board other ships, he would pay his men by the crossing in order to encourage them to achieve the fastest time possible since a record time for the crossing would influence the buyers just as much as the ship's appearance. The majority of other captains paid their men by the month, which did not incline them to hurry since a longer crossing would give them a bigger wage. If the destination was in England, Scotland or Ireland, Captain Bernier would pay £8 to £10 per crossing, when the average wage paid by other ships was £15 per month. Thus higher wages ensured a better performance and a crew that would not jib at following his orders.

Bernier favoured the Strait of Belle Isle between Newfoundland and Labrador in order to achieve a faster North Atlantic crossing. He usually made his decision off the eastern tip of Anticosti Island. If wind and weather were favourable, he would head for the Strait of Belle Isle; otherwise he would steer for Cabot Strait. For most of the voyage he preferred to be at his post, on deck, to show his men that he was indeed the master of the ship and to be able to react quickly in case of need.

On every ship he commanded, new or old, he insisted that orderliness and impeccable cleanliness be maintained at all times. These qualities became especially important when he was delivering a ship to Britain. Since the sale was also one of his responsibilities, he always organized things so that he had everything going for him:

> Not only were masts, spars, sails and gear kept in perfect order, but on approaching the Irish Coast I set some of my crew to painting, and this was completed on arrival after unloading. Hulls were usually painted black, poops white, bulwarks brown. All bright wood surfaces were oiled and varnished. All spots chafed by the timber were planed down and oiled, even in the hold. The hold was swept up. The masts and yards were cleaned and oiled; the decks scraped, polished with the "holystone," and oiled. Deckhouses were cleaned and tidied. Sails were dried out and unbent and stowed away. Ropes were coiled and stopped

Loading timber on a square-rigged ship. [J.-Ernest Livernois Collection, ANQ, P560, S1, P118]

on the pins or up to the fairleads. And a mat was placed at the gangway. The ship was advertised for sale, and I remained on hand to receive prospective customers.[7]

The prudent businessman that he had become did not hesitate to invest in the ships he was delivering or the cargoes he was transporting. Indeed as the years passed and his responsibilities increased he learned how to transform himself into an accomplished, competent, polyvalent seaman, capable of tackling every step connected with the building, rigging, navigation, and sale of new ships.

In the course of his long association with the Ross company, he was appointed ship's husband, in charge of fitting-out for the entire fleet. Thus in the early 1880s Bernier was responsible for inspecting all Ross & Co. ships arriving in the port of Québec. He would recommend and regulate any necessary repairs, arrange dockings and sailings, oversee loading and unloading, order provisions and equipment, and even supervise insurance contracts. As the company representative, he had to know at all times where ships were in order to relay orders to them, and make enquiries in the event of shipwrecks or accidents. Here is a sample of the orders he might receive from head-office:

> Captain Bernier: You will please proceed to Cardiff and arrange to get the ballast out of the barque *Underwriter* as quick as possible, and place the vessel in graving dock to examine her metal, and have her stripped if you think it necessary; thoroughly caulked, and re-sheathed with yellow metal.[8]

It is fortunate that this great seaman had a mania for keeping everything. The certificates of all the ships that he commanded and the numerous letters of recommendation and congratulation from his employers make it possible to confirm his exceptional abilities and the confidence that he inspired in the shipbuilding community. On 4 March 1874 when he was applying to the Quebec Gulf Ports Steamship Co., 22 influential individuals lent their support to his application. This is an indication of the extent to which he was appreciated.

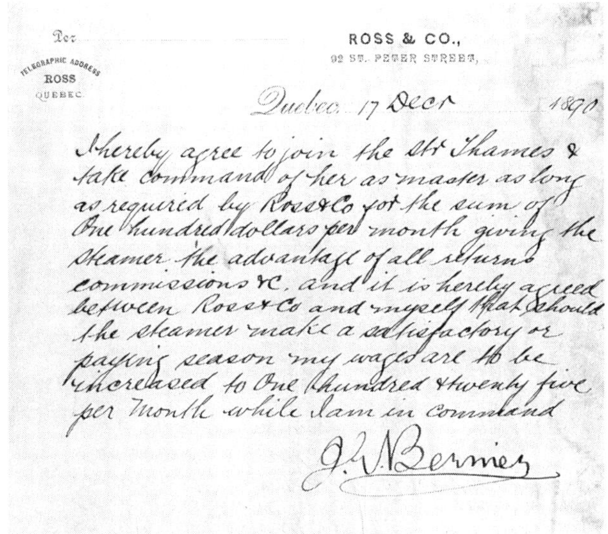
Per

TELEGRAPHIC ADDRESS ROSS QUEBEC

ROSS & CO.,
92 ST. PETER STREET,

Quebec 17 Decr 1890

I hereby agree to join the Str Thames & take command of her as master as long as required by Ross & Co for the sum of One hundred dollars per month giving the Steamer the advantage of all returns commissions &c. and it is hereby agreed between Ross & Co and myself that should the steamer make a satisfactory or paying season my wages are to be increased to One hundred & twenty five per Month while I am in command

J. E. Bernier

Letter of intent between Captain Bernier and the Ross Company. [Archives of Carol and Louis Terrien]

Bernier also had the excellent initiative to have several paintings done of the fabulous three-masters that represented an era and earned him his reputation. In 1885 he ordered portraits from the Canadian marine artist, who had settled in Liverpool, William H. Yorke (1847-1921).

> [...] portraits of three ships, symbols of his exploits, and of which he doubtless wanted to retain a visual souvenir [...] Every element of each of these ships—sails, cordage and construction, *sensu stricto*—is rendered with the greatest skill of the portraitist. In this respect Captain Bernier's paintings, inseparable one from the other, form an ensemble of very high quality.[9]

The Musée du Québec holds three works commissioned by Captain Bernier: paintings of the *Felicitas*, the *Germanic* and the *Cambria*. Since portraits of ships built at Québec yards are somewhat rare in public collections and on the Canadian market, "the gift of this exceptional grouping, well documented and relatively well preserved, thus constitutes a major acquisition for the Musée du Québec."[10]

The *Germanic*, 1885, oil on canvas 76x51 cm, by artist William Howard Yorke. [Photo: Jean-Guy Kérouac, Musée national des beaux-arts de Québec, No. 95.10, donated by Clément Gauthier]

The death of Senator Ross on 2 October 1888 deeply affected his trusted agent, who had developed, over his many years in his service, an immense respect for the "king of ship-building," and for his integrity and his rectitude. On leaving Ross & Co. on 8 December 1891, Elzéar Bernier received a very fine tribute on the part of its president, who described him as a master mariner whose competence was unequalled since he could take any sort of ship, sail or steam, to any port in the world and that he was familiar with all the practices and regulations that might be involved.

Captain Bernier achieved his Atlantic crossings in record times for the period; on average he took 22 days from quayside to quayside. He is credited with about 44 crossings in ships newly built in the Québec yards, more than half of which represented record times. Amazingly, he holds 11 records for crossings made in wooden ships, under sail, without the aid of sophisticated instruments, and at the mercy of the wind and storms:

1. The three-masted barque, *Felicitas*, 750 tonnes, left Québec on 18 August and moored at Liverpool on 5 September 1874—a passage of 17 days, 15 days and 16 hours from pilot to pilot.

2. The square-rigged three-master, *Dominion*, 1287 tonnes, left Québec on 1 June and arrived at Liverpool on 23 June 1875—a passage of 22 days.
3. The three-masted barque, *Queen's Cliff*, 611 tonnes, left Québec on 17 August and moored at Liverpool on 5 September 1875—18 days from quayside to quayside, 15 days from pilot to pilot. After the ship was sold Bernier caught a steamer that landed him back at Québec 29 days later.
4. The three-masted barque, *Tarifa*, 634 tonnes, left Québec on 25 October and moored at Liverpool on 14 November 1875—a passage of 19 days, 17 days from pilot to pilot.
5. The three-masted barque, *Supreme*, 762 tonnes, left Québec on 21 May and moored at Liverpool on 8 June 1876—a passage of 17 or 18 days.
6. The three-masted barque, *Modern*, 757 tonnes, left Montréal for Glasgow with a cargo of wheat and arrived on 27 November 1877—a passage of 19 days, 17 days from pilot to pilot.
7. The square-rigged three-master, *Germanic*, 1296 tonnes, left Québec on 1 June and moored at Liverpool on 23 June 1878—a passage of 22 days. Bernier returned to Québec in the same ship in 22 days, then returned to Liverpool in 24 days.
8. The square-rigged three-master, *Quorn*, 1242 tonnes, left New Orleans on 24 March and moored at Liverpool on 26 April 1880—a passage of 32 days. Bernier made another crossing in her; she left Québec on 6 July and moored at Glasgow on 29 July 1880—a passage of 22 days.
9. The square-rigged three-master, *Royal Visitor*, 1220 tonnes, left Glasgow on 6 April and reached New Orleans on 12 May 1881—a passage of 36 days. In the same ship Bernier left Québec on 1 November and reached London on 25 November 1881—a passage of 24 days.
10. The square-rigged three-master, *Lanarkshire*, 1439 tonnes, left Greenock on 15 July and moored at Québec on 7 August 1883—a passage of 22 days. Bernier made another passage of 27 days in the same ship—between Mobile, on 10 February 1884 and Liverpool on 8 March 1884.
11. In the three-masted barque, *Cambria*, 1252 tonnes, Bernier raced the three-masted barque *Cheshire*, of 1307 tonnes. Both ships were launched on the same day in May 1885, the former from Samson's yard and the latter from Charland's yard. The *Cheshire* left Québec on 11 June and Bernier, in command of the *Cambria* followed her two days later. He made a crossing of 21 days and moored at Liverpool four hours before his rival.[11]

CHAPTER 18

They sang "Charley-Man"

In publications on the era of the big sailing ships, specialists in maritime history generally cite Captain Bernier because his memoirs represent one of the few testimonies to shipbuilding at Québec in the 19th century. Apart from the memories of Narcisse Rosa (1823-1907) recorded in his book *La construction des navires à Québec et ses environs* (1897), Bernier's writings remain the most important source on working conditions in the shipyards and on various aspects of the industry.

In the spring of 1874 Joseph-Elzéar accepted the offer of Peter Baldwin (1839-1917)[1] to manage his Hare Point yard on the Saint-Charles River for a salary of $100 per month, which represented a very reasonable salary for that time. This important shipbuilder and outfitter would not have called upon this young man of 22 to supervise his lucrative projects and head his teams, if Elzéar had not been a leader of men and if his rigour, attention to detail, experience, intuition, and practical mind had not impressed him.

Some writers have suggested that he accepted this position "at the instance of his wife."[2] Bernier has refuted this assertion, revealing rather that he was delighted at getting this opportunity to round out his knowledge of shipbuilding and that he lost no time in moving to the Saint-Sauveur district with Rose.[3] He does not specify the location of this first dwelling in the Québec suburb, but he did say that he had to walk a little over a mile to reach the Baldwin shipyard. In fact he bought a house in this district that would represent his "first investment in Canada."[4] This dwelling had the unique characteristic of facing four streets: "Aqueduc, de l'Église, Massue, and Sainte-Gertrude." If this house had not disappeared in the great fire of 1899, it would nowadays be located at the intersection of the following streets: Aqueduc, Saint-Sauveur, and Père-Grenier.

Between 1830 and 1870 the districts of Saint-Sauveur, Saint-Roch, and Hare Point on the Saint-Charles River were at the heart of Québec's shipbuilding industry, responsible for large sailing ships. The numerous shipyards located there were so crammed together, that they gave the impression that this was a single vast shipyard.

Joseph-Elzéar Bernier in his early twenties. [Archives of Carol and Louis Terrien]

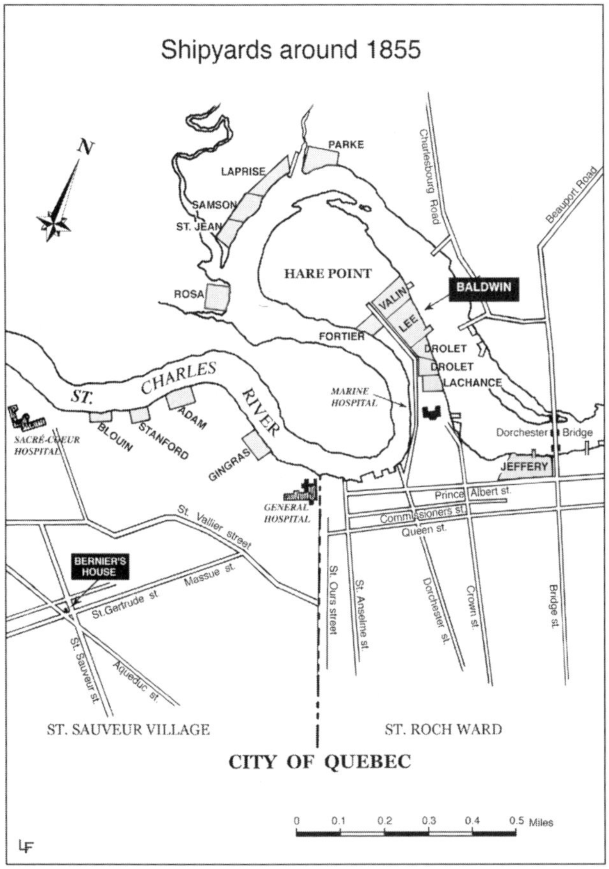

Shipyards along the St. Charles River, west of the Dorchester Bridge. This map shows the importance of this area in the shipbuilding industry at Québec around 1855. Twenty years later when Captain Bernier took over the direction of the Baldwin shipyard, the number of yards had decreased considerably. According to research by Eileen Reid Marcil, there were no more than four still in operation, namely those of: Narcisse Rosa, on the site of the former Valin yard; Pierre Valin, located on the site of the former Jeffery yard; Jean-Élie and Pierre-Élie Gingras, still on the same site; and William and Peter Baldwin, located on the site of Thomas C. Lee's former yard from 1870. The site of Joseph-Elzéar Bernier's house in Saint-Sauveur is indicated to reveal the route he travelled daily to get to work.

> Superintending a shipyard was an interesting but arduous occupation. To a shipmaster there could be nothing more interesting than to see the members and planking of a staunch ship rise under his eyes, almost under his own hands, and for a man who loved ships and knew them the watchful attention to the small details of the finishing, the rigging, and the outfitting, became almost a labour of love.[5]

His days were long and his responsibilities heavy and demanding. He would get up at 5 a.m. to prepare his breakfast and his lunch-box, and in order to be at his post at the yard well before the first workmen arrived, between 6 and 7.

When the 7 o'clock signal sounded, over 400 men were already busy, working with enthusiasm, precision, and confidence, and the blows of their hammers, axes, saws, and mauls resonated everywhere, echoing the sounds of the hundreds of other workmen at work in the neighbourhood in the yards located along this section of the Saint-Charles River.

In the Baldwin yard, just as in the yards of Narcisse Rosa, Pierre-Vincent Valin and elsewhere on Hare Point, almost all the shipbuilding was done outdoors, even during the lowest winter temperatures. According to Captain Bernier, during that period of the great shipyards the men were more stalwart and less demanding, and they carried out their tasks with good humour. Narcisse Rosa's memories are in the same vein:

> I still like to recall those good old days when the workman, pouring with sweat, would work to build a ship with the same enthusiasm and the same cheerfulness that he would have put into building his own home. But there were no limits to that good humour when it was a matter of transporting the components just by man-power, whether it be the keel, the stem or the stern-post. Then the "shipyard concert" would take place. If the components were not too heavy, one of the best voices would strike up a song and all the others would reply in chorus. But if the wooden component was very heavy, they would sing "Charley-Man."

View of the Saint-Sauveur district before the 1866 fire. The very long building is the rope-walk that specialized in the manufacture of rope and cordage. [ANQ, PA 122757]

> Who could listen to "Charley-Man," sung by these deep, sonorous voices the notes of which would be lost among the noise of the waves, without feeling moved to the depths of one's soul? One felt that beneath the rough exterior of the workman there was the heart of a good, honest worker.[6]

"Charley was a good man"... and the men would respond in unison: "Charle'—Man!" The accent placed on the first syllable provided the rhythm to the group's efforts ... from 7 o'clock in the morning to 5 or 6 in the evening.

The building of a ship might take over ten months and demanded the participation of about 15 trades such as carpenters, joiners, planking fitters, makers of tre-nails and wedges, caulkers, block-makers, mast- and spar-makers, ship's painters, riggers, blacksmiths, cart-ers, etc. Some of these workmen were paid by the day, others by the piece, depending on whether they were permanent employees or itinerants.

> After the winter's work came the great day of launching. The workmen were required to be on hand before dawn. On his arrival each man was served a stiff drink of Canadian whisky. At dawn the work of removing blocks was begun, starting from the stern. Amidships, the men were served another drink of whisky. By this time there were many spectators; the owners' families and friends, the workmen's families, curious strangers, and all the stragglers of the town. Just before the key was knocked out, a final drink was served to the men. Then a final blow knocked the key out, and the ship slid gracefully down the ways into the water amid thundering cheers. Her god-mother stood on a platform near the bow, and as the ship started down the ways a bottle of Madeira or port, secured by a ribbon, was broken against the bow.
>
> Ships were launched without rigging, but usually with masts and deck-houses in place, and with all spars lashed on deck. As a ship reached the water she dropped her anchor and came to rest in the stream. She was then towed in to a wharf to await her gear. In the meantime, the work-men and the guests gathered around long narrow tables loaded with sandwiches, cheese and biscuits, cookies, ale and spruce-beer. The owner and his guests retired to the shipyard office where fine wines and other refreshments awaited them. On launching day, every workman was given a full day's pay.[7]

Bernier would take pride in contributing to the real-ization of a magnificent ship and, on launch day, he could share that satisfaction for a job well done with his bosses, his workmen, and his wife.

In spring, as soon as the new ship was fitted out and loaded with timber, he would don his master mariner's cap again, and again would become a ship-deliverer, then sales agent. After the sale and before taking the steamer for the return voyage he would purchase the metal components required for building the next ship: anchors, chains, iron bars of varying sizes, handles, and hooks, as well as hemp for making sails and cordage.

A transaction that he concluded with William Baldwin in July 1878, at the end of his long association with that family of shipbuilders, provides evidence of Captain Bernier's business-sense:

> This time the *Germanic* sold readily, and I was free of her soon after my arrival. Mr. W.H. Baldwin was then in Hull with the *Roma*. She had turned out to be a veritable white

View of Pierre Valin's shipyard established on the site of the former Jeffery yard, beside the Dorchester Bridge. [Paul Gouin's Collection, ANQ, B.B.-7]

elephant, and was such a constant source of worry to him that his wife appealed to me to help him get rid of her. At first he wanted to sell her to me outright. But finally I bought a half share in her, paying down the money I had made out of the [private] butter shipment and the savings that I had in English banks. I put the *Roma* in dry-dock, cleaned and painted her, and set everything shipshape. Within three weeks after I had acquired a half interest in her, the *Roma* was sold to a Londonderry firm of distillers for thirty-six hundred pounds. My profit on the deal was three hundred pounds.[8]

This small profit allowed him to spend the winter in Liverpool, with his darling Rose, and to celebrate his birthday in Glasgow.

CHAPTER 19

On board the *Quorn*

In the spring of 1879 the Ross Company entrusted Captain Bernier with the command of their full-rigged three-master, the *Quorn*, which had reached the ripe age of 25 years. It goes without saying that after a quarter century of sailing, her frame of red pine was considerably weakened and her joints dangerously strained. In reality Ross was quite keen to get rid of her.

The *Quorn*, built and fitted-out at Kingston, Ontario, was a spiked ship, which meant that, contrary to normal custom, her planks had been spiked onto the frames with large spikes with wide heads, instead of copper bolts. As they rusted, these spikes had created numerous leaks.

Bernier owned eight of the 64 shares in the ship, which had a displacement of 1242 tonnes. As soon as he took command of her, he put her on dry dock to be caulked and generally overhauled; he also changed her rig from that of a full-rigged ship to a barque, which meant that instead of square sails on all three masts, he opted for square sails on the main and fore masts and for a gaff sail on the mizzen mast. The full rig required a large crew to set and furl the sails, whereas the fore-and-aft sail could be handled from the deck and required less men since the trapezoidal sail was bent obliquely. At that time all sailing vessels were rigged in the same manner to allow sailors to serve on any ship and to be able to work in total darkness.

Rigged like this, Joseph-Elzéar was convinced that the *Quorn* would be capable of handling further alarming incidents.

In March 1880[1] the *Quorn* was moored to the quayside in the river port of New Orleans, while waiting for a cargo of cotton, staves, and rock ballast bound for Liverpool.

Since Rose was along for the voyage, she and her young husband took advantage of the trip to tour the "Old Square" that had preserved numerous reminders of the French and Spanish past of this Louisiana city that survived thanks to its trade in cotton and sugar.

Every day, around noon, Elzéar would go to the office of his agent, Hall, Vaughan & Co. to pick up his mail and any orders from his owners.

On one of these occasions he made the acquaintance of Captain Tannock, who was well known in maritime circles for frequently participating in races between sailing ships that were then very much in fashion. Tannock commanded a large four-master, with the fine lines of a clipper, namely a stream-lined sailing ship built specially for achieving record speeds.

Intrigued by this colourful character and by the prospect of spending an evening in good company,

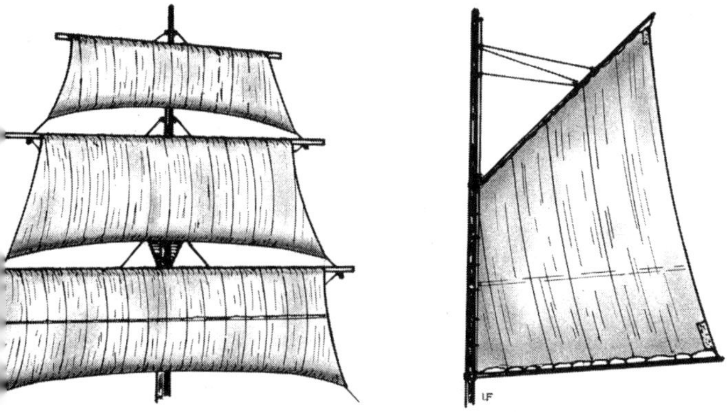

Square sails and gaff sail.

Bernier invited Captain Tannock to dine on board the *Quorn.*

On spotting the three-master's less than elegant appearance Tannock could not help bursting out in laughter. And, as he surveyed her almost vertical stem, the battered figure-head representing a huntress, and the unusually steeply inclined bowsprit of the Canadian vessel, his hilarity only increased.

Stung by his outburst of laughter, outraged by his unkind remarks about "his ship," and insulted by the lack of consideration with regard to his hospitality, Bernier exclaimed: "Captain Tannock, the *Quorn* may look like an old ballyhoo to you, but I want to tell you she carries her sail well, and for an old ship she can keep company in a fair wind with most vessels of her class." This statement amused Tannock even more.

His pride as captain/owner injured more and more, the young L'Isletain reacted immediately and threw out a challenge that his interlocutor refused to take seriously. "Hot words ensued and he finally strode away in anger refusing to dine with me, while I went aboard to nurse my wrath."

The next day, when Joseph-Elzéar got wind of the fact that Tannock was making fun of him all around the port, spreading the word that "that Frenchman has the nerve to say that his old ballyhoo is good company," he immediately went to the agent's office to wait for his rival and to challenge him again. With eight or 10 captains as witnesses he wagered $1000 that his old tub would easily win a race to Liverpool against his fast ship.

For a few moments Tannock was left gaping, open-mouthed, amazed at the amount of the bet and by the mettle of this young puppy. But he recovered quickly and made the pretext that he was not interested in stealing $1000 from him.

Joseph-Elzéar stuck to his guns and told him that if he was too cheap to stake $1000 on his ship, a beaver hat would do just as well. But he did not fail to add that he was sure he could beat him on the run to Liverpool and that, if Tannock refused the wager, all those present would know that he was right.

Tannock was caught in his own trap. The race was on! Each man deposited the price of a beaver hat, before starting to prepare for the voyage.

> A few days later Captain Tannock sailed, his ship loaded with staves, cotton seed, oilcake, grain and cotton. Nearly forty hours after him the *Quorn* set out on his track loaded with cotton, staves and rock ballast. Both ships were bound for Liverpool. My cargo was a little lighter than his, and the *Quorn*'s registered tonnage was about 250 tons lighter. But my ship was twenty-seven years old and his barely three or four. Mine was a stout timber-carrying ship, and leaked like a basket; his was a real clipper and was sound and dry. And mine had less sail than she had originally been designed for, and very much less than his ship carried. All things considered he had the advantage over me. But with fair winds and good seamanship I hoped to overcome the advantage.

Clearly, Bernier enjoyed challenges that aroused his competitive nature and his hunter's instinct. Moreover there can be no doubt that he took a certain pleasure in trying to show this pretentious captain that one should not judge a man by his clothes, nor the worth of a captain by the appearance of his ship.

Now to get on with the story of the race! Generally when trying to make a fast passage Captain Bernier

Joseph-Elzéar-Bernier in his thirties. [Archives of Carol and Louis Terrien]

Rose Caron, aged about 30. [Archives of Carol and Louis Terrien]

would not hesitate to spend most of his time on deck, allowing himself only a few hours of rest, sitting along the rail. On this occasion, since Rose was on board and because she was worried about the ill-effects of his lack of sleep, Elzéar was obliged to break with his usual habit to please his wife. "Nevertheless, I spent by far the greater part of each day on deck, and saw that every advantage possible was taken of any breeze that blew." No doubt this meant that he spent the nights in his cabin with Rose.

Despite her age, the *Quorn* made very good time. On one occasion her day's run was 280 miles, then 260 miles the next day, and 237 miles the day after that… onwards, always onwards, her sails swollen to the maximum and the huntress at her prow parting the waves in her passage, like Delacroix's *Liberté guidant le peuple [Liberty leading the people]*... Undoubtedly a happy moment for Bernier.

Victory awaited him at Liverpool, 28 days later. He had beaten his rival by more than two days.

"It was Captain Tannock's turn to be furious," announced the happy winner, in conclusion.

Captain Bernier was always in the habit of personally checking the state of the ship's pumps before undertaking a crossing. He did so at Greenock after discharging and cleaning the *Quorn*'s hold. In addition to undertaking a meticulous inspection he decided to add canvas filters to prevent the pumps from becoming choked. Once these precautions had been taken the ship was ready to sail and, with earth for ballast, she was able to put to sea from this Scottish port on the Firth of Clyde, bound for the North Channel and the Atlantic Ocean.

The ship's log tells of the tragedy that put an end to the long career of this gallant sailing ship. The condensed style, quoted verbatim, is typical of this type of seaman's report and has scarcely changed since that time.[2]

> November 17th 1880. Weighed anchor today for my 70th sea voyage. Left Greenock in tow of the steam tug *Flying Dutchman*. Draft, 13 feet for'ard, 13 ½ feet aft. Wind N.E. Sky threatening. Tug left us in the Firth of Clyde. By nightfall off Rathlin Island to the north of Ireland. Wind favourable.
>
> 18th. Strong breeze from N.E. Doing 9 knots. Pass two ships. Latitude 55.7. Longitude 12.50.
>
> 19th. Fine breeze from W. Running well. At 10 p.m. wind veered to S. with rain. At midnight strong breeze from S.W. Lat. 54.19. Long. 16.46.
>
> 20th. Heavy gale from S.S.W. All sails reefed. Ship is straining and making water. (…) The carpenter building up a wooden frame about the pumps to keep the ballast from the pumps.
>
> 21st. Gale veers to S.W.; and increases to hurricane. In a furious squall, the ship takes a heavy list to starboard. Seas coming from all directions. We are in the midst of revolving gales. Forced to pump constantly from 8 a.m. until noon. At 6 p.m. wind blows from N.W. with squalls. All sails reefed.
>
> 22nd. Heavy gale from W. Forced to heave to. Lat. 53.46. Long. 18.11.

23rd. Wind W.S.W. Foresail set with a reef. Pumping in each watch.

24th. Furious storm from W. Angry sea. Ship is rolling and pitching very heavily. Leakage increasing. All hands exhausted from pumping. Storm slackens shortly after sundown.

25th. Sea is very heavy and breaks over the deck, forcing the ship to roll more than ever and to make more water. The pumps are kept going without stopping, each man being served with hot coffee as he is relieved at the pump. By noon the hurricane is blowing furiously, the ship is pitching violently. In a sharp dive into the crest of a wave the bobstay chains break and the bowsprit starts to rise. We unshackle one anchor chain and pass it over the bowsprit to secure it in place, heaving it tight with the windlass (if the bowsprit had broken we might have lost our foremast). Four feet of water in the hold and all hands to the pumps until night. Barometer is lower than I have ever seen it, 28.10. At midnight terrific hurricane strikes us from the N.E., and veers to N.N.W. with such force that our yards are stripped of all sail. Listing very heavily to port.

26th. At 4 a.m. five feet in the hold. Set mizzen staysail to keep the head to the wind. At 8 a.m. storm slackens a little. At noon we set our lower topsails. Lat. 54.34; Long. 16.49. Have lost one degree 11 miles of longitude.

27th. Storm from S.W. Ship is hove to and rolls very heavily, making more water; 6 feet in the hold. One of our fresh water tanks, battered by the rolling, bursts, and 1500 gallons of water pour into the hold; this is half our fresh water supply. Only canvas set is half of main topsail. All hands at the pumps. We are losing ground and driving to the E.N.E. Lat. 55.6; Long. 16.1. At night sea is very bad.

28th. At 2 a.m. the water is gaining on the pumps. At 8 a.m. we rig up a stage with a ladder and plank, lower it over the starboard side, and then lower the carpenter, Philip Wiseman, and a helper, to caulk some loose planking. Both these men are washed off the stage and recovered with considerable difficulty. I then have myself lashed to the staging and caulk the spots myself. Storm veers to W. In a terrific squall, the ship quivers like a leaf, but our topsails hold. Pumping constantly; the men complaining bitterly, but I reassure them as best I can. By lashing spars to the handles of the pump, and rigging them up in a "balance-wheel" movement, the effort of the men at the pumps is made somewhat easier. Serve out regular rations of liquor. Pass the night hove to. Rolling heavily.

29th. Storm abated somewhat. Set upper topsail for'ard with a staysail. Water in hold is 6 ½ feet. Carpenter and I work all day caulking on the starboard side abreast the foremast. Seas sweep over our stage at intervals. Men pump all day. By nightfall water reduced to 5 feet. Crew very much discouraged; I bring them into the cabin, talk to them encouragingly, and serve out a ration of rum. Then back to the pumps.

30th. At 2 a.m. I go down to the hold with six men to clear the ballast away from the pumps. We work in water above our knees until 8 a.m. when the pumps are clear of silt. Still 4 feet in the hold. Wind is N.W. and weather clearing. Lat. 54.39; Long. 16.30. At 4 p.m. wind freshens and the sea grows heavy.

December 1st. Wind nearly dead. Grasp the opportunity to work on the outer topsides. Run out of oakum, using strips of sail tightly rolled and nailed over joints of planking, until our supply of nails runs out. At noon dead calm. Ship is rolling heavily. At 2 p.m. wind sets in from S. with a fine rain. At 4 p.m. forced to clew up topsail. Terrific storm from S.S.W. The sea is like a boiling caldron, and all covered with scum. Despite constant pumping water is gaining on us; 5 feet in the hold. In the evening set the fore topsail, but at 10 p.m. it is torn away by a squall. At midnight I go aloft myself to bend a new topsail.

2nd. At 4 a.m. 6 feet in the hold. All hands worn out by lack of sleep and constant pumping. Two men overcome with exhaustion and I treat them as best I can. At noon sun appears for few minutes and I obtain observations. Lat. 53.33; Long. 19.16. Shortly after noon I relieve the mate at the pumps and take charge until midnight, when I take the wheel for an hour.

3rd. After one hour's sleep I am wakened with the report that there is 5 ½ feet in the hold. On descending to the hold find that water is rolling about above the ballast and that it is impossible to reach the pump shafts. The hold is a desolate sight. Wind is fair and we set some sail.

Sailors on the pump during a gale at sea. [Artist unknown, Carol and Louis Terrien Collection]

4th. Heavy gale from S.W. All sails reefed. Gale increases to hurricane. Furious sea running. Pumping all day and most of the night. Hurricane increases steadily through the night.

5th. Hurricane blowing with unbelievable force. Mountainous seas breaking over vessel. Ship is rolling and pitching, and is straining and groaning horribly. Topside planks are starting, and springing apart. Water is gaining steadily on the pumps; 7 feet in the hold. Crew completely discouraged. Plead with me to put back or take to the boats. All my energy and persuasion required to keep them at the pumps. Hearing rumours that they are planning to abandon the vessel, I bring them one by one into the cabin, and explain the position of the ship and convince them of the impossibility of a boat living in the mountainous seas now running.

6th. Storm abates slightly. Set a topsail to keep the ship under control. At 8 a.m. the crew come to the cabin and beg me to put back the ship. I call my officers in consultation, and we agree to put back towards the Irish coast and run for the nearest port. I enter in the log-book the names of the two officers and eleven members of the crew who made the request to put back. Fortunately I have an excellent crew and first class officers, 18 men all told. With a poor crew or even an average crew we would have been lost long ago. My efforts to save the ship have been well seconded by the mate, Patrick Meaher, the second mate, Martin Abrahamson, the carpenter, Philip Wiseman, and the entire crew. Today the pumps are kept going the full 24 hours. There is 8 feet in the hold.

7th. Strong breeze from W. Ship has been tacked and is running eastward at 8 knots. Lat. 54.34; Long. 22.55.

8th. Strong gale from W.S.W. Pump steadily all day. No sleep for any one. Barely time to eat a little in the galley. One man kept constantly cleaning out silt from the pump. At noon the wind-mill pump breaks down.

9th. At 4 a.m. there is 10 feet in the hold. At 8 a.m. the crew decide to take to the boats and abandon the ship. I remonstrate forcibly with them, tell them that within three days we will be off the coast, explain that they would be lost in the boats, and even threaten to knock a hole through each boat if they attempt to lower them. They are to do their best for another two days, and return to the pump.

10th. Strong breeze from the W. Heading for Ireland. Crew spend the night at the pumps and are all worn out. But the pumps are still kept going. Now and again a man falls down exhausted. I have him carried to the galley where I give him brandy and coffee. Lat. 55.11; Long. 9.27.

11th. Heavy storm from S.W. Water still gaining on the pumps. Men very much discouraged. At 11 o'clock I send Wiseman, the carpenter, aloft to watch for land. I stand at the wheel. Most of the crew at the pumps; a few lying exhausted on deck. Every five minutes he reports: "Nothing in sight, sir." The men are growing more discouraged. Ship rolling heavily. At noon Wiseman sings out exultantly: "Land ahead, sir. Two points on the starboard bow." A cheer goes up from the deck, and the men crowd the rail to see if they can catch sight of the land. Then they return to the pumps and bend to the work with renewed energy. The land is Tory Island. I decide to round Inishtrahull Light and to run for Lough Foyle, and attempt to make Londonderry. At 8 p.m. we sight Inishtrahull and prepare the anchors. There is 11 feet in the hold. The ship is taking sickening lists, first to one side and then to the other, and is griping so badly that it takes two men to hold the wheel. All evening we are firing rockets. Running before the wind, we are shipping so much water that we are obliged to heave to. But the ship lists badly and threatens to capsize, so we are forced to run before the wind again.

12th. Shortly after midnight the crew come aft and plead with me to beach the ship in the first safe spot we see, and I agree. I had hoped to run past Magilligan Point into Lough Foyle, but the tacking to port required to run through the narrow channel very nearly capsizes us. There is now 12 feet in the hold and the water is awash of the beams. I drive her before the wind and luff her alternately six times. At 1 o'clock my officers agree that we can not stay afloat until morning. At 2 o'clock I turn her bow to the shore, steering for the middle of Magilligan Strand, to the east of Lough Foyle. At 3 o'clock we are almost in the breakers, and I order all hands to the poop aft to keep clear of the masts and yards in case they fall. I also order them to lash themselves to the rail, and I tell the wheelsmen to jump clear of the wheel the moment she touches.

The shock was terrible. The *Quorn* struck violently on the bar on the Irish coast, and ploughed into the sand with a series of terrifying impacts, worse than earthquakes. But her tribulations were only just beginning. The first sea swept the poop with great force, half drowning the seamen lashed to the rail. A second wave, with unbelievable force, lifted the poor ship some 10 feet over the bar then dropped her on to the rocks. The stem and keel disintegrated immediately, disembowelling both decks and uprooting the fore mast. Then a third wave hurled the dying ship over the natural coastal bar, pushing her irrevocably towards her end and towards *terra firma,* while the terrified men clung desperately to the poop.

By 4 a.m. the sea was still not ready to relinquish its prey. Just as the captain was going below to his cabin to retrieve his log and other important documents, it was the main mast's turn to become unstepped, and to crash down on the ship's deck.

The sailors, soaked to the skin, continued to endure, hour after hour, until it became light enough for them to make out human figures in the distance, on the beach. But the sea was still too dangerous to try to launch a boat.

Wait! Survive!

Another seven hours elapsed while they clung like this, imploring the gods of the sea, until their captain decided that it was time to act. He asked for volunteers to help him carry a lifeline to the shore. The carpenter Wiseman and seamen John Patrick and Martin Carl agreed to attempt this manoeuvre and began to strip while their captain wrapped a cable around his waist.

> The first wave fills our boat to the gunwales, the second washes my three men away and I remain alone, clutching desperately to the thwarts. At the third wave the boat touches ground, but is dragged back on the receding wave. In and out again goes the boat several times, but finally the men ashore manage to pick me out of the stern-sheets, more dead than alive, half-choked with the sand I have swallowed, and my right arm useless from the knocking about I have received from the boat. My three companions are fortunately washed ashore and picked up before they swallowed too much water.[3]

Grabbing the line wrapped around the captain's waist, the men on shore hauled ashore a thicker cable, the other end of which was firmly secured to the fore mast and one by one, despite their exhaustion, the crew members grasped it and braving the current managed to drag themselves to the beach. The last to leave the dying *Quorn* were the mate and, wrapped in his arms, the ship's mascot, a Newfoundland dog named Jack, which had survived the shipwreck.

The rescued men found refuge in a nearby farmhouse belonging to the Henry family. This was certainly not the first drama of this kind that these modest peasants of Scottish-Irish origin had witnessed, but they welcomed the strangers warmly and offered them a simple but abundant supper.

Calm returned to the eyes of the men, tested severely by the ferocity of nature. Gradually the fire in the hearth, the woollen blankets, the familiar smells, and the warmth of the soup, soothed their bodies, battered by the fury of the sea. One by one the seamen stretched out on the beaten-earth floor in the single large room of the cottage, and immediately dropped into a deep, long sleep.

Stretching out on a straw mattress, Joseph-Elzéar did not even have time to thank his lucky star or even to think of Rose. A heavy sleep robbed him of all his senses and held him, a prisoner lost to the world, for more than 24 hours.

When he awoke the young captain's muscular body would no longer respond to commands from his brain. Elzéar could open his eyes, but his swollen throat was incapable of uttering a sound. There followed several hours of great anxiety for the captain, normally so powerful, who had always been proud of his exceptional physique. What if he were permanently paralyzed?

For hours he tried to stimulate his limbs and to reprogram his memory with movements that had been instinctive. One finger, then another; one muscle, then another… until he had mustered enough strength to try to lift his body. An unbearable pain in his shoulder suddenly riveted him to the spot. The pain was so intense that he could not breathe.

That evening, he was able to move with assistance. He had to send a telegram to the Ross Company to inform them that the *Quorn* was finished, but that her entire crew was safe.

Next day Sir Harvey Bruce, Member of Parliament for Coleraine, and his wife Lady Bruce, invited him to stay at their castle, near Magilligan Strand, in order to look after his shoulder and to regain his strength.

Elzéar recovered some personal belongings from the wreck and sold it by auction, before traveling to Liverpool to give evidence to an enquiry into the shipwreck.

> My story was corroborated by the officers and some of the crew. When the presiding magistrate saw our "rust-eaten" hands he said he was convinced that we had all done our duty to the ship. [4]

The conclusions of the tribunal were shared by his employers, who promised to entrust him with another command as soon as possible.

Joseph-Elzéar reported that Rose was badly shaken by the shipwreck and that, to reassure her, he promised not to go on any more transatlantic trips.

CHAPTER 20

A paddle-pump

At the time of the great sailing ships storms on the high seas were just as frequent, unpredictable, and dangerous as nowadays. One has only to watch single-hulled or multi-hulled vessels racing on television to realize that these modern vessels do not always measure up, despite their radar, computers, hydraulic masts, and sophisticated gadgets, in face of the tough laws of meteorological hazards. Even today demastings, broken spars, and torn sails are commonplace and the records are full of violent rolling, and material and human losses.

When Bernier had to face a furious sea he could count solely on the qualities of his ship, his own competence and experience, the tenacity of his men, and their ability to make the right manoeuvre at the right time… splicing, hoisting, shoring up, adjusting … actions that had to be synchronized and precise, despite the vessel's rolling and pitching. In their unequal battles with nature wooden ships always suffered material damage and leaks. Since motor pumps had not yet been invented, the seamen were obliged to operate hand pumps to discharge the water that had percolated through the seams in the planking and accumulated in the bilges and the hold; this represented exhausting, demoralizing physical labour for the crew, victims of the fury of the elements.

To save his ships and their cargoes during these assaults by the sea, Joseph-Elzéar Bernier had no choice but to rely on the strong arms and the good will of his officers and seamen. As the episode of the *Royal Visitor* proved, however, it was not enough to increase their rum ration or their wages to encourage them to work to their utmost, sometimes 24 hours a day, until total exhaustion.

> During my service as ship's-husband for the Ross fleet I had kept my eyes open for a likely ship in which I could invest. The Ross firms were interested in my plans and put many offers my way, but I was determined to act slowly and to make a good investment. Finally in March 1881, I bought a half interest in the ship *Royal Visitor*, the other half being owned by the Ross partners.
>
> The *Royal Visitor* was a full-rigged ship built in 1860 by Thomas Oliver for William Jeffery of Quebec. That was the year of the visit to Canada of the Prince of Wales, later King Edward VII. The young prince while in Quebec had been taken to visit the Oliver shipyard, and in his honour one of the ships then on the ways was named the *Royal Visitor*. She was 192 feet long, 1220 tons register. My interest had cost me twelve hundred and 50 pounds.[1]

Captain Bernier was quite pleased with his purchase, which displayed a proud appearance. Despite her many years of service the ship was fairly sound and very fast. Her only fault was a tendency to make water.

Early in April Bernier took command of the three-master and sailed in ballast from Glasgow, bound for the Franco-American city of New Orleans. Right from

The *Royal Visitor* after being changed from a square-rigged ship to a three-masted barque. This canvas was probably in Captain Bernier's private collection. [F.W. Wallace, *In the Wake of the Wind-Ships*, 1927]

the start he realized that a change in her rig might improve the ship's performance and might ease the work of the seamen.

> The opportunity came sooner than I had expected. Ten days out of the Clyde we were becalmed for a little more than a day. Before the wind failed us the look-out had reported a large log floating on the starboard bow. I had a boat lowered and the log secured. It turned out to be a fine piece of timber sixty-one feet long and thirteen inches square, probably thrown off the deck-load of a ship weathering a heavy sea. I set the carpenter working with helpers and within a short time the spar was shaped into a topmast and fixed in position on the mizzen-mast. Rigging and sails were also changed, and when the wind set in again the *Royal Visitor* was a barque-rigged ship.[2]

This modification allowed him to make a successful crossing of 36 hours from port to port. However his luck abandoned him completely once he had reached Louisiana. Not only was he forced to proceed to the port of Pensacola, Alabama, to find another cargo, but eight of the seamen took advantage of this to desert while the ship was being loaded. Bernier had to pay crimps to obtain a new crew, although he had the nasty impression that it was these same procurers who had lured his men away in order to offer their services to another captain.

As she left Pensacola Bay, the *Royal Visitor*'s keel touched on the bar, which started a leak but this did not prevent her from continuing into the Gulf of Mexico.

Five days later she ran into a tropical storm in Florida Strait southwest of Key West and the Florida keys. The seas were so high that water was spurting in through bow loading ports, used for loading timber. The men were forced to pump continually, but still were not gaining on the inflow of water.

> After two days of pumping the water had run up to six feet in the hold, and the ship was listing heavily. The men were afraid that we would capsize and pleaded with me to jettison the deck-load. I ordered two-thirds of the deck-load thrown overboard, and the balance brought aft. This raised the bow, which eased the strain on the bow ports.[3]

There could no longer be any question of crossing the Atlantic with a ship in such a condition.

Elzéar headed north past Miami and West Palm Beach on the east coast of Florida, bound for Cape Canaveral. Taking refuge in a small bay near that cape he dropped both anchors and let the entire length of chain run out, to lighten the bows. Then, with the help of his carpenter he managed to caulk and repair the bow-ports effectively, thus allowing the pumps to discharge the bulk of the water that had accumulated in the hold.

The *Royal Visitor* immediately resumed her voyage towards the North Atlantic, pointing her bowsprit towards Scotland, confident that an evil fate had been thwarted. Barely four or five days later, she encountered another powerful storm that resulted in another major leak that could not be located.

She was little more than a quarter of the way across the ocean. Should she put back to Canada, which would mean the loss of any profit on the cargo, or continue the voyage with the help of the pumps? Captain Bernier was faced with a major dilemma: should he return to North America to put his ship in dry-dock and repair the leak or continue to a British port and force his men to pump continually even though they were already discouraged by the turn of events,. He reasoned as follows:

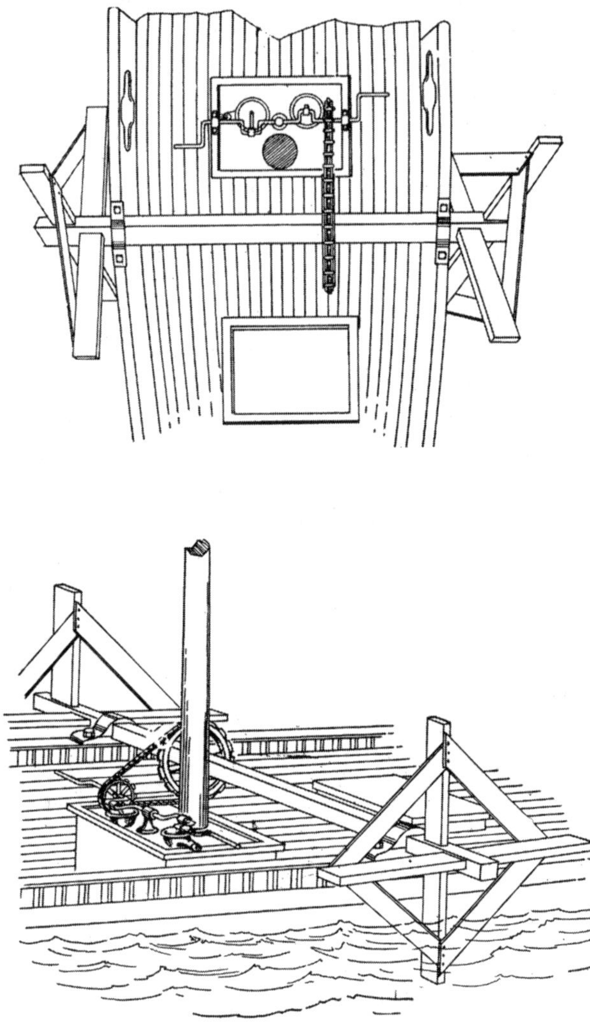

The Bernier pump. [Bernier Collection, *Master Mariner*]

> If the *Royal Visitor* had been equipped with a windmill pump the matter would have been simple as the windmill pump alone would probably have taken care of the leakage. This reflection suggested to me a solution of the problem. Lacking a wind-mill, why not construct a water-mill?[4]

To resolve his problem he invented the "Bernier pump," a paddle-pump on the principle of the paddle steamers that he had certainly seen on the Mississippi.

So a great square timber was taken from the deckload and laid athwart the ship near the main-mast from rail to rail, about four feet projecting beyond each rail. Where the timber rested on the rail it was rounded like a mast, and two blocks were fashioned to hold it. One block fitted below and one above, each with a semi-circle rounded out, so that, with the use of grease, the timber could turn in the blocks. The blocks were bolted together about the timber, and later bolted to the rail.

In the middle of the timber, near the pump, a wooden wheel was fitted. This was connected by a chain belt to the fly-wheel of the pump. Before the blocks at the bulwarks were bolted to the rail, the entire arrangement was lifted a few feet by means of tackles fixed to the mainmast. The paddles were then put in place at the ends of the timber. These paddles were broad planks, mortised and bolted onto the timber at right angles so that, when the timber was lowered again, one end of one plank was always in the water. These planks were made rigid by cross-pieces.[5]

Once the sails were set and the ship was under way again, the pump functioned just as the astute captain had anticipated. Bernier's invention "worked splendidly, and much faster than any men could pump."[6] Without this paddle-pump the three-master would certainly have suffered a disaster, since, en route, she encountered five more storms.

In the Firth of Forth the vessel and her strange machine aroused many enquiring looks among those with whom she crossed paths. Abeam of the island of Inchkeith the captain/inventor had the protruding ends of the axle sawed off, to permit the ship to go alongside the dock.

> The Norwegian timber-droghers may have immortalized the windmill pump, but Bernier's water-mill pump was probably the only rig of its kind.[7]

The *Royal Visitor* had taken 51 days to reach Scotland. She was unloaded in the port of Leith before going on dry-dock and being completely recaulked, allowing her co-owner to sell her one year later to a rich Danish ship-owner for a net profit of £250.

CHAPTER 21

Sojourn in Southeast Asia

After the sale of the *Royal Visitor* I returned to my duties of ship's-husband for the Ross fleet. At that time there was a Ross ship that was causing a great deal of worry to the Ross partners. She was the full-rigged ship *Lanarkshire* [211 feet and 1439 tonnes], built in Quebec in 1864 by J.E. Gingras [and L.-S. Labbé], backed by Senator Ross. She had made many passages to various corners of the earth. Her last voyage had been to Singapore with coal from Cardiff. Off Mauritius she had run into a typhoon and started to leak badly. The crew had been obliged to pump all the way to Singapore. On coming to anchor her master had called Lloyd's surveyor and two other masters on board for a survey.[1]

They were unanimous. The ship had leaks that were invisible. They therefore recommended that she put on dry-dock, that her copper sheathing be stripped off, that a detailed inspection be made of the seams between the planks, that her hull be recaulked and retarred before new copper plates were fitted, and that new wooden sheathing be applied above the waterline.

When surveyors make a recommendation for repairs, these repairs must be made before insurance can be secured for her or her cargo, or even before the ship can obtain her clearance papers from the port she is in. However, if the owner disagrees with the Lloyd's survey he can obtain an independent survey by three masters, and if the recommendations of this survey are complied with the ship can be cleared out of port but no insurance can be obtained until the Lloyd's recommendations are fulfilled.[2]

As ship's-husband Joseph-Elzéar had had occasion to see the *Lanarkshire* in dry-dock and was convinced that the survey of the Singapore specialists was inaccurate and their verdict unjustified. He had noticed many times that wooden vessels that regularly carried coal tended to leak just above the copper sheathing. According to him this was due to the gas that formed from the bilge water coming in contact with the coal, and working on the strained joints in the planking. Captain Bernier was certain that the survey of the *Lanarkshire* had been made before she was unloaded.

The repairs recommended by Lloyd's survey would have cost five thousand pounds, much more than the ship was worth, and the Ross partners were seriously considering abandoning the ship to the insurers. Before doing so they asked my advice. I had so much confidence in my analysis of the situation that I offered to buy the ship, or the major interest in her. The partners agreed and the ship, as she stood in Singapore, was valued at two thousand pounds. I bought forty-five of the sixty-four shares. Then I purchased some equipment I knew would be required in the repair of the *Lanarkshire* and shipped the lot by the steamship *Gleneagle,* bound from Liverpool for the East Indies. With the shipment went a windmill pump.[3]

Shrinking from nothing, Bernier decided to see to the repairs to his ship and to bring her back to Canada. In July 1882 he made the trip from Liverpool to Singapore. He first landed at Calais and travelled to

Paris to buy tropical clothes. He took advantage of the opportunity to be a tourist, travelling across France and Northern Italy. According to members of the family this was when he saw the Côte d'Azur for the first time, as well as a dozen tourist cities such as Lyon, Marseilles, Milan, Verona, Venice, Florence, etc.

He took a steamer from the port of Brindisi, on the Adriatic Sea, to Alexandria on the northwest tip of the Nile Delta in Egypt, then on to the Suez Canal. This master-piece of canal building[4] considerably reduces the distance between Europe and Asia by avoiding the need to round Africa.

Bernier noted that "Not harassed in every port by the worries of loading and unloading, of chartering and of shipping crews, I was able to view and to visit our stopping-places with unaccustomed enjoyment."[5]

From the Red Sea, his steamer crossed the Gulf of Aden, then the Arabian Sea to the port of Colombo, the capital of Ceylon, now Sri Lanka, and an important stopping point on the sea route along the south coast of Asia.

While waiting for the arrival of the next ship that was to take him to the Malay Peninsula, Joseph-Elzéar had the leisure to visit this exotic island and to taste some of its charms and contrasts. He even acquired numerous sapphires and natural pearls which would generate a good profit when he resold them to a jeweller in London. As a souvenir of his voyage he had one of these valuable sapphires set in a ring of white gold, which he wore for the rest of his life.[6]

He made the last leg of his voyage in the steamer, *Grange*, running across the Andaman Sea and through the Strait of Malacca, with stops at George Town on the island of Pinang and at the port of Melaka.

Clearly Captain Bernier was not a writer by profession and he has left no vivid descriptions of the landscapes he was seeing for the first time, nor did he make significant analyses of the customs of the peoples along whose shores he was coasting. In any case, only one thing was on his mind during this great adventure, and that was the condition of the *Lanarkshire*.

As soon as he reached Singapore he introduced himself to the captain of his ship, Captain Scott, in order to show him his title of ownership and to offer him the position of mate for the return voyage.

> I then went ashore, called on Lloyd's surveyor, presented my papers, and asked him to make a fresh survey of the *Lanarkshire*. He strongly resented my request and refused to examine the ship again. So I boarded several ships in the harbour, until I had located two masters who expected to be in port for at least three weeks, one an American, the other a Norwegian. They agreed to hold a survey with me next day, and promised to come aboard at 8 o'clock. I then went down to Chinatown on the other side of the harbour where I located a Chinese carpenter who did ship contracting and who was strongly recommended to me by some of the masters familiar with the port. Owah Chaung also promised to be on hand next morning bright and early.[7]

By the time they all came aboard the ship was already anchored off Chinatown, beyond the jurisdiction of Singapore. As had been agreed the inspectors proceeded to make a careful inspection while the carpenter took notes as to the repairs to be made.

Owah Chaung's estimate was less than 2000 Straits dollars; this represented less than half the original estimate presented by the Lloyds inspector. Bernier could only congratulate himself on having relied on his own judgment.

> Owah Chaung's price was low, but he asked for a month to do the work in. I gave him fifteen days, and I promised him that if he delivered me the ship within that time I would give him as a bonus a very fine seventy-five-foot spar on the *Lanarkshire*'s deck, which he had endeavoured to buy from me to fit as a mainmast into a schooner he was then repairing.[8]

At dawn, next morning, the owner watched a dozen sampans crammed with Chinese people boarding his ship. The men immediately went to work with their small, primitive tools.

The repairs were completed on the fourteenth day. Owah Chaung was able to leave with his spar, and Captain Bernier called his two inspectors on board again.

> They examined everything closely, sounded the pump, and gave the *Lanarkshire* a clean bill of health. I then went ashore, shipped my crew of Lascars and Malays, and cleared the ship through the consul's office. Late in September I sailed for Moulmein in Lower Burma.[9]

Despite his willingness and his determination Captain Bernier had not seen an end to his troubles, however. It took him a further two months, trudging the streets of Moulmein, Rangoon and Mandalay before he finally secured a charter for a cargo of teak bound for Queenstown in Ireland. Loading the timber took a further month.

> My three months stay in Burma was one of the most interesting quarters that I have ever spent. There were so many sights strange to my Occidental eyes: the pagodas, the temples, the use of elephants as beasts of burden, the strange rites and customs of the inhabitants.[10]

If he had had a camera at his disposal he would certainly have immortalized several of these amazing scenes. George Eastman (1854-1932), founder of the Kodak Company had invented the first photographic plates using gelatino-bromide of silver five years previously, but the photographic apparatus was still not portable. Not to mention the fact that one had to develop the plates in a dark room on site. Joseph-Elzéar's interest in photography and cinematography would manifest itself later, when he had access to more portable cameras to fix events in time. Until then, he always called upon professional photographers and their magic boxes in their studios, to mark important moments in his life.

During the homeward voyage he encountered his first typhoon in the Indian Ocean:

> It lasted twenty hours and carried away three of our sails and smashed part of our rigging, all of which we replaced immediately. On April 1st I rounded the Cape of Good Hope for the first time, but only after fighting contrary winds for ten days in its vicinity. On May 5th we passed St. Helena, and forty days later we were in Queenstown, a total passage from Moulmein of 127 days.[11]

When he returned to Québec Captain Bernier almost interrupted his sea-going career. To please his wife who begged him to abandon that crazy way of life and to settle down ashore, Elzéar entered into negotiations to buy the Île aux Ruaux, opposite the Île d'Orléans.

> This island was a particularly pleasant spot for anyone who knew the neighbourhood and did not mind the lonesomeness. It is about two miles long by a quarter-mile wide, has fine beaches and fishing coves, and excellent hay meadows and pasture lands. It had an old stone manor-house. My intention was to import a certain hardy breed of sheep from the north of Scotland and raise sheep for the wool and meat markets.[12]

The owner, by the name of Blouin, drew up a sales contract for the sum of $2200 but since he could not provide a clear title, the deal fell through. Probably relieved, and aware that he was not really cut out for a sedentary life, Captain Bernier went to sea again on board the *Lanarkshire.*

In April 1884 he turned over command of this vessel to his friend and relative, Captain Charles de Koënig from L'Islet-sur-Mer, who had bought 16 of his shares, the others being taken up again by the Ross Company. This three-master was sailing under the Norwegian flag in 1891 and was abandoned at sea in 1893.

CHAPTER 22

The ill-fated *Jeannette*

DURING HIS SOJOURN IN QUÉBEC in the summer of 1883 a firm of brokers proposed to Captain Bernier that he might invest in the building of a schooner that was to be 100 feet in length and was to displace 197.67 tonnes. Joseph-Elzéar accepted the challenge and advanced $3000 to Captain Théodore Bouchard of the Île aux Coudres. He was not the only one to become involved in this business since part of the mortgage had been sold to François Audet, Charles Robichaud, and Raymond Blakiston. The reason that the brokers had approached him to make such an investment was that he was already recognized in the maritime community as a man of means.

Later that summer Captain Bouchard took command of his *Jeannette* and sailed from the port of Québec with her first cargo of timber, bound for St. John's, Newfoundland. But it was an unlucky maiden voyage:

> He was driven ashore in a gale among the Saint-Pierre and Miquelon Islands, and the *Jeannette*'s hull was badly damaged. She was repaired by unloading her cargo and canting the ship in the water. For these repairs I had furnished another three thousand dollars by telegraph.[1]

The repairs had just been completed when another storm drove her violently ashore. This time Bernier refused to lend any more money and the schooner was taken to St. John's where the firm of Harvey & Co. was to undertake the repairs.

In the spring of the following year Joseph-Elzéar learned that the schooner was still not yet seaworthy. This was when he relinquished his shares and command of the *Lanarkshire*, to go to St. John's to see to the problems of the ill-fated *Jeannette*.

> I found Bouchard's affairs hopelessly involved. He had been entitled to insurance on the ship and to salvage on his cargo. But he had failed to follow the proper procedure to obtain either, and it was now past the period provided in the policies. Finally the ship was libelled by Harvey & Co., put up at auction, and bought for $4,004 by my representative. The ship was now mine, so I proceeded to repair her and make her ready for sea. This cost me $1,200, plus my own expenses, which I placed at $1,050. The *Jeannette* had cost me, all told, $12,254, a big price for a schooner.
>
> But I was not through with bad luck over this trim little ship. The first master I placed in charge of her stranded her on Ciberus Rock outside the Gut of Canso, but failed to report it as he floated her again. Her hull was now damaged again, sea-worms got in under the paint and before long she was leaking badly again.
>
> But before I had discovered this, the *Jeannette* had made two trips to the West Indies under a new master. It took all the freight money of these two trips, about two thousand dollars, to make her seaworthy again. After these repairs she made one trip from Halifax to Quebec, where I berthed her and posted her for sale. In 1886 I sold her to a firm of Quebec ship-owners for ten thousand dollars. I was paid five hundred on account, and given notes for the balance. I had accepted this arrangement as the

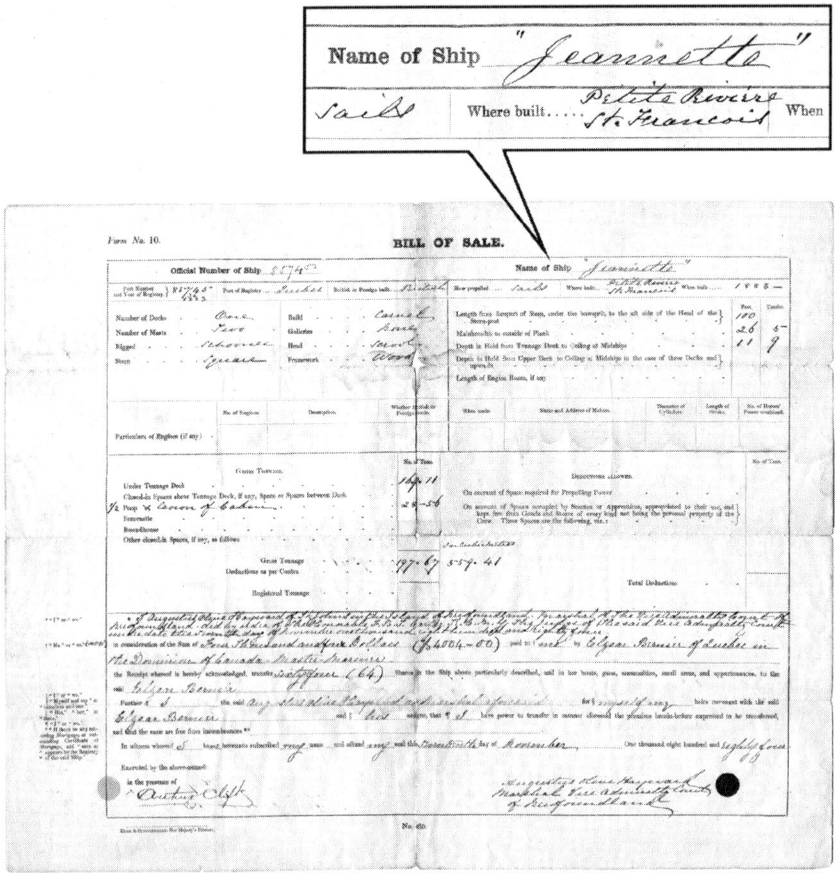

Contract for the purchase of the *Jeannette,* a schooner built at Petite-Rivière-Saint-François in 1883. This document indicates that on 17 November 1884 Captain Bernier paid $400 for 64 shares in this sailing vessel. [Private collection])

firm was of previous good repute, and quite a fleet of vessels was operated by it. However, before the second note was paid the firm went bankrupt and all its ships turned out to be heavily mortgaged, including the *Jeannette.* All I ever realized on this unlucky boat was that first payment of five hundred dollars.[2]

The unlucky ship was seized and sold at Buenos Aires.

During a stay of six months in Newfoundland Bernier struck up a friendship with one of the partners of the New York company, J.E. Simpson & Co., who operated the dry-dock in St. John's. Simpson offered him the position of dockmaster, but the government refused to approve the appointment of somebody who was not a Newfoundlander. Joseph-Elzéar therefore decided to return home, in time for the Christmas festivities. He left St. John's on the steamer, *Portia*, bound for New York via Sydney and Halifax. By coincidence J.E. Simpson was occupying the stateroom next to his. On the night of 20 December, during a severe storm with hail and snow, the *Portia* ran aground at Sydney Mines, at the entrance to Sydney harbour:

> The ship was fast on the rocks, but pounding in the breakers. She was making water for'ard, but not seriously. The captain was ill in his room and the mate was in charge. He decided to land the passengers. I knew that with the sea running so high and with the furious gale blowing the attempt to land would be more dangerous than remaining on the ship. But the mate thought otherwise. Two of the boats were manned, the mate taking charge of one and the second mate of the other. I decided to remain on board and advised Mr. Simpson to do so too. All the other passengers and the entire crew with the exception of the captain, the engineer, a fireman and a stoker, left with the boats.
>
> At the captain's request I took charge of the vessel. I instructed the engineer to fill her tanks for'ard and aft in order to steady her and keep her from pounding. Then I had the fireman build a fire in the galley, made coffee, explored the pantry, and had a night lunch served to the few of us on board.
>
> In the meantime our siren had been heard from on shore, and a steamer had put off to help us. At dawn it was standing near us, but could not approach owing to the heavy seas breaking about us. Our two boats had been unable to land in the violent surf, and were still pulling about in the vicinity of the ship.
>
> The wind had now abated, but the sea was still heavy. At full daylight I told the engineer to empty his for'ard tanks and to half-empty his aft tanks. I then set the engines reversing, throwing the helm hard a'port. With her bow lighter than the stern, the swinging motion set up by the reversing made her slip sternwards off the reef on which she had stranded. Helped by a rising tide she was soon free. I had the tanks aft pumped out, and turned her nose towards Sydney, bringing her safely to anchor off the Archibald wharf. The two boats, which had set out to pull for Sydney three and a half miles from the reef, were picked up by the steamer which had come out to assist us.[3]

Captain Bernier caught the train at Sydney and reached Québec in time for the Christmas celebrations.

CHAPTER 23

Mina

New Year's Day, 1885, was my first birthday at home for some years, and my family celebrated the event by presenting me with an address and a gift.

Late in January I was invited by my old schoolmaster in L'Islet, Brother Jean-Chrysostôme, to be godfather to a new bell for L'Islet College. I went down with my wife and assisted at a class reunion which brought back vividly the days when I had attended the school, a care-free barefoot boy, and had enjoyed such thrilling hours in my father's shipyard as the *Saint-Joseph* rose on the stocks.[1]

This return to their roots also allowed the couple to realize an adoption plan that had been close to their hearts for a few years already. At that time it was common for children from a large family to be "adopted," or raised by childless close relatives. This was the case for Marie-Elmina Clémence Caron (1875-1972), sixth in a family of 12 children.

Elmina, or Mina to close friends and relatives, was the daughter of Philomène Boucher (1844-1937) and master–tanner Louis-Joseph Caron (1840-1899), and a second cousin of Captain Bernier. Philomène was a younger sister of Rosalie (or Rose) who had accompanied him on the *Zillah* in November 1854, while Louis-Joseph was a good childhood buddy.

Joseph-Elzéar had broached the question with his cousin two years earlier: "Philomène, you have seven daughters, whereas I have only one god-daughter, Mina. I would like to adopt her."[2]

Philomène was neither surprised nor offended by her relative's proposal and his rather direct approach. Her husband Louis-Joseph was not in good health, and her little Mina was also showing signs of illness. Clearly this solution would lighten the family's burden and would ensure security and a great future for her daughter. She had replied: "Not before speaking to Mina."

Mina was an inquisitive, intelligent, vivacious little girl and the idea of embarking on an adventure with this famous godfather and the nice Rose did not intimidate her at all. On the contrary, she already understood that with them she would enjoy a privileged life, quite out of the ordinary and different from that of her brothers and sisters. She agreed to be "adopted;" this did not mean that she disowned her own parents, for she would always call her adoptive parents "Captain and Aunt Rose," and she would always maintain close, fraternal ties with her own folk. Moreover she never took the name Bernier.

"Not before her First Communion," Philomène had insisted. "Not before she is 10." As a loving mother she wanted to give her a chance to cement her attachment to her own family, so that she would never feel abandoned.

When the formalities of the adoption were completed, in January 1885, Mina had still not reached the age of 10, since she was born on 24 September 1875. Nonetheless she turned her back on L'Islet, her school, and everything she had known so as to embrace the realities of her new life.

The following winter and spring provided an opportunity for the young girl to discover the house on the Rue Sainte-Gertrude, and to gradually put down roots in the Saint-Sauveur district, while her Aunt Rose took delight in dressing her as a "real princess" and in teaching her to read, write, sew, and knit. Her grand-uncle, the Captain, also settled into his new role of guardian, but simultaneously he was assessing the inevitable decline in shipbuilding at Québec.

> By this time the industry was fast approaching dissolution. The previous year there had been only a barque and a schooner launched from Quebec yards. This year there were two small barques, a larger barque, and two large ships.[3]

The timber trade was on its last legs and the era of the large square-rigged sailing ships was drawing to a close, victim of technological evolution.

> Yet the day arrived when it was all too apparent that the large wooden ships had become obsolete and the clock could not be put back—metal ships were stronger, they rarely leaked, their annual depreciation was far less, and their insurance rate far lower.[4]

At the same time, Québec, which was the first large-capacity seaport as one ascended the St. Lawrence, was losing its status as the Atlantic terminus of Canada, unable to rival Montréal, centre of a large catchment area experiencing intense economic dynamism. In Montréal "the population was growing at lightning speed, reaching 35,000 inhabitants in 1839, 90,323 in 1861 and 219,616 in 1891."[5]

The only consolation on the horizon was the industrial activities that were gradually taking over from the shipyards in the area of manufacturing. "The leather trades were replacing the timber trade and, between 1880 and 1890, 3000 workers were recruited in the shoe-making factories alone."[6] The shoe-making industry along with tanning and furniture manufacturing would become the spear-head of the city's economy.

Captain Bernier, Rose Caron and their adopted daughter, Elmina "Mina" Caron in 1885. [Bernier Collection, *Master Mariner*]

With the support of Québec's elite, however, the enlargement and modernization of the city's port (the Louise Basin was inaugurated in 1890), and investments in the railroads that converged on Québec, the city succeeded in regaining the upper hand and in displaying a new look. Then grain delivered to Québec by rail was to replace timber as the main product exported.

Captain Bernier was never more aware of the decline in the shipbuilding industry, which he loved passionately, and which had supported him well, than in that spring of 1885. Was the 33-year-old seafarer afraid for the future? Where would his place be in this world that was modernizing as one watched? Would he see his people turn away from his river and lose all memory of their sea-going exploits, their ingenuity, and their close links to the water?

Joseph-Elzéar certainly found what was happening around him deplorable but he was not a man to regret the past or to worry about the future. He would always say: "Go with the flow. What is done, is done!"

The port of Québec around 1880 with sailing vessels and steamships lying side-by-side.
[S. Flemming Collection, LAC, C-008048]

In that year of 1885 two events held his attention in particular: his new responsibility as a parent, and the building of two sailing vessels in the Pointe-Lévy yards.

Bernier loved children. His second cousin, Germaine Bernier, has testified to this:

> [...] I can recall those evenings when the captain, in the midst of his family circle would reply patiently to the questions from us curious kids about all the countries he had visited [...]. He always had some new details to give us.
>
> These conversations were the equivalent of real lessons for his young listeners [...]
>
> On one holiday a whole group of us cousins and friends were taken for a trip by the captain and his wife (he loved to surround himself with young people) and we were coming back from the Île d'Orléans by boat [...]
>
> A holiday procession, memories of holidays and childhood, it all rolls past, along with the recall of the old sailor who is no more and who really enjoyed our blooming youth.[7]

Despite this figure of authority, severe and demanding to the seamen who worked with him, he was said to be especially kind, sensitive and attentive to women and children. In adopting his god-daughter, Joseph-Elzéar had undertaken to bring her up well, to protect her, and to prepare her to receive her inheritance. By the same token he was providing a companion for his wife, who had probably wept copiously over the loss of her baby and suffered from not being able to conceive more. His Rose was getting older. She evidently took less and less pleasure in long overseas voyages and was talking increasingly of life as a "normal" couple, on shore.

This new presence in his wife's daily life perhaps allowed him to rejoin a little more freely the world of men, and to take an interest in the building of some splendid sailing ships financed by J.G. Ross: the *Cambria,* a full-rigged three-master, 202 feet in length and displacing 1,252 tonnes, built in the yards of Étienne Samson (1815-1893), and the *Cheshire*, also a full-rigged three-master displacing 1,307 tonnes and 198 feet long, the handiwork of Guillaume Charland Sr. (1824-1901).[8] Samson and Charland were two of the greatest shipbuilders in Québec. Between 1855 and 1893 they were alone responsible for building 62 ships of substantial tonnage.

Étienne Samson wanted to retain ownership of the *Cambria* rather than selling her to a British owner and offered command of her to Captain Bernier. The command of the *Cheshire* was assumed by the latter's friend, Captain Zéphyr Charron.

Since the two shipyards were next-door neighbours in Pointe-Lévy, a lively rivalry had quickly developed between the two old friends as to which of their ships would be launched first. The result was a tie, since the ships left their respective yards on the same day in early May 1885.

> A fresh wager was made regarding the cost of getting the ships to Liverpool, and the challenge to race across the Atlantic with the traditional beaver hat at stake was inevitable.[9]

The two friends registered their square-riggers at the Customs House in Québec on the same day.

In the preparations for the voyage the *Cheshire* managed to take the lead and on 11 June, at 4 p.m. she sailed from Québec loaded with timber bound for Liverpool. The *Cambria* weighed anchor two days later, at 6 a.m. on the 13 June.

Pointe-Lévy seen from Québec, 1870-1880.
[Photo: Louis-Prudent Vallée, LAC, C-087032]

We encountered a storm on the 14th and were forced to anchor in the lee of Cap-au-Diable (Devil's Cape), about sixty miles below Quebec. In weighing anchor as soon as the wind turned favourable, one of the hams of the windlass snapped.

We raised the rest of the chain and the anchor with great difficulty and stood in for Rivière-du-Loup, where I hoped to obtain a quick casting of a new ham. But the little foundry there cast metal only on Wednesdays and Saturdays, so I boarded the noon train for Levis, with the broken piece in the baggage car. At Rivière-du-Loup station I telegraphed Mr. Charles-William Carrier, head of the engineering firm of Carrier, Lainé & Co., of Levis, explaining the situation and asking for quick service. As the train slowed down in approaching Levis, I pitched the broken ham out of the car opposite the Carrier shops. Mr. Damase Lainé, Mr. Carrier's partner, was waiting for me. The ham was placed in sand, the mold was taken, and during the night the iron was run and allowed to cool. Next morning I was given the new ham still too hot to touch. I carried it hooked to a piece of wood to the station where the train was ready to pull out for the Lower St. Lawrence. By rare good fortune there was an empty flat car onto which I threw the iron, jumping aboard myself as the train pulled out.[10]

In recounting the story of this extraordinary round-trip that lasted about 28 hours Captain Bernier clearly intended rendering homage to these men who were watching their trade being eclipsed along with the majestic sailing ships that sailed all over the world.

> This was a fair sample of the service extended to its customers by Carrier, Lainé & Co., a standard of service that made its name known throughout the shipping world of the Atlantic. [...] Its great shops in Levis were the pride of the south shore and furnished a livelihood to many hundred skilled workmen of Quebec and Levis. Like the other great industries of Quebec, such as shipbuilding and timber-exporting, it rendered great services to a generation or two, and then passed almost into oblivion.[11]

This sea-dog's literary style is impregnated with his forceful character, his sense of the dramatic and seaman's expressions:

> We sighted the *Cheshire* off the Old Man of Kinsale [or Old Head of Kinsale, on the southeast coast of Ireland facing the Celtic Sea], and the run to the Mersey was a brisk and stubborn race. We were bow to bow when we drew abreast of the pilot anchorage, but the *Cheshire* took the first pilot and preceded us by a few lengths as we both drew in on the tide. Both of us were bound for Canada Dock, and the first to berth would reap the honour, although the race was already mine, having left nearly two days after Captain Charron.[12]

The authorities at the Canada Dock refused to let Captain Charron enter because the tide was not high enough for them to be able to open the gates to the dock. When Bernier realized that his old friend was going astern in the Mersey estuary, he ordered his pilot to head for the Canada Half-Tide Dock, a smaller, deeper basin, from which he could more easily reach the Canada Dock. Thus, when the *Cheshire* moored in the Canada Dock on the next high tide, his rival was already half unloaded. Including the delay caused by the incident of the capstan ham, Captain Bernier had won the race by four days!

Some time later Rose and Mina arrived in Liverpool by the steamer *Sardinian* to rejoin the captain.

The emotions of this child who was discovering the world and its marvels in the company of the impressive captain and her Aunt Rose must have been quite obvious. Unfortunately Mina spoke little of her childhood memories. Sometimes, when she was questioned, she would reply with shining eyes: "I had a great life. I have seen extraordinary things and the most spectacular landscapes in the world. I learned English. I have no regrets." Undoubtedly she realized that her life would have been very different had she remained sitting primly on the benches of her country school.

In taking her aboard the *Cambria*, Captain Bernier was able to offer her the world as her heritage. He would teach her geography, history, the arts, the sciences, and the reality of human nature, as his father had done with him in his youth.

In October the family threesome were passing the famous Sugar Loaf, at the entrance to the magnificent Guanabara Bay, and discovered Rio de Janeiro that stretched amidst luxuriant tropical vegetation, colourful and fragrant.

The *Cambria* left Brazil in early December, heading south with granite slabs as ballast. Emotions must have been running high among the crew as they prepared to realize that dream of all sailors: to round Cape Horn, located at the southern tip of Chile.

> Since its discovery by Magellan in 1520 Cape Horn, separating the Pacific and Atlantic oceans, has always been the greatest challenge for sailing ships. More ships have disappeared without trace in its wild waters than anywhere else in the world, and sailors who returned from it knew that they had faced the worst test that the sea could set for men. But, other than sailing around the world by way of the Cape of Good Hope—which does not offer an easy passage either—until the building of the Panama Canal in 1914, there was no other means of getting to the west coast of the American continent than by way of the "tough cape" as its victims called it.[13]

Was it a feeling of humility at this important achievement of rounding the southernmost tip of South America that led the captain to remain silent on the subject? Did he consider himself lucky at not having been vanquished by the Cape Horn route?

> The Pacific Ocean being higher than the Atlantic Ocean, a strong current that may on occasion run at 50 miles per day, but whose speed averages between 10 and 12 miles per day, is encountered in these waters. The sea bed rises in steps, making these currents even more turbulent and violent winds, known as williwaws, blocked by the Andean Cordillera for 1200 miles to the north, break free from them in fury, blowing 22 days out of 30 at anywhere from 45 to 120 miles per hour, and are capable of throwing a ship on her beam-ends in minutes.[14]

Bernier, the new "Cape Horner" wrote simply:

> We made extra quick time around the Horn, having the rare experience of rounding the Horn on one tack. Just after Christmas we hove to off Valparaiso, after a record run of thirty-one days out of Rio.[15]

During that same month of December 1885, he took only 36 days to sail from Valparaiso, Chile, to Astoria, Oregon. Since this had never been done before, the American press marked his exploit by coverage worthy of the greatest news stories of the day.

Mina was too young to be aware of the sea-going feats of her famous grand-uncle and the risks that he faced on each voyage. Nowadays her descendants believe that she was stricken by the early stages of tuberculosis and that her memories of tropical seas were coloured by that disease and especially by the treatment that the captain imposed upon her. Elzéar had installed a barrel of salt water on deck so that the little girl could soak there for hours in the open air, to benefit from the curative properties of the mineral salts combined with the warmth of the sun. The fact that she lived to the age of 97, they believe, was probably thanks to his initiative.

Her grand-children would have liked to learn more about her unusual adventures at sea, which lasted over a year. But they say that Mina was not a story-teller. She never showed any interest in resurrecting all that ancient history. She preferred to concentrate on the present moment.

Fortunately Captain Bernier saw things differently. To him, talking about his voyages was to leave a testimony to his profession as a seafarer in the age of the great sailing ships.

> I left the *Cambria* at Astoria and proceeded to Portland, Oregon, to secure a charter. [...] Finally, after nearly three months of waiting, I secured a satisfactory charter, and the *Cambria* was loaded at Portland with grain consigned to Queenstown [or Cork, Ireland] for orders. Our passage was marked by alternate fair winds and storms. We had some fine day's runs, one of them being 260 miles, but we also ran into squalls and gales when sails had to be clewed up, or taken down. Our rounding of the Horn was very stormy, and later we ran into several "Pompero" blows, the violent squalls that blow out of the River Plate. Just after one of these blows we narrowly missed being caught in a waterspout which passed within half a mile of the ship. [...] Our run from Astoria to Queenstown was one hundred and seventeen days.[16]

At Queenstown the captain received orders to take his cargo to Le Havre on the Seine estuary. There Rose and Mina said goodbye to their companion before boarding a Cunard steamer, *British Queen,* bound for America.

Shortly afterwards Captain Bernier resigned from his functions with W.H. Ross & Co. and turned over command of the *Cambria* to his mate, and cousin, Guillaume Bernier.

> I was not to see her until nearly 20 years later when she was tied up in the Louise Basin at Quebec and posted for sale by Ross & Co. She had served on all the oceans, had traveled many sea-lines, and had come back to rest at her birthplace, weary and worn. She was still sea-worthy and could have been made shipshape without too great expense, but the day of sailing vessels had long passed, and the only purchaser that could be found was a wrecker.[17]

In October 1886 Joseph-Elzéar returned home. He was 34 years old and did not know what awaited him in Québec. His passage on the steamer *Carthaginian* perhaps represented his last Atlantic crossing. He had no way of knowing.

The sea-rover had finally bowed to his wife's wishes. Henceforth he would put down roots ashore!

CHAPTER 24

Dockmaster at Lauzon

On 26 October Captain Bernier submitted his application for the post of dockmaster of the new dockyard at Pointe-Lévy.

He was not the only candidate to seek an interview with the Québec Harbour Commission. The Commissioners eliminated the less serious or less experienced candidates and lingered over only four names: his own, that of his former boss, Peter Baldwin, his friend, Captain Zéphyr Charron, and Alfred Samson, son of the shipbuilder Étienne Samson. The latter withdrew in his favour.

To support his application and to improve his chances Joseph-Elzéar appealed to influential individuals in maritime circles such as Charland, Marquis, Gingras, Robitaille, Valin, and Massicotte, as well as powerful friends such as Sir Hector Langevin, Sir Adolphe Caron, Sir François Langelier, the Honourable Justice Bossé, the Honourable Thomas-Chase Casgrain, Senator Philippe Landry, the Honourable Joseph Shehyn, and others. They all interceded in his favour and signed a letter of recommendation.[1]

Despite these efforts there was no guarantee that he would get the job. He therefore also applied for the position of harbour-master at the government harbour in British Columbia and manager of New York operations of the Quebec Steamship Co., which dispatched a fleet of steamers between Montréal, Québec, Halifax, Boston, New York, and the West Indies.

> I went to New York to further my application and there learned with considerable surprise that Mr. Baldwin had also applied for the position.
>
> By coincidence on my return to Quebec, I met Peter Baldwin in St. Peter Street one cold winter day. We went into a small restaurant for a pot of coffee together [...] When we separated an hour later we had reached a happy understanding. He wrote the Quebec Harbour Commissioners withdrawing his application and strongly recommending me, and I wrote the Quebec Steamship Company withdrawing my application and strongly recommending Peter Baldwin.[2]

As a result of this manoeuvre, Baldwin ended up in New York at an annual salary of $3,000 and Captain Bernier was confirmed in his new position at Lauzon (Pointe-Lévy) for a term of three and a half years at a salary of $1,200 per year. The salary was lower but the position was just as prestigious as the one in New York. On 1 April 1887, as his mandate began, Bernier wrote in his diary: "This ends my career as a sailor. I am giving up the sea for ever!"

Since 1870 the Lévis shore had become the most coveted area of the port of Québec because its piers, warehouses, mills and links to the railroad network were attracting a large part of the timber trade.

> Another important factor, rarely mentioned, was that the wharfage fees were much lower at Lévis than at Québec, which greatly favoured the operations of loading and

Captain Bernier, aged about 40. It was said that he never smiled for the camera to avoid displaying his gold teeth! [Photo: R. Roy, Archives of Carol and Louis Terrien]

transshipment on the wharves of the young town. In the early 1870s the business climate was still euphoric and its journalists even sounded arrogant: "Let Québec figure out her remaining share of shipbuilding and the timber trade, once we have taken our due share."[3]

If there is one name that is synonymous with the socioeconomic rise of Lauzon-Lévis, it was incontrovertibly that of Davie. The Allison C. Davie shipyard,[4] whose origin dates back to 1832, was the oldest marine shipyard in Canada still functioning. It also had the distinction of being the first to be equipped with a hauling-slip to haul ships ashore.

> Captain Davy's [sic] Marine Railway constructed at Pointe Lévi [sic], opposite the lower town loading place, was tried for the first time on Saturday, when one of the Steam Companies' barges was hauled up. We believe this is the first establishment of the kind formed in British America. It will be very useful. The principle is that of a common railway, the carriage on which the vessel is taken at high water, moving on iron rollers & being drawn up by an iron chain, the largest vessels may be drawn up in this manner.[5]

Benefiting from its easy access to deep water, the Davie dockyard was also equipped with several floating dry-docks. In this way several ships could be repaired at the same time; this allowed the company to retain a true monopoly on ship maintenance in the port of Québec.

> Until 1886, in the absence of any dry-dock, beaching a ship between two tides was the only means of repairing or maintaining ships' hulls. However, from 1827 onwards, thanks to their great ingenuity Québec shipbuilders perfected the floating dock for careening ships. They were the first in North America to develop this technique for lifting ships. Until 1878 Québec's shipyards boasted nine floating drydocks.[6]

The river-front at Lévis when Joseph-Elzéar established himself there. [Illustrated postcard, ANQ, P547,DL287,P48]

The Lorne Dry-Dock at Lauzon, beside the Davie & Sons shipyard. [Photographer unknown, Musée maritime du Québec (Musée Bernier), No. 80.26.75]

Wishing to take advantage of the Lorne dry-dock, the property of the federal government, the George T. Davie[7] and Sons expanded and modernized their yard in order to repair larger metal-hulled ships. Thanks to its specialization in building and repairing steamships and to its involvement in refloating wrecks, the Davie company would be the only one to survive the decline in shipbuilding in the Québec area.

The Lorne dry-dock and wharf, which had been opened in 1886 by Sir Hector Langevin, Minister of Public Works, and named in honour of the Marquis of Lorne, Governor General and son-in-law of Queen Victoria, were part of a vast plan for the re-equipping and modernization of the port of Québec.

It must be said that this new dry-dock at Lauzon was impressive: it was 484 feet long, 110 feet wide, and over 25.5 feet deep at high tide. It took no less than six years of hard work to achieve this technical marvel that could have held an entire football field! It had been excavated out of the beach. Then, using dynamite, it had been blasted out of the Lévis cliff, consisting of gneiss as hard as granite, and of the same mineralogical composition. The three sides and one end were made of reinforced concrete poured to form giant steps that were reinforced with enormous granite blocks from the Deschambault quarry set in cement. The fourth side was the dock entrance closed by a single large gate. The floor was also lined with Deschambault granite.

Captain Bernier was the first dockmaster of the Lauzon graving dock and, as such, it devolved upon him to establish the routine of the dock, or its modus operandi on both short term and long term, and also to supervise the activities at the dock, to look after tidal surveys, and to control the entry and launching of ships from the dock.[8]

Between 1 April 1887 and 18 November 1890, he supervised the berthing and maintenance of 21 vessels of varying tonnages.

Where was he living at this time?

> I was a few months over thirty-five years of age when I received my appointment. I immediately moved my belongings to Lauzon where I made arrangements for board and lodging not far from the dock. Later I was to build myself a very handsome buff brick house on the cliff overlooking the dock, a house now the home of George D. Davie.[9]

The impressive Lorne Dry-Dock. [Artist unknown, Bernier Collection, *Master Mariner*]

The Bernier Villa at Lauzon.
[Archives of Carol and Louis Terrien]

On 19 July 1887, in the presence of M. Cyprien Labrèque, Québec notary, Mrs. Marie-Louise Raymond, estranged wife of Isidore-Noël Bellau Esq., barrister, sold to J.-E. Bernier Esq., superintendent of the graving dock, and residing at Saint-Joseph de Lévis, "the Bourassa lot in the village of Lauzon, between the government road leading to the graving dock on one side, and the Marquis shipyard on the north and the Intercolonial Railroad on the south and southwest."[10] Mrs. Raymond had acquired this triangular lot from the local sheriff after Michel Dorval's law-suit against Joseph-Onésime Bourassa, on 24 November 1881, and

The Bernier Villa when it was owned by George D. Davie. [ANQ, N477-43-14]

George Duncan Davie was the son of George T. Davie. On the latter's death he took charge of the Davie Shipyards, along with his brothers, John Lovett Davie and Allison Cufaud Davie. [Archives of Carol and Louis Terrien]

she sold it to Captain Bernier for the sum of $500. The lot in question was quite large since on the survey map it included numbers 50 to 55, 72 to 81, 105 to 111, and 139-141.

It was on this site, on the cliff overlooking the shipyards of François-Xavier Marquis (1828-1911), that he had the house-of-his-dreams built, the Villa Bernier. It was apparently admired by all and after George Duncan Davie bought it in August 1903, he liked to show it off to the numerous visitors who appeared at his door, intrigued by the residence of the famous master mariner. Furthermore George Davie was as proud of this property as he was of his shipyard and converted the gardens "into a horticultural showpiece, remarkable for the beauty of its rows of majestic trees bordering its walks, the profusion of flowers in the flower beds, its fruit trees and bushes and its kitchen-garden that was a cook's delight."[11]

⚓

Apart from his functions at the Lorne dry-dock, Captain Bernier also found time to involve himself in some investments. On 16 April 1888, in the presence of notary Charles-Isaïe LaBrie,[12] he bought from Tancrède Bourget, gentleman, a property with the number 652A on the survey map, with appurtenances, measuring 42 feet in width by 166 feet in length. He paid $200 cash. Two years later, in the presence of the same notary,[13] he sold this property to Elvina Turgeon, estranged wife of François Edouard Verreault Esq., for the sum of $400 or an annual rent of $17. Mrs. Turgeon undertook to build a house within 18 months. When this obligation was not met the sale was annulled and, on 1 September 1890, the ownership reverted to Captain Bernier. A few months later he succeeded in selling the property to Pierre Plourde, a Lauzon blacksmith, for the sum of $400.

On 30 November 1888 Joseph-Elzéar received an agricultural property, made over to him by Marie-Luce Bourget,[14] widow of Charles Bourget, and her daughter Camille, in exchange for an annual life-rent of $80. Two years later,[15] he bought a neighbouring property owned by Étienne Patris for the sum of $700 and, on 6 March 1895, probably on the death of Mrs. Bourget, he sold the combined properties, with animals and buildings to Alphonse Poirier, a Lauzon boatman. This double property was located in the second *rang* in the parish of Saint-Joseph, with a frontage of five and a half arpents and a depth of 30 arpents. According to the terms of the contract Mr. Poirier was to pay the Captain and his wife an annual life annuity of $200, payable in two equal instalments. The seller reserved himself the annual rights to 8 cords of 3 foot logs, half hardwood and half softwood.

Joseph-Elzéar also took the time to look after his elderly parents. It appears that Thomas and Célina joined him in the Villa Bernier after the 1889 fire that devastated the Saint-Sauveur district. Thomas died a few years later at the age of 70, after a "short" illness.

Thomas had drawn up his will[16] a month before he died and had named the parish priest Édouard Fafard as executor. He left half his possessions to his wife Célina and the other half to his three children: Joseph-Elzéar, ship's captain, Alfred, ice-merchant of Montréal, and Henriette, wife of George Boisjoly of Schenectady, New York. At the time of his death he owned two properties: a house with six apartments in Saint-Sauveur and another in the village of Lauzon.[17]

Thomas Bernier in 1893 shortly before his death. [Bernier Collection, *Master Mariner*]

Célina probably stayed with Elzéar and Rose for a few more years. But at the time the house was sold, on 1 February 1897, she was residing in Québec.[18] She died in 1906 at the age of 74.

⚓

During the three and a half years that he held the post of Lauzon dockmaster, Captain Bernier had been acting counter to his deepest inclinations in order to please Rose. But … "the sight of the great timber droghers and smart clippers setting their white sails as they rounded the Pointe-de-Lévis, their bowsprits straining eagerly for the first briny scent of the sea, always filled me with a longing for a return to my life afloat."[19] A longing for the wide-open spaces still stirred his heart-strings and "by the summer of 1890 I could not resist the call of the bridge any longer. For my holidays I accepted the job of navigating two yachts bound for the lower St. Laurence. This was the only kind of work I could undertake in the short time at my disposal."[20]

It was inevitable that he would return to the sea since he had salt water in his veins. The sea was his entire life and, in November of that year Joseph-Elzéar did not renew his contract with the Lauzon dry-dock.

The captain was again sailing to the warm waters of Rio de Janeiro, Santos, and Saint Lucia. He also roamed the Atlantic waves on voyages to Baltimore, Sydney, Boston, New York or Portland. Once again he was enjoying moments of pleasure at the helm of great wooden ships built in his Québec.

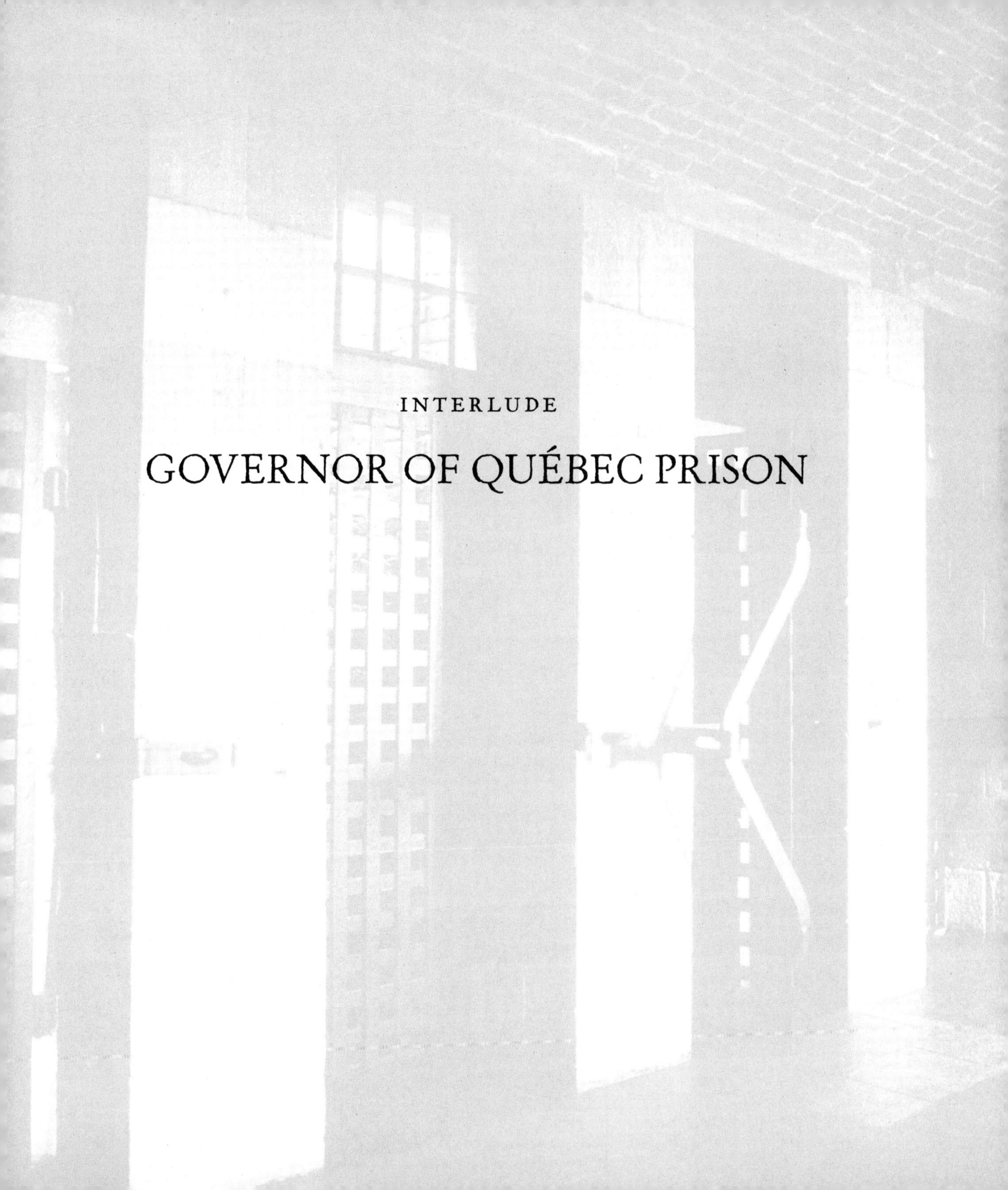

INTERLUDE

GOVERNOR OF QUÉBEC PRISON

BY THE BEGINNING OF 1894 Joseph-Elzéar seemed to be bogged-down in irresoluteness. Admittedly he had obtained his Canadian certificate as a coastal pilot that allowed him to take command of ships in the St. Lawrence and along the Atlantic coast, and had also passed the Baltimore exams for working as a pilot in those American near-shore waters. He had commanded superb yachts for rich owners and influential political personalities or had inspected ships and checked compasses for the Richelieu and Ontario Navigation Company's fleet. He had even established a record of 104 hours from Québec to Portland, Maine, on board the screw steamer *Lilac,* owned by the American government.

Judging by the numerous letters of reference[1] and congratulations, at the age of 42 Captain Bernier was still in demand, and his services were greatly appreciated. Why then did he appear distracted whereas he had always been able to pursue his ambitions with ardour and passion?

While witnessing the decline of shipbuilding at Québec and the end of the extraordinary epoch of the great sailing ships, did he also discern the end to his own magnificent adventure without hopes of challenges to be met or of projects worthy to be undertaken? Could he see the years slipping away and the idea of retirement creeping ever closer with each grey hair?

Neither his forceful character nor his legendary toughness could stop the passage of time or prevent the world from changing around him. Rose, his Rose, no longer had a wasp-waisted figure. At the age of 41 the wrinkles furrowing her soft face were steadily increasing in number. She could only reflect the image of his own aging. And Mina, the little girl with round, blue, laughing eyes and a mischievous smile, had become a beauty with a mother-of-pearl complexion. She was a woman already! Early in the year, at the age of 19, she had linked her destiny with that of Dr. Joseph-Odilon Bourget (1868-1904) of Lévis.[2]

The young married couple, Elmina "Mina" Caron and Dr. Joseph-Odilon Bourget. [Collection of Suzanne Audet and André Normandeau]

Bernier was not the type to brood or to regret the past. Nonetheless in 1894 one had the definite impression that the man of action had lost impetus and was unable to find a fair wind that would swell his sails again.

In the spring he went into partnership with his brother Alfred and his cousin Joseph[3] to found the Dominion Ice Company "in order to make some money." He did not hide the fact that he needed money to live. Other motivations also pushed him into this initiative, namely his desire to help his brother, something he would do throughout his life, and his search for stimulating projects. He would certainly have taken great pleasure in starting such an enterprise since the Dominion Ice Company was the first of its kind in Montréal.

It is strange to imagine a time when fields of ice were manufactured for human consumption:

> A basin 500 feet square was constructed in a vacant lot in the village of Saint-Henri, now a ward of Montreal. Earth walls were built around it to the height of six feet. The walls and bottom were lined with clay. Water pipes led into the basin. The only machinery was the water valve, and the freezing agent was the prevailing cold west wind which came sweeping down through the fields and orchards of Côte Saint-Antoine village, now the prosperous city of Westmount.[4]

The blocks of ice were sawn by hand then transported to customers on horse-drawn carts.

Throughout that year Elzéar commuted between Lévis and Montréal, dividing his time between the Villa Bernier, his responsibilities as manager at the Dominion Ice Company, and a room at the Viger Hotel or the Grand Pacific Hotel on Notre-Dame Street.

Then, one fine day in February 1895 he received a telegram from an old school buddy, Joseph-Isaac Lavery: "Come down immediately!" Nothing more. A surprising and rather incongruous message from his friend, who had become one of the most important barristers in the city of Québec.

> Much puzzled by this, I decided to run down to Quebec in a day or two to see what bee my old friend was harbouring in his bonnet. The same afternoon came another insistent wire, and nearly as brief, this time from the Hon. Thomas-Chase Casgrain, law partner of Jos. Lavery, and provincial attorney-general in Premier Marchand's cabinet. "You had better come down at once!"[5]

Joseph-Elzéar did not hesitate a moment longer. He caught the five o'clock train to Québec.

Next morning, 12 February, he was offered the job of Governor of Québec Prison, replacing William McClaren,[6] who had died a few weeks earlier.

> His first reaction was to refuse point-blank, but when he was told that this was his wife's wish, since she had always been afraid for his life when he was at sea, he accepted, although it went a little against the grain.[7]

Was the captain trapped by his over-zealous friends or by Rose's concerns, as several writers have assumed?[8] Since he never elaborated on it in his writings, this presumption remains unverifiable. He stated simply that his two friends insisted that he come down to Québec immediately. That's all.

The captain was greatly flattered by this proposition since the post was normally reserved for former ministers, or retired members of Parliament. Was this a political appointment?

Joseph-Elzéar was passionate about politics and had declared himself as a Conservative in the federal election of 1887. He had also assisted his cousin, the independent candidate, Phydime Bélanger, who had tried to win the riding of L'Islet from the incumbent Liberal, P.B. Casgrain:

> I entered the fray on my cousin's behalf and spent several weeks in January and February traveling through the villages and "concessions," of the back part of the country. Voting day was February 22nd, 1887, and ended with Mr. Casgrain thirty votes ahead of my cousin.[9]

During the provincial election of 1892 the captain was among the regional campaign-workers and took part in the Conservative meetings in Lévis, Québec, and L'Islet. He wrote in his personal journal:

> Worked very hard in Lévis for our candidate. At 6 p.m. we learned that we had won in the village of Lauzon.
>
> [...] The government of the Honourable de Boucherville remains in power with a majority of 40. The Mercier government is out.[10]

It is claimed that when the post of Governor of the Québec Prison became vacant, Bernier laid claim to this political nomination by making the most of his devotion to the Party.[11] One thing is certain: the captain would not have had access to this privileged position without the help of his powerful Conservative friends.

The prison on the Plains of Abraham. Its construction began in 1861. [*Franck Leslie's Illustrated Newspaper*, 9 September 1865]

Joseph-Elzéar loved to surprise his listeners by remarking, point-blank: "Did you know that I spent more than three years in prison?" When they swallowed the hook, he would add, laughing: "As Governor!"

On 13 February 1895 he agreed to become prison governor, entering a milieu that was not his own, and which he would be stuck with for an indeterminate period. The man of action had found a real challenge. He certainly did not anticipate that he would find a new passion in this position or that he would find the vitality of youth that would carry him to a surprising future.

Seven days later he was confirmed in his new role:

> I have been instructed by the Honourable Provincial Secretary to inform you that, by an Order in Council dated 20 February inst., it has pleased His Honour the Lieutenant Governor to name you gaoler of the Common Prison for the District of Québec, replacing the late M. McLaren, at a salary of 900 dollars per year, starting from 13 February 1895.[12]

Rose was appointed Head Matron of the Québec Prison on 23 April 1895, at an annual salary of $200.

Bernier's appointment was widely underscored by the popular newspapers that had long been following his exceptional career, so frequently in the limelight.:

> Today Captain J.E. Bernier bids farewell to the sea, not without regret, no doubt, but the position he has just accepted, that of Governor of Québec Prison, will be some small consolation, and will give him the opportunity to again demonstrate the remarkable activity that he has always displayed previously [...] This appointment has been looked upon favourably by the public and we hope that Monsieur Bernier will enjoy good health as he fills his new office which certainly does him honour.[13]

The severe, massive building that now greeted the new Governor had been inaugurated in 1867. It was the work of Charles-Philippe-Ferdinand Baillargé of the famous family of Québec sculptors and architects of the 18th and 19th centuries. The building was located on the highest point of the Plains of Abraham within the area used by the military; it consisted of four storeys, and

The former Québec Prison and the Wolfe monument, prior to construction of the hospital wing behind the main body. "Decommissioned" in 1970 the prison temporarily became the "Petite Bastille" a youth hostel, in connection with some major popular festivals. It is now part of the Musée du Québec. [J.-Ernest Livernois Collection, ANQ, N974-140]

was extended by several annexes. Its façade faced north, in parallel with the Grande Allée, while the rear faced the St. Lawrence. The central block housed the administrative offices, private apartments, visiting rooms, a reception room, and the guard-room. The wing that ran back from this central structure housed on its various floors services such as kitchens, dining hall, men's and women's infirmaries, and the Catholic and Protestant chapels. The tiers of individual cells and the workshops were located in the lateral wing and its extension. The small prisoners' cells were separated from the outer wall by a corridor, and they had only a single opening, a stout latticed iron door, that certainly discouraged any attempt at escape. To isolate it even more from the city, the complex was encircled by an insurmountable wall.

As an example of prison architecture, for its time, the building was avant-garde since it consisted of a complex comprising several distinct entities, but that were interconnected by a central bridge crowned by a watchtower. All three corridors and walkways converged on this central structure that was surmounted by a light shaft.

The furniture was of fire-proof construction, at least in the sections inhabited by the prisoners. The outer walls were three feet thick, and made from grey dressed stone, whereas the corridor walls and those of the vaulted cells were lined with painted brick.

⚓

While touring his new premises from top to bottom Captain Bernier could not but be impressed by the solidity and austerity of the place. Grasping immediately that he would be solely responsible for the welfare and safety of the 107 men and women incarcerated under this roof, he decided to take a look elsewhere to compare and understand. He inspected the Montréal Prison at Pied-du-Courant and the one at Saint-Vincent-de-Paul on Île Jésus. Before settling into his role of jailer, he wanted to comprehend his obligations and the functioning of this establishment and especially to adapt them best to the different groups of prisoners who included those waiting to be tried, those who were serving their sentence, and those condemned to death.

As T.C. Fairley and C.E. Israel wrote:

> He waded zealously into his new duties, administering the jail in true nautical fashion. The guards were his officers, the prisoners his crew.[14]

This was the essence of logic; he would adapt the knowledge, the structures, and the methods of organization that he had learned, tested and implanted in his seaman's world to this new reality. The prison would become his ship, the guards his officers and the prisoners his crew! Furthermore he would insist on being called Captain.

His first task was to get to know those who would be working with him. To his surprise he discovered an elderly group, somewhat undisciplined and set in old ways of doing things. Since he had the excellent habit of listing everything, we know who these 20 men were and what he thought of them:[15]

Name	Position	Age	Arrived	Language	Remarks
S.B. Jennings	Sergeant	71	1852	English	Too old
R. Mulholland	Assistant	68	1853	English	Too old
W. McCabe	Guard	65	1867	English	Too old
J. Boulanger	Turnkey	65	1868	Both	Too old
M. Bamon	Guard	56	1872	English	Slow/grumbler
E. Delage	Guard	52	1874	Both	Responsible
T. Dussault	Guard	63	1878	Both	Too old
A. Boiteau	Sergeant	39	1887	Both	Responsible
F. Savard	Guard	58	1887	French	Too old
W. Crafton	Guard	48	1887	English	Responsible
R.J. Modler	Turnkey	40	1888	Both	Responsible
I. Fortier	Turnkey	55	1888	Both	A spy
T. Gagnon	Guard	52	1888	French	Good officer
A. Vézina	Guard	34	1891	French	Undisciplined
F. Vézina	Guard	37	1892	French	Undisciplined
A. Bélanger	Guard	44	1892	French	Good/stubborn
E. Carbray	Guard	64	1892	English	Undisciplined
L. Marcoux	Guard	44	1894	Both	Undisciplined

H. Siméon & J.B. Gagnon, guards[16]

Captain Bernier had always counted on the knowledge and discipline of the group he commanded to carry through his appointments. It was clear that the administrator who had preceded him had been surprisingly lax with his personnel. The prison officers had simply gone their own way for a long time and they certainly had no intention of submitting to the demands of the newcomer. Naturally Bernier saw things differently.

On 9 November 1895 the Governor wrote to his sergeants:

> I wish the Sergeant on duty to inform the Guards of their having to wear their uniform on Sundays, holidays and visiting days or whenever the Sheriff comes on his official visit or whenever any other high Personage is expected. Also to see that the rooms used by the Guards are kept clean and their beds made up in military form. Also the Guards on duty shall report to the Gaoler if any prisoners neglect their work or any conduct he thinks is not according to the rules of the Gaol.[17]

Joseph-Elzéar Bernier in his uniform as Governor of the Québec Prison. [Archives of Carol and Louis Terrien]

On 13 November he was forced to suspend Hector Siméon from his duties. Here is how he justified this decision to Sheriff C.A.E. Gagnon:

> It is with regret that I have to inform you that I have been obliged to suspend Mr. Hector Siméon, Prison Guard, for failing in his duties. On several occasions he has failed in his duties because of drunkenness. Yesterday evening he got into a fight and this is why he could not handle his duties today. It is absolutely necessary to put an end to this type of conduct on the part of some of the guards at the Prison, who are providing a bad example, and who are forcing the other, more conscientious guards to do double duty.[18]

On that same date he made another report to the Sheriff:

> Yesterday being visiting day, I stood on watch at the entrance to the Prison to determine how tobacco and various other objects were entering the Prison without the officers being able to spot them. I noticed that each visitor was bringing in these items either in their pockets or clothes, or by hiding them on the outside. I hope, Monsieur, that you will assist me in order to prevent this abuse on the part of visitors.[19]

The indefatigable Bernier tackled every problem with remarkable energy. This emerges from the reports of the prison inspectors:

> A thorough inspection visit was made to this prison today by Inspectors Desaulniers and De Martigny. They admired the useful changes that the energetic Governor of the Prison has introduced during the short time that he has been in charge of this institution. Everything has been renovated or repaired to such a degree, and cleanliness is maintained everywhere to such a degree, that one would think oneself in a new prison.[20]

The remarks of the Assistant Attorney-General were in the same vein:

> Without wishing to diminish the merits of the former Governor of this prison, it is only fair to observe that an appreciable change for the better has been effected in the general running of the institution and in the bearing of the entire personnel, the officers and even the prisoners.[21]

Everyone, from the worst criminals to young delinquents, was surprised at having to suddenly emerge from their repugnant filth and lethargy to be forced into a prescribed program. It was quite simple, as Bernier pointed out:

> At six o'clock a bell awakened everyone. Cells were opened and prisoners sent to the ablution rooms. Washing was compulsory. At seven breakfast was served in refectory, where each man was given his portion of porridge, bread, salt and water. Hunger strikes were unknown in those days. At 7.30 another bell sent the prisoners to the yard for exercise, under the watchful eye of guards posted on the walls. From 8 to 11 there was work of various kinds. No talking was allowed. After a half hour recess, dinner was served at 11.30. From 12 to 1 prisoners were locked up in the "waiting room" while officers and guards had their own dinner. A prisoner's dinner was made up of pea soup or vegetable soup, beef and potato, bread and water. There was more work from 1 to 4, and one hour's exercise before supper, which consisted of bread, clear gruel, and tea. At six all men were locked in their cells, the gaol entry was barred and the day's state was entered in the books.[22]

The new Governor introduced improvements and soon the Québec newspapers began describing the major changes that he had imposed. All the interior walls were given a new coat of white-wash, the floors cleaned and waxed, the hospitals painted, and new bathrooms built for the prisoners. The walls, ceilings, and woodwork in the lobby of the entrance-way as well as the staircase and corridor leading to the Governor's quarters were painted. The two rooms used as a reception hall were wall-papered and a new hardwood floor laid there, while bookcases with shelves for the director's office were built to one side.

> Everything is maintained at a high level. [...] It was especially with regard to hygiene that changes were needed at the prison. Hence the Governor goes to extraordinary lengths to force his inmates to conform to them. They are obliged to change their clothes twice per week and the clothes are then washed by the prisoners.[23]

Bernier saw to everything: repairs to the metal roof on the building, replacing lightning rods that had become defective and dangerous, improvements to the grounds around the prison, organizing a greenhouse and a garden to feed all the personnel and the prisoners, and even the installation of a plaque behind the monument to Wolfe that read, in large letters, "Wolfe died here, 1759." He requested writing paper for the personnel. He organized the collection of funds to buy a harmonium for the Catholic chapel. He solicited 500 loads of stones for paving the road leading to the Grande Allée. He ordered

Prisoners' cells in the former Québec Prison.
[Photo: Lynn Fournier]

straw hats to protect the guards and prisoners from the sun while they were working outside. He demanded that a horse be bought for the prison and the farm. He even demanded furniture for a reception room: "a table measuring 9 feet by 10, 12 chairs, a sofa, 4 mats for the entrance doors, and a large rug for my office."

Indeed he did his work so well that the chairman of the prison inspectors, Dr. de Martigny, proposed that he organize the central prison in Montréal. Bernier replied:

> [...] you can count on my support in your work to make the Central Prison in Montreal a model prison and at the same time to achieve an effective, but not expensive solution. If you would like to mention my name to the Premier with regard to supervising that establishment, you can count on me to fulfil that responsibility to the satisfaction of both yourself and the Premier.[24]

This project came to nothing.

⚓

In his memoirs Captain Bernier did not linger for long on his position at the Québec Prison. He covers these three years in less than two pages. Is it because he did not have pleasant memories of those years? This is highly likely since the prison records reveal that his employees were trying to discredit him in order to get rid of him.

As early as 31 December 1895 Bernier was informing the Sheriff that some of the guards were taking pleasure in reporting "on the outside" what was happening inside the prison walls. On 23 January 1896 he confirmed that it was particularly Hector Siméon and J.B. Gagnon who were the agitators because they bore him a grudge for having suspended them from duty.[25]

To stop the malicious gossip and to prevent the few members of this hard core from interfering with the smooth functioning of the prison, Bernier asked the members of his team to declare in writing that they had nothing to say against the conduct of their boss. Twelve French guards and eight English guards signed two separate declarations, dated 31 July 1896.[26]

A year later, on 27 July 1897, 17 employees certified, in writing, that it was untrue that they had demanded their director's dismissal. Was this the captain's method of identifying and isolating the trouble-makers from the rest of the group? Did he think he could thereby counter their influence and wear them down? What appears evident is that he had misjudged the hate and rancour of the hard cases which had been festering in the prison environment for many years. He had been wrong to imagine that he could run a prison like one of his ships. He did not succeed in enforcing his discipline and his authority. The affair would soon degenerate to become the "Bernier inquiry."

The fine details of the accusations made against Bernier cannot be determined. However press clippings allow us to deduce that they perhaps focused on the greenhouse and the garden produce that exceeded the needs of the prisoners.

> Yesterday afternoon Mr. Charest, an engineer in the Department of Public Works, and Mr. J.B. Gagnon visited

the greenhouse and the prison stall to obtain certain information requested by the commissioner of the inquiry.[27]

Captain Bernier recalled that greenhouse in a letter in 1909:

> When I was appointed Governor of the Québec Prison, the effects belonging to the former jailer were sold by auction, including a greenhouse that I bought for $100.00 cash. Later, through the intervention of Premier Flynn I obtained permission to lengthen this greenhouse and I spent a total sum of $1200.00 to lengthen the greenhouse by 100 feet.
>
> As emerged at the inquiry that took place at the prison, and on the basis of the documents that I produced, I was exonerated of the charges that had been made against me.[28]

And that's all!

The local newspapers specified that 100 complaints were lodged with the Commissioner of the Inquiry, Mr. L.J. Cannon, by attorneys Messrs. Joseph Turcotte and Achille Larue and that Charles Langelier was defending the accused. The inquiry was held *in camera*.

The Attorney General concluded that there was insufficient proof to justify Captain Bernier's dismissal and, on 12 February 1898, the Sheriff of Québec brought closure to the confrontation that had lasted over two years:

> All the officers and employees of the prison must understand that everything must now return to normal with discipline and hierarchical obedience being restored; absences without permission and reports outside the prison without just cause must no longer take place. Those culpable of any such offences are liable to punishment or even dismissal in the case of serious transgressions.[29]

The following month Bernier turned over the keys of the prison to the new jailer, Nazaire Bernatchez; the latter wrote:

> [...] I would like to pay homage to him [Bernier] and that he was very kind to me, in informing me as to surveillance at the prison and as to all that is involved with governing it. It gives me great pleasure to report that this institution was turned over to me in a very good state of cleanliness.[30]

Despite the difficulties he experienced, this sojourn at the Québec Prison represented an important period in Captain Bernier's life. This interlude of three years gave him the time he had never had when commanding his ships and finally the leisure to read and to study a subject that had interested him for over 20 years: navigation in ice.

Since the last polar expedition of the American explorer Charles Francis Hall (1821-1871), Joseph-Elzéar's library had consisted almost entirely of treatises and analyses on the Arctic or Antarctic, as well as accounts by navigators and biographies of explorers who had engaged in adventures to the end of the Earth. What became a true hobby motivated him to seek out, in every new port that he visited, the company of experts, sailors, whalers, and sealers who could instruct him in this area and answer his numerous questions on winds, ocean currents, tides or ice thicknesses according to the seasons.

> Ploughing away in both languages, he sought knowledge about the north. Because people liked him, they forgave his relentless quizzing and before long Bernier himself became an authority on the Arctic.[31]

There was nothing northern in his antecedents, but by dint of questioning and ferreting he became an expert on the subject.

His duties at the Québec Prison allowed him to devote himself seriously to this hobby. It is no exaggeration to say that his enthusiasm for polar geography, science, and exploration rapidly became a veritable obsession. Soon a deep desire began to infiltrate his consciousness: why not he?

ambitious dreams for the first time. And by 5 a.m. next morning when he reverted to his role of jailer and opened for them the heavy gates of the Québec Prison, where they had been voluntary prisoners, he had converted these sincere friends to his plans and knew that he could count on their most absolute support under any circumstances.[33]

Fired with the idea that a French Canadian might win the most important competition of the *fin de siècle*, his buddies concluded that not only was his plan realistic, but that it ought to be executed as soon as possible.

Captain Bernier surrounded by the books that adorned the walls of his office in the Québec Prison. [Archives of Carol and Louis Terrien]

In his office the jailer developed the extraordinary plan of discovering the North Pole. He was fascinated by the polar enigmas and by the fact that no explorer had yet reached the imaginary most northerly point on Earth. The North Pole was a real challenge worthy of his passion for life.

> With the help of a prisoner serving the maximum gaol term for forgery I made a large map of northern lands and waters, incorporating all that was then known about them and tracing the routes of all the explorers. This map was completed on the last day of 1896.[32]

Armed with this wall map and certain of his knowledge, Joseph-Elzéar decided that he was ready to undertake the race for the Pole. He published his map before sounding out the receptivity of his friends, members of the *Société de géographie de Québec*, who often met in his library to discuss the doughty deeds of the great explorers, geography or other subjects of the moment. Messrs. Timms, Baillargé, Bignell, Fréchette, and LeVasseur were among his first confidants.

> Over the course of a dramatic night that those who witnessed it still remember, Captain Bernier revealed his

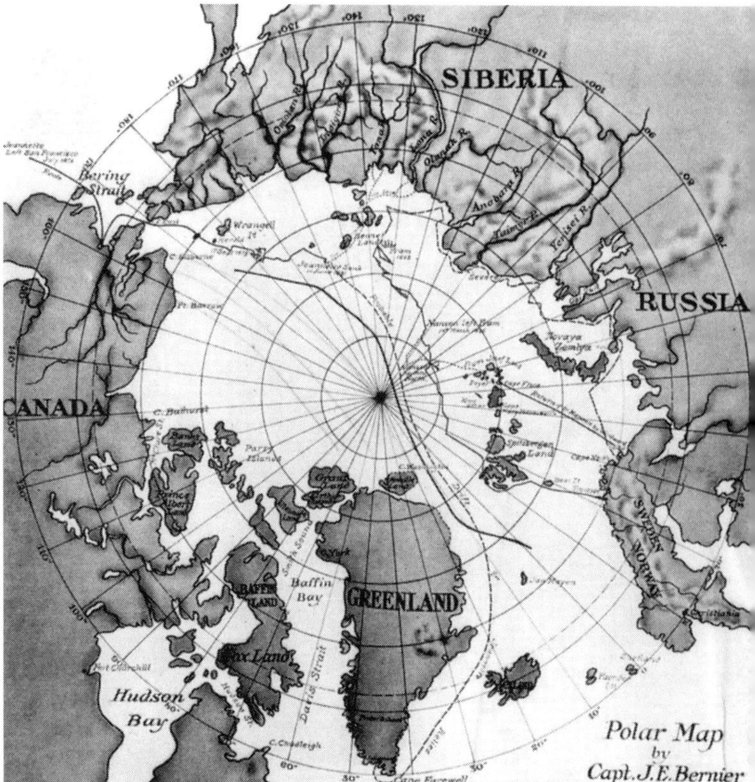

The Polar map established by Captain Bernier with the help of a prisoner serving time while he was Governor of the Québec Prison.[Archives of Carol and Louis Terrien]

PART 2

"KAPITAIKALLAK," THE ICE MAN

"We in our turn, followed in the wake of the master
mariner as far as northern Baffin Island,
what the Inuit call the 'backside of the Earth.'
There we met the 'elders.' They recalled
the man they called affectionately
'Kapitaikallak, Captain Bernier'."

STÉPHANE CLOUTIER, spring 2001

CHAPTER I

The plan

If only by his thirst for discovery, Joseph-Elzéar Bernier was definitely fascinated with the Arctic at a time when the only unknown regions on the globe that remained were those surrounding the North and South Poles.[1]

The trip he was proposing to make was inspired particularly by the expedition of a Norwegian, Doctor Fridtjof Nansen (1861-1930). On board the *Fram*, and seconded by his compatriot Otto Sverdrup, Nansen undertook to explore the Arctic Ocean between 1893 and 1896, by allowing himself to drift with the currents from east to west, from the New Siberian Islands to Denmark Strait. Nansen thereby reached the most northerly point attained by any explorer before him, namely 86° 14'N.

The Norwegian explorer had been influenced by the unfortunate polar voyage of the *Jeannette*, and especially by the fact:

> [...] that in 1884 Eskimos discovered near Julianehåb debris from the *Jeannette*, that had been wrecked three years earlier near the New Siberian Islands, namely: a list of provisions bearing Captain De Long's signature, a pair of oilskin breeches, the peak of a cap, and a list of the ship's boats. Whether this wreckage was authentic or not mattered little, since it had given rise to a hypothesis that pointed to the only possible way to reach the Pole.[2]

Indeed Nansen calculated that this wreckage, imprisoned in the ice, had drifted northwest across the Arctic Ocean, passing between Svalbard and the Pole before heading south along the east coast of Greenland.

Captain Bernier had come to the same conclusions as Dr. Nansen: if the American ship had been able to withstand the ice pressures it would definitely have reached the Pole and then would have naturally reached the shores of Greenland. Thus the itinerary for reaching the North Pole was traced out.

Fridtjof Nansen had tested this theory by letting his ship drift with the ice for 33 months, but he did not succeed in achieving his dream. It was now the turn of the man from L'Islet to pick up the baton and try his luck. Furthermore he was convinced that Nansen would not have failed if the *Fram* had entered the ice at the right place.

From early in 1889, that is when his position as Governor of the Québec Prison was being scrutinized by the Attorney General of the province, Bernier began to talk publicly about his plans for polar exploration. "He was a great talker, with a fine Québec sense of humour and a flair for telling a story."[3] Speaking to people was a real pleasure for him. His direct style, his picturesque expressions, and his passion for polar themes could not but captivate the groups he encountered.

His first public speaking engagement was to the members of the *Société de géographie de Québec* at its annual meeting on 27 January 1898:

> In order to pass through the Behring Strait and navigate through the polar ice pack, your humble servant

would build a small, modern vessel, fitted with sails and steam-powered.

We would set sail from Vancouver on or about the first of June, stopping at Port Clarence, Alaska, to load the remaining provisions for our dogs. We would then follow the coast of Siberia as far as the New Siberian Islands. We would complete exploration of Bennet Island and Sannikof Island, the latter sighted by Dr. Nansen, and perhaps other islands in the area.

Next we would study the movement of the ice and, at a given moment, direct our small vessel into the ice as far as possible at a point some three hundred miles east of the spot where the *Fram* entered.

[...] Once we are held fast in the ice pack [...] we shall be henceforth in the hands of nature. We would have only to build ourselves a shelter in which to store provisions, in the event our ship is destroyed by the crushing ice [...]

We would have to take care of our ship and supplies for the first winter; we would hunt polar bear, walrus and seal, and have no difficulty building ice shelters in which to store our provisions. Moreover, we would have sufficient time to make all the scientific observations required of an expedition such as this.

We would remain fixed in the same spot, in all likelihood, for nearly three years, except, of course, for the current pulling us north thirty-six degrees west. We shall then be able to begin our journey to the pole, planting aluminum markers containing provisions every half mile. Several times during the year, however, there are openings in the ice which, after closing, form hummocks. We shall have to know where to deposit our provisions during the first year.

By the second winter, the ice pressure will have almost completely subsided. There will be fewer openings as well and the hummocks from the previous year will be filled with a very light powdery snow (there will be very little moisture in the air); the ice will be more uniform and easier to walk upon. It will be easier to go out on excursions, each time closer to the Pole, carrying our new provisions as well as the markers that will guide us back to the ship. We plan to use wireless telegraph during the spring, and later that summer we should reach the pole. After exploring the area and making scientific observations we shall plant the flag of our country at the Pole. With the help of God nothing is impossible to man.

The *Jeannette,* an American vessel commanded by Captain DeLong, being crushed by the arctic ice in 1881. [G. Vallat, *À la conquête du pôle Nord,* 1897]. Concerning this tragedy William Chapman wrote: "They died, leaving their task unfinished, without having penetrated into the zone they had dreamed of, without reaching their splendid, radiant goal [...] amidst the horrors of the eternal ice."

After completing our exploration of this much sought-after area, which, in my opinion, is no more than a vast expanse of ice with great water depths and ice fifteen to sixteen feet thick on the average, and a compass variation of nearly fifty degrees deviation west, we would be looking southward in every direction. [...] To leave the area surrounding the pole, one necessarily heads south. Before doing so we shall erect a monument of ice in honour of our divine Pilot, whom we will ask for divine guidance back to our families and our fellow countrymen, who will be awaiting our return.

All this time, we will have remained in contact with our ship by wireless telegraph. Each month we shall instruct them to send a message attached to a small balloon, as planned. These balloons will be prepared in such a way as to float for several days attached to a guide-rope that will prevent them from reaching too great a height. I am certain that they will make their way south from the polar basin, then east, as dictated by nature and daily need. Upon our return to the ship, we shall continue our drift through the ice in a direction of south thirty-six degrees east towards the channel between Greenland and Spitzbergen, a journey that should take at least eighteen months. We shall then do our best to free our ship from the ice and make or way back to Canada.[4]

One should not be surprised at the naivety of his proposal nor by its lack of detail; they simply demonstrate that at the time there was a great deal of ignorance as to the realities of the polar regions. Captain Bernier's "grand plan" was a plan for exploration driven by his passion for making discoveries. The challenge was to test his theories and to succeed where so many others had failed.

This initial presentation was clumsy, unprofessional, improvised, and rendered in poor French. Joseph-Elzéar was self-taught; even in the elementary classes at the village school he had not been very motivated. His working language for the previous 30 years had been English. Yet the man had sufficient charisma and dynamism to compensate for these weaknesses and, over time, he would learn to express himself better, to refine his proposals and to use projected images to communicate his ideas.

Two weeks later Nazaire LeVasseur, an influential member of the *Société de géographie de Québec*, set forth Bernier's strategy to the Minister of the Interior, Clifford Sifton:

Embedded in the ice and carried by the arctic current northwards from the Novosibirskiye Islands (New Siberia), Bernier's ship would drift eastwards and towards the Pole among mountains of ice. On reaching a point located about 720 miles from the Pole, Bernier and some men would leave the ship with dogs, reindeer, kayaks, a prefabricated house and sufficient provisions to reach the Pole and return to Svalbard, where they would board one of the steamers that ply regularly between Norway and that archipelago. In the meantime the polar current would have carried the expedition ship to those same Svalbard shores.[5]

On Saturday 19 November 1898 Captain Bernier was the guest-of-honour at the opening of *La Patrie*'s lecture-hall in Montréal and, on the following Monday the newspaper published the first detailed account of his polar project, introduced in glaring headlines:

THE NORTH POLE

Captain Joseph E. Bernier and a few brave, stalwart companions will discover it.

The audacious exploits of Nansen and his predecessors—the interesting lecture by our Canadian explorer.

Beneath these headlines there was a large portrait of the man-of-the-hour, followed by several pages of text, a copy of the enormous polar map that he had drafted, and a map of the winds in the northern hemisphere that supported his theory about the currents. For the benefit of the readers, also included was a sketch of the reindeer-skin clothing that he would have made for all the members of the expedition and of the revolutionary equipment that he was counting on using for transport across the ice: aluminum sledge-boats with steel runners built in sections to make them unsinkable, portable folding canvas boats, and aluminum boats with crankable screws.

Captain Bernier had grasped that to give his project a certain credibility he not only had to garner the

M. LE CAPITAINE JOSEPH ELZEAR BERNIER

support of the important *Société de géographie de Québec*, but also capture the attention of the general public and the press. This is what he achieved by his lecture on 19 November. By illustrating his proposal with lantern slides in the manner of our modern slides, by describing the dangers and the obstacles to be overcome, and by inserting numerous unusual and spectacular details, he succeeded in fascinating and arousing the enthusiasm of the 215 people in attendance.

On 8 December he made the same presentation to a crammed hall in Lévis.

> The town of Lévis has undertaken to supply Captain Bernier with a large part of the articles needed for his expedition: sledges, boats, etc. The lecture he gave in Lévis was extraordinarily successful.[6]

Bernier had proved that his project was sufficiently well formulated to captivate the people of his province. He could now widen his horizons and hope to recruit a vastly larger public beyond Québec's borders. Before thinking of the practical aspects of realizing his dream, the French-Canadian adventurer had first to conquer English Canada.

CHAPTER 2

Stirring public opinion

"It's not dots on the map that people want, it's adventure and bravery." The Norwegian explorer, Roald Amundsen (1872-1928) was correct in saying that at the end of the 19th century people did not want to hear about imperialism or territorial expansion, but rather romantic adventures and valour. In trying to reach the North Pole Amundsen had thought he would earn the love and respect of the whole world. In penetrating the mysteries of the Arctic he had hoped to gain access to the select club of arctic heroes such as Nansen, Franklin, Parry, and M'Clure.

Was the same true for Joseph-Elzéar Bernier? Did the 46-year-old seafarer want to leave his mark by achieving a task that would assure him a place in his country's history and the world's gratitude? Definitely. As a man of action he was driven to excel. His ego craved honours and glory. His extraordinary talents demanded challenges worthy of him. The quest for the Pole could satisfy all his needs.

The Arctic has always captured popular imagination. This was especially true during the Victorian era.[1] Exploration of the icy wastes and the sacrifices that this required—isolation, privations, starvation, sometimes even death—appealed to the masses hungry for heroic, dramatic or tragic accounts and served as inspiration for poets and painters who wanted to take advantage of this strange fascination.

> The proud adventurers, captives of the pack-ice,
> Exiled for ever in their tombs of ice,
> Had dreamed that their glory would be immortalized:
> The Pole, like the Sphynx, remains inviolate.[2]

The Far North has always evoked a feeling of freedom associated with escape towards horizons with limitless possibilities. It has always symbolized man's affirmation and his passion for life.

Even today the Arctic remains:

> one of the least-known mega-regions of the world [...] that has encouraged imaginative creations and the circulation of a whole series of clichés more symbolic than real. What one thinks one knows about the North may derive more from the imaginary than from a measurable, palpable and verifiable reality.[3]

And the northern adventurer still benefits from a very positive and likable image.

At the end of the 19th century Captain Bernier seemed to personify the perfect polar explorer. When he said that he was ready to solve the enigma of the land of the midnight sun, nobody would have listened to him or even taken him seriously, if he had not been up to the job.

On 2 October 1900 Israël Tarte, Minister of Public Works, confirmed this aspect to Lord Strathcona, Canadian High Commissioner in London:

Captain Bernier's visiting card. He wanted to show that he would be attacking the North Pole, despite the threat of the Russian bear and American and Scandinavian eagles. In the popular imagery of the day Bernier, the Canadian beaver, would be the conqueror of the Pole. [Archives of Carol and Louis Terrien]

> The Captain has made up his mind to discover the North Pole. I do not know of any other living man who, in my humble opinion, would be more able to accomplish that object than Captain Bernier is.[4]

Stalwart, virile, bold, proud, energetic, determined, and passionate… the seafarer with vivid blue eyes was every bit the adventurer "who embodies all the desires for escape of the ordinary man."[5]

In general his Canadian contemporaries were no different from the rest of the Victorian world. They knew almost nothing about the arctic regions apart from its excessive cold, its empty, icy spaces, and its romanticism reflected in popular imagery. The lack of information stimulated the imagination, while scientific treatises, which were popular in Canada at that time, proclaimed the superiority of the northern race and the benefits of its cold climate. A race of iron and steel fashioned by the North: "We are the Vikings of this continent."[6]

The intrepid Bernier and his plans to brave the unknown and to sail stormy seas simply confirmed that the spirit of the Vikings was still alive on the North American continent. The symbol of the contemporary North was just as powerful and evocative for Canadians as the symbol of the West for Americans. The colossus with a glorious past was the sort of individual who could respond to the quest for a national identity and who flattered the image of the superior man whom Canadians made themselves out to be.

Very soon the country's major newspapers were publishing numerous articles on Bernier's plan, linking it with praise for Canadian pride. Why not Canada?

> […] what nation has a better natural right and a fairer chance and a stronger incentive to supply the conqueror of the Pole than Canada?[7]

His personal ambition thus became that of an entire people:

> […] with perseverance, with courageous men, we can certainly out-distance our predecessors and plant our flag on the top of the world.
>
> […] Why should Canada not harvest the prize for all her work? Why […] should we allow other countries to precede us? We have been making giant steps in terms of progress for several years; we are forging ahead.
>
> […] Why should Canadians not reach the heights in attaining the geographical position of 90°N, and in placing our flag on that part of the globe that is the northern limit of our Canada, that belongs to Great Britain.[8]

Captain Bernier in 1898. [Archives of Carol and Louis Terrien]

CHAPTER 3

An *idée fixe*

BEFORE DEVOTING HIMSELF entirely to the quest for the North Pole, Joseph-Elzéar Bernier first had to ensure sufficient income for his family and for the major expenses associated with the numerous lectures and interviews necessary for bringing-on-side and convincing the Canadian public and the prestigious scientific societies. He therefore accepted a series of short appointments as captain, as well as tackling a major project, that of refloating the steamer *Scottish King*, that had run aground during a storm on the east coast of Newfoundland a few years previously.

> The work on the *Scottish King* stands out as the most difficult and trying in my career out of the Arctic regions.[1]

In fact the winter that marked the start of the 20th century was one of exceptionally violent weather on the east coast of Newfoundland. The winds were so strong, the seas so heavy, and the cold so intense that the work could be tackled only in brief snatches. Despite this foretaste of polar climatic conditions and a tough task that would consume over seven months of effort, the salvage and sale of the steamer in question succeeded in re-establishing Captain Bernier's financial situation.

Hence from September 1900 Joseph-Elzéar could freely dedicate himself to his *idée fixe*.

> To get his expedition under way Bernier would be contributing his own time, his competence as a navigator, and his desire that the operation should succeed; but he still had to obtain funds for the material and human resources necessary for the enterprise. [...] In light of the high costs of such an expedition and its limited commercial prospects, the government, or rather Prime Minister Laurier, became the primary target of Bernier and his supporters.[2]

The *Scottish King* aground on the Newfoundland coast. [Archives of Carol and Louis Terrien]

In 1898 Bernier had already prepared a memorandum of over 20 pages in which he presented the main outline of his plan to conquer the Pole to the Liberal leader. By writing "and what an honour it would be for you to have one of your compatriots harvest this fruit,"[3] he had hoped to touch a sensitive cord in the heart of the first French Canadian to exercise the functions of Prime Minister of Canada. In his letter of acknowledgement Sir Wilfrid Laurier (1841-1919) remained cold and distant and gave him no sign of encouragement.

Fortunately, his friends at the *Société de géographie de Québec* believed firmly in his project. On 7 October 1898 Charles Baillargé had supported his approach to the Prime Minister by writing to the federal Minister of Public Works, Israël Tarte:

> The discovery and exploration of the North Pole by one of our countrymen, a French Canadian, is perhaps not a matter of urgency for the material advancement of Canada, but such a feat will cast such a lustre on the country, will throw it into such relief vis-à-vis the whole world and will contribute so greatly to completing geographical knowledge that, truly, one should not hesitate for a moment in assisting a man of the calibre and will-power of Captain Bernier in this project.[4]

On 5 April 1899 another influential member of the *Société de géographie de Québec*, Nazaire LeVasseur, well-known writer and journalist with the Québec newspaper *L'Événement,* wrote directly to Wilfrid Laurier, stressing the "popular" aspect of the enterprise:

> Until now Captain Bernier's project has been greeted with great acclaim by the public. It has piqued the curiosity and provoked the interest of the masses who naturally have a great passion for adventures and especially for a somewhat adventurous expedition such as an expedition to the North Pole.[5]

Thus Prime Minister Laurier was being constantly sensitized to the fascination that Bernier's project was arousing in the Canadian population. The "greatest poet of the 19th century," Louis-Honoré Fréchette (1839-1908)[6] also tackled the task:

Sir Wilfrid Laurier. [Photographer unknown, LAC, C-016741]

> My dear Laurier,
>
> Captain Bernier has asked me to tell you what I think of his plan. I have studied the question a little, and I find it most practical. As for the project itself, what reverberations and what an advertisement for our country if it succeeds![7]

Louis Fréchette was perhaps not an expert on polar questions, but his opinion as a public figure counted, especially since the poet and playwright had been a member of Parliament.

Even before his friend Fréchette intervened, Prime Minister Laurier, pressed from all sides, had agreed to grant an interview to the famous captain. There is no record of their meeting on 16 April 1899 but the fact that the "Bernier personage" was squarely the opposite of the "Laurier personage" would let one suppose that their initial contacts were somewhat reserved. The stocky build of the man of action who had spent his life outdoors could not but contrast with the appearance of the thoroughbred politician who had never liked physical exercise:

> His physical appearance emitted a sort of natural *majesté*. Tall, straight, thin, with a pale, sickly face, right from the start he gained the sympathy of the listener by his grave, serious face, tinged with melancholy. His silver hair floated in an aureole, while his voice was agreeable and sonorous.[8]

Bernier's fire and candour could only displease the delicately-attuned, well-balanced mind of the skilful lawyer, who held a degree from McGill University and was accustomed to conciliation and to compromises in order to survive in the political arena of his day. As much as Bernier was direct in his approach, Laurier was known for his ambivalence. The captain's lack of education and the simplicity of his proposals must inevitably have made a poor impression, as against the man whom the newspapers had nick-named "the silver tongue," "one of the greatest orators of his time," and one of "the most charming causeurs in the Dominion."

Moreover Fréchette wrote of Laurier, whom he had met in 1870:

> I was struck by the power of his intelligence, by such a philosophical cast of mind, possessed of such an astonishing range and variety of knowledge in a country where professional men believe that they are compromising themselves if they read anything apart from books dealing with their own specialty.[9]

The intellectual impressed by his culture, his presence, and his elegance while the captain captivated by his joviality, his enthusiasm and his determination. Two giants who, however, had one thing in common, their French roots, the identity that Laurier had defended during a debate in the House on 28 March 1889, when faced by attacks by the Member MacCarthy, a Conservative from Ontario .

> [You said] yesterday that French Canadians sometimes forget that Canada is a British country. [...] I am French by origin and I am proud of that origin, and I know my Anglo-Saxon fellow-citizens only too well to know that if I did not have pride in my origins in my heart, they would never look at me except with the scorn that I would deserve. I am French by origin, but I am a British subject.[10]

Laurier and Bernier were both French Canadians, ambitious to succeed in a British country.

> It is claimed that at that first meeting the Prime Minister asked his interlocutor: "But what guarantee can you give that your enterprise will succeed?" and that the captain, drawing himself up to his full height, replied: "Sir Wilfrid, my grandfather, father and eleven members of my family [were seamen] and they all died in their beds. I don't plan to break with tradition.[11]

Laurier was not convinced but "at the request of Savard, his French Whip in the House of Commons,"[12] he agreed that the captain should submit his plans to the members of Parliament, who certainly wanted to hear them.

> In 1900 and later the following year, Bernier appeared before parliamentary committees to tell federal politicians of his plan. Most of the committee members would later speak before the House urging Parliament to endorse Bernier's expedition project.[13]

In a country dominated by Liberals at both federal and provincial levels, the ex-Governor of the Québec Prison had to forget his Conservative past if he wanted to realize his dream. He appears to have succeeded in motivating the politicians to the extent of setting aside their partisanship, since early in 1899 the Québec Premier, Félix-Gabriel Marchand (1832-1900). who in 1897 began a Liberal reign that would last for almost 40 years in Québec, agreed to sponsor his presentation to the members of the Québec Parliament. And then towards the end of that year it was the turn of the Mayor of Montréal and the newspaper, *La Patrie*, then under the control of Israël Tarte, to organize a meeting of patriots, motivated by the idea that a Canadian could win the race for the North Pole.

The storm of publicity around the future arctic hero meant that he was invited everywhere. Everyone wanted to meet him, to invite him or to attend his lectures. People dreamed of heading north with him. People wanted to be part of his team. Bernier became so overwhelmed by all these requests that he recruited a special secretary to help with his correspondence.[14] That correspondence would have cost him $1000 in stamps. Moreover, since he never accepted payment for his lectures, he calculated that his travel and promotion of his expedition between 1898 and 1904 cost him a total of $21,000.

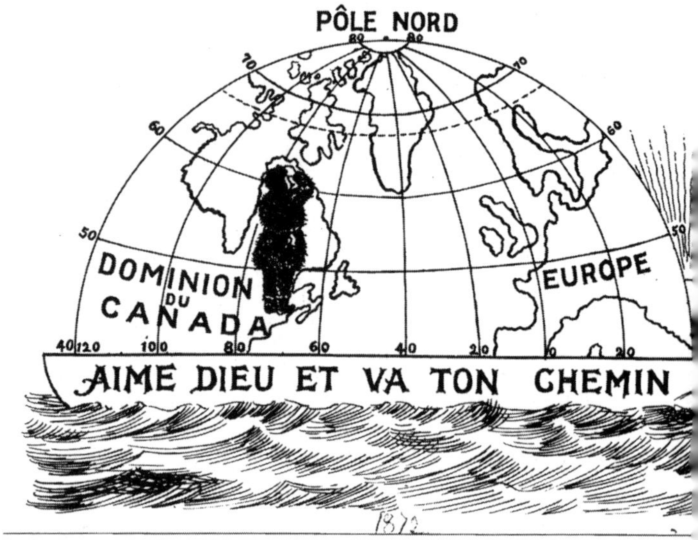

Joseph-Elzéar Bernier adopted the motto "Aime Dieu et va ton chemin" in his early twenties and linked it to his polar voyages early on. [Archives of Carol and Louis Terrien].

Despite all his efforts, in the spring of 1900 Bernier received Laurier's refusal to subsidize his polar expedition for the current year. Disappointed and perhaps aware that he was wasting time by marking time, the indefatigable captain decided to focus his energies elsewhere and to extend his campaign outside Canada. It was his friends at the *Société de géographie de Québec* who established the first contacts with the learned societies of Europe, while ministers Israël Tarte and R.R. Dobell, as well as Lord Strathcona, Canadian High Commissioner in London, introduced him to the inescapable Royal Colonial Institute in London.[15]

On 17 January 1901 over 300 guests attended an event at the Royal Colonial Institute. Among the people of note who had travelled to hear the first Canadian who aimed to rival the great British explorers:

> were notably Sir Frederick Younge, supporter of the Empire and of territorial expansion, and Sir Clements Markham, the explorer whose influence had impelled the British Admiralty to dispatch Sir George Strong Nares' polar expedition in 1875-76.[16]

His personal diary for 1901 records that Rose accompanied him on this trip and that on 8 January they spent long hours at the British Museum "to study Eskimo clothing."[17] On 13 and 14 January they were at the port of Dundee on the North Sea coast of Scotland to photograph and examine the details of ships for sailing in arctic waters. Then they travelled to Newcastle upon Tyne, in Northumberland to meet Sir W.G. Armstrong of Whitworth & Co. Ltd. "to enquire about a vessel for Arctic exploration." In fact, in his letter of introduction[18] the captain stated that he had plans and detailed sketches of the ship that he wanted to build for his expedition and that he hoped to study them with Sir William Armstrong.

Despite the enthusiastic reaction of the Londoners Bernier did not succeed in finding the financing that he wished for his project. But he did not return home empty-handed since the approval of the prestigious British societies represented an important trump-card that gave him the credibility he needed to carry on with renewed vigour.

In that year, 1901, he sent out a flood of letters … to the House of Commons, the Minister of Trade, the Minister of Finance, the Royal Scottish Geographical Society, the Minister of the Navy and Oceans, the Governor-General, the Archbishop of Québec, and many more!

More and more Canadian associations declared themselves in support of his plan: the *Société littéraire et historique de Québec*, the Toronto Astronomical Society, the Committee on Polar Research, the Ontario Land Surveyors' Association, and the Natural History Society of Montréal. Even the famous singer, Albani, encouraged him to realize his dream. Bernier continued to work public opinion and to capture imaginations.

Children collected cigar bands with the captain's photo; and poets such as the French Canadian William Chapman acclaimed the Tarzan of the pack-ice.[19]

In March a certain E.C. Leigh of Toronto, inspired by the polar expedition, forwarded these lines imbued with admiration to the future conqueror of the Pole:

O! for the North! Who fears to go
Into the regions of the snow
The pure, white glittering snow!
Not by the ice-bound, frozen sea
That thwarts man's restless energy;
But over-sea to go.

* * *

Are there not daring hearts and strong
The sons of Canada among?
There are. We know there are!
Who dread not danger, who would die
To place the "Maple Leaf" on high
Beneath the Polar Star […].[20]

A M. LE CAPITAINE J.-E. BERNIER

Amant des grandes eaux, des vastes horizons,
Dans l'âme te sentant la flamme des Jasons,
Tu brûles de voguer vers la zone lointaine
Qui vit sombrer, hélas! tant de puissants agrès,
Et, pour collaborer à l'œuvre du progrès,
Tu vas risquer tes jours, ô vaillant capitaine!

Oui, chez toi c'est le sang des découvreurs qui bat;
Le danger te séduit, nul vent ne te courba,
Nul fardeau n'est trop lourd pour ta robuste épaule,
Et, vers le but rêvé tournant ton front d'airain,
Tu jures de vouloir distancer tout marin,
Tu promets de porter ton pavillon au pôle.

Guidé par les jalons que des preux immortels
Ont semés à travers les glaçons éternels
Que l'Arctique sans fin bouleverse et tourmente,
Tu vas, j'en suis certain, écarter tout revers,
Tu vas toucher du doigt le bout de l'univers,
Réaliser bientôt le projet qui te hante.

Tout ce que la nature a de rude et d'amer,
Toute l'horreur qui doit régner sur une mer
Que l'hiver boréal incessamment entoure,
Tu l'auras à combattre, ô noble aventurier!
Nul tourment ne fera fléchir ton cœur d'acier,
Rien ne triomphera de ta mâle bravoure.

Tu sortiras vainqueur de ce combat sans nom
Où jamais ne devra dominer le canon,
Mais bien plutôt ta voix, ta grande voix qui vibre,
En faisant répéter à de mornes échos,
Qui n'ont jamais frémi qu'au grondement des flots,
Les allègres refrains d'un jeune pays libre.

Sur le sommet nacré d'un iceberg géant,
— Semblant un vaste autel bercé par l'Océan, —
Pour remercier Dieu qui retient les désastres,
Un soir, tu planteras quelque modeste croix,
Et tes fiers compagnons, ces marins de ton choix,
Avec toi fléchiront le genou sous les astres.

Un ardent *Te Deum* montera vers le ciel,
Et dès qu'aura vibré cet hymne solennel,
Des frissons inconnus traverseront l'espace,
Le gouffre des grands flots engourdis tremblera,
Et l'esprit des déserts dans la brume dira :
— Banquises, courbez-vous! c'est le maître qui passe! —

Captif du fier progrès, proscrit du saint devoir,
Tes amis ne pourront de sitôt te revoir;
Mais, durant les longs jours de ta longue croisière,
Ton souvenir en eux sera toujours vivant,
Et les soirs radieux les verront bien souvent
Pensifs et l'œil tourné vers l'étoile polaire.

Et quand tu reviendras du parage ignoré
Où tant d'audacieux espoirs avaient sombré,
Ton large front aura la pâleur glaciale;
Mais dans l'ombre sereine où la gloire enfin luit,
Ton nom rayonnera comme parfois, la nuit,
Brille dans notre ciel l'aurore boréale.

W. CHAPMAN

Poem by William Chapman, dedicated to Captain Bernier. [*Les Aspirations, poésies canadiennes*. Motteroz: Martinet, 1904] Chapman (1850-1917) was haunted by the desire to surpass Louis Fréchette. He exploited the same patriotic themes as the latter but according to the *Dictionnaire des œuvres littéraires du Québec*, "he will never be a subtle artist."

Also in March 1901 Chapman expressed the infatuation of an entire people for this hero with the "heart of steel":

Oui chez toi c'est le sang des découvreurs qui bat;
Le danger te séduit, nul vent ne te courbe,
Nul fardeau n'est trop lourd pour ta robuste épaule,
Et, vers le but rêvé tournant ton front d'airain,
Tu jures de vouloir distancer tout marin,
Tu promets de porter ton pavillon au pôle.

Laurier could no longer ignore this man who was attracting so much attention and who was winning the support of so many people among his electorate. Following a poll of his members, Laurier agreed that Bernier should appear for a second time before the members of Parliament.

This presentation in Room No. 16 in the House of Commons represented an important occasion for the captain. He was only too well aware of it. This was his last chance to convince those elected by the people. His arguments had to be well prepared, solid, and convincing. The text of his presentation no longer exists. Its gist was probably identical to that of the letter that he sent to the Prime Minister in August 1903. Bernier had already refined his thoughts over a number of years and used the same arguments in all his lectures and interviews.

> I come to you today not with the intention of demonstrating the utility and feasibility of my projected exploration of the Artic [sic] Seas as far as the North Pole, nor the great good this exploration would bring to science and to Canada generally, because most of you have already told me long ago, that you were converted to my ideas, and some of you have even said they were ready to subscribe $1,000 of their own money towards it. But I come because the time for action has arrived. [...] It is a national [project], because it will be a great benefit to Canada. The geographical position of our country gives us the right to extend our frontiers as far as the North Pole, and we should take actual possession of the Islands, Lands and Seas of the Arctic Ocean, where it is known there are coal fields and other mineral wealth. The Government of Canada should not let the United States take actual possession of those lands and seas, nor should the task of discovering the North Pole, where the Canadian flag has the right to float, be left to any foreign country. [...]
>
> I state that the time for action has arrived because, if the government of Canada does not act this year, other countries may, and their representatives be at the Pole before us. The time has also arrived because I have devoted six years of my time, my money and used my energies in the particular study of this question
>
> [...] and I may state that I have now everything ready, down to the most minute details, so as to ensure success.
>
> I have lectured throughout Canada and England, before many scientific societies and boards of trade, and I can boast that my plans have been approved everywhere and by everyone, and I can assert that public opinion in Canada is thoroughly with me [...].
>
> The time for action has now arrived as I am at present in the prime of physical and intellectual strength, but these gifts of God sometimes wear away very quickly, and to undertake an exploration of the Northern seas which might last four or five years, it requires strength, determination and knowledge. These qualifications I now possess and I would require thorough fitness of the men I would take with me and I know where to find such men.
>
> [...] and if this Government desires to attach its name to such a national undertaking a start should be made now [...].[21]

After his presentation to the House of Commons Bernier wrote proudly in his personal diary: "success complait [sic]." He had reason to be pleased with his performance before a packed house. Even Lord Minto, Governor General of Canada was among the enthusiasts.

On the following day Senator William C. Edwards took pleasure in reporting to the Prime Minister:

> A meeting was held in Room No. 16, House of Commons, yesterday, attended by, I would say, fully 60% of the members of the House and from 15 to 20 Senators, as well as a number of citizens. In fact, the room was filled to overflowing.
>
> [...] At the close of the meeting a motion was moved by Mr. Monk, M.P., seconded by Mr. Wallace, M.P., thanking Captain Bernier for his address and recommending to Parliament his scheme and also recommending to the government that Parliament should contribute the necessary funds for the carrying out of the same. This motion was unanimously carried.[22]

Two months later it was the turn of the Royal Society of Canada to approve the exploration project and to recommend that public funds should be devoted to it.

Despite these important successes and his numerous requests of elected members, Bernier did not receive a government grant. It was Israël Tarte's *La Patrie* that, on 25 May 1901, best expressed this refusal to get involved on the part of the Federal Government:

> Prompted by the Minister of Public Works, *La Patrie* reports that the Government has come to the definite conclusion that it will not be voting funds this year for Captain Bernier's expedition. Many people who, he says, have been taking an interest in this venture—if I may be allowed to use this expression—will regret the government's decision. But we are in a century of positivism. There is no lack of people who believe that when a thing brings no immediate profit, one should definitely not engage in that thing.

Was this the end of a dream for Joseph-Elzéar Bernier?

CHAPTER 4

A subscription campaign

The financial assistance that Captain Bernier was soliciting from the Government came to $100,000 which represented a very considerable sum for the time. This money was to be used to build a ship designed especially to resist the pressures of the polar ice, as well as for provisions and the salaries for 15 men for an expedition that might last for six years.

In the spring of 1901 the Prime Minister, who was still hesitating about involving his country in a race for the Pole, seemed nonetheless ready to accept a compromise that would gain him some time and that would respond to the strong national feelings that the project was arousing among his countrymen.

> Distrustful, Laurier demanded from Bernier concrete proof of public interest in the form of subscriptions. The government would provide $60,000 if Bernier managed to raise the same amount from the Canadian public. Encouraged by this proposition, even if equivocal, Bernier prepared to approach the Canadian public directly.[1]

Did the idea for a subscription campaign come from the Prime Minister or from Captain Bernier who hoped to force the government's hand? The letter that the latter addressed to Laurier on 15 April 1901 rather suggests that his was the brain behind the new "Polar Expedition Committee" and the public appeal:

> Sir,
>
> Would you [be] so kind as to give your assent to become the "President" of the General Committee in charge of the Canadian North Pole Expedition which I propose taking charge of as already explained to you.
>
> His Excellency Lord Minto, Lord Strathcona and Mount Royal, Sir Clements Markham, and the Hon. R.R. Dobell, have already consented to act on said committee and it is my intention to appeal to the public for subscriptions.[2]

Laurier refused the Presidency.

Three days later the Canadian newspapers announced that the Government had finally decided to yield to the wishes unanimously expressed by the population and that it would provide Captain Bernier with a suitable ship and all the scientific instruments required for his expedition to the North Pole. In return an appeal would be made to the generosity of the Canadian public to pay the crew and to provision the ship for the long voyage into the unknown.

Encouraged by the support in principle of numerous federal politicians, by that of several provincial premiers, and by even that of the Governor General, Lord Minto, Bernier did not hesitate to put his plan into practice. Moreover, in reading his impressive private correspondence, one gains the clear impression that the man from L'Islet had made great strides over the past few years and that he had become quite at ease, some-

April 1902
THIS IS OUR BUSY DAY
RUSTAP.
CAPT. BERNIER—"Wouldn't the Government of Canada put up $100,000 to help discover the North Pole?"
SIR WILFRID LAURIER—"I wouldn't give ten cents to discover any place colder than where we had to live for eighteen long years."

Cartoon of Laurier and Bernier, 1902.

times even intimate, with the "princes of this world," with whom he was in regular communication. This letter, which he addressed to Lady Minto at Rideau Hall, is proof:

> Mrs. Bernier is here, in Ottawa, with me and I am so busy that I cannot attend to her as I would like to; but I have given her the freedom of the capital and she goes on her own hook. But she never fails to put in her appearance at meal times and in the evening.
>
> I may possibly go on a lecturing tour later on. Just fancy a sailor on the stage; I would look like a fish out of water; but I have been so long on salt water that I think I would keep anywhere for some time. If it be God's will I shall go and return from the North Pole all right.[3]

Premises at 117 Bank Street in Ottawa were quickly transformed into an administrative centre and, by mid-May 1901, over 60,000 circulars had been sent to geographical societies, scientific bodies, private companies and a host of individuals who might contribute to "Captain Bernier's North Pole Expedition." The persons of note identified in the circular would confer a certain prestige and great credibility on the organizing committee, even if the French text left something to be desired.

This subscription campaign became the event of the year and Bernier the man of the hour. In Québec all the Catholic parish priests received a poster from the famous adventurer. The Canadian newspapers fell into step, delighted that their top story should arouse the interest and curiosity of their readers. The *Société de géographie de Québec*, always very supportive of the project agreed to make an appeal to public and private bodies to raise funds. The letter that its president Nazaire LeVasseur sent to the chairman of the Finance Committee of Québec City, Georges Tanguay, on 26 July 1901, perfectly expresses the strong national feeling associated with the Bernier expedition. Increasingly Canadians saw in it a common project, other than the transcontinental railway, capable of raising pride in

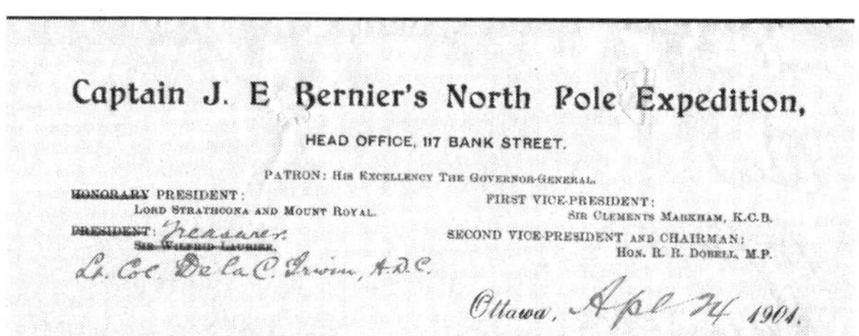

Captain J. E Bernier's North Pole Expedition,

HEAD OFFICE, 117 BANK STREET.

PATRON: His Excellency The Governor-General.

~~HONORARY~~ PRESIDENT: Lord Strathcona and Mount Royal.

~~PRESIDENT~~: Treasurer: ~~Sir Wilfrid Laurier.~~ Lt. Col. De la C. Irwin, A.D.C.

FIRST VICE-PRESIDENT: Sir Clements Markham, K.C.B.

SECOND VICE-PRESIDENT and CHAIRMAN: Hon. R. R. Dobell, M.P.

Ottawa, Apl 24 1901.

Letter-head used by the Committee for Bernier's polar expedition. It is interesting to note that Wilfrid Laurier's name, as President, has been stroked out. This would lead one to suppose that the stationery had been printed before the Prime Minister's approval had been obtained. [Private collection]

EXPEDITION POLAIRE CANADIENNE

DU CAPITAINE BERNIER.

PATRON: SON EXCELLENCE LE GOUVERNEUR GENERAL.

isée et Approuvée par le GOUVERNEMENT DU DOMINION, et des PROVINCES, LA SOCIÉTÉ GÉOGRAPHIQUE DE QUEBEC, &c.

President,
LORD STRATHCONA
ET MONT ROYAL.

2eme Vice President et avec Siege.
HON. R. R. DOBELL,
M. P., C. P.

1er Vice President,
SIR CLEMENT MARKHAM,
K. C. B.

Tresorier,
LT.-COL. De La C. T. IRWIN,
Hon. A. D. C. au Gouv-Gen.

CAPITAINE J. E. BERNIER.

UN vif intérêt s'est éveillé dans les coeurs tous les Canadiens à la nouvelle que le Capitaine Bernier, un Canadien de naissance, est à pré[illegible] une expédition au Pôle Nord. Le bâtiment qui doit le conduire sur l'océan glacial sera bâti dans le Canada. Le Capitaine Bernier partira d'un port Canadien. Ce brave marin offre ses services gratuits à son Roi et au Canada, et ne demande au gouvernement et au peuple Canadien que de fournir les frais de construction et d'equipage du bâtiment. La somme requise est de $150,000 et nous en appelons à votre générosité, par l'entremise de cette circulaire, pour un aide quelconque à une souscription nationale. Le gouvernement a promis d'accorder une somme substantielle comme sa contribution à cette souscription nationale. Il est du devoir du Canada d'envoyer un Canadien à la découverte du Pôle Nord pour l'honneur du Canada, de la Mère Patrie, et de l'Empire.

Il y a une vive compétition entre toutes les grandes nations du monde pour la découverte du pôle, et le Canada a été trop longtemps, à la tête, pour reculer maintenant et permettre à un autre pavillon que le drapeau Canadien de flotter à la plus éminente position. Diverses tentatives à découvrir le Pôle Nord en pour résultats d'importantes découvertes et de précieux acvntages pour le genre humain. La région du Pôle est d'une immense étendue et les résultats scientifiques que l'on obtiendra par l'examen de cette vaste région sont d'une importance également considérable. Il n'y a point de doute qu'il est à désirer que l'on achève l'exploration de ces Mers du Nord, au point de vue physiographe, zoologique et magnétique. Les Canadiens ont un trop grand interêt dans ces Mers du Nord, pour laisser aller à des nations étrangères la gloire de cette déconverte.

Le Captiaine Bernier est bien connu non seulement dans le Canada, mais dans tous les pays du monde son nom est familier, et toutes les sociétés scientifiques l'ont proclamé le Capt. Bernier l'homme le plus capable et le plus compétent pour ce voyage.

On demande avec instance que les souscriptions, nécessaires soient fournies sous le plus court délai possible. Vous êtes prié de souscrire à l'instant, et votre contribution sera acceptée avec appréciation. Les souscriptions seront immédiatement déposées à la Banque de Montreal, Ottawa, toute somme sera dûment accusée, et le nom du souscripteur sera enrégistré dans le régistre officiel de l'entreprise. Les souscriptions peuvent être adressées à tous les Banques ou Journaux dans le Canada, ou envoyée directement par la malle au "Comité de l' Expédition Polaire," 117 Rue Bank, Ottawa.

Des arrangements peuvent être faits pour une lecture illustrative sur le voyage du Capitaine Bernier au Pôle Nord, en communiquant avec le bureau central de l' expédition

Circular used for the subscription campaign for Bernier's polar expedition. [J.E.Bernier Fonds, LAC, dossier No. 38]

belonging to this vast country that was trying to emerge from the shadow of the British Empire:

> The first individual who can claim the honour of having discovered and explored the North Pole and the circumpolar regions will also be able to make a gift of them to his country, whether he be Norwegian, American or Canadian, by hoisting his national flag there. At one swoop he will give his country control of fisheries, hunting, mineral resources and habitable lands in the arctic zone. This country will be able to register all of these to its credit [...] the important thing is to take possession of them.
>
> Is Canada, adjacent to the Pole as she is, to allow the possession of these immense regions to be taken from her, no matter that they are glacial, and no matter that they may appear disinherited?
>
> When, for many years now, many nations have been agitating about extending their spheres of action and influence towards the Pole, is Canada, that is in the process of taking a significant place among the nations of the world, to remain inactive and impassive faced by this trend? Even occupied as she is with domestic affairs should she not also look beyond her borders and work at pushing them back as far as the Pole?[4]

In the meantime the indomitable captain criss-crossed the country giving lectures to interested groups. He travelled so often between Toronto, Ottawa, Montréal, Sorel, Trois-Rivières and Québec that he had no scruples about asking for free tickets from the Canadian Pacific Railways. After all, wasn't he working gratis for his country? The railway company saw things differently! This refusal did not put the brakes on his efforts aimed at the Montreal Board of Trade, the Ontario Legislative Assembly, Queen's College in Toronto, the Knights of Columbus, the Hamilton Astronomical Society, the Toronto Engineers' Club... Between two lectures he took the time to inform Laurier of the progress of his subscription campaign, while trying to drag a formal contract out of him.

Then it was the turn of his "executive commissioner" J.-X. Perrault to present the matter strongly to the Prime Minister:

> The entire world will know that we have retained the vigour, the endurance and the virility of the first discoverers, that our soil and our climate can still produce this vigorous race that knows no obstacles [...]; we will have won a world-wide reputation for physical vigour; we will be the first nation in the world [...].[5]

Seven days later Laurier sent Perrault his reply.

I've always believed that it would be almost impossible to induce the public to subscribe the amount necessary for the success of this enterprise [...]

Do not forget, however, that an expedition, that of Peary, left three years ago. If he succeeds our project will no longer be of any value; if he does not succeed, there will be little hope that Bernier can succeed.[6]

This speaks volumes about Laurier's indifference with regard to the conquest of the North Pole. But Joseph-Elzéar refused to be discouraged by the hesitant reaction of the man who could destroy or advance his dream with a single wave of his wand.

He had a persistence that refused to recognize defeat, a determination that dissipated discouragement when it was offered to him.[7]

On 25 November 1901 he informed Lord Minto that he was returning to Great Britain to interest the British in his project and to raise funds. For two months he knocked on every important door in London... those of the Astors, Chamberlain, Pearson, Lipton, Furness, Wills, Gordon, Edwards, and Mount Stephen.

The emotive response on both sides of the Atlantic was intense and there were numerous promises to contribute. Despite this the subscriptions were slow to accumulate in the coffers of the organizing committee. By the spring of 1902 the campaign had brought in only $20,000.

Nonetheless Bernier waged the most vigorous one-man campaign ever witnessed in Ottawa. He continued to address audiences of non-government people: business men, factory workers, housewives [...] He sought out individual members of Parliament, invading their offices, their clubs, even their homes.[8]

It was impossible to ignore Bernier. Through his relentlessness the captain obtained the signatures of 113 members of Parliament on a petition[9] asking the Government to grant him the funds necessary to put his plan into effect. This new demonstration of support, he believed, ought to stimulate his subscription campaign, especially since the governments of Ontario and Québec

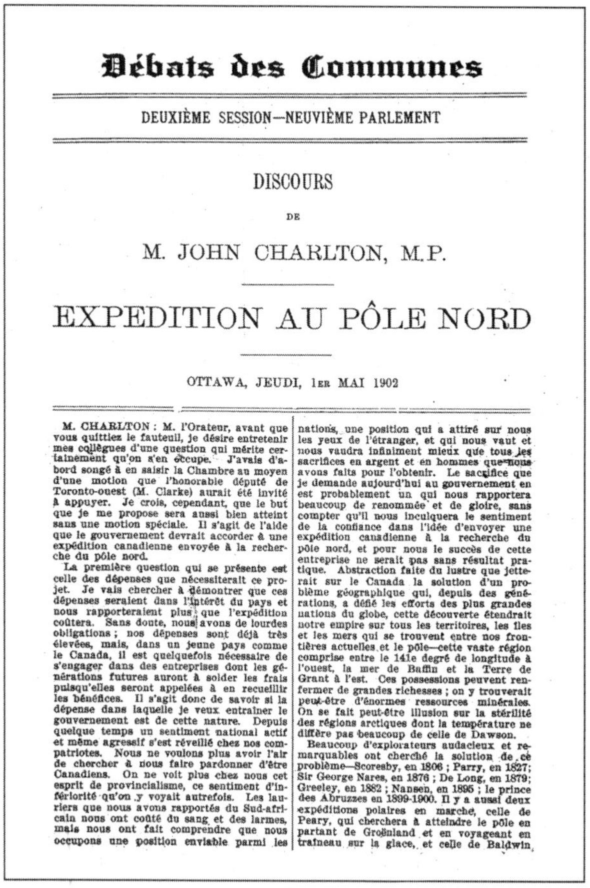

Débats des Communes

DEUXIÈME SESSION—NEUVIÈME PARLEMENT

DISCOURS

DE

M. JOHN CHARLTON, M.P.

EXPEDITION AU PÔLE NORD

OTTAWA, JEUDI, 1ER MAI 1902

M. CHARLTON : M. l'Orateur, avant que vous quittiez le fauteuil, je désire entretenir mes collègues d'une question qui mérite certainement qu'on s'en occupe. J'avais d'abord songé à en saisir la Chambre au moyen d'une motion que l'honorable député de Toronto-ouest (M. Clarke) aurait été invité à appuyer. Je crois, cependant, que le but que je me propose sera aussi bien atteint sans une motion spéciale. Il s'agit de l'aide que le gouvernement devrait accorder à une expédition canadienne envoyée à la recherche du pôle nord.

La première question qui se présente est celle des dépenses que nécessiterait ce projet. Je vais chercher à démontrer que ces dépenses seraient dans l'intérêt du pays et nous rapporteraient plus que l'expédition coûtera. Sans doute, nous avons de lourdes obligations ; nos dépenses sont déjà très élevées, mais, dans un jeune pays comme le Canada, il est quelquefois nécessaire de s'engager dans des entreprises dont les générations futures auront à solder les frais puisqu'elles seront appelées à en recueillir les bénéfices. Il s'agit donc de savoir si la dépense dans laquelle je veux entrainer le gouvernement est de cette nature. Depuis quelque temps un sentiment national actif et même agressif s'est réveillé chez nos compatriotes. Nous ne voulons plus avoir l'air de chercher à nous faire pardonner d'être Canadiens. On ne voit plus chez nous cet esprit de provincialisme, ce sentiment d'infériorité qu'on y voyait autrefois. Les lauriers que nous avons rapportés du Sud-africain nous ont coûté du sang et des larmes, mais nous ont fait comprendre que nous occupons une position enviable parmi les nations, une position qui a attiré sur nous les yeux de l'étranger, et qui nous vaut et nous vaudra infiniment mieux que tous les sacrifices en argent et en hommes que nous avons faits pour l'obtenir. Le sacrifice que je demande aujourd'hui au gouvernement en est probablement un qui nous rapportera beaucoup de renommée et de gloire, sans compter qu'il nous inculquera le sentiment de la confiance dans l'idée d'envoyer une expédition canadienne à la recherche du pôle nord, et pour nous le succès de cette entreprise ne serait pas sans résultat pratique. Abstraction faite du lustre que jetterait sur le Canada la solution d'un problème géographique qui, depuis des générations, a défié les efforts des plus grandes nations du globe, cette découverte étendrait notre empire sur tous les territoires, les îles et les mers qui se trouvent entre nos frontières actuelles et le pôle—cette vaste région comprise entre le 141e degré de longitude à l'ouest, la mer de Baffin et la Terre de Grant à l'est. Ces possessions peuvent renfermer de grandes richesses ; on y trouverait peut-être d'énormes ressources minérales. On se fait peut-être illusion sur la stérilité des régions arctiques dont la température ne diffère pas beaucoup de celle de Dawson.

Beaucoup d'explorateurs audacieux et remarquables ont cherché la solution de ce problème—Scoresby, en 1806 ; Parry, en 1827; Sir George Nares, en 1876 ; De Long, en 1879; Greeley, en 1882 ; Nansen, en 1895 ; le prince des Abruzzes en 1899-1900. Il y a aussi deux expéditions polaires en marche, celle de Peary, qui cherchera à atteindre le pôle en partant de Groënland et en voyageant en traîneau sur la glace, et celle de Baldwin,

Speech by Liberal Member from Ontario, John Charlton, during debate in the House of Commons on 1 May 1902, to persuade the Government to vote the funds required for the Canadian polar expedition. [Courtesy of Rosaire Saint-Pierre]

were waiting only for a gesture from Laurier to confirm their financial contributions.

It was inevitable that at some point the question of the polar expedition would resurface in the House of Commons. Captain Bernier's spokesperson declared:

[...] We have recently awakened to the possibility of having an active and aggressive national life in Canada. We no longer feel like apologizing for being Canadians [...].

> I wish now to state that we have among Canadian navigators a nautical man, whose experience, whose courage, whose length of service in seafaring life, and whose knowledge of all the conditions pertaining to Arctic exploration, probably render him better fitted than any other man in this country, and as well fitted as any in the world, to take command of an expedition and attempt to reach the North Pole. I refer to Captain Bernier, who belongs to the race of La Salle, which has penetrated to the heart of the continent, and who has the courage to undertake to penetrate to the North Pole, and will do it if the government will afford him the means. Captain Bernier is 50 years old. If the government had done their duty and sent him at the time they should have, he would have started on his trip at 48 years of age […].
>
> It would be an expedition undertaken and joined in by both races and it would be an advertisement to the world and more than this it would be an incentive to aspiration, to great achievements, to high resolves, to self-reliance and to development in national character that would be worth infinitely more than it would cost.
>
> I urge, Mr. Speaker, upon the government the advisability of giving the money to place this expedition on foot, to draw the attention of the world to the fact that Canada has sent a polar expedition with the good hope that in due time Canada's effort will be crowned by success and that Capt. Bernier will reach the pole.[10]

TORONTO, FRIDAY, JULY 10, 1903—TWELVE PAGES
WANTED
RECRUITS FOR CAPTAIN BERNIER'S EXPEDITION TO THE NORTH POLE
A HOT WEATHER SUGGESTION FOR CAPTAIN BERNIER.

Cartoon in the *Globe*, suggesting that Torontonians should sign up for Bernier's expedition in order to combat the problem of the hot weather. Clearly the volunteers did not take much persuasion. [Courtesy Season Osborne]

The Prime Minister was obliged to recognize the strength of the national sentiment that was involved:

> If a son of Canada were to plant his country's flag at the North Pole, if he were to accomplish what so many brave men have tried in vain to accomplish, there is not a single Canadian heart that would not beat with pride. Canada would be more than happy to achieve such glory.

Laurier was able to give way briefly to lyricism in fulsomely praising Bernier's talents since that did not commit him to anything. But he was worried about what federal participation would cost: "I was not expecting that we would be asked for $100,000." He wanted more time to evaluate the practical aspects of the enterprise before formally committing his government.

Laurier remained cautious. This nationalist fervour that was becoming inseparable from the Bernier expedition, preoccupied him. It could only provoke political disorder.

CHAPTER 5

Arctic boundaries for Canada

> What we consider to be "the" original feature of Canada's arctic borders [...] is closely linked to the person of Captain Joseph-Elzéar Bernier.[1]

How can this be?

Bernier's project became so well known in Europe and in America that it focused the gaze of other nations on the Canadian government. Was it going to participate in the race for the North Pole, yes or no? The longer it delayed in declaring itself, the more the captain gained in popular support and the more Laurier risked being ridiculed and criticized. Within the country the idea of a Canadian expedition led by the dynamic Bernier succeeded in stirring up interest in the public-at-large in these territories—forgotten, icy, uninhabited, yet filled with natural resources and, in the same vein, it gave rise to a totally new national pride, and a very strong pan-Canadian movement that included the North Pole within the territories delimited by Canada's arctic boundaries.

In reality nothing was very clear as to this entire question of the arctic borders and it deserves to be examined.

By an Order in Council of 23 June 1870 Great Britain had formally transferred to the Dominion of Canada all its possessions designated as "Rupert's Land and the North-Western Territory."[2] The arctic islands were included in this transfer by a second Order in Council of Her Majesty, Queen Victoria's Imperial Government on 31 July 1880. The vast archipelago, covering some 550,000 square miles, located north of the Canadian continental mainland up to some point near the Pole took the name of the "Northwest Territories." The event

Photograph that Captain Bernier used to promote his polar project. He was then 50 years old. In 1901 a journalist with the *Toronto Daily Star* wrote that Bernier's eyes were such a piercing blue that he could read one in a few seconds. [Archives of Carol and Louis Terrien]

The Dominion of Canada at the time of Confederation in 1867.

passed unnoticed, or nearly so, on both sides of the Atlantic, and for a number of years Canada did not appear to be very aware of the boundaries of its "northern empire," nor ready to assume responsibility for it. In reality nobody at the time could attest to the extent of these lands and islands, nor define precisely their boundaries, nor even identify the actual title that Great Britain had to these polar regions. This explains why the Imperial decree that formalized the 1880 transfer, was formulated in somewhat innocuous terms:

> From and after the first day of September 1880, all British Territories and Possessions in North America, not already included within the Dominion of Canada, and all Islands adjacent to any such Territories or Possessions, shall (with the exception of the Colony of Newfoundland and its dependencies) become and be annexed to and form part of the said Dominion of Canada; and become and be subject to the laws for the time being in force in the said Dominion, in so far as such laws may be applied thereto.[3]

One could not be less precise about nameless, unknown territories without boundaries.

The uncertainty of the British authorities as to the validity of Great Britain's title to ownership[4] is clearly revealed in the correspondence of the Colonial Office. Not only could they not delimit the boundaries of the territories that were transferred, but they revealed themselves to be in a hurry to rid themselves of their possessions and rights in the region in order to prevent the Americans from moving in:

> The object of annexing these unexplored territories to Canada is, I apprehend, to prevent the U.S. from claiming

CANADA -- 1898

The political components of Canada in 1898.

them, and not from the likelihood of their proving of any value to Canada.[5]

Thus it was presumed that the United States would protest less against Canadian ownership as against that of the British, and it was claimed that it would be easier to oversee these vast ice fields from offices in Ottawa than from those in London.

Until then only explorers, fur traders, missionaries, and whalers had dared to penetrate into these vaguely defined regions, inhabited only by a very small population of semi-nomadic Inuit, and only the Hudson's Bay Company[6] had established fur trade posts and a form of administration there.

The vagueness of the Act of Transfer of 1880 as well as the lack of interest on the part of Canada did not help to change anything as regards the status of "no man's land" of the polar region. Certainly the Canadian government had dispatched a few expeditions to study the ice in Hudson Strait[7] and in 1895 had divided the immense Northwest Territories into four provisional districts: Mackenzie, Yukon, Ungava, and Franklin.[8] But the fact remained that the absence of any permanent Canadian presence in the region meant, in the eyes of the international community, that everyone had freedom of access and freedom of action in the Arctic Archipelago.

One can better understand Laurier's ambiguous and hesitant attitude; he preferred "letting sleeping dogs lie:" the *status quo* rather than a public debate, controversy, and international tensions. Furthermore hadn't he shown his colours as new leader of the Liberal Party in 1887:

> The time has come to abandon the policy of revenge, and to show the American people that we are brothers and to stretch out a hand to them, but without losing sight of the consideration due to our mother country.[9]

Laurier was, above all, a conciliator, who believed that the best path was that of prudence and that compromise was the key to the peaceful evolution of his country. As a statesman he had grasped that Canada was only a very small under-populated country that lived in the shadow of the United States and that her future depended on her partnership with the British Empire. This is how this realist politician would retain power for 15 years, by cultivating ambiguity.

In any case the question of the North did not merit the Prime Minister's attention. First of all, the entire south of the country had to be developed and he was counting on achieving this through immigration. Immigration would ensure the profitability of the railway; it would people the vast spaces of the West; it would produce the wheat that the hungry world wanted; and it would provide an important consumer market for Canadian industry. His efforts in support of immigration were considerable. Between 1896, the year that Laurier took power, and 1911, the year his party was overthrown, more than a million immigrants from all countries of origin settled on the Prairies.

Laurier was an authoritarian accustomed to encountering submissive men prepared to bow to his decisions. Of course Captain Bernier was not a submissive person since he had been master of his ships and crews from the age of 17. This sailor, born under the sign of Capricorn, was just as ambitious and realistic as the leader of his country. His strength of character and his discipline were as well-known as his physical capacities and when he committed himself to an enterprise, it was always with a view to succeeding. The Prime Minister was perhaps more educated, more refined and charming in terms of manners and speech, but he had neither the robustness nor the endurance of this natural phenomenon who had always been accustomed to facing the worst of bad weather. Both men were dominant, determined beings, who knew how to put their plans of action into execution. One had the political power, while the other had the support of the public.

The more Wilfrid Laurier equivocated, the more Bernier insisted. The more talk there was of the polar project that was inflaming all sorts of passions, the more the Prime Minister feared that:

> the publicity resulting from such a discovery might precipitate a new Canadian/American or international conflict over the ownership of the arctic territories at this point. Fearing this possibility and, on the other hand, not wishing to shock the voters who favoured the polar project, Laurier found that his best defence against the adventure proposed by Bernier lay in silence and temporization.[10]

Laurier was no dupe. The indefinite status of the Northwest Territories, at a time when the United States was in full flight and the British Empire was starting to become exhausted, could only usher in years of uncertainty for the country. To counter American expansionism and the claims of other nations on Canada's northern boundaries, his government had to impose its authority over the arctic archipelago.

It is difficult to pinpoint when the Prime Minister conceived the idea of substituting the project of conquering the Pole for the administrative organization of Canada's northern regions. On 1 May 1903, when Captain Bernier got wind of the government's decision to allot $75,000 for an expeditionary project, everything seemed cut and dried. And a few months later the civil servant A.P. Low and his party were already on their way north to the archipelago on board the steamer *Neptune*.

Speaking to his fellow parliamentarians in the House of Commons on 30 September 1903, the Minister of Marine and Fisheries, Raymond Préfontaine justified the decision of his government thus: "We have just dispatched an expedition to northern Hudson Bay. And why? Simply to organize the territory, to protect our interests there and to preserve it for Canada."

The *Neptune* expedition consisted of A.P. Low, of the Geological Survey of Canada, Captain S.W. Bartlett, and Major J.D. Moodie of the Northwest Mounted Police, five policemen, a crew of 25 sailors, and five scientists; its mission was "to patrol the waters of Hudson Bay and those adjacent to the eastern Arctic islands; also to aid in the establishment, on the adjoining shores, of permanent stations for the collection of customs, the administration of justice and the enforcement of the law as in other parts of the Dominion."[11]

In October of the same year the question of the Alaskan border appeared to confirm Laurier's fears vis-à-vis the Americans. The new President of the United States who had replaced President William McKinley, assassinated in 1901, the impetuous Theodore Roosevelt (1858-1919), pursued an authoritarian and violent foreign policy. He envisaged imposing his government's claims unilaterally and, if necessary, enforcing them militarily.

Fearing retaliation and reckoning that Canada would emerge the loser, Britain's Prime Minister, Lord Salisbury, and Canada's Prime Minister, Sir Wilfrid Laurier, yielded to the tactics and bad faith of the Americans and accepted their claims with regard to the boundary with Alaska.[12]

Following this incident many Canadians, like Laurier, wanted a stronger Canada that would assert herself more with respect to Britain and the rest of the world. His desire for political autonomy would lead the Liberal government to underscore its presence in the arctic archipelago and to introduce its administrative authority there.

From his room in the Windsor Hotel the imperturbable Bernier was still biding his time. It is claimed that he was thinking seriously of accepting the offer of the explorer Jean Charcot (1867-1936) to work for France, as well as proposals by American merchants who wanted to finance his project. This is highly likely. However, the announcement of the bitter defeat of the Canadian representatives at the Alaskan boundary tribunal, which raised strong anti-American feelings, gave him the spring-board he needed to relaunch his campaign in support of his project and to set aside solicitations from other countries. He could argue that if he planted the Canadian flag at the North Pole that would affirm, in the eyes of everyone, Canada's claims to the arctic archipelago. Moreover he was convinced that the geographical situation, alone, gave his country the right to extend her boundaries to the North Pole. And he would repeat endlessly the same key statements: "Why let ourselves be outwitted? I can succeed in this race for the Pole as well as anyone! In the near future the North will become a strategic point for Canada. Why wait for other nations to plant their flag there?"

On 4 December 1903 the following appeared in the Trois-Rivières newspaper the *Trifluvien*

> I have not abandoned my plans for seeking the Pole [...]. The statements to that effect are false. Why would I abandon them when I have the promise of $47,000 towards the expenses of the expedition. I am lacking no more than $13,000 to be able to obtain a government subsidy. It is up to Canada to help me and to prevent me from dying of despair!

CHAPTER 6

The *Gauss* affair

By the end of 1903 Joseph-Elzéar Bernier had devoted more than five years to promotion of his polar project, without attaining a satisfactory result. Aware that he was getting older he arranged for two eminent doctors[1] to assess his physical condition.

The captain was built like a bear: "weight 203 lbs; height 5' 4 ¼"; circumference of abdomen: 41 ½"; circumference of chest: 43 ¾" (inspiration); 40 ½" (expiration)."

Dr. Quinlan confirmed that he was in excellent health and that, barring a serious accident or an infectious disease, his patient might live for another 15 years and could survive an expedition lasting five years.

Since he was no longer often at home and since he might expect to set off on his great adventure at any time, Joseph-Elzéar sold the Villa Bernier to his friend George Davie on 21 August 1903, and stored his personal belongings with his adopted daughter on Rue Saint-Joseph, Lauzon. His wife, Rose, who did not always accompany him on his numerous moves, also stayed with Mina and Odilon Bourget to help take care of their four children.

The man who anticipated succeeding in the race for the Pole and who was floating on the electrifying current of his *idée fixe* must have felt very far from the daily preoccupations of family. A brief letter from "your little niece till death, Rosalie of L'Islet," informing him of her imminent marriage,[2] reveals that nonetheless he maintained affectionate ties with his family:

> Little Rosalie, who used to like to please you so much [...]. I could not let this critical moment in my life pass by without acquainting you with it, you who are so good and generous [...] I am going to stay very close to Elmina. This will help me to pass the time.

These family contacts must have been rather rare during these years when he was concentrating all his energies on promoting and realizing his polar dream.

Captain Bernier did not manage to pierce Prime Minister Laurier's armour but what is certain is that, over time, his continuous efforts brought some benefits.

> The funding campaign for his polar project had allowed Bernier to acquire in Canada the reputation of the man of the Far North. At that time he was the only Canadian to reveal publicly his plans for exploring the Arctic. Yet, whereas before 1904 he was a captain in great demand for intercontinental voyages, Bernier had still not sailed the waters of the arctic archipelago. Be that as it may, in the mind of the Canadian public and in his own mind, Bernier represented the frontier explorer, the man who would bring the country the political and cultural satisfaction that was so keenly desired.[3]

This reputation as the "man of the Far North" would stick with him. Every question concerning the Arctic as well as the publicity surrounding every Canadian expedition to the Arctic revolved around him, to the great chagrin of the politicians: "The Canadian government was eclipsed by the public figure of Captain

Bernier who, in the people's eyes, symbolized Canada's occupation of the Arctic."[4]

Without knowing it, Joseph-Elzéar Bernier had already won the wager since, even before setting off to reach the Pole, he had assured himself a place in the history books by awakening Canadian awareness as to northern realities. Henceforth Bernier's name became synonymous with the arctic boundaries of his country.

At the beginning of 1904 the preoccupations of this man of action were quite different. He was determined to carry out his project before he was too old. Hence, on 28 February he gave an important lecture to several Federal ministers and the members of the Canadian Institute in Ottawa. Unfortunately for him, the man who pulled the strings of political authority was not in the auditorium.

Laurier would have preferred to continue ignoring this entire polar question, but the political stakes were pressing him to act.

> The discoveries, the acts of taking possession, and successive British and Canadian expeditions within the arctic territories that the Canadian government had acquired by the transfer of 1880 conferred on it sovereignty-in-the-making. Even although no other nation had acquired similar rights to the Arctic by means of official acts of occupation, for the moment Canada had to continue to occupy the arctic archipelago effectively in order to insure her sovereignty. Albert Peter Low's expedition in 1903-4 was crucial but not absolutely decisive. The Laurier government found itself faced with a programme of regular expeditions across the entire archipelago.[5]

Bernier was ready-to-hand to undertake this enterprise and his expertise was undeniable. The time had finally come therefore, for this dynamic man in his early fifties!

Without informing him as to his government's true intentions, Raymond Préfontaine, Minister of Marine and Fisheries, who had administrative responsibility for all expeditions to the Arctic, asked Captain Bernier to choose a ship that would be suitable for navigation in ice.

The Berniers and Elmina Caron at the end of 1905, a year after the death of Dr. Joseph-Odilon Bourget. The Bourget children are, from left to right: Marie-Reine, Marie-Albert, Marie-Jeanne and Marie-Marthe. [Suzanne Audet and André Normandeau Collection]

"Rather than choosing a faster ship like the *Neptune*, a Newfoundland whaler, which the owners wanted to sell to the Department of Marine and Fisheries, Bernier finally decided on a sturdier ship [...]."[6] The ship in question was the *Gauss* a three-masted barquentine, built in the Howaldt yards in Kiel in 1900-01.[7]

This vessel, built of oak and pitchpine, had wintered in the Antarctic over the previous two years and was considered to be one of the best polar ships of the time, comparable to a larger version of Nansen's *Fram,* with a length of 165.4 feet and a beam of 37.2 feet.

> She [...] was fully square rigged on the foremast, and had an economical triple expansion engine which could push her sturdy double-ended hull at seven knots. She even had a steam driven generator which was something of an innovation in such a ship.[8]

On 9 April the Deputy Minister of Marine confirmed Benier's mission in preparation for a "Northern Expedition."

The *Gauss* on her arrival at Québec, summer 1904. It is said that the reason that the Germans sold her to the Canadians was that the scientific expedition to the Antarctic in which she participated was not a great success. [Bernier Collection, Department of Indian and Northern Affairs, LAC, PA-118134]

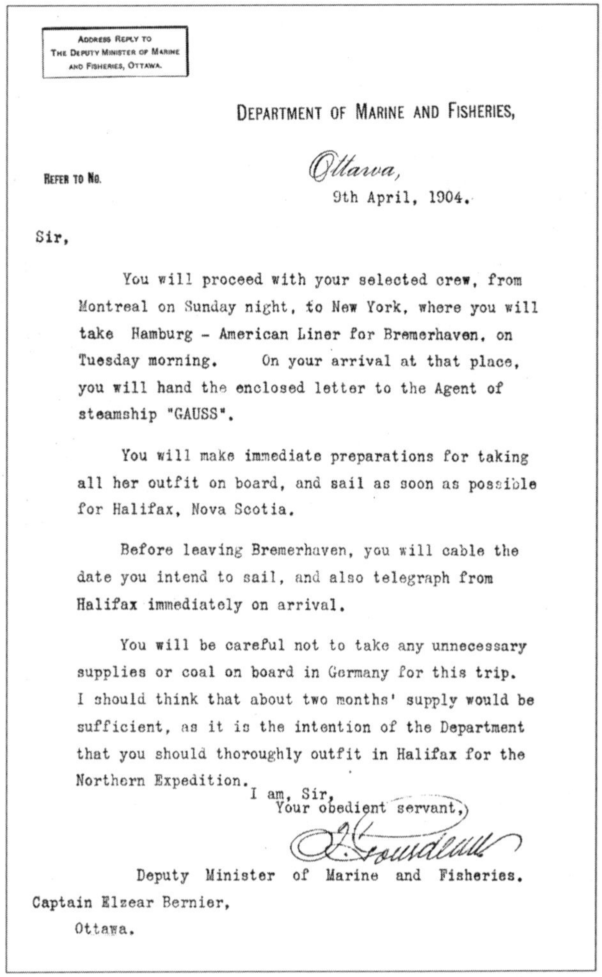

ADDRESS REPLY TO
THE DEPUTY MINISTER OF MARINE
AND FISHERIES, OTTAWA.

DEPARTMENT OF MARINE AND FISHERIES,

REFER TO NO.

Ottawa,
9th April, 1904.

Sir,

You will proceed with your selected crew, from Montreal on Sunday night, to New York, where you will take Hamburg - American Liner for Bremerhaven, on Tuesday morning. On your arrival at that place, you will hand the enclosed letter to the Agent of steamship "GAUSS".

You will make immediate preparations for taking all her outfit on board, and sail as soon as possible for Halifax, Nova Scotia.

Before leaving Bremerhaven, you will cable the date you intend to sail, and also telegraph from Halifax immediately on arrival.

You will be careful not to take any unnecessary supplies or coal on board in Germany for this trip. I should think that about two months' supply would be sufficient, as it is the intention of the Department that you should thoroughly outfit in Halifax for the Northern Expedition.

I am, Sir,
Your obedient servant,
F. Gourdeau
Deputy Minister of Marine and Fisheries.

Captain Elzear Bernier,
Ottawa.

Instructions from the Deputy Minister of Marine and Fisheries to Captain Bernier concerning the *Gauss*. On the same day Colonel Gourdeau sent him a cheque for $4000 "being an advance to defray the expenses incurred by you in taking the crew to Bremerhaven, outfitting, and bringing to Canada the steamer *Gauss* lately purchased from the German Government." He recommended that he keep all his receipts since on his return he would be called upon to submit a detailed record of his expenses. [Benoît Robitaille Fonds, ANQ]

Bernier did not set off alone for the major fishing port of Bremerhaven, located 61 kilometres north of Bremen. He was accompanied by his crew of 30 men, those he had chosen or who had been imposed upon him, to experience the first stage of this polar adventure that was the dream of young men throughout the world. Evidence of this interest abounds. Many were sons of good families who wanted to follow the man of the Far North. Those who were beyond the age for dangerous challenges would take the initiative and recommend one of their own family:

> Just a line to offer one of my grand-nephews, grandson of my deceased brother Charles; his name is Octave Jules Morin.
>
> He has been sailing with me almost constantly for seven years, i.e. for seven seasons. He wanted to learn about sailing foreign. He is a good helmsman. He can readily serve as your "wheelman", and it is in that position that he wants to go with you.
>
> He has a coastwise mate's certificate, but has never served on board a steamer. He has a sharp grasp of all kinds of things.[9]

Octave-Jules Morin was on the voyage to Germany, early in April 1904, along with the other members of the crew.

J.-E. Bernier, Captain
Zéphirin Caron, First Officer
René Pelletier, Second Officer
F.V. Moffet, Captain's Secretary
Reverend Labelle, Priest
John Van Koënig, Chief Mechanic
Septime Laferrière, Head Gunner
Bâetke, Chief Engineer
Adolf Gobbard, Engineer
K. Carruthers, Electrician
Charles Savage, Chief Steward
J.-Arthur Boucher, Assistant Steward
Émile Mackenzie, Stoker
J.-A Ladébauche
Michel Fortin
Ernest Caron
Joseph Vigneault
C.-R. Mongin
Désiré Morin
L.-J. Papineau
Joseph Duquet
Ludger L'Heureux
Alex Simard
Adolf S. Lyzzell
Octave Bélanger
Alphone Demers
Gaston Chaput
W. Lameke
Friedrick Marx

We'll let young Arthur Boucher recount part of this voyage.[10]

The departure

> *April 9, 1904, Saturday*
> Supper at the Mountain Hill Hotel in Québec with my friend and companion for the voyage, Ernest Caron of L'Islet, and at 11 p.m. we leave for Montréal en route to Germany where we are going to pick up the SS *Gauss*, under the command of Captain J. Elzéar Bernier, John Koënig, René Pelletier, and several others from L'Islet.
>
> *April 10, Sunday*
> Reached Montréal at 8. Breakfast at the Hotel Meunier, and then I went to O. Caron's place with Ernest and I had lunch with my brother Norbert at the Collège St.-Henri where he is a teacher, and spent part of the afternoon with him. At 4 p.m. met the Captain to see about our baggage. Supper at the Hotel Lalonde. Left for New York at 7.45 on the Delaware-Hudson Railroad express.
>
> *April 11, Monday*
> Changed trains at Albany and all had coffee together between trains. Reached New York at 10.50 and crossed to Hoboken N.J. Lunched at the Mayers Hotel at 11.50, and in the afternoon I wrote postcards to my parents and friends. Had supper at this hotel and went to bed after having had quite a good time.
>
> *April 12, Tuesday*
> After breakfast went aboard the *Kaiser Wilhelm II* at 10 o'clock, bound for Bremerhaven, Germany. Sailed from Hoboken at 1.30 p.m. in fine weather. Dropped the pilot at 3 at Sandy Hook, and passed a steamer that later sank in a collision. Finally en route to Germany aboard a ship steaming at 23 knots—not a bad speed.

The voyage out

April 14, Thursday
Really foul. Fog, rain, and strong southeast wind; the deck awash [...] Distance run in last 24 hours, 525 miles.

April 15, Friday
Fine clear weather, wind SE. Received a visit from our officers [...] Spent a good day and stayed up until midnight raising hell, Johnny, Ernest, and I.

April 16, Saturday
[...] Threw a bottle into the sea with our names and addresses inside.

April 17, Sunday
A French priest, M. Labelle, has come with us; we're going to say our rosaries. Fair weather, but there is a strong wind blowing. We are writing home [...]. In the afternoon the *Kaiser*'s steward took three photos of *Gauss*'s crew [...]. I bought three, one of each.

Met three sailing vessels. Tour of the *Kaiser.* Went to bed early. Johnny bunks aft. In a word all goes well.

April 18, Monday
Strong wind and very cold. Impossible to go on deck [...] Reached Cherbourg at 7.30. We can't see very much; it is starting to get dark, but we certainly saw the English coast. It looks very beautiful; the grass is green. To get back to Cherbourg, I assure you that it is a very well guarded sea-port; a very narrow entrance and breakwaters all equipped with the latest guns. I'm sorry that it was not daytime; we could have seen things better, but we were in a port in the Mother Country. A *Canadien* who has any blood in his veins feels moved while thinking about this as one should.

April 19, Tuesday
Towards evening we had a lot of fun. At 6 o'clock, arrived about a dozen miles from Bremerhaven and anchored to wait for high tide, and the 1st and 2nd class passengers disembarked in two tugs but we immigrants remained on board [...]. We stayed on board again tonight, but didn't sleep; we fooled around all night.

The arrival

April 20, Wednesday
Got up at 4 but did not disembark until 9 o'clock. We were like real immigrants ... sad times for those unfortunate travellers. Had breakfast and lunch together at the steamer company's hotel. Since lunch was paid for by the government we decided to have claret and beer; but ultimately we had to pay out of our own pockets, and since some of us had no money it was quite a laugh; ah well, what can you do. When travelling one has to take these incidents as they come.

At 3 o'clock we went aboard the SS *Gauss* and began working right away, then got ready for supper.

April 21, Thursday
We are at Bremerhaven, cleaning and rigging the *Gauss.*

April 22, Friday
Same routine work. Our Montréal seamen are already tired and we haven't even put to sea yet; their problems are only just starting.

April 24, Sunday
The sea is the prettiest thing I have found here. The promenade along the sea shore, where the sea runs up onto an even slope of stones set in cement, and extending down to a certain depth of water; it is ideal. And this beautiful river, immensely long, with a scattering of beautiful islands. I was with Ernest Caron and Michel Fortin and we walked around the town, smoking like "sports." I didn't have time to be bored at all.

April 26, Tuesday
Always get to work at about the same time and we are doing the same work, while waiting to get ready to put to sea. We don't know when we'll be leaving. The crew is working on deck, rigging the ship, but the weather isn't the greatest for them; it hails for half an hour and then five minutes later the sun is really hot. Smoked a cigar and to bed at 10.

April 27, Wednesday
Nothing really important around here today, but up on deck not one of the "Able Seamen" from Montréal is

capable of going aloft, but the lads from L'Islet distinguish themselves at this.

Went to bed early. Goodnight.

April 30, Saturday
Foggy weather; various work. This evening the Captain gave a lecture on his plans for the trip to the North Pole. Many people. I went with Ernest Caron and Michel Fortin.

May 1, Sunday
I went to Mass at 7 o'clock with Z. Caron for the second and last time in Bremerhaven. I've noticed that the people are extraordinarily devoted; and this method of taking up the collection with this big "what's it" with a little bag at the end with a little bell in the bottom.

May 3, Tuesday
Fine, hot weather. Around 4 in the afternoon the Captain received some bigwigs from on shore, including the British Consul and his lady, and a dozen others for a big TEA. The steward and I prepared it as best we could but we had nothing, not even a table-cloth or serviettes, but despite everything we succeeded in producing something that was presentable.

May 5, Thursday
Today I am 25 years old. Hence, for the first time I would much rather have been at L'Islet, i.e. back home, to at least shake hands with those who brought me into this world, but this is impossible; the distance separating us just won't allow it. I'll just have to imagine it, that's all. After supper went ashore and bought a nice small watch (pocket watch) as a souvenir of my 25th birthday in Germany. I paid 27 marks or $6.75 for it.

May 6, Friday
Still the same weather, and it is hard to know what to do. We are to sail at any moment; finally it was put back until evening, but we still haven't left. We'll leave tomorrow, I suppose. Had a smoke and went to bed at 10.

Homeward, 7 to 24 May

May 7, Saturday
Nothing decided until 3 p.m. when the Captain suddenly ordered the engineers to have steam up by 5 o'clock, and indeed we sailed for Québec at 5.20, and when we started he told us that we were bound for Halifax. I'm not at all upset to hear this news. Finally under way ... under steam, and we set sail a little after we put to sea. By midnight we'd covered 45 miles. Goodnight.

May 10, Tuesday
Running north along the Scottish coast; saw it quite clearly around 4.30 and were passing Edinburgh at 6.30. I notice that one encounters many small steamers throughout the North Sea.

May 12, Thursday
Ascension. Rolling in the morning. The wind picked up again during the day, with rain. I'm below, as every day; I have to get up at 5, to serve coffee to the Captain and the officer of the watch; at 8 breakfast; at noon lunch; and at 6 supper. There was no thought of celebrating, but all is well. Goodnight.

May 14, Saturday
Gale out of the northwest; heavy sea. Spent the day under reefed sails. Making 4 knots. Some problem aloft. A piece of wood fell to the deck; by good luck it did not hit anyone.

May 15, Sunday
Today we celebrated Holy Mass, in our minds, for lack of anything else; something one must do. Below decks here still the same, but up on deck they spent the day manoeuvring in pouring rain all day long. Sunday at sea; but we are at sea only in body, because our minds are often back before Germany, each of us back home.

May 19, Thursday
Strong wind out of the southwest and seas from every direction; they had their hands full on deck today because of some problem in the rigging, which kept all hands on work on deck for 4 to 6 hours.

May 20, Friday
Fine, clear weather; very heavy sea, wind northwest swinging to west. I enjoy watching the sea. After supper, not feeling very well I went to bed early.

May 22, Sunday
Strong wind; almost gale-force out of the southwest, and a raging sea. Yesterday evening I went on deck to speak to M. Caron, First Officer; I can assure you that I amused myself for about 10 minutes watching how the ship was riding in this hellish sea. She is doing very well, but it has the shortcoming of all ships, it rolls like hell.

Last night from 10 to midnight 21/22 May I was convinced that I saw the *Gauss* taking water wholesale to leeward above the waterline; and all night long they were heaving like hell; they don't give a damn, the ship is good, but this morning they had to reduce sail and several of the sails were ripped.

This morning when I got up I found that the ship was rolling and pitching in an extraordinary fashion; it was no problem for me below here, but those poor devils on deck in the driving rain, and as black as pitch.

May 23, Monday
Wind from the northwest, not as strong as yesterday but the sea is very high, although it is dropping. *Gauss* is rolling gently as if she hadn't a care. All is well. I spent the evening on deck; it is good to enjoy the fresh air after spending the day below. Nothing important today. Goodnight.

Unfortunately the pages of the diary covering the rest of the crossing have disappeared.

The impressions of the second steward attain their full importance when one considers the turn of events at the end of the voyage.

The German ship entered Québec harbour at 3.30 a.m. on Monday 13 June without fanfare and without attracting the attention of the media since the *Canada* had sunk the day before not far from Sorel, having been struck broadside by the collier *Cap-Breton*. The headlines of the Canadian newspapers were devoted to the terrible disaster involving this imposing steamer of the Richelieu and Ontario Company, to the eight fatalities, and to the coroner's inquest. Only *L'Événement* of 13 June mentioned briefly "The arrival of the *Gauss* after a crossing of 27 days."

> Captain Bernier anchored his ship in the middle of the river, opposite the Quai du Roi. [...] It looks rather miserable out in the middle of the river. [...] As seen from the piers her appearance is quite untidy. [...] This ship can't be very fast, in that she took so long to make the crossing [...] If Captain Bernier is heading for the Pole in this vessel he'll need four or five years.

And then, the next day, the front page of *La Presse* of Montréal displayed the following headline, alongside the *Canada* tragedy: "The arrival of the ship, *Gauss*, occurred without fanfare but is giving rise to an outcry of protests." The article, which occupied two pages of five columns and included seven photos, was so well structured and documented that it appeared evident that it had been composed well before the ship reached Québec. When one digs a little, it transpires that the person responsible was none other than the Chief gunner, Septime Laferrière, a journalist with *La Presse* signed on "under false colours" since the ship had no guns.

The root of the problem was that Captain Bernier had had his choice of his three officers and six or seven other professional seamen from L'Islet-sur-Mer, and that the rest of his crew had been foisted on him by the authorities at the Department of Marine. With the exception of the engineers and the German sailors there were two camps on board the *Gauss,* the lads from L'Islet and those from Montréal.[11]

According to *La Presse* several participants claimed to have been ill-treated during the voyage to Germany in third class:

> [...] the horrible conditions in the steerage on German ships is well known. It has been called "hell on the high seas" and this is accurate. We do not understand how the Department of Marine and Fisheries could have left cit-

izens in its employment in such a terrible position when, for a modest balance of $280, they could all have been accommodated in 2nd class.

We spent 8 long nights and 8 even longer days there, all crowded together in the most intimate contact with immigrants and individuals of every denomination, in the bottom of the ship's hold and in the most disgustingly dirty conditions.

The journalist accused the captain of being solely responsible for this terrible situation and especially that he and his offices were travelling first-class. According to him Bernier provided:

> [...] ample proofs of incompetence and lack of foresight in his command every day [...] that Captain Bernier's main thought, right from when he left Montreal, seems to have been his own vainglory and his personal interest in preparing for a voyage to the North Pole—rather than the full, entire and true interest of the Department of the Marine, namely the comfort and safety of the crew.

Sixteen seamen, some of them from L'Islet, signed an affidavit prepared by the Chief Steward, Charles Savage and addressed to Commodore Spain, in command of the Canadian government fleet. This document stated that:

1) Of four barrels of salt beef that were part of our provisions for the crossing from Germany to Canada, the contents of one were totally rotten; the contents of two others, due to their bad smell and taste, were not fit to be put on the table.

2 a) The brown sugar, lard and butter were, to my certain knowledge, of very inferior quality, although the latter was listed and labelled as being first quality butter.

b) One box had to be tossed overboard almost as soon as we had left Bremerhaven since its contents, namely 10 lbs. were terribly spoiled.

c) Several men complained that the lean part of the bacon was unusually tough.

d) The contents of some of the cans of preserved meat appeared to be old and the meat seemed very inferior.

e) Moreover, sugar and syrup ran out more than 10 days before we reached Québec.

3) For various reasons we had to throw large quantities of meat and other provisions overboard.

4) Obeying Captain Bernier's orders I had to force the crew to accept a diet of exclusively salt food from 9 April until 5 June.

5) In general the crew—officers and men—was fed in a manner that would be far from doing credit to the Canadian Department of Marine and Fisheries, if that Department were responsible for this state of affairs.

6) All transactions with regard to the provisioning of the *Gauss* were handled solely and personally by Captain Bernier.

Other Québec newspapers fell into step:

> One of *Gauss*'s stokers, M. Mackenzie, who lives at 15 Rue St-Elizabeth, came this morning to protest against the name "creek sailors" used by Captain Bernier with reference to members of the crew. [...] M. Mackenzie says that the entire crew, with the exception of seven men, were in a rush to resign on reaching Québec [...] The Chief Gunner, Septime Laferrière, was interviewed and made serious statements about the crossing and also against the ship's master, with regard to the manner in which he treated the crew. The Chief Gunner declared that the *Gauss* left Bremerhaven 26 days ago, and that for 19 days the *Gauss* was tossed like a cork by the waves and strong winds. This, no doubt, is due to the curved shape of the ship's hull, designed to help when she encounters ice.[12]

They began to cast doubt on the veracity of the accusations made by the journalist from *La Presse:*

> *La Presse* is at the bottom of this affair.
>
> One of its correspondents sailed with Captain Bernier. The latter has just stated that *La Presse*'s mouthpiece was on board in the capacity of gunner. Naturally there were no guns on board the *Gauss*.
>
> In an interview Captain Bernier said that the crew was imposed on him by political influences.
>
> The correspondent of *La Presse* made the voyage at the expense of the government. He appears not to have been too happy with the menu on board!
>
> Hence all the noise we have been hearing.[13]

LE CANARD
5
SAGE PRECAUTION
MINISTÈRE DE LA MARINE.
GAUSS
CAP BERNIER
— Va mon enfant, mais garde toi bien de rapporter le pole avec toi; nous avons assez d'hiver comme ça.

Cartoon from the newspaper *Le Canard.*

Captain Bernier had indeed agreed to make some comments to the journalist from *L'Événement.* He did not mention the fact that he had received only $4000 from the Canadian Government for the entire expense of crew-hiring and the cost of provisioning. He said that he would defend himself in front of relevant authorities at the right time and place.

> All that I can tell you, he added, is that the vast majority of the young fellows comprising my crew had never been to sea. And that a large number had never even seen the sea.
>
> It was by dint of importunities and by making the most of more-or-less valid qualifications that the majority of my crew managed to get hired, without my having the liberty to make my own choice. For these young people this was only a pleasure jaunt, a delightful free trip that would allow them, on their return to tell fabulous stories to their parents, friends and even to strangers.
>
> As regards work, I had to bring them to their senses. They were hired to work the ship, i.e. for hard work, and that obligation they found totally disenchanting.
>
> They claim to be of good family; this is possible, I do not contest it; but in that case they might have stayed at home rather than taking the place of good, experienced, disciplined seamen that I could have chosen and who, certainly, would not think of complaining on their return, aware that life on board the *Gauss* was no different from all the other crossings they had made previously, on whatever ship.
>
> The *Gauss* is not a pleasure vessel and her crossing from Germany was not a pleasure cruise.
>
> Life on board a sailing vessel especially, is rough, even for the sailors, and I imagine that these young fellows of good family, accustomed to the pleasant things of the paternal home, experienced a great disappointment to find themselves subjected to the tough toil of a seaman, whereas they had been dreaming of a tourist cruise, sheltered by an awning, or with a cigar between their lips, rocking in soft rocking chairs in the captain's cabin, enjoying a drink or an ice-cream depending on the occasion.
>
> [...] I will add only that when the matter is presented to the Minister the roles may have changed and that from being the accused I may become the accuser, complaining of a conspiracy against me, something that the facts will bear out.[14]

The *Gauss* affair proves one thing: Bernier was a man subject of controversy. He upset people.

> The purchase of this vessel stirred up numerous criticisms on the part of some fanatics who could not stand to see a French Canadian receive such a great mark of confidence.[15]

Was there a campaign to discredit him? In light of the extremist reaction of the *Montreal Gazette* of 17 June 1904, one certainly has grounds for wondering:

> He [Captain Bernier] actually makes threats... This sort of language cannot be permitted. It makes a mockery of

> constitutional methods; it is not merely insubordination; it is rank, open mutiny, not on high seas, but certainly on the Quebec docks. If the Hon. Sydney Fisher was Minister of Marine we all know what would happen to Capt. Bernier. He would be fed to crate-fattened chickens.

Surely he deserved better than to be fed to fat chickens. Pretty strong words! And all this because the Captain dared to complain of political influences that had prevented him from choosing his own crew. And all that, too, because there was a French Canadian at the head of the Department of Marine and Fisheries and that French Canadians, according to some, were taking up too much room in a country that was largely English. Moreover, Wilfrid Laurier, the first French Canadian to accede to the post of Prime Minister of Canada, the man who had dreamed of contributing to the harmony between the two races and the union between the two cultures, would admit "[that] a Francophone can do nothing for his own people in Ottawa."[16]

To retain power Laurier, the realist, had realized that he would have to renounce his aspirations and bow to the majority.

CHAPTER 7

Preparations for the voyage

On 27 July 1904 young Arthur Boucher ended his personal diary as follows:

> It will soon be two months since we reached Québec, and no news as to our sailing date and nothing settled as to the Captain. It appears that that matter is not over yet; time will tell whether he will survive. Since we arrived in Québec we have spent three weeks on dry dock, and after coming off the dry dock we had to return to it since the ship was still making water. This time we were on dry dock for only three days, and then came back to the Quai du Roi where we have remained ever since. The steward, M. Savage, disembarked on the 18th and the Captain has authorized me to remain as Steward, which is OK; we await events impatiently, either putting to sea or else changes.

This is to say, then, that between mid-June and the end of July, independently of his negotiations with those responsible at the Department of Marine and Fisheries, Captain Bernier was busy cleaning, repairing and provisioning the *Gauss*. Despite the "*Gauss* affair" he still anticipated that he would be attempting his grand northern adventure, like Nansen, Markham and Franklin.

He was everywhere at once, and he noticed everything. He supervised the electrical repairs, the work of restoration and fitting-out, as well as the installing of steel plates in order to reinforce the oval-shaped hull, made of oak and pitchpine. In Québec harbour he renamed the *Gauss* the D.G.S.[1] *Arctic*, and negotiated the purchase of the vast quantity of coal, provisions, and equipment that were to fill the bunkers, the hold and the tween-decks of the little ship.

One question arises right away with regard to this technical aspect: how could a master mariner who had never sailed arctic waters, "foresee the unforeseeable" and conceive the actual needs as to foodstuffs, clothing, and tools for about 40 men and the same number of dogs, for a voyage of five years to one of the emptiest, most dangerous and least productive regions of the globe?

Fortunately there is abundant documentation to demonstrate his organizing genius and his methodical mind. For example, according to his calculations, for a voyage of 1200 days one man would require:

1	Uniform for use in harbour.
1	Reindeer suit (young) with mitts same skin.
2	Pairs Esquimaux Boots.
2	Suits blue pilot clothe [sic], wool lining.
2	Leather caps, heavy lining.
1	Fleeced cap with nose piece.
1	Fleecy knitted traveling cap.
2	Suits of oil skin short with sou-westers.
2	Pairs of knee rubber boots.
1	Pair stout Arctic boots cow hide.
1	Pair black Clarence fleeced slippers.
1	Pair seaman's bluchers (leather shoes).
1	Pair brown slippers.

The *Gauss/Arctic* in dry-dock in the port of Québec, July 1904. View from astern of the barquentine, 165.4 feet in length with a beam of 37.2 feet. Loaded she drew 22 feet and could attain 7 knots. Her gross registered tonnage was 436 tonnes and, loaded, her displacement was 650 tonnes. [*Canadian Life and Resources Magazine,* 1905]

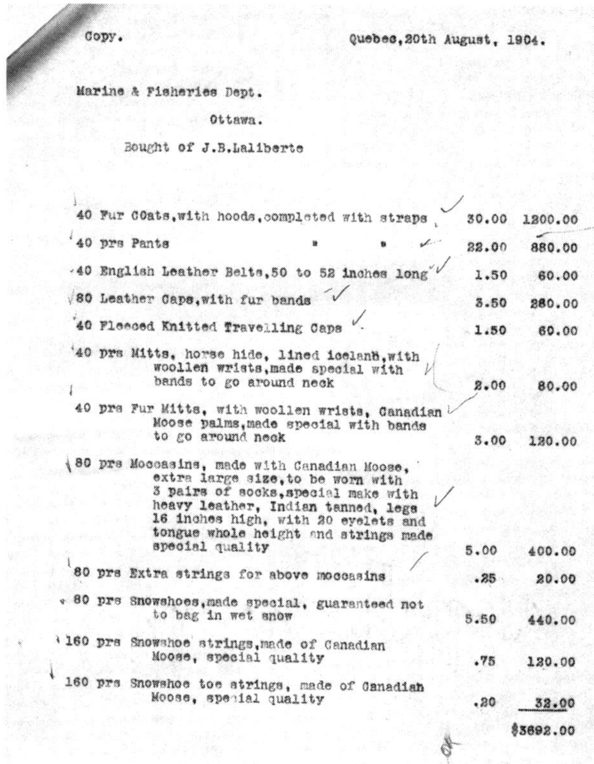

Copy. Quebec,20th August, 1904.

Marine & Fisheries Dept.
Ottawa.

Bought of J.B.Laliberte

40 Fur COats,with hoods,completed with straps	30.00	1200.00
40 prs Pants " "	22.00	880.00
40 English Leather Belts,50 to 52 inches long	1.50	60.00
80 Leather Caps,with fur bands	3.50	280.00
40 Fleeced Knitted Travelling Caps	1.50	60.00
40 prs Mitts, horse hide, lined icelanB,with woollen wrists,made special with bands to go around neck	2.00	80.00
40 prs Fur Mitts, with woollen wrists, Canadian Moose palms,made special with bands to go around neck	3.00	120.00
80 prs Moccasins, made with Canadian Moose, extra large size,to be worn with 3 pairs of socks,special make with heavy leather, Indian tanned, legs 16 inches high, with 20 eyelets and tongue whole height and strings made special quality	5.00	400.00
80 prs Extra strings for above moccasins	.25	20.00
80 prs Snowshoes,made special, guaranteed not to bag in wet snow	5.50	440.00
160 prs Snowshoe strings,made of Canadian Moose, special quality	.75	120.00
160 prs Snowshoe toe strings, made of Canadian Moose, special quality	.20	32.00
		$3692.00

One of the numerous lists describing Captains Bernier's purchases in preparation for his polar expedition. [Courtesy of Benoît Robitaille]

1 Pair sleeping socks long.
12 Pairs woolen stockings, assorted.
12 Pairs of woolen socks.
2 Pairs of mocassins, large.
3 Undervests double breasted to button on shoulder.
2 Pyjamas full suit.
6 Navy blue shirts.
3 Navy knitted guernseys.
2 Pairs of camel-hair blankets.
2 Colic bands.
1 Carrigan jacket with hood.
2 Heavy mufflers.
3 Pairs of buckskin mitts.
1 Pair Para-buck double wrists.
3 Pairs of woolen gloves.
2 Pairs of camping blankets.
1 Woolen sleeping bag.
1 Green leather jacket.
1 Royal blue mackinaw shirt.
1 Rubber duck lined ulster.
1 Mole lined jacket, pants and hood.
1 Camel hair pillow.
1 Dozen wool undershirts.
1 Two inches leather belt.
1 Pair suspenders (Leather).
1 Knitted wool hood.

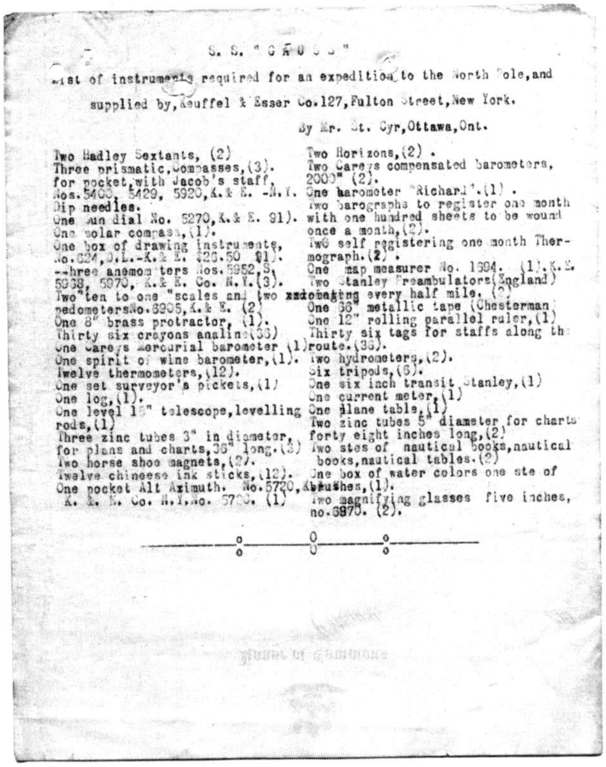

S. S. "[illegible]"

List of instruments required for an expedition to the North Pole, and supplied by, Keuffel & Esser Co. 127, Fulton Street, New York.

By Mr. St. Cyr, Ottawa, Ont.

Two Hadley Sextants, (2)
Three prismatic, Compasses, (3). for pocket, with Jacob's staff, Nos. 5400, 5429, 5920, K. & E. -N.Y.
Dip needles.
One Sun dial No. 5270, K. & E. 91).
One solar compass, (1).
One box of drawing instruments, No. 624, D.L.-K. & E. $26.50 (1).
Three anemometers Nos. 5952, S, 5968, 5970, K. & E. Co. N.Y. (3).
Two "ten to one "scales and two pedometers No. 6905, K. & E. (2)
One 8" brass protractor, (1).
Thirty six crayons analine (36)
One Careys mercurial barometer (1)
One spirit of wine barometer, (1).
Twelve thermometers, (12).
One set surveyor's pickets, (1)
One log, (1).
One level [illegible]" telescope, levelling rods, (1)
Three zinc tubes 3" in diameter, for plans and charts, 36" long. (3)
Two horse shoe magnets, (2).
Twelve chineese ink sticks, (12).
One pocket Alt Azimuth. No. 5720, K. & E. Co. N.Y. No. [illegible]. (1)

Two Horizons, (2).
Two Careys compensated barometers, 2000" (2).
One barometer "Richard". (1).
Two barographs to register one month with one hundred sheets to be wound once a month, (2).
Two self registering one month Thermograph. (2).
One map measurer No. 1894. (1). K.E.
Two Stanley Preambulators (England) registering every half mile. (2)
One 36" metallic tape (Chesterman)
One 12" rolling parallel ruler, (1)
Thirty six tags for staffs along the route. (36).
Two hydrometers, (2).
Six tripods, (6).
One six inch transit Stanley, (1)
One current meter, (1)
One plane table, (1)
Two zinc tubes 5" diameter for charts forty eight inches long, (2)
Two stes of nautical books, nautical books, nautical tables. (2)
One box of water colors one ste of brushes, (1).
Two magnifying glasses five inches, no. 6875. (2).

List of instruments required for the 1904 expedition. For those accustomed to Global positioning systems, echo-sounders and radar, these instruments may appear rather rudimentary. [Courtesy of Benoît Robitaille]

1 Sheep's skin sleeping bag seven and a half feet long.
2 Navy blue undershirts flannel.
2 Large black silk handkerchiefs.
2 Pairs snowshoes one round one half round.
2 Pairs of skies [sic], not less than seven and a half feet long.
1 Camel hair fleeced suit and helmet or woolen felt.

... not to mention the underpants! If these are the necessities for one sailor, just imagine the volume of the requirements for 40 men!

And this was not all! Each area of specialization had to be equipped adequately, since there were no "corner convenience stores" in the Arctic. One had to think of

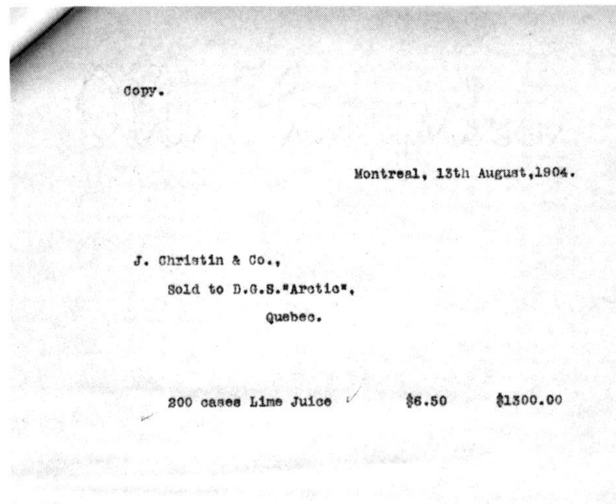

Copy.

Montreal, 13th August, 1904.

J. Christin & Co.,

Sold to D.G.S. "Arctic",

Quebec.

200 cases Lime Juice $6.50 $1300.00

Sailors and explorers used the Vitamin C in lime or lemon juice to prevent scurvy. [Courtesy of Benoît Robitaille]

the carpenter, the quartermaster, the doctor, the electrician, the laundryman, the cook, the fireman and the engineer ...from a simple nail to a boiler, from soft soap to toilet paper, from sewing needles to turpentine, from a toboggan to leather thonging for repairing snowshoes, from gun cartridges to snow shovels, from beeswax to playing cards ... pipes, matches, flags, writing paper, cough drops, carbolic acid, tents, bear traps ...Tonnes of material to anticipate, in addition to navigation instruments and tools that would facilitate a voyage in the icy kingdom.

The reason that Bernier invested so much effort in the preparations was that he was responsible for the safety, the well-being, and the autonomy of the expedition members. After all, he was not embarking on this great adventure with the aim of risking his life, but to come back south to enjoy the glory that would accompany his victory.

And indeed, what would they be eating, apart from the game and fish that they obtained in the field? Captain Bernier calculated that 40 adults would consume in a year:

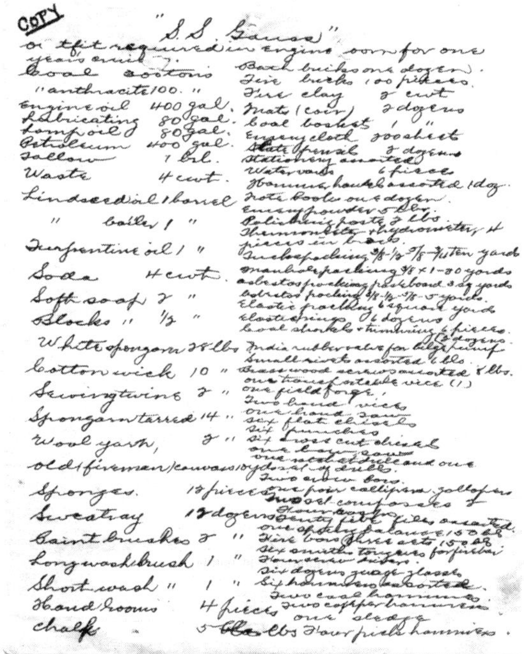

COPY

"S.S. Gauss"

[illegible] required in engine room for one year's [illegible].

Coal 200 tons
" anthracite 100. "
Engine oil 400 gal.
Lubricating 80 gal.
Lamp oil 80 gal.
Petroleum 400 gal.
Tallow 1 bbl.
Waste 4 cwt.
Linseed oil 1 barrel
" boiled 1 "
Turpentine oil 1 "
Soda 4 cwt.
Soft soap 2 "
Blocks " 1/2 "
White spongarn 28 lbs
Cotton wick 10 "
Sewing twine 2 "
Spongarn tarred 14 "
Wool yarn, 2 "
old (fireman) canvass 10 yds
Sponges. 12 pieces
Sweat rag 12 dozens
Paint brushes 2 "
Long wash brush 1 "
Short wash " 1 "
Hand brooms 4 pieces
chalk 5 lbs

Back bricks one dozen.
Fire bricks 100 pieces.
Fire clay 2 cwt
Mats (coir) 2 dozens
Coal baskets 1 "
Emery cloth 200 sheets
Slate pencil 2 dozens
Stationery assorted
Water [illegible] 6 pieces
[illegible] assorted 1 doz.
Note books one dozen
Emery powder 5 lbs.
Polishing paste 2 lbs.
Thermometers & hydrometers 4 pieces in boxes.
[illegible] packing 3/8-1/2-5/8-7/8 ten yards
Manhole packing 3/8 × 1-20 yards
asbestos packing pasteboard 3 sq yards
Asbestos packing 3/8-1/2-5/8-5 yards.
Elastic packing 6 square yards
Elastic rings 6 dozens
Coal shovels + [illegible] 6 pieces.
India rubber valves for bilge pump [illegible] dozens.
Small rivets assorted 6 lbs.
Brass wood screws assorted 8 lbs.
one [illegible] vice (1)
one field forge.
Two hand vices
one hand saw
six flat chisels
six punches
six cross cut chisels
one [illegible]
one [illegible] and one dozen of drills.
Two [illegible] bars.
one pair callipers [illegible]
[illegible]
[illegible] files assorted.
one spring balance 150 lbs.
[illegible] three sets 150 lbs
six smith tongues for [illegible]
[illegible]
six dozens gauge glasses
six hammers assorted.
Two coal hammers.
Two copper hammers.
one sledge
Four pick hammers.

Materials required annually for the engine room. [Courtesy Benoît Robitaille]

Lbs		
15,000		wheat biscuits
1,344		assorted biscuits
12,000		wheat flour
6,000		oatmeal
500		rolled oats
500		hominy (corn cereal)
240		corn flour
400		corn meal
600		crushed oats
200		buckwheat flour
500		pea flour
600		green peas
600		split peas
600		whole peas
1,200		round beans
1,500		pork and beans
200		kidney beans
100		sago
100		tapioca
600		pearl barley
600		rice
500		rice flakes
192	cans	canned soup
2,500		assorted canned fish
108		ham
250		sausages
35		bacon
3,000		Bovril concentrate
6,800		canned beef and mutton, roast or boiled
4,000		salt beef
5,000		salt pork
250		smoked tongues
4,000		pemmican
300		mincemeat
500		potted tripe
744		brown, granulated sugar in blocks
24	gals.	maple syrup
3		saccharine
150		molasses
1,000		tea
1,000		coffee
1,200		chocolate and cocoa
200		chocolate products with 10% albumen
600		pickles
10	gals.	vinegar
192	pots	assorted sauces
1,000		dried fruit
600		marinated fruit
1,000		cheese
1,776		canned potatoes
960		canned beetroot, onions, carrots, cauliflower
240	cans	tomatoes
1,500		dried vegetables
300		dried apples
24		mustard
35		black and white pepper
3		red pepper
10		dried herbs
2		fresh herbs
10		celery salt
1,644		condensed milk
361	cases	raisins

150		currants
96		baking powder
25		yeast cakes
5		hops
500		coarse salt
500		fine salt
30		assorted spices
		25 bottles assorted essences
25		lemon and orange peel
24		corn starch
50		gelatine
50		lime lozenges
24	bottles	olive oil
250	pots	red currant jelly
250	"	black currant jelly
96		marmalade
144		strawberry jam
400		honey
35	bottles	curry
40		bicarbonate of soda
500		tobacco
½	barrel	whisky
40	gals.	rum
40	pure alcohol	
3	cases	brandy
4		port wine
600		macaroni
300		assorted nuts
300		assorted candies
144	cans	concentrated eggs
250		candles
750		back fat or suet
750		lard
7		ginger powder

One wonders how the little vessel would stay afloat with all this load! One also wonders where the men were going to be accommodated with all this cargo!

These purchases certainly benefited the merchants and the local economy.

> The dispatch of government expeditions automatically created jobs for sailors of every category […] As far as possible the government attempted to recruit competent candidates from among its "friends." Protection, like patronage, are political responsibilities that every government has to meet.[2]

Even the journalist Nazaire LeVasseur hoped to profit from it:

> You will understand that apart from my congratulations, I may have a favour to ask of you. I should like my son to accompany you […] he loves traveling and adventure as indeed do all French Canadians.[3]

Paul LeVasseur would be signed on as second steward, in the place of Arthur Boucher. The same would happen in the case of a protégé of Senator William Ross, Frank Douglas McKean, a young artist who was recruited as the expedition photographer although he had no experience in photography. It would seem, indeed, that Captain Bernier did not have much say in the choice of men who were to accompany him, except in the case of Octave-Jules Morin, who was promoted to second Lieutenant, engineers Joseph Lemieux and John Van Koënig, and perhaps also a few French-speaking sailors. All the others, the English-speaking sailors, the historiographer, the doctor, the artist, the eight Newfoundland sailors, Superintendent Moodie of the Royal Northwest Mounted Police, his son, his wife, and ten Mounted Policemen, were appointed by government representatives.[4]

The Minister of Marine and Fisheries had not been above-board with Captain Bernier. He waited until the end of July before informing him that his polar expedition would not be taking place and that the *Arctic* would be used to resupply the *Neptune*, to establish police posts in Hudson Bay, and to study ice conditions and currents in that area.

Outraged and his pride hurt, the man of the Far North tendered his resignation.

> Without warning I was suddenly ordered to put ashore three years supplies and proceed to Hudson Bay, prac-

> tically under the orders of the Mounted Police to ascertain whether a certain well-known and highly respected ship captain was engaged in selling liquor to the natives.[5]

What a disappointment for the man who had hoped to be able to offer the North Pole to Canadians and to add to the scientific knowledge of the world by exploring the arctic regions alongside an oceanographer, a geologist, a meteorologist, and a biologist. Instead, his government was proposing that he accept the role of patrolling the Arctic and helping the police!

When Bernier agreed[6] to resume his command of the *Arctic*, it was because he had been persuaded that he was the only seaman capable of bringing such an endeavour to fruition, and because he had been promised that this North Pole project had not been cancelled, but simply postponed to a later date. The captain was a realist who certainly understood that this voyage to Hudson Bay would give him a golden opportunity to learn about the Arctic at first hand. He could test his knowledge and judge the performance of his ship in arctic waters. This new experience would give him an opportunity to prove himself to the politicians.

> Much later, after having kept silent on the subject for years, Bernier told a newspaper reporter his views on why he had not been allowed to go to the Pole. He felt it was a political move. In 1904, Canada's foreign policy was controlled by England, who was extremely anxious to maintain friendly relations with the United States. A few weeks before Bernier's trip was cancelled, Commander Peary had decided to make another attempt on the Pole, this time using a ship as a base. Peary drew up plans with the official approval of the U.S. government. It is indeed possible that when Laurier heard about this, he decided not to send out an expedition which would compete with the Americans. In some of his papers, Laurier has written that he thought it would be better to leave the discovery of the Pole to private enterprise.[7]

The co-founder of *Le Droit* interpreted the facts differently:

AU POLE NORD !

I—Démarches Préliminaires

Bernier—Tout ça pour faire un voyage de plaisir ? Très obligé, Sir Wilfrid.

Laurier—Prenez, prenez, mon ami, c'est autant de sauvé, que, les autres ne gaspilleront pas. Mais donnez-nous de vos nouvelles.

Bernier—All this to go on a pleasure trip? Much obliged; Sir Wilfrid. Laurier—Take it, take it, my friend, it's all the more saved that the others won't waste. But let us know how you get on.

> Instead of allowing the "Polar Bear" to attempt the conquest of the pack ice and the glaciers, he was sent to simply transport a detachment of the Northwest Mounted Police to Hudson Bay. He wanted to resign and was prevented from doing so only by the promise that he could take up the task again on a later voyage [...] He was fed successive disappointments [...]
>
> If the North Pole was not discovered by a Canadian it was not the fault of this valiant sailor. He was the man for the job.

> But the Laurier government never had the courage to face Anglo-Canadian censure in the house and to grant Captain Bernier a well organized expedition. He was not an officer in the British Royal Navy, and it is claimed that a Governor-General had whispered that a French Canadian should not be given the opportunity to attain the glory that had been sought in vain by the most celebrated British seamen.[8]

Naturally Laurier never justified the political reasons that led him to block the expedition to the North Pole. But the idea of expending resources and significant sums of money on a public relations project, or one of national fervour, cannot have weighed heavily in the politician's immediate preoccupations. The quite real threat of American domination in the Arctic and the dubious activities of foreign whalers in the Canadian archipelago represented much more pressing problems that obliged him to initiate a series of measures aimed at ensuring gradual, but effective control of the northern territories.

> [...] the *Arctic* will be under the command of Captain Bernier and [...] is to sail on August 15. This boat will carry an officer and ten men of the Mounted Police, apart from the crew of the ship [...] Their instructions are to patrol the waters, to find suitable locations for posts, to establish those posts and to assert the jurisdiction of Canada [...] At the present time there are whalers and fishermen of different nations cruising in those waters, and unless we take active steps to assert [...] that these lands belong to Canada, we may perhaps find ourselves later on in the face of serious complications.[9]

For the Prime Minister and his government, patrolling arctic waters and establishing police posts constituted concrete gestures that would guarantee a permanent Canadian presence in the Arctic Archipelago and would counter any claims by other countries, especially the Americans.

CHAPTER 8

To Hudson Bay, 1904-1905

On 12 September 1904 Captain Bernier received his instructions from Deputy Minister Gourdeau. The sharing of responsibilities was clearly established:

> You will be held responsible for the navigation and the safety of the *Arctic* in every way, but in all other respects she is to be subject to the commands of the Officer in Charge of the expedition.[1]

The same applied to the *Arctic*'s itinerary:

> Until otherwise ordered by the Government, Major Moodie's instructions are that the route of the *Arctic* will be limited to Hudson's Bay, Hudson's Straits, Davis Straits, Baffin's Bay, Smith Sound, Kennedy Channel, Lancaster Sound, and other bays and channels on the west coast of Hudson's Bay, Davis Strait, or Baffin's Bay.

The mandate of the government expedition, commanded by Superintendent J.D. Moodie[2] of the Royal North-West Mounted Police was to winter at Fullerton in the northwest corner of Hudson Bay, and to ensure the change of personnel and re-provisioning of the Mounted Police post at that location. In the following summer the *Arctic* was to patrol in the Eastern Arctic to locate new sites for Mounted Police posts.

The *Arctic* sailed for Hudson Bay on 17 September. It was a colourful and noisy departure.

> [...] the ships in harbour were dressed overall. The Canadian colours were flying from the tall, white mast that stands watch near the upside-down cannon that serve as mooring bollards. The *Arctic*'s three masts were each flying a flag. The band from the Citadel battery was on the quay, serenading our commander. From the quays, the terrace and the *Arctic*'s decks the arrival of the Honourable Minister of Marine was greeted with enthusiastic cheers.[3]

The annotations, the descriptions, and the states of mind revealed in the personal diary[4] of the expedition's historiographer are particularly eloquent as to what he called his "15 month cruise in the North."

> *Saturday, 17 September, 10 a.m.* Finally all's well that ends well. The Minister of Marine and the main officers have arrived. The misunderstandings are straightened out; we will sail at noon.
>
> To the sound of cannon shots from the Citadel Captain Bernier orders the *Blue Poter* [sic] hoisted to the main masthead. The *Blue Poter* [sic]... means "I am ready to sail—let's go."
>
> We are still short of two men to complete the crew, namely a First Mate and a quartermaster, but the Captain will find them at Sydney, where we will be calling next Wednesday; from here to there Captain Alfred Bernier will assist his brother as First Mate. Mr. Elzéar Normand, a pilot from L'Islet, will guide the ship as far as Bic.
>
> He is already on deck ... waiting for the signal to give the helm the turn that will take us to sea. The weather is magnificent with sunshine, a blue sky, and a gentle south-easterly breeze that invites the sailors to set their sails.

The members of the crew, "slightly the worse for wear from the generous wines of Québec," had long been

The *Gauss/Arctic* in dry-dock in the port of Québec, summer 1904. One can clearly see the egg-shaped design of the hull that prevented it from being crushed by the polar ice. [*Canadian Life and Resources Magazine, 1905*]

experiencing the emotions of the departure. There was a risk that this separation would be permanent. Perhaps they would never again see their families, the magnificent skyline of the city of Québec, or the autumnal colours of Charlevoix, or the verdant slopes of the South Shore.

As they headed towards Sydney on the northeast coast of Cape Breton Island, they were all hoping to take advantage of this last "civilized" port since "we will spend the rest of the three years of this expedition to the North on ice- and snow-covered shores in the midst of savages." The expedition members could only imagine what really awaited them in Hudson Bay.

As they sailed along the coast of Newfoundland heading for the Labrador Sea, some of the neophytes woke up for the first time to the effects of a gale in the open sea.

> The gale makes itself felt both below and above decks. First of all, we find it impossible to walk around without rolling from one side to the other [...] and banging our heads on the bulkheads [...]. In our bunks we have to hang on tightly to ropes to prevent ourselves from rolling out. All the lights on board are extinguished.

The storm pursued them without respite all the way along the Labrador coast and into Hudson Strait. To exorcise his fear Vanasse resorted to writing once again:

> It would not be prudent to approach the coast more closely because of the reefs that dot the sea. [...] The captain is not in a good mood; his compasses are getting dizzy; of the

The *Arctic* leaving for Hudson Bay, September 1904. Captain Bernier had immortalized the event on postcards like this one, that he distributed to friends and fans. Note that for this first voyage the ship had not been repainted. [Archives of Carol and Louis Terrien]

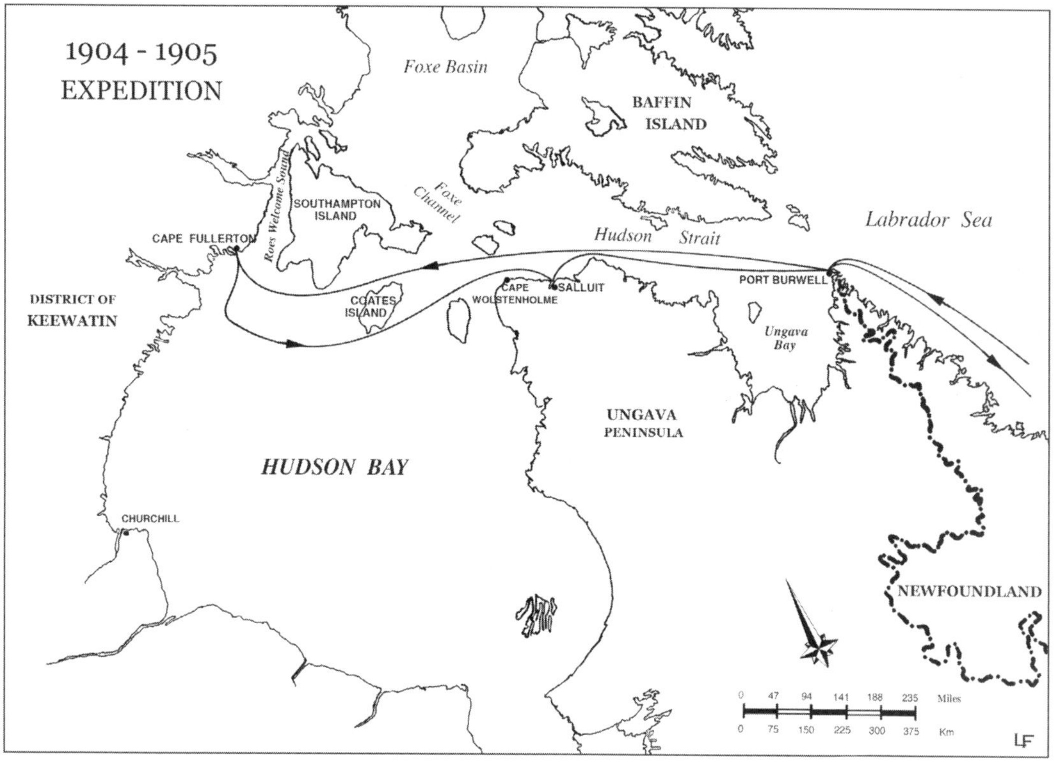

The *Arctic's* track during the 1904-1905 expedition.

three compasses not one agrees with the others. [...] The potatoes left on the deck will be frozen rock-hard. [...] The commander has had fur caps distributed; [...] the snow is increasing. The water is starting to freeze along the ship's sides. It is cold [...] the wind is very strong; the ship is running at full speed under sails and steam. Where are we going?

⚓

Captain Bernier anchored the *Arctic* in Fullerton Harbour a month later. This harbour is formed by several small islands located about five miles from Cape Fullerton. It was so small that it could accommodate only three ships at a time.

Fullerton is a little hole hidden among rocks and very difficult of access because of reefs. Breakers and numerous rocks surround it, over an area more than 12 miles in diameter.[5]

When they arrived there was a solitary whaleship lying in the corner, Captain George Comer's *Era* from New Bedford in New England. The schooner was already well ensconced for her third consecutive wintering, during which she was transformed into a major trading post that served a well established Inuit clientele. The trappers and their families would congregate at Fullerton with their sledges loaded with furs that they would trade for manufactured goods from the South.

Bernier quickly imitated his sole neighbour and organized his ship for a wintering. As early as 28 October

The *Arctic* working through ice in Hudson Bay. [Archives of Carol and Louis Terrien]

he had weighed anchor since the ice surrounding the ship was 22 inches thick and strong enough to hold the ship in a stable position against currents and the prevailing northerly winds. To increase the closed space on deck, he had a temporary wooden frame built, which was then roofed in with sails, and the deck covered with several feet of snow. A thick wall of snow blocks was also built against the ship's sides to insulate the ship and ensure that the ship's heat would be retained during the long cold months. "Windows" were cut in these protective walls to let daylight penetrate the interior. Snow gangways were built across this unusual structure to facilitate access to the ship.

To provide his men with drinking water Captain Bernier had a large number of ice-blocks sawed from a freshwater pond located near the Mounted Police post. He issued fur coats and pants to allow his men to move about as normally as possible in this tough environment, where almost nothing was familiar.

Without disrupting the Americans' trade, the *Arctic* presence offered the Inuit another centre of activity. They now had the choice of living in the vicinity of the "Canada Hotel" or that of the "United States Hotel." However "trading with the natives was prohibited." The Canadians could hunt and could obtain traps free of charge from the police stores, but they could not hire an Inuk to trap for them.

Bernier reported that throughout the winter the Inuit of the Fullerton area "were starving and it was considered our duty to feed them to such an extent as to prevent their being exterminated. It was quite a drain on some of the supplies, namely: biscuits, sugar, molasses, oatmeal, meat and flour."[6]

At times the precarious situation of the indigenous population touched sensitive souls such as Fabien Vanasse:

> *8 November, Tuesday.* It is a cold night outside; it is very warm inside the ship. I am almost ashamed to mention the

Nansen's *Fram* in winter quarters. Captain Bernier was inspired by the methods used by the Norwegian explorer when it came to organizing the *Arctic*'s wintering. [Gustave Vallat, *À la conquête du pôle Nord, 1897*]

> comfort we enjoy here. When I think that two paces away from the ship the Eskimo families are lying in their snow houses or in improvised tents in the cold wind, without any fire inside to moderate the cold.

The Hudson Bay region was cruel. Bernier realized that man had to come to terms with it. Since the safety and success of the expedition devolved upon him, he had to take things in hand to establish some sort of routine and to create a semblance of a family from this disparate group, whom he had not chosen and whom he did not know very well. His experience as a ship's master had taught him that human solidarity was of prime importance to the harmony of a group forced to live in close confinement. To survive a wintering over nine months in length the captain was determined to keep the men occupied and to provide some diversion.

His effective approach and his numerous initiatives are impressive. He used windmills lent by the Aeolian Company of New York to light the ship. He had a tele-

Hattie, Suzie and Jennie, Inuit women from the Fullerton region in their traditional dress. This photo was probably taken by Geraldine Moodie who accompanied her husband, Commander J.D. Moodie, to Hudson Bay. [RCMP Collection, LAC, C-089352]

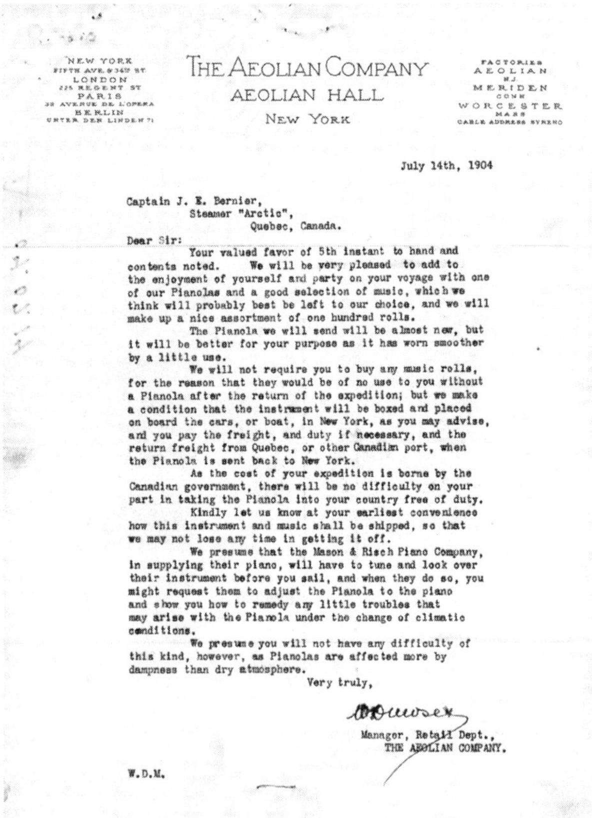

NEW YORK
FIFTH AVE. & 34th ST.
LONDON
225 REGENT ST
PARIS
32 AVENUE DE L'OPERA
BERLIN
UNTER DEN LINDEN 71

THE AEOLIAN COMPANY
AEOLIAN HALL
NEW YORK

FACTORIES
AEOLIAN NJ
MERIDEN CONN
WORCESTER MASS
CABLE ADDRESS SYRENO

July 14th, 1904

Captain J. E. Bernier,
Steamer "Arctic",
Quebec, Canada.

Dear Sir:

Your valued favor of 5th instant to hand and contents noted. We will be very pleased to add to the enjoyment of yourself and party on your voyage with one of our Pianolas and a good selection of music, which we think will probably best be left to our choice, and we will make up a nice assortment of one hundred rolls.

The Pianola we will send will be almost new, but it will be better for your purpose as it has worn smoother by a little use.

We will not require you to buy any music rolls, for the reason that they would be of no use to you without a Pianola after the return of the expedition; but we make a condition that the instrument will be boxed and placed on board the cars, or boat, in New York, as you may advise, and you pay the freight, and duty if necessary, and the return freight from Quebec, or other Canadian port, when the Pianola is sent back to New York.

As the cost of your expedition is borne by the Canadian government, there will be no difficulty on your part in taking the Pianola into your country free of duty.

Kindly let us know at your earliest convenience how this instrument and music shall be shipped, so that we may not lose any time in getting it off.

We presume that the Mason & Risch Piano Company, in supplying their piano, will have to tune and look over their instrument before you sail, and when they do so, you might request them to adjust the Pianola to the piano and show you how to remedy any little troubles that may arise with the Pianola under the change of climatic conditions.

We presume you will not have any difficulty of this kind, however, as Pianolas are affected more by dampness than dry atmosphere.

Very truly,

Manager, Retail Dept.,
THE AEOLIAN COMPANY.

W.D.M.

Captain Bernier had appealed to the generosity of several private companies for his 1904-1905 expedition. The Aeolian Company of New York had agreed to lend him a pianola and a good selection of music to entertain the expedition members during the long months of wintering. [Private collection]

phone link installed between his office and that of Commander Moodie in the wooden house that also served as barracks and customs-house, and was located about 1200 feet from the ship.

Bernier also organized various forms of entertainment, including a banquet on November 9 aboard the *Arctic* to celebrate the birthday of King Edward VII of England. Toasts in honour of the King were made by Commander Moodie, Captain Comer, and Bernier himself. Following the banquet, a dance was organized on the ship's deck and Bernier invited local Eskimos to join in the festivities. In addition to these events, the captain also organized hunting and fishing parties in the surrounding region.[7]

To enhance their evenings and to entertain his shipmates, he played old Canadian tunes, waltzes, popular songs, and religious songs on the phonograph that had been supplied free-of-charge by the Berliner Gramophone Co. Ltd. of Montreal in exchange for a photograph of the expedition members listening to their discs in the Arctic. "One has to do something to amuse oneself, otherwise one would go mad," Vanasse admitted in his diary on 16 November. "Loneliness weighs upon us. This is the greatest—indeed the only—stressful aspect of the voyage."

Occasionally the captain would organize lectures on his favourite subject—the race for the Pole. Thus at 22.30 on Sunday, 20 December, "before an audience of the crews of the *Arctic* and the *Era*, the men of the Mounted Police, and all the Inuit, men, women and children," he retraced the exploits of all those who had tried to reach the Pole and explained how he anticipated meeting the challenge. "The presentation was of interest to everyone," the expedition historiographer concluded. "There was plenty to satisfy both the eyes and the mind."

To fill the moments of idleness and to combat homesickness, the captain took care of everything: religious functions, daily exercises, sporting matches, fishing or hunting trips, concerts, literary evenings, holiday menus, etc.

The captain observed the natural environment around him and collected data on temperature, ice thickness, and tides. He was interested in the Inuit and questioned them endlessly on their manner of living and surviving in these icy wastes. His career in the Arctic was only beginning. Hence he had to acquire as much experience as possible and collect all the information that might help him on future voyages.

By mid-June the ice at Fullerton was still 49 inches thick. Summer had arrived in Hudson Bay, but had not freed the *Arctic* from her ice prison. The wintering had to end with the arrival of summer. They had to put to sea, come what may, to avoid compromising the rest of the mission.

By 1 July the ice had shrunk by only 13 inches. The captain ordered his men to saw away this solid layer of ice to remove it from the metal hull. Then using the powerful steam engine and his skill, Bernier got his ship under way again. Little by little he would charge forward, pull back, stop then push forward again, like a ram attacking an obstacle!

The *Arctic* advanced cautiously along the channel that she had slowly broken across the confines of Fullerton Harbour. On 5 July, after a wintering of nine months, she was finally free to pursue her mandate. Her sails breathed again, shaking and filling to the northern winds.

> Initially the vessel cruised around the western part of Hudson Bay, but suffered damage to her screw while manoeuvring among the pack ice. The ice concentrations were such that ultimately the ship was unable to reach Churchill.[8]

The remainder of the expedition consisted of patrolling these waters to observe the activities of foreign whalers and to collect as much information as possible on the whaling industry in Hudson Bay and the Baffin Island area, and looking for a more accessible site than Fullerton in order to establish another Mounted Police post.

Blocked by the pack ice 400 miles from Churchill, and unable to see any open water either to the south or west, Captain Bernier decided to head back north to Cape Southampton on Coats Island.

From 14 July onwards the ice no longer presented any obstacle to the ship's progress and she ran rapidly towards Hudson Strait. She came-to in a long bay that the Inuit then called "Salluk" and that is now known as the fjord and settlement of Salluit.[9]

Bernier wrote:

> About 40 miles east of Erik Bay we found a natural harbour where quite a beautiful river empties into it. At this point on the coast the land rises to a considerable height with good flat beaches around the bay. At this time of year the surrounding hills were covered with grass. We determined that a bar exists at the entrance to this stretch of water, preventing ships from entering except at high tide.[10]

This natural basin, fed by numerous streams full of fish, was an ideal location for a police post. It measured about one and a half miles in width and "the natives of this part of the country assure us that Préfontaine Bay is free of ice by 1 June and that the heavy pack ice never invades it from the Strait."[11]

It was in Salluit harbour that Bernier participated in his first ceremony of taking possession, which took place on the *Arctic*'s deck on 20 July 1905:

> All personnel were ordered to be on deck. Just as the anchor was dropped opposite the future town, the flag of the Canadian Navy rose to the main masthead. Then the Commander, in full-dress uniform, and surrounded by his officers, declared that henceforth this bay will bear the name Préfontaine Bay, in honour of the Honourable Raymond Préfontaine, Minister of Marine; and that the immense cape, so graceful and imposing in shape, is named Cape Laurier, after Sir Wilfrid Laurier, Prime Minister of Canada, and that the natives' "Round Island" will be called White Island, for the services that this excellent officer has rendered to Canada. These declarations were greeted with vigorous cheers in honour of the abovementioned illustrious sponsors, and the ceremony was finished.[12]

This symbolic gesture was of fundamental importance since it affirmed for the first time in the eyes of the world that Canada was finally taking an interest in its northern boundaries.

Subsequently the *Arctic* shuttled between Préfontaine Bay and Erik Harbour, near Cape Wolstenholme with a view to meeting the ship that was to resupply her. It had been anticipated that this rendez vous would be around

22 July, but by 9 August the collier had still not arrived. It was therefore agreed that the *Arctic* should proceed to Port Burwell located at the eastern end of Hudson Strait, at the entrance to Ungava Bay in order to replace the propeller blade that had been broken off, and to await orders from the government.

At Port Burwell, Bernier met the Governor of Newfoundland, Sir William McGregor on board a British frigate, but he did not find the facilities adequate for making repairs to the propeller. He was surprised to find a constant going-and-coming of Newfoundland ships and sailors who were freely fishing for cod and hunting whales and seals in Canadian waters, without paying any customs dues. This strong "foreign" presence at the entrance to the sea route represented by Hudson Strait and Bay, he believed, could only be prejudicial to the sovereignty of his country in this area.[13]

The problem with the propeller forced Captain Bernier to terminate his mission of patrolling and to return to Québec earlier than anticipated. It was only at Château Bay in the Strait of Belle Isle that he finally met the *Neptune*, that was to resupply the *Arctic*.

Fabien Vanasse was probably not the only member of the crew who was delighted by this early return. Within sight of Anticosti Island the historiographer gave free rein to the emotions that were overwhelming him:

> *8 p.m.* All our sails are set and the *Arctic* is flying from wave to wave, like a beautiful swan. It is a superb night. The stars are shining like golden nail-heads that are fastening a hanging of black cloth to the vault of the firmament. It is the night sky of home; these are definitely our stars; that is definitely our moon, with its calm, soft light.

The *Arctic* reached Québec on 7 October 1905 and passed the winter on the dry-dock in the Sorel yards.

CHAPTER 9

The *Arctic* scandal

> Late in the evening of 10 October 1905 the town of Sorel is celebrating the return of the *Arctic*. Everyone has gathered on the quays and Préfontaine, the Minister responsible for this expedition, has joined the crowd, which deafens him with enthusiastic cheers. Sorel crackles with the sound of fireworks. Pyrotechnic displays light up the quays.[1]

Raymond Préfontaine died two months later and was replaced by Louis-Philippe Brodeur, who had the reputation of being an honest man and an irreproachable employee. Unfortunately, in accepting the portfolio of Minister of Marine and Fisheries, Brodeur was also inheriting stigmas of corruption associated with the reign of his predecessor and as soon as he was in office, he became the target of the opposition party that was trying by every means to destabilize the government of Wilfrid Laurier, who had been holding firmly onto power since 1896.

The Conservative team, which, in general terms, had strongly supported Captain Bernier's polar project, judged that it would succeed in discrediting the Liberals by attacking the 1904-1905 expedition. Borden, Fowler, Bennett, Bergeron, and Stockton took great pleasure during debates in the House of Commons in taking aim at what they perceived as the Achilles heel, the weak point of the whole affair, namely the *Arctic*'s cargo:

> [...] it is perfectly well known that on the streets of Montréal and Québec certain individuals accosted the Minister [Préfontaine] or certain officials of his Department and sold them merchandise for the steamer *Arctic*. [...] The expedition is a giant scandal [...].[2]

They did not hesitate to go over the list of provisions with a fine tooth comb and to concentrate their fire on items that they judged to be non-essential to the expedition. Thus M.P. Bennett amused himself by listing the cards, checker boards, pipes, cigarettes, and the 4000 "Laurier" cigars: "Is the Minister unaware that there exist plenty of other well-known brands of cigars that sailors particularly prefer?"[3]

In this game of politics M.P. Fowler, succeeded in taking the debate where he wanted, namely to denounce

Louis-Philippe Brodeur, Canadian Minister of Marine and Fisheries. [Bernier Collection, *Rapport officiel de l'expédition de 1908-1909*]

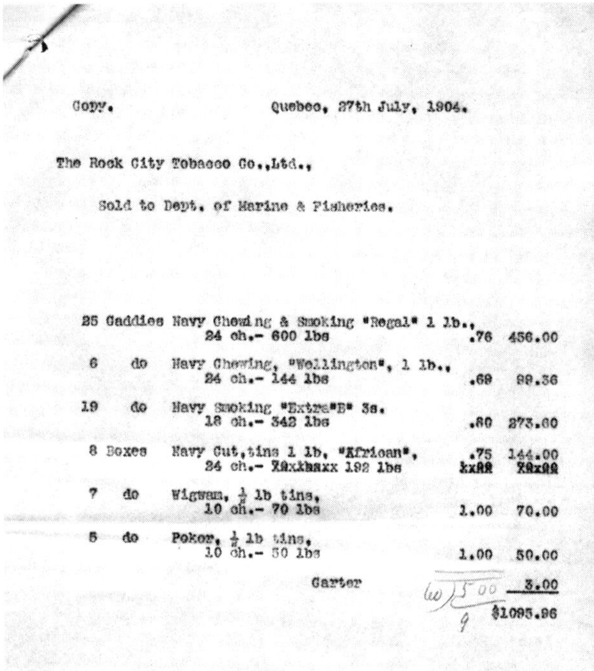

Copy. Quebec, 27th July, 1904.

The Rock City Tobacco Co.,Ltd.,

Sold to Dept. of Marine & Fisheries.

25	Caddies	Navy Chewing & Smoking "Regal" 1 lb., 24 ch.- 600 lbs	.76	456.00
6	do	Navy Chewing, "Wellington", 1 lb., 24 ch.- 144 lbs	.69	99.36
19	do	Navy Smoking "Extra"B" 3s. 18 ch.- 342 lbs	.80	273.60
8	Boxes	Navy Cut,tins 1 lb, "African", 24 ch.- 192 lbs	.75	144.00
7	do	Wigwam, ½ lb tins, 10 ch.- 70 lbs	1.00	70.00
5	do	Poker, ½ lb tins, 10 ch.- 50 lbs	1.00	50.00
		Carter		3.00
				$1095.96

One of the lists concerning the purchase of tobacco for the 1904-1905 expedition. [Courtesy of Benoît Robitaille]

what he perceived as the extravagance of the Liberal administration:

> In my opinion this is the most extraordinary, most iniquitous and most scandalous list of expenditures that one could conceive of [...] Such a list would certainly be such as to alarm our population if the present government hadn't already accustomed it, to some degree, to this type of behaviour.[4]

Despite himself, Bernier again found himself involved in a controversy when the Liberal Member L.G. McCarthy tried to absolve Minister Brodeur by throwing the blame for the presumed abuses in provisioning onto the *Arctic*'s captain. For a short time this manoeuvre succeeded in diverting the attacks of the Conservatives, until Member Borden realized that a scapegoat outside the government would serve as a way-out for the people in the Department of Marine and Fisheries. The opposition then resumed its denunciations, dwelling on the $2,870.60 spent on tobacco and the $1,608.86 invested in alcohol for the said expedition. They deplored the five cases of gin, the port, the "Salsapareille Special," the five cases of V.O. cognac, the seven octaves of "Old Jamaica" rum and the five cases of "Burmeister's Fine Old Crusted Port vintage 1878!"

> [...] The Conservatives maintained that the prices paid for provisioning the *Arctic* were extravagant, that the quantities purchased were excessive and, finally, that not all the cargo could have been put aboard the *Arctic*. The Conservative opposition believed it was on the track of a gigantic scandal and demanded a thorough enquiry.[5]

On 16 May 1906 Prime Minister Laurier finally acceded to the Conservatives' demands by striking a special committee of six Liberal members and four Conservative members to study the price, quality, and quantity of all the items in question.

It goes without saying that the opposition members who were on the committee attempted by all possible means to drag out the debates in order to exploit the "public scandal" to the limit. Nonetheless the Liberals managed to wind up the enquiry by June 1906. The results were published in the pamphlet "Arctic Expedition, the facts of it."[6]

> [...] the quantity and variety of stores [...] were reasonable and necessary and were of the best quality [...]. No part or portion of the said stores, merchandise, supplies and provisions were, in whole and in part, improperly diverted for uses other than originally contemplated [...] that fair and reasonable prices were paid [...] with the exception of a quantity of tobacco purchased in Québec [...] and provisions not consumed during the progress of the expedition [...] are now in possession of, and under the control of the Department of Marine and Fisheries.

The imbroglio derived from the fact that the Government had not been frank with Captain Bernier as to the *Arctic*'s true role and itinerary. Right from the start Bernier had organized the provisioning of his ship in the belief that he was preparing for a polar expedition

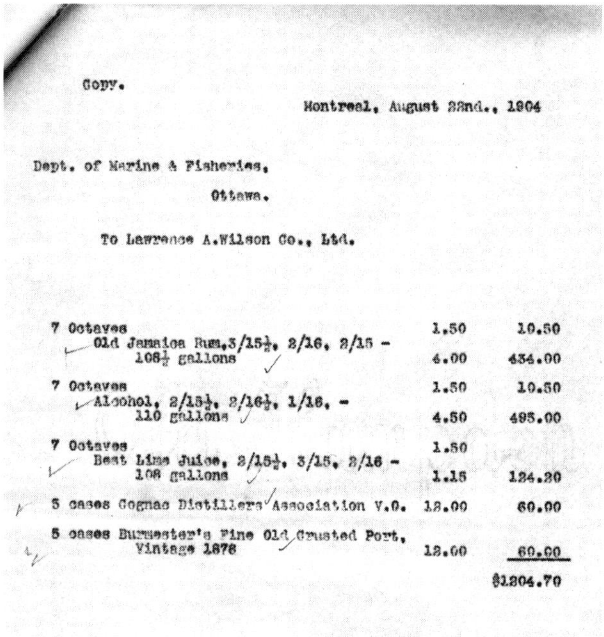

Copy.

Montreal, August 22nd., 1904

Dept. of Marine & Fisheries,
Ottawa.

To Lawrence A.Wilson Co., Ltd.

7 Octaves	1.50	10.50
Old Jamaica Rum, 3/15½, 2/16, 2/15 – 108½ gallons	4.00	434.00
7 Octaves	1.50	10.50
Alcohol, 2/15½, 2/16½, 1/16, – 110 gallons	4.50	495.00
7 Octaves	1.50	
Best Lime Juice, 2/15½, 3/15, 2/16 – 108 gallons	1.15	124.20
5 cases Cognac Distillers' Association V.O.	12.00	60.00
5 cases Burmester's Fine Old Crusted Port, Vintage 1878	12.00	60.00
		$1204.70

One of the lists concerning the purchase of alcohol for the expedition to Hudson Bay. [Courtesy of Benoît Robitaille]

lasting five years. It was only later that he was compelled to withdraw part of the supplies for the patrol voyage to Hudson Bay that was expected to last about three years. Since the *Arctic* had entered the shipyard at Sorel earlier than anticipated, a complete inventory of the materiel and provisions that remained had been approved by Deputy Minister Gourdeau, Colonel White and a certain Mr. Semple. To recoup a little of the money these government representatives had then decided to auction off the portion of the stock that had been damaged during the voyage.

Questioned as to this dispute, the *Arctic*'s commander was well-qualified to defend himself since he had always conformed to the regulations of the Department that had appointed him. "Bernier spent long hours on the witness stand. His name was cleared of even a breath of scandal, and he received a special commendation from both parties for his direct, no-nonsense answers."[7] Clearly the Conservatives were upset by the results of the enquiry, but they had not said their last word.

From 1904 onwards the Conservative opposition persisted in trying to discredit the government expeditions sent to the Arctic with Captain Bernier. Not that they were truly aiming to criticize the actual purpose of the expeditions, since they could not have justified such a position and would have made themselves very unpopular. But while having approved the political gesture that the expeditions represented vis-à-vis foreign countries versus Canada, they continually attacked the administration of the expeditions, in order to disparage the Liberal government that was responsible for them. Since from time to time there was some material related to the affairs of the expeditions that might shock public opinion a little, the Conservatives would renew their attacks by exploiting the smallest details concerning the budget of the expeditions, the provisioning of the ship, the functions, discipline and competence of the expedition members, the nature of their relations with the indigenous population, and so forth.[8]

CHAPTER 10

And the North Pole?

On 12 March 1906 Joseph-Elzéar Bernier submitted a request for copyright to the Federal Government for his book *Captain J.E. Bernier's Plan for the Conquest of the Pole.*[1] This text, which was never published, reveals that the captain was still in the race for the North Pole. The voyage to Hudson Bay hadn't diverted him at all from his *idée fixe*.

While the *Arctic* was lying in the anchorage at Port Burwell, he had given a lecture to an audience of over 300 sailors and whalers on the subject of "How to reach the Pole." Shortly afterwards, on 26 September 1905, while anchored at Château Bay, he had sent a telegram to Raymond Préfontaine to ask him for authorization to prepare his expedition to the Pole. On the following 21 October, having received no reply from the Minister, Bernier wrote to him again to inform him that the ship was re-provisioned and ready for the voyage to the North Pole, but also to remind him of his promise: "I remember your kind words when we left Québec and I know you are a man of your word."[2]

Inspired by the encouragement of Dr. Fridtjof Nansen and stimulated by the fact that another great explorer of the Arctic Basin, Roald Amundsen, was also in the race and had just finished his second wintering in the Arctic Archipelago, Bernier was very keen to take the field again. He sent a copy of Nansen's letter of support to the Minister of Marine and solicited the patronage of the Governor General of Canada, Earl Grey. Although the latter refused to endorse the project, the bold navigator did not lessen his efforts, giving a new series of lectures and organizing an intense publicity barrage. Despite his volunteer efforts to stir Canadian opinion, the Liberal government did not reverse its decision of 1904 and in the spring of 1906, when the Minister of Marine and Fisheries decided to entrust him with the organization and command of the *Arctic*'s next voyage,[3] the North Pole project had been permanently laid aside. From all the evidence:

> The Government had never thought of sending him to discover the North Pole. Parliament had never voted funds for that purpose. The Government having decided to establish permanent posts at various points on the northern coasts, the expedition was equipped towards that end [...] It was never a question of the North Pole.[4]

Was Bernier thereby abandoning the dream that had consumed him for more than 10 years?

Captain Bernier's snowshoes, in the private collection of Carol and Louis Terrien.

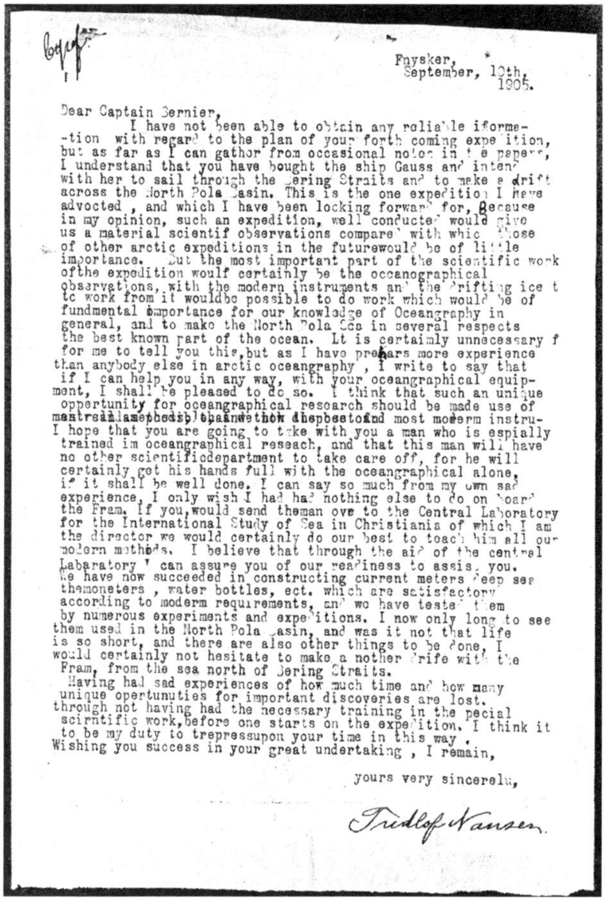

Fnysker,
September, 10th,
1905.

Dear Captain Bernier,

I have not been able to obtain any reliable informe-
-tion with regard to the plan of your forth coming expedition,
but as far as I can gathor from occasional notes in the papers,
I understand that you have bought the ship Gauss and intend
with her to sail through the Bering Straits and to make a drift
across the North Pola Basin. This is the one expedition I have
advocted , and which I have been locking forward for, Because
in my opinion, such an expedition, well conducted would give
us a material scientif observations compared with which those
of other arctic expeditions in the futurewould be of little
importance. But the most important part of the scientific work
ofthe expedition woulf certainly be the occanographical
observations, with the modern instruments and the drifting ice t
to work from it wouldbe possible to do work which would be of
fundmental importance for our knowledge of Oceangraphy in
general, and to make the North Pola Sea in several respects
the best known part of the ocean. Lt is certaimly unnecessary f
for me to tell you this,but as I have prehars more experience
than anybody else in arctic oceangraphy , I write to say that
if I can help you in any way, with your oceangraphical equipment, I shall be pleased to do so. I think that such an unique
oppertunity for oceangraphical research should be made use of
[illegible] most moderm instru-
I hope that you are going to take with you a man who is espially
trained im oceangraphical reseach, and that this man will have
no other scientificdepartment to take care off, for he will
certainly get his hands full with the oceangraphical alone,
if it shall be well done. I can say so much from my own sad
experience, I only wish I had had nothing else to do on board
the Fram. If you,would send theman ove to the Central Laboratory
for the International Study of Sea in Christiania of which I am
the director we would certainly do our best to toach him all our
modern methods. I believe that through the aid of the central
Labaratory I can assure you of our readiness to assis. you.
We have now succeeded in constructing current meters deep sea
themoneters , water bottles, ect. which are satisfactory
according to moderm requirements, and we have tested them
by numerous experiments and expeditions. I now only long to see
them used in the North Pola Basin, and was it not that life
is so short, and there are also other things to be done, I
would certainly not hesitate to make a nother drife with the
Fram, from the sea north of Bering Straits.

Having had sad experiences of how much time and how many
unique opertunuties for important discoveries are lost.
through not having had the necessary training in the pecial
scirntific work,before one starts on the expedition. I think it
to be my duty to trepressupon your time in this way .
Wishing you success in your great undertaking , I remain,

yours very sincerelu,

Fridtjof Nansen

This letter from Dr. Nansen was waiting for Captain Bernier on his return from Hudson Bay. The Norwegian explorer was encouraging him to implement his plan of drifting towards the North Pole. For a clearer version see Appendix VIII. [Archives of Carol and Louis Terrien]

Definitely not. So long as he had hope the dream remained alive in his heart. He would not let go until three years later when the American Robert Edwin Peary (1856-1920) claimed to have reached the Pole.[5]

During his lecture to the prestigious Empire Club of Canada on 20 December 1909 Captain Bernier took advantage of the presence of Prime Minister Laurier to express himself on the subject.

Well, gentlemen, when I came here some six or seven years ago, I did mention that I wanted to get to the Pole, and I proposed two plans–one to go walking over the ice, up to the Pole and back, for glory. I furnished half the money I had, and I was giving my time to the people of Canada for nothing; that shows you that I was in earnest. I could give no more, but I offered that, and they did not think it was worth while. Perhaps they were right; perhaps to go to the Pole only for glory, would not be worth what it cost; but in the North we have a good deal of spunk and time will prove it. It has already proved that we have got all these Northern, lands annexed. Of course, I did not submit only one plan, but two. The second was a drifting plan to take a ship and put it in the ice, and let her drift with natural conditions, and during that time she would be a perfect observatory. We want an observatory to take soundings and find out what there is during that long drift from ocean to ocean.

When I did submit these plans you do not suppose for a moment that I was not prepared to carry them out–that I had not studied the question. Do you think I would risk my life and the lives of those with me to go about that way on no prepared plan? Oh no! No, sir. I am not in that habit. I am in the habit of going from one part to another. I wanted to have the honour of reaching the Pole for Canada, and at the same time of reaching the islands and giving them to Canada; and if any were discovered to annex them. They were ours; they were given to us by Britain on the 1st of September, 1880. We have annexed them–we want the people to settle there now! I am glad that you approve of that because progress moves not only westward but northward too. Therefore it is a northwest course and that is what we are doing. Immigration is going northwest. We are following the setting sun; we are running towards the light; we are inclined to go that way; and, in doing so, when we scratch the ground we find something in it. In northern Ontario, not so very long ago, there was nothing to speak of. Now, today, what do we see? Silver, as much as you can take out of the ground. Therefore, Canada is today, I consider, one of the greatest countries in the world. Because you have vast, immense places, where you can search for something, and is it possible to think that God did not put on earth in the far north what is good for man to live on?

Everywhere I have been there is something for man to live on. Even on Melville Island I found thousands of

A postcard that Captain Bernier distributed to promote his voyages to the Arctic. [Courtesy of Jeanne Coudé]

musk-ox and deer. We killed no less than 24,000 pounds of fresh meat during our stay there, and we spared many herds because we could not utilize them. We did not kill a single animal we could not use; we left them for those who come after us. I found an American gentleman in the North who had been hunting musk-ox and deer, and one fine night in Baffin Land, inside a bay, I noticed a small light. [...]

All the rivers in the North are full of fish, and you can send fish to England, and as soon as your railways are built to the Hudson's Bay, you can bring fish here to Ontario, and have it cheaper than you have it now. The fishing in Hudson's Bay has been reduced very much from twenty years ago, but I am glad to say there is only one American vessel in the Strait. We met that vessel one year. We wandered alongside of her. During that year she caught seven whales, but now the whale fishery is much reduced from what it used to be. Whales are gone to the other side, that is, they have gone through Lancaster Sound, Barrow Strait, Melville Sound, McClure Sound, and on the other side the American whaler comes in from San Francisco, calls in at Herschell Islands, and still proceeding eastward on our territory, she goes as far as Bank Land and Victoria Island. Inside of the Strait they winter sometimes at Cape Hatterass and deal with the Esquimaux, selling their trash for skins. Their revenue has been about forty thousand dollars per ship. Now I think it is time that our American cousin should be looked after. That is, he should be asked for that little fifty dollar bill for the present, until such time as we see fit to have a close season, and that I would advise as soon as you can make up your mind to have a close season in those northern waters. In annexing those lands we have annexed probably in the neighbourhood of eight thousand Esquimaux, and when I took possession of Bank Land on the ninth of November, the King's birthday, I told them that they had become Canadians and therefore they were subject to our laws. Well they could not see that, but I tell you they saw it when they came on board my vessel to a dinner to which I had invited them, and they had everything they wanted, and then they commenced to realize that it was a good thing to be a Canadian.

With reference to Sir Wilfrid Laurier, Captain Bernier added:

That man holds in his hand today everything that belongs to Canada; whatever he says goes; if his Government says we are going to do a thing it is done, because he has the power. He is exactly like a captain when he is on board ship; he can do what he likes but you must remember that he must give an account of himself when he comes home. And it is exactly the same with the Government; they have to render to the public an account of what they have done. I am proud that the present Government has had occasion for striping towards the North. I did work out this problem long ago. If I had come sooner, very likely I might have been farther ahead, but I did not want to come before the Government to ask any help before I was convinced that my plans were correct, and it was only when Nansen returned that I said, "Yes, my plans are now fully developed, and there is the proof; and if I put my ship in the ice, I will come out;" and since that time I have been before the Canadian people from Vancouver to England. I have lectured in England; I am not much of a lecturer; I am more of a worker. Yes, I can do any amount of that.[6]

These statements were very touching. The sailor was perhaps not as eloquent as Laurier, but he was sincere. He was convinced that he would have succeeded in conquering the Pole if the Canadian government had supported him in his efforts. Despite the fact that he was able to re-orient his career as a result, his inability to realize his dream was certainly a bitter blow for him. The man of action, who rarely spoke of emotions wrote in his memoirs:

> I will not dwell on the disappointment that overwhelmed me when this turn in events occurred. However, since the opportunity to make a drift across the North Pole was denied to me, I determined to devote my efforts in the Arctic to what, after all, may be regarded as a more important object, that is to say, to securing all the islands in the Arctic archipelago for Canada.[7]

CHAPTER II

A frontier to explore, the expedition of 1906-1907

WHILE THE SUFFRAGETTES IN BRITAIN AND FRANCE were becoming militant to obtain the right to vote, while the city of San Francisco was surviving the terrible consequences of its worst earthquake, and while Captain Alfred Dreyfus of the French Army was finally coming to the end of his nightmare and was receiving the Order of the *Légion d'Honneur*, Joseph-Elzéar Bernier was gearing up again to carry out his first far-reaching voyage to the Arctic.

He had a mission: to issue fishing licences, to patrol the waters of the northern regions, to annex the islands and lands ceded to Canada by the British government, to winter there, and to return to Québec in the fall of 1907.

It was not only the début of a series of three official expeditions that he would command between 1906 and 1911 to affirm Canadian sovereignty in the Arctic Archipelago, but also the launching of his career at the top of the world, a milieu to match the man.

The captain was ready. He knew his ship very well; he knew where he was going and what he had to do, and he had chosen the majority of the officers and seamen who formed his crew:[1] 41 competent men, several of whom were originally from L'Islet-sur-Mer and the South Shore, and who were disciplined and could obey orders.

At 1.10 a.m. on the night of 17 July 1906, while the *Arctic* was anchored off the Quai du Roi, ready for her great arctic adventure, a Norwegian steamer, the SS *Elina*, fouled her bows as she passed. The midnight sky was clear, almost luminous, the night watchman was at his post and the anchor lights were lit. This is an indication of the extent to which sailing at night contributed to the accident. The pilot's false manoeuvre shattered the bowsprit, the jib-boom, and all its gear, so that the *Arctic*'s departure was delayed 11 days.

She sailed from Québec on 28 July, dropped the pilot at Pointe-au-Père, ran through the Strait of Belle Isle, and headed north along the Labrador coast before steering for the west coast of Greenland, which at that time of year was the area least troubled by icebergs. Captain Bernier was determined to avoid these immense bodies of ice which break off from glaciers and which sometimes weigh a million tonnes. Driven by currents and wind, icebergs drift south from the coast around Kap York, Greenland, and Baffin Bay, and float slowly towards the Strait of Belle Isle and the Atlantic Ocean until they disappear naturally. Some of these monsters might take three years before melting away in the warmer waters off Newfoundland.[2]

> The coast of Greenland was followed until we reached 70° 42' N latitude, and 63° W longitude, then the course was changed towards Lancaster Sound. Bylot Island on the south side of the Sound was passed, and the voyage con-

The S.S. *Elina* after colliding with the D.G.S. *Arctic* in Québec harbour. [Bernier Collection, LAC, C-071495]

> tinued until Navy Board Inlet was reached. The inlet was entered and a course made to Albert Harbour, where the *Arctic* anchored. Notices were issued to inform the whalers requiring them to procure licences on payment of $50. These notices were left in charge of an agent at the whaling station, to be delivered to captains of whalers which make the station a calling place.[3]

The expedition headed right to the heart of the archipelago, traversing Davis Strait, Baffin Bay, and Lancaster Sound and Barrow Strait. While carrying out a series of ceremonies whereby he took possession in Canada's name, Captain Bernier had the time to explore the main access routes, as well as Bylot, North Somerset, Cornwallis, Griffith, Bathurst, and Byam Martin islands.

On 29 August the Canadian vessel reached Arctic Point on the east coast of Melville Island where Bernier made his usual proclamation whereby he took possession not only of Melville Island, but also of all the adjacent islands including, Prince Patrick and Eglinton islands. He completed this first phase of taking possession of the Arctic Archipelago by adding Lowther and Russell islands in Barrow Strait on 30 August 1906. "Records were left at the different places touched and cairns built as tokens of the annexing all of these islands to Canada."[4]

Since the season was already quite advanced Captain Bernier took his ship back towards Lancaster Sound with a view to going into winter quarters. Along the way, he took advantage of the opportunity to immortalize the memories of friends by bestowing their names on various locations that he was passing in Admiralty Inlet: "Baillargé Bay" in honour of the former President of the *Société de géographie de Québec*, "Brodeur Peninsula" after his superior, the Minister of Marine and Fisheries, "Vanasse Bay" to flatter the ego of the historiographer who accompanied him, "Levasseur Inlet" in homage to another president of the *Société de géographie de Québec*, "Moffet Inlet" in recognition of the Chief Editor of the Ottawa newspaper, *Le Temps*, and "Prud'homme Inlet" to commemorate the contribution of his friend O. Prud'homme, "the first person to assist me on my arrival in Ottawa," as he would justify in his official report, published in 1909.

> During this voyage and the others that followed he [Bernier] was sailing in the wake of British explorers. He would restore the provisions depots that had been established

The *Arctic* departing on the 1906-1907 expedition. The ship is now displaying her new colour scheme. [Archives of Carol and Louis Terrien]

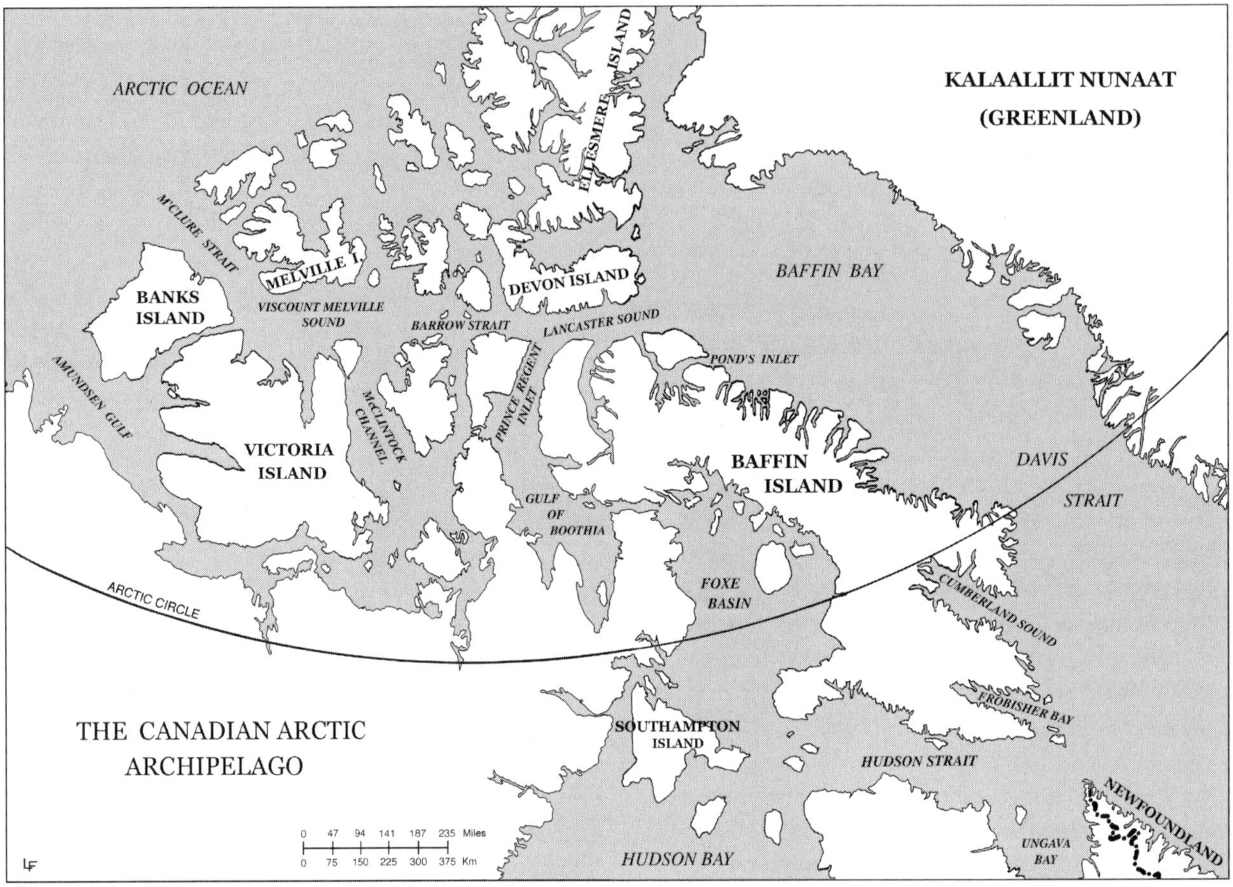

The Canadian Arctic Archipelago.

during their numerous expeditions, retrieve messages left by his predecessors and would take care to renovate the commemorative plaques or gravestones. These were symbolic gestures whereby the Canadians were trying to assimilate as episodes in their own history the epic of the British explorers and to affirm that they were their legitimate successors.[5]

Thus on Beechey Island on the west coast of Devon Island he had repaired the monument erected during the previous century by the expeditions charged with finding traces of Sir John Fanklin (1786-1847) and his men. On the shores of a neighbouring bay, named Erebus in memory of one of the ships of the unfortunate Franklin, Bernier recovered the yacht *Mary*, that the Scotsman Sir John Ross (1777-1856) had left at this location in 1850. He had it hauled to the top of a beach where it was left high and dry. These relics linked him physically with the arctic heroes that he had studied in history books over many years. Each glorious expedition had claimed its victims. Bernier was well aware of this.

> On a snowy island, acknowledging defeat
> And with bitterness in their hearts, without food, without hope,
> They carved their names, homicidal conquest,
> And sad, resigned, they died in the evening.

(René Chopin, *Paysages polaires*)

The *Arctic*'s track during the 1906-1907 expedition.

In their strange little vessel, under sail and steam, Captain Bernier and his men were facing the terrible white desert that had made adventurers dream since the beginning of time. They were alone among more than 3000 miles of pack ice, icebergs, ice caps, and glaciers, often embellished with circular currents, fog banks and showers of ice. How could they not be aware of their vulnerability and their human limits in the presence of a landscape so tortuous, extreme and inimical to life? How would their corporal envelope, accustomed to the more temperate climate of southern regions, manage to tame the cold and survive in this polar universe? A modern writer who attempted to ski to the Pole has written:

> To desensitize myself to the effects of cold I started taking a cold shower every morning from December onwards. Initially, it takes one a little by surprise, but then one gets accustomed to it. One can't talk of methods of acclimatization, but rather of exercises of desensitization aimed at making low temperatures less uncomfortable.[6]

This expert took two years to train his body, to increase his hardiness and endurance, to plan the nutritional balance of his special diet, and to assemble the sophisticated equipment that was to help him subsist during his expedition to the North Pole: the Kanuk tent capable of withstanding gusts of over 60 miles per hour, Thermolactyl underwear and anoraks, pants and anorak

The flag is raised on Bylot Island at a spot that Bernier named Canada Point. This ceremony, that took place on 21 August 1906, was one of Bernier's first ceremonies to take possession of the Arctic Islands in the name of Canada. The date and the name *Arctic* were carved into the rock, which has resulted in the Inuit calling this place Titiralik, the place where there is writing. Joseph-Elzéar Bernier is the second from the left. [Photo: George R. Lancefield, LAC, PA-139394]

made of Qualofil, a very light, waterproof and insulating fabric, a Gore-Tex windbreaker, leather boots lined with felt, the super Kanuk mouflons, gloves, goggles, and masks!

Bernier and his men were starting "from cold" with the equipment of the day. In order for their bodies to function and survive they had no other choice but to observe the habits of the Inuit and to adopt their clothing made from caribou, bear, fox, seal or bird skins. Over the centuries the Inuit had developed complex, layered clothing: double layers of skins—one with the hair inside, the other with the hair outside—that were well ventilated and waterproof, that retained body heat, insulated against the cold, and even controlled humidity and prevented overheating.

The European explorers who had preceded Captain Bernier in the Arctic had been reluctant to dress like the Inuit, often to their great peril. At that time, "the British wore wool uniforms and clothing that made the wearer overheat, and perspiration soaking into the thick wool would freeze, encrusting it with thick ice."[7] Since there was no method of drying the frozen clothing and underwear, they frequently became their shrouds.

Bernier, on the other hand, had had the good sense to study the matter thoroughly before embarking on his great adventure. Moreover, to this day, the elders living

The ceremony for taking possession of Baffin Island and adjacent islands, 9 November 1906. Bernier described the event in his memoirs: "King's Birthday. We fired the Royal salute. The holiday was celebrated on board and on shore. Fifteen natives came to the ship upon our invitation to take part in the celebration. The party then went up on the mountain and took possession of the island in the name of the King. We caused the flag of the Dominion of Canada to be hoisted and it was left floating in both places. I addressed the natives, telling them that they had become Canadians, that they must live in peace with one another and conform themselves to the laws of Canada. We held a rifle competition and discovered that there were some good shots aboard and that the natives are accurate with the rifle. All the Eskimos were invited to have dinner on board, and they certainly enjoyed the celebration very much."
Captain Bernier is standing in the back row, to the left of the flag. [*Master Mariner,* p. 320-321 and Archives of Carol and Louis Terrien]

at Pond Inlet still talk about the unforgettable *Kapitaikallak* who treated their forefathers as equals, who respected their ability to survive in the Arctic, who wore their traditional outfits, and who entrusted himself to their expertise as guides.[8]

> Legend has it that Bernier never even froze a finger in the Arctic [...] The savoir-faire of the Inuit women is undoubtedly responsible for this, for it is they who clothed the captain and the other members of the crew from head to toe, in *qulittaq, silapaaq, pualuuk,* and *kamiik* of caribou skin or sealskin. Unlike certain explorers Bernier knew that this people of the cold undoubtedly possessed the technology and the best techniques to survive in an environment that appeared hostile to the outsider.[9]

The wintering at Albert Harbour (or Port Albert), near the whaling station of Pond Inlet lasted for 10 months. Held in the ice as if in a vice, the *Arctic* was a prisoner of a severe, desolate, inhuman region. The 41 members of her crew, crammed among the provisions and the merchandise, had to come to terms with the cold, the isolation, the silence, the waiting, and themselves. It was up to the expedition leader to see to the safety and well-being of his men.

> A winter's routine in the arctic is concerned largely with making the expedition comfortable, providing for the safety of the men from fire, sickness and accident, keeping them in fit condition by exercises ashore and on board, and keeping them interested and amused by concerts, reading, music, lecture, church services and light duties.[10]

Despite all the efforts and the good will of the *Arctic*'s master, this long period of immobility, between September 1906 and July 1907, was not without incident. Even if Fabien Vanasse took pleasure in remarking that "after God there is the captain," Bernier was not a superman who could control everything. The majority of his fellow-winterers were experiencing this incredible adventure for the first time and each of them reacted to, and survived the arctic shock in his own way. Tensions and frictions were inevitable.

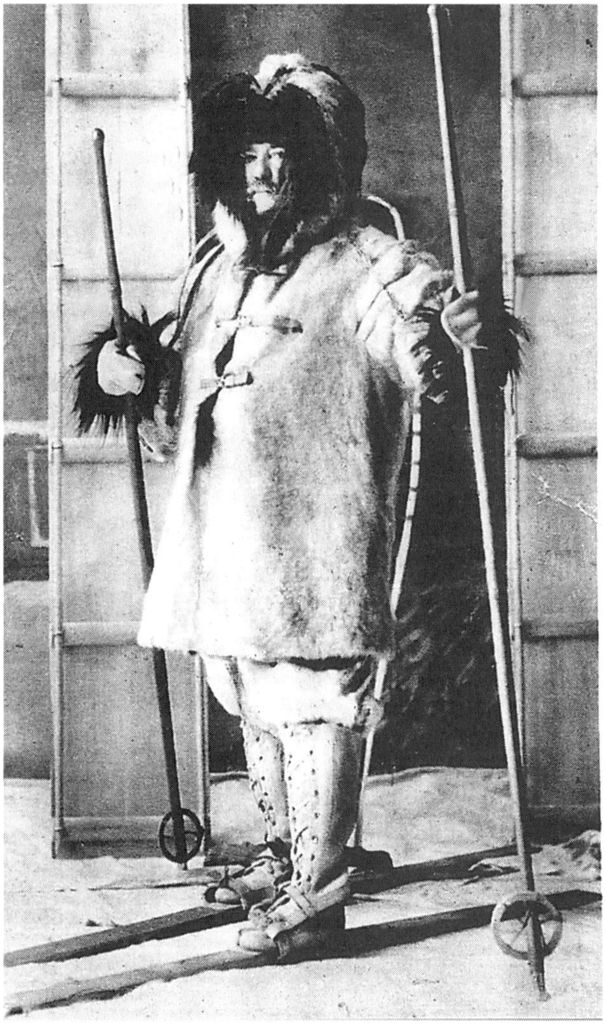

A rare photo of Bernier in his fur outfit and on skis, ready to explore the area around Pond Inlet. [Archives of Carol and Louis Terrien]

Such was the case with photographer George Lancefield who, according to Vanasse, did not get on well with the rest of the crew:

Some colleagues around the pianola in the *Arctic*'s saloon, winter of 1906. From left to right: Paul LeVasseur, Dr. Joseph R. Pépin, Captain Bernier, and Fabien Vanasse de Vertefeuille. The expedition members spent a lot of free time in this luxurious saloon, with its dark, oak-panelled walls and shelves filled with books. There were handsome copper lamps and well-upholstered chairs and benches. It was a comfortable spot and here one could forget the cramped quarters elsewhere in the ship. [LAC, PA-149035]

> Yesterday the photographer had an argument with the captain on the subject of the pups. He used some uncouth insults, such as "Son of a bitch" [...] Yesterday evening he did not come for supper. The little kid was sulking [...] At 7 p.m. the captain summoned him to his cabin. There were explanations. It was a solemn business. Ultimately everything was settled, in light of the major importance of the photos, since the photographer swore by the hairs of his dirty blonde wig and his dirty white beard, that he could not work on the photos with the pups living above his cabin. Faced with this supreme argument, the man of steel folded and promised the kid that he would have the little trouble-makers moved.[11]

It should also be mentioned that after the expedition returned Lancefield refused to turn over some of the photos of the voyage to his government employers. Subsequently no professionals were recruited as official photographers for the 1908-1909 and 1910-1911 expeditions.

The solitude, the remoteness, and the long period of darkness must have played on the nerves of some of the young men, such as John A. Simpson, who had anticipated a great and fine adventure, but who regretted having embarked on this hell-on-earth: "Feb. 17, 1907. A great event, John A.'s 25th birthday which was duly celebrated by myself. I am certainly not getting any younger and should have more sense than to be up here."[12]

But it is especially the writings of Fabien Vanasse[13] that reveal the human side of life on board the *Arctic* during the winter of 1906-1907. This intellectual was well aware that the Liberals had offered him the position of historiographer to get him away from political journalism. He saw the Bernier expeditions as a penance that he had to undergo to expiate his Conservative past. This Vanasse was a strange fellow; although he accepted this situation as a political exile, once under way, he never stopped complaining:

> I spent a very bad night. My beef dinner contrived to make me a present of a serious case of indigestion. I've been feeling bouts of dizziness, cramps and sweats from head to toe [...] ended up the year 1906 by taking a purgative. [...]
>
> We're truly treated like pariahs whom the authorities have deported to islands lost in the ocean to rid society of us. It is not known what they want to do with us, or where we should be shipped in these difficult, dangerous seas [...] Deportees go where the jailer takes them.[14]

Fabien Vanasse took a malicious delight in criticizing everyone: the "captain who claims never to be mistaken," "the youngster Lancefield or the captain's brown-noser," "Captain Gargantua," "Lancefield took a photo and the captain took pains to be very conspicuously front-and-centre, out of modesty!" His notes are full of complaints, reproaches, and nasty gossip that compromise his credibility as the historiographer of the expedition.

Despite this individual's frustrations, spleen and affectedness, his testimony allows us to penetrate into the lives of the expedition members and to discover that

Christmas menu on board the *Arctic*, 1906.
[Vanasse Fonds, ASTR]

all was not going as smoothly as it might during the wintering of 1906-1907.

Apart from the wrangling and the interpersonal tensions, Vanasse's observations reveal problems of discipline, such as the thorny question of contacts between the Whites and the Inuit: "The Protestants have discontinued their church services. They have had only one today; they are either sleeping or have gone to see the native women."[15]

The Inuit population of the Pond's Inlet region[16] participated quite regularly in the social life of the *Arctic*, by attending lectures and taking part in games, sporting competitions, and hunting parties. The Inuit men and women would party and dance with expedition members during recreational evenings. It is therefore plausible that loneliness, libido, a holiday ambience, and alcohol pushed certain members of the crew into the arms of Inuit girls who were, on the whole, quite pretty and appealing, with their round faces, their almond eyes, and their firm, attractive breasts. Naturally Bernier could not curb the sexual appetites or the fantasies of his men who were already enduring several constraints in their everyday existence.

> […] The Eskimo women were prey to the forwardness of the sailors rather than heroines of a frontier romanticism. Some expedition members made love to them without ceremony in their cabins on board the *Arctic* during dance evenings, and even in the snow-houses while their husbands were away hunting […] despite Dr. Pépin's posters describing the hygienic conditions of the natives, several sailors had a "coonie" in the village of Pond Inlet.[17]

On 14 January 1907 one of them, James Ryan, got lost coming back from the village. After searching for him for nine hours, the assistant quartermaster, Napoléon Chassé, and the laundryman, Joseph Goulet, found him half-dead from cold, three miles from the ship. His ears, cheeks, nose, and eyes were completely frozen. It took Ryan no less than three months to recover from this misadventure.

Vanasse, who was very religious and preferred to distribute medals of the good Saint Anne to the young Inuit women rather than making love to them, summed up this eventful day as follows: "May this terrible lesson serve for all the coureurs de bois frequenting igloos on the scent of the female savages and may God be praised for having spared the life of this wretch who is perhaps not ready for the great journey into eternity from which nobody returns."[18]

On 11 February Frederick Brockenhenser died of a heart attack. As Bernier admitted: "A funeral of a comrade in the loneliness of an Arctic night is a very sad affair and added much to the gloominess and depres-

Napoléon Chassé posing proudly with a hunting trophy. [Archives of Carol and Louis Terrien]

sion of the men."[19] Fortunately there was hunting to relieve tensions!

Captain Bernier loved to go hunting and trapping. It comes as no surprise to note that on all the expeditions to the Arctic that he commanded, these sports occupied an important place in his calendar of recreational activities along with football games, snowshoe races, shooting competitions, and other competitive sports. This was particularly the case during the 1906-1907 expedition, not only to allow the men to relieve their stress or to forget their isolation, but also to stimulate them by giving the opportunity to make a little money. They really enjoyed themselves trapping and hunting. White and blue foxes, caribou, muskoxen, polar bears, and seals fell to the guns of these hunters from the South who shot and trapped almost everything that moved!

Moreover during this same wintering Bernier, the businessman, missed no opportunity to indulge in fur-trading with the Inuit trappers, and he allowed his crew to follow his example.

There again he was unable to restrain his men's excesses, and the situation degenerated rapidly. Soon provisions and ship's materiel were being disposed of: condensed milk, canned meats, confectionery, alcohol, woolen sweaters, tuques etc. According to the historiographer's observations the expedition members quickly exceeded the point of excess and would not even hesitate to strip themselves of their own uniforms in exchange for furs: "The men are all naked, from the first mate right down to the lowest of the waiters."[20]

This was certainly a tough lesson for Bernier, who had always prided himself on his talents as a leader and his mastery of situations.

The *Arctic* leaving Port Albert, July 1907. [Bernier Collection, *Rapport officiel de l'expédition de 1908-1909*]

From mid-May onwards the snow-covered surfaces began to thaw, breathing a little energy into bodies overwhelmed by the excessive cold.

As the days lengthened the monotony vanished and good humour took charge of the minds of the exiles more firmly.

On 18 June the temporary roof that had covered the *Arctic*'s deck during the wintering, was removed. A glimmer of hope then revived the looks of men exhausted by the endless arctic whiteness.

Then, on 20 July, the ice in Albert Harbour began to move with the tides. The *Arctic* rocked enthusiastically.

> With indescribable exhilaration, on the morning of 27 July officers, technicians and sailors felt the ship's hesitant vibrations. Like the first beatings of a heart that is coming back to life. They were liberated![21]

If there was jubilation it did not last long since their trials were not yet over. Captain Bernier got under way the same day to patrol in Lancaster Sound.

On the following Friday, 2 August, the *Arctic* passed Coburg Island at the entrance to Jones Sound. After taking possession with an appropriate proclamation, Bernier returned to Lancaster Sound, and from there attempted to reach Port Burwell by using the natural route provided by Prince Regent Inlet and Fury and Hecla Strait. Stopped by the ice, he had to abandon this attempt and retreat.

Bernier was groping his way, uncertain of the coasts or passages that he might discover or the risks he might be running. He was relying only on his eyes, his judgment, the experience of his sailors, and the manoeuvrability of his small vessel. A single false move, faced with the pack and this impenetrable wall where giant blocks of ice collided violently and became interlocked, could mean the end of his expedition.

The *Arctic* retraced her original route and after patrolling in Lancaster Sound again, she reached the southern tip of Ellesmere Island. But the ice fields stubbornly blocked her access to Smith Sound. Unable to push any further north, she was forced to return to Baffin Bay.

Running south along the Baffin Island coast the expedition leader had the leisure to explore its access routes and the inhabited settlements and to make a census of the Inuit: "Earjuvat Station—160; Button Point—100; Cape Adair along the south coast—200; Kekerten—150; Blacklead—260; Cape Haven and along the shore -- 100."[22] He inspected the whaling stations at Kekerten and on Blacklead Island in Cumberland Sound before continuing his patrol, crossing Hudson Strait and stopping at Port Burwell in Ungava Bay.

> The *Arctic* remained at Port Burwell from September 2 to October 5, during which time Bernier observed the activities of the Newfoundland fishing fleet, compiled data received from Moravian missionaries concerning ice movements and weather conditions, and had the ship's purser assess the value of goods owned by the Port Burwell missionaries. Bernier also had a series of navigation markers set in place and recorded topographical data along the coast of Killinek Island, where Port Burwell was located, in order to improve existing sea charts of the area.[23]

Shortly afterwards Dr. Pépin informed the captain that it was urgent that they return south:

> I regret to inform you that in light of the large number of sick on board, especially in the last few weeks, a number that is tending to increase rather than decrease, and also because the cases are becoming increasingly serious, it is my duty to ask you to do something for your part, and to warn you that, for my part, I am almost at the end of my resources, given the impoverished nature of the medical department on board at present.
>
> Captain, I have no more medications or the most essential drugs even for those sufferers who are already in bed. [...] I have reason to fear that there will be even more cases of sickness due to the advance state of fatigue and stomach exhaustion among the crew.
>
> [...] I can no longer assume responsibility for the lives that have been entrusted to me with the limited resources on which I can count in the future. However, although sick myself, I will still do my best for some time, but if the voyage is prolonged indefinitely, I am afraid my best may not be enough.[24]

On 19 October the *Arctic* finally reached Québec harbour. A moment of great relief, no doubt, for the crew, who finished this trip with a pay cheque and a Sunday mass.

Captain Bernier supervised the unloading of his ship in Louise Basin before catching the first train to Ottawa.

CHAPTER 12

The apogee of his career, the expedition of 1908-1909

THE STREETS OF QUÉBEC had never been so decorated. The city was literally enveloped in banners, hangings, flags, and bunting in rich and contrasting colours. In that summer of 1908 Québec was celebrating its three hundred years of existence. To commemorate the arrival in America of its founder Samuel de Champlain, the proud city was dressed overall, as she overlooked an imposing gathering of warships of the three great allied world powers, Great Britain, the United States, and France.

> The ceremonies will be grandiose: march-past, solemn open-air mass, reconstruction of Champlain's "Abitation" guarded by soldiers in period costume, re-enactment of major historic scenes in the history of Canada, fireworks in Victoria Park, organization of a park on the Plains of Abraham, and the installation of historic plaques. Officially starting with the inauguration of the Laval Monument on 22 June 1908, the activities will actually take place from 19 to 31 July.[1]

Streets had been widened and some boulevards broken through. A monumental triumphal arch had even been raised in front of the Parliament buildings to underscore the visit by the Prince of Wales, the future George V. His arrival on Wednesday 22 July was the signal for a series of receptions, balls, military reviews, concerts, regattas, symbolic tree plantings, and children's holidays. The fine weather co-operated and the Governor-General of Canada, Earl Grey, declared himself very satisfied with the welcome accorded the King's representative.

The tricentennial of the City of Québec, 1908. The view of the Château Frontenac, the Champlain Monument and the river, taken from the roof of the Palais de Justice. [Photo: John Woodruff, LAC, C-019930]

"We are justified in anticipating that a new imperialism will flourish in Québec," he wrote to the British Prime Minister, Lord Chamberlain.

In the midst of this collective euphoria, the 42 members of the crew[2] of the *Arctic* were "looking lively" under the vigilant eye of the "Old Man." Preparations for the voyage were under way and Bernier was checking and double-checking everything: coal, construction lumber, tool-boxes, guns, canned goods, flour, husky dogs, so indispensable for sledge trips, and even pigs and cows that he had decided to take to provide the group with milk and fresh meat for part of the winter. It was an original idea, but the experiment was a fiasco, since the animals consumed all the fodder in a flash. At least Bernier and his men had the pleasure of varying their diet with fresh pork roasts and some beef steaks.

There had been a great deal of coverage on the new expedition in the press and the name of the captain from L'Islet, the intrepid seafarer, was on everyone's lips. At 56 years of age Bernier was at the apogee of his career. He was highly regarded by the most illustrious explorers of the day, such as Nansen, Amundsen, Scott, Shackleton, Peary, and Byrd. He was admired by Canadians who recognized that this countryman of theirs was impelled by a powerful vocation as an explorer and adventurer-extraordinary. Above all, his was an enviable mission, that of affirming Canada's arctic boundaries.

His instructions from the Deputy Minister of Marine and Fisheries, G.J. Desbarats,[3] took into consideration what he had accomplished during his previous voyages and designated the sections of the archipelago that he was to survey, explore or annex. However his superior left him free to make two successive winterings, if he judged it to be opportune.

Before she sailed, the *Arctic* was duly inspected by Minister Brodeur and by Rear-admiral Kingsmill, Commander-in-Chief of the Canadian Navy, who found the ship to be seaworthy and adequately equipped for an expedition of over two years. On this occasion it was agreed that the wives or families of expedition members would receive part of their salaries during their absence.

On departure day while last-minute checks were under way, two British Navy officers came aboard the polar vessel to inform Captain Bernier that His Royal Highness the Prince of Wales wished to make his acquaintance. This was one of the most memorable meetings of his career. "On appearing before the Sailor Prince I was questioned closely about my previous voyages and my career at sea. I took advantage of the occasion to indicate to His Royal Highness my plan to take possession for Canada of all the islands discovered and annexed by British explorers, and was warmly commended for my persistence in urging this matter upon the Canadian government."[4]

At 13.30 on 28 July the captain steered his ship past the British squadron and several French and American vessels lined up to honour the *Arctic,* as well as a large number of ships of various nationalities that were lying at anchor.

> We passed by the naval vessels, saluting them, and were greatly honoured by the cordial manner in which the salute was returned by all vessels within sight, as our little vessel passed down abreast of the harbour.
>
> The most stirring circumstance to us personally, was the display of comradeism shown by the offices and crew of the British fleet.[5]

Indeed, high above them, on board the HMS *Indomitable,* commanded by the Prince of Wales, a band broke into *Auld lang syne*, in honour of the Canadian crew, who immediately replied with joyful cheers.

This emotion-charged departure could not but move these brave lads who were heading for the "roof of the world." Despite the enthusiasm of their fellow-seamen, the acclamation of the crowd, and the splendid weather that buoyed their spirits, they must all have had a presentiment that the adventure that they were about to embark upon, would not be a pleasure trip.

This astonishing departure set the stage for the remainder of the voyage since the 1908-1909 expedition represents the most important of Captain Bernier's missions to the polar regions, that on which he asserted himself as the principal architect of Canadian sovereignty in the Arctic, and that which conferred on him the title of the greatest navigator and explorer in the history of Canada.

Let us first take a look at the early part of this remarkable voyage. After an uneventful trip along the coast of Labrador and the west coast of Greenland the *Arctic* dropped anchor at Etah on the afternoon of 19 August in order to land provisions intended for the American explorer Frederick A. Cook,[6] who was aiming to reach the Pole, but while keeping his movements in the North a close secret. It was his wife who had arranged that the Canadian vessel would leave provisions in the area where he would normally be located.

Landing this depot and replenishing the fresh water tanks were completed during the night and at 9 the next morning the *Arctic* sailed from Etah harbour, at the entrance to which several icebergs had grounded. With the wind in her sails the little schooner headed off in a southwesterly direction across Baffin Bay, bound for Coburg Island.

> These are dangerous waters since the sea is infested with icebergs and fogs are frequent. Indefatigable as always Bernier would often spend 24 hours at a stretch on the bridge, watching over the—relative—comfort of his men and the safety of his ship.[7]

At noon on 22 August the *Arctic* was at 74° 45'N and 78° 45'W, and was encountering large quantities of melting ice, in the middle of which were giant icebergs that were drifting in Lancaster Sound until they were driven out by a strong tidal current from the west.

> On the morning of the 23rd, the sun rose clear from the horizon, gilding North Devon and presenting a fine sight. The whole of the land is a high plateau with ravines where glaciers once formed and discharged into the sea, and this is shown by the glacial action on the banks.[8]

Throughout that day the ship was heading for Erebus Bay with the aim of establishing a provisions depot for the expedition's own use in case of necessity. On the morning of the 24th she dropped anchor in a depth of 13 fathoms,[9] just opposite the monument erected to the memory of Sir John Franklin which Bernier had re-erected during the 1906 voyage. They landed four boatloads of supplies of all sorts that they stowed in a cache and left a document outlining their intention of pushing further west. "We remained in Erebus bay, making magnetic observations and securing geological specimens until 4 p.m."[10] For, unlike the *Arctic*'s previous voyages this one included scientific personnel equipped with instruments for studying meteorology, the magnetic elements, mineral resources, fauna, flora, topography, and the geology of the lands visited, as well as the thickness and movement of the ice. The information obtained would paint a realistic portrait of the islands of the archipelago, previously unknown, and would advance knowledge of navigation in these icy seas. Captain Bernier, who had always wanted to include this scientific side in his expeditions, tried to facilitate the scientists' work and involved himself personally in the soundings, the study of tides and currents, the search for precious metals, and the organization of sledge expeditions.

The sun was dropping for longer and longer periods below the horizon, although it still was never totally dark. Despite dense fogs, a strong north wind and the menacing presence of the pack ice, the *Arctic* continued to push west, first running along the steep coast of Cornwallis Island, then slipping between the pack ice and the snow-covered peaks of Baker Island, lying off Bathurst Island.

On the morning of 26 August she was rounding Cape Cockburn. The sky was overcast and it was snowing a little. At noon she was at 75° 8'N and 103° 15'W, near Viscount Melville Sound, which, incredibly for this time of year, was completely free of ice. This situation allowed her to reach Byam Martin Island and finally Melville Island.

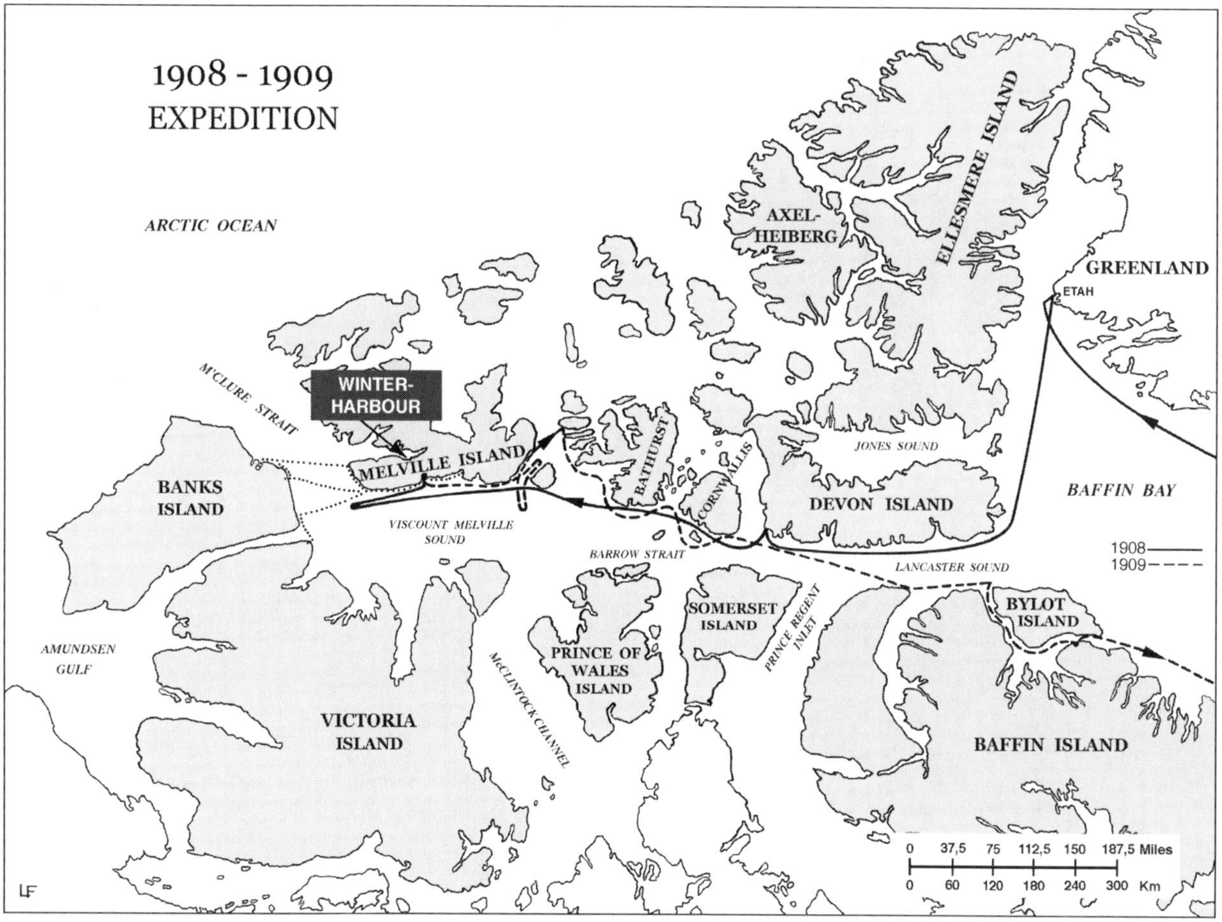

The *Arctic*'s track during the 1908-1909 expedition. The dotted lines indicate the trips by sledge and on foot to Banks and Victoria islands.

On 27 August she rounded Cape Providence and taking advantage of her good fortune pushed on to 20 miles south of Cape Hay.

> No ice was visible to the westward, but heavy Arctic ice was seen to the southward; we were then about half-way through M'Clure Strait, and if our instructions had included making the Northwest passage, I feel confident that it could have been made.[11]

The captain concealed his emotions well. Imagine the possibility of being the first sailor to make the transit of the Northwest Passage in a single season. If he had wanted to, Bernier might have surpassed the exploits of Roald Amundsen who traversed the legendary Passage in three seasons, 1903-1906.

Novelist Gilberte Tremblay, who had interviewed Joseph-Elzéar's family members, imagined this decisive moment as follows:

> He [Bernier] raised his eyebrows as he scanned the horizon:
>
> "No ice, not the least sign of ice! Inconceivable! [...] We could be in Vancouver in a few weeks!"

Since there were neither telephones nor satellite communications, Captain Bernier and his shipmates would build cairns or piles of rocks and earth to prove that they had been there and to leave documents providing information on the *Arctic*'s expedition. This one was erected at Key Point, the northwestern point of Vanier Island, in 1909. [Bernier Collection, *Master Mariner*]

There followed a brief silence. The water was sparkling. The sun was shining. The sea stretched away, free! Some of the sailors were humming songs in the tranquil air. Then came the whispered temptation: fame is extending a hand to you, Bernier!

"We have the chance of a lifetime," Braithwaite raised the stakes.

"You can beat Amundsen," an inner voice assured him. "Wasn't Amundsen covered with honours when he completed the Northwest Passage? But he took three years! You would be achieving the same exploit in one season, just a few months, just a few weeks! Bernier… you would be famous! Famous! Make up your mind!"

"You're hesitating, Captain?"

Braithwaite had brought him back from his dreams.

"You know our orders, George!"

"Of course. But…"

"Is there any mention that we'd been sent to attempt the Northwest Passage?"

"It's not part of our mission, but… wouldn't the Government be the first to agree to it on a morning like this?"

"Can you telegraph them?"

"No, unfortunately!"

"Or make contact with the Minister immediately?" suggested Bernier drily.

"No. But we have an unexpected opportunity here! Think about it, Captain."

"George," Bernier broke in, "We're going where we've been asked to go!"

"I'm sorry, Sir. But I thought that…"

Bernier spoke slowly, with visible effort:

"Mr. Braithwaite, we will fulfill our mission, that of ensuring the ownership of the arctic islands for Canada!" And, brusquely, he left the bridge.

But in his diary, completely alone, he wrote: "I had tears in my eyes a moment ago! I could have really wept. It was a tragic moment. Perhaps somebody else would have acted differently! But for me, 'Orders are orders.'"[12]

Fame had passed Bernier by for a second time. He might have been the first to discover the North Pole. He might have been the first to make a transit of the Northwest Passage in one season. But this man of decision was able to distinguish the relative importance of his obligations as against his possible actions. Much as he enjoyed recognition and honours, he was fully aware that his duty and the work he undertook for his country took precedence over his personal interests.

Since the season was already quite advanced the captain decided to turn back and to take up winter quarters in Winter Harbour.

> An examination of the harbour was an important matter, and I began to familiarize myself with its features as a place of safety for the ship. It was soon apparent that no more favourable one could have been selected in these regions, for it is well sheltered from outside pressure of ice; Hearne Point runs in a southeast direction for about 3 miles and Reef Point and Shoal in a southwest direction. There is an inner harbour, suitable for vessels drawing less than 18 feet of water, with an area of about one mile in length and half a mile in width [...] Stone beacons were built by the crew for leading marks for entering and departing, so that a stranger may now enter the harbour by the marks.[13]

Preparations for the wintering began on 1 September, with the rigging of a housing over the ship's deck and the collection of heaps of rocks for ballast. This latter precaution was ingenious since throughout the winter it allowed the rocks to be used as weight to replace the coal and foodstuffs that were consumed, thus insuring the ship's stability.

Throughout the year that the wintering lasted, there was never any lack of activities. The fall was devoted mainly to hunting muskoxen and caribou. As Captain Bernier explained, this was an absolute necessity.

> We had before us a long winter, with 43 souls on board, in an Arctic climate, where nature demands animal food containing a large amount of fat, to maintain within the body sufficient heat to withstand the rigours of the winter, whilst moving about outside the ship. We had an abundance of salt meat, both pickled and canned, but had not sufficient fresh meat. With the continuous use of salt provisions scurvy would be inevitable [...].[14]

The *Arctic* reaching Winter Harbour, 1908. [Bernier Collection, *Rapport officiel de l'expédition de 1908-1909*]

Aware of the custom of polar explorers of depositing messages at certain locations, either to prove that they had been there and to inform as to their discoveries, or to indicate the route they intended taking, Bernier took advantage of the short fall season to search for caches and cairns. Not only did he hope to find travel accounts of the first British explorers and useful information on navigation in northern waters, but he also had a presentiment that the natural resources of the Canadian archipelago would one day be coveted, which in fact was a more important reason impelling him to engage in this treasure-hunt. During all his government expeditions he therefore did his utmost to search out these messages and to replace them systematically with his own messages, proclaiming Canadian sovereignty over the area.

> In the entire history of exploration of the Canadian Arctic, Bernier has the distinction of recovering the greatest

One of the many muskoxen killed by expedition members on Melville Island in 1908. Bernier wrote: "To our great surprise we noticed that the muskoxen were not afraid of us and continued to graze while we fired at them." [Bernier Collection, *Master Mariner*]

number of documents and other articles left behind by previous expeditions. The largest such recovery was made during his 1908-1909 voyage. In each case Bernier made a point of turning over to the Department of Marine and Fisheries all material that he and his men had gathered.[15]

By mid-September the winds blowing from the north were announcing the approach of winter. Hence, since all the rigging was dry, the captain had the ship unrigged and all the gear stowed away carefully in convenient locations. Until then the "Old Man" had stayed in his room in the deck-house, as a precaution, so as to be always ready to navigate the ship.

> The life was rather of a hermit nature; orders were given to clean my room in the cabin and put it in order. I found the exchange of quarters more agreeable as I came in contact with the officers and found the social conditions more pleasant, after the long strain of the voyage outwards.[16]

Contrary to what one might imagine, his report on the 1908-1909 expedition makes for interesting reading, full of comments and details that reveal a more human side of this seafarer. Since he was solely responsible "next to God" it appears evident that all aspects of this communal life "in a goldfish bowl" were of concern to him—regulations, physical exercise, distribution of warm clothing, diet, as well as the morale of the group.

> September 26 being the anniversary of the entrance of Sir William Parry into Winter Harbour, we raised our flag in honour of the brave mariners who discovered so many of the islands of this Arctic archipelago. I took advantage of the occasion to refer to the bravery and courage of the early mariners who had endured hardship in their voyage of discoveries, in the same waters as we were now exploring, and commended their example to the men on board. The life on board ship, in Arctic regions, where men are frost bound and in darkness for over 90 days, is by no means a pleasant one. It, therefore, was considered my duty as commander, to employ every means to encourage the men to look forward to accomplishing something that will be recognized by their fellow men as more than an ordinary voyage.[17]

As to the crew's health:

> The doctor made an examination of each individual on board, and remarked when doing so that pimples were appearing on some of the crew. This was attributed to neglect in changing their clothing, and an aversion to the use of proper precautions in this matter. In the Arctic regions there is a disinclination on the part of some individuals, owing to the cold, to take baths. Orders were issued for all on board, to exercise the utmost care with regard to cleanliness. This order was not necessary in most cases, but the precaution against the breaking out of any disease compelled the most rigid observance of rules for baths and changing of clothes. The rule applied also to bed clothing, and reporting any dampness observed in the sleeping apartments. The men were given a half holiday on Saturdays for washing their clothes.[18]

During the winter the crew had been making preparations for sledge trips that were to take them across M'Clure Strait to Banks and Victoria islands. Four sledges were specially built for these missions aimed at taking possession, then loaded with sleeping bags, clothing, maps, compasses, cameras, guns, and foodstuffs.

As an introduction to these journeys of exploration, it is important to examine the "thorny" subject of the contribution of the captain's companions. Even today, one often hears the following statements:[19] "Not Captain Bernier again!" "Don't you think enough has been written about him?" "No, but why not write a book about the men who did all the work for him and have been left out of the picture?" "It was the young lads with him, who made the sledge trips at the peril of their lives, but Bernier has always enjoyed the limelight."

Of course, apart from being the leader of these government expeditions, it was Captain Bernier who had interested the Canadian public in the question of the Arctic frontier. Bernier's name had become an enormously popular headline that sold the newspapers of the day.

As one studies the official report of the 1908-1909 expedition, it emerges clearly that the *Arctic*'s commander never attempted to diminish or suppress the crew's contribution to the success of his enterprise. The details of the sledge trips, and the reports of the officers were included and commented upon, on par with the accounts and research results of the scientific personnel. There even emerges a certain pride from the fact that these young fellows overcame all the difficulties and succeeded in the missions that he had entrusted to them. Moreover, in his memoirs Bernier sings their praises as follows: "Officers Morin and Green and their men deserve the highest praise for the able manner in which they carried out their orders to annex Victoria and Banks islands, and search the shores for evidences of former explorers."[20] And then, on returning from the expeditions, he never prevented his men from responding to the questions of journalists who were looking for anecdotes that might interest their readers.[21]

The *Arctic* wintering at Winter Harbour, 1908-1909, surrounded by a wall of snow designed to insulate the ship to increase the crew's comfort. The windmill on the ship's deck provided electricity, quite a futuristic technique for the time. [Bernier Fonds. Musée maritime du Québec (Musée Bernier)]

Naturally these young seamen would never have experienced "the greatest moment of their lives"[22] had it not been for Captain Bernier. It is no exaggeration to add that the "Old Man" "was able to create a true family among his men and that it is among that courageous group of sailors that one finds the greatest admiration for Captain Bernier."[23]

But let us return to the sledge expeditions in that spring of 1909. Despite his age and the potential dangers, Bernier nonetheless took charge of the first group of 17 travellers who left the *Arctic*, early on the morning of 30 March, bound for Banks Island. They covered 13 miles before pitching a provisional camp near a colossal iceberg, nine miles west of Point Hearne.

> The following day, the appearance was threatening, and in the morning, finding that our sleighs required altering, and that the packages of biscuit which had been opened were found unfit to send with a party on so perilous journey as our men under Mr. Morin and Green were about to

Some of the *Arctic*'s sailboats were mounted on wooden runners so that they could travel both in the water and on the ice, after the manner of modern amphibious craft. [Collection Bernier, *Rapport officiel de l'expédition de 1908-1909*]

take, was sufficient reason for all the parties to return to the ship.[24]

Le Soleil of Québec had a somewhat different version of this false start.

On the expedition's first day one of the sledges landed in a jam, and, while working at hauling it out of there, Captain Bernier became exhausted and when a severe storm struck at the same time, the expedition returned to the *Arctic*.[25]

Could Bernier have been embarrassed to admit that he had exhausted himself and was therefore incapable of taking command of one of the sledge trips? It is possible that he altered the facts in his official report so as avoid the impression that he was a "quitter."

On the April 2, 3, 4 and 5, the wind was too stormy to attempt a start. But on the April 6, since the weather was calm again, the various groups of explorers were able to get started. The second officer, Octave-Jules Morin, was in charge of the first sledge, Charles Green, the third officer led the second sledge; Napoléon Chassé, second quartermaster, was in charge of the third sledge and Claude Vigneau,[26] also second quartermaster, was at the head of the third sledge. A fifth group accompanied them to provide assistance for part of the trip.

Officer Morin's account[27] reads almost like the scenario for a film.

April 8. [...] our faithful dog, Arctic, had accompanied us to this point. As we marched along I noticed at a few miles distance, in a ravine, a herd of musk oxen, and sent Bodeker out to hunt them, and he was lucky in killing one, which provided us with a luxury of fresh meat for our journey and to leave a quantity in a cache in case of future need. When Bodeker fired to kill his ox he had the misfortune to hit with the same bullet our dog, Arctic, which was playing havoc with the herd; the bullet struck him in the thigh and he soon after died [...]

April 11. At 8 a.m. the thermometer registered 20 degrees below zero, the wind blew northwest, velocity 16 to 17 miles. We had but time to remember that it was Easter Sunday, so well celebrated throughout the world, and marched on till 10.30 a.m., when we found ourselves opposite Cape Providence, where we camped. [...]

April 12. [...] We were now marching on thick packed ice on the Strait. Great difficulty was experienced and the full force had to be put on one sledge, and all sledges had to be hauled over one by one. Owing to these difficulties only a short distance could be covered and the men were tired out; we then set our camp for the night and while cooking our supper we had the visit of a splendid specimen of a bear which I was lucky enough to kill.

April 13. The thermometer indicated 27 degrees below [...]. Green, who had taken a different route, expecting an easier road, reached camp only at 7 o'clock with two sledges.

April 14. [...] Green informed me that one of his men had a foot frozen. I then decided that Green, with seven men, should return to the steamer *Arctic* [...] and I, with the seven men left, headed for the land on Banks Island [...].

April 15. The ice was now becoming so irregular that I decided that it was not practicable to go any further with our large sledge, with its heavy load, and I ordered it to be returned to Cape Providence at the cache, and sent back five of my men. I kept on the journey towards Banks Island with the smaller sledge and two men,[28] and took provisions for fifteen days. [...]

April 20. [...] The ice was in the shape of pyramids and peaks, and we experienced great difficulty in getting through. At 12 noon, we stood at a distance of 19 miles from Banks Island, and I took advantage of the sunshine to make an observation and ascertain at what latitude we stood. [...]

April 25. [...] We were now camping at a distance of 5 miles from Russell Point; all felt tired out. The roughness of the ice and snowdrifts were beyond description, and we often sank down to our necks in the drifts accumulated during the last storm. Nevertheless we felt in good spirits at the idea that possibly we would reach the mark on the next day.

April 28. [...] I dispatched my two companions, Napoléon Chassé and Reuben Pike, to Peel Point on Victoria Island to take possession of this island in the name of Canada and to visit Capt. Collinson's cairn, erected in 1851. As for myself I headed through Prince of Wales Strait, I made for M'Clure's Mount Observation, situated on the east coast of Banks Island, being 16 miles from the mouth of the Strait. Throughout this journey I travelled over smooth new ice [...]. I kept walking on the Strait till I was nearing Cape Parker, on the east side, and I only reached camp after a tramp of thirty-three hours. I was in an exhausted condition and suffered much from being snow-blind. I could hardly see at all. [...] My companions had made Point Peel on Victoria Island, and had returned after a twenty-six hours trip. [...] During our absence polar bears visited our igloo, and destroyed our blankets [...] and also completely destroyed our sleeping bags, and had eaten up most of our provisions. [...]

April 29. [...] a terrific blizzard on the Strait made it impossible for us to make a move; our rations this day was one biscuit each, and when night came we retired to our snow hut for a night's sleep, not fearing to be troubled with indigestion.

The return trip to Cape Providence was a real nightmare for the three men, who were suffering from cold, snow-blindness, fatigue, and "severe thirst, which is even worse than hunger." Fortunately on 3 May they had the good fortune to spot the uprooted trunk of a red spruce on a block of ice. Chassé, axe in hand, immediately went to work to transform it into an invigorating fire. They all took advantage of it by melting snow and sleeping for a few hours, their first good sleep in five days.

This painting illustrates clearly the effort that Morin and his men had to expend when faced with the pack ice of M'Clure Strait, 50 to 55 miles in width. On 13 April officer Morin wrote: "As far as the eye could see, the pack presented irregular floes of varying heights that barred our way." [Painting by S. Gurney Cresswell, "Sledging over hummocky ice," *A Series of Eight Sketches in Colour*. London: Day and Son, 1854]

May 5, Wednesday. [...] Not being able to resist our thirst any longer, I made up my mind to sacrifice our sledge, in order to make a fire to melt snow, to assuage our thirst, and give us a sufficient provision of water to allow us to finish the journey. We had only four biscuits left, so I considered that we did not need the sledge to carry them the 32 miles which still separated us from Cape Hay, Melville Island.

Finally, on 7 May, on their last legs, famished and almost blinded by snow-blindness, the three fellows got back to the camp at Cape Providence. They found Green and his fellow-travellers sleeping comfortably in their tent.

May 9, Sunday. We left the depot at Cape Providence on Saturday night at 8 o'clock, for Winter Harbour, where we arrived that evening at 9.30, having covered in twenty-five hours the 37 miles between the cache and the ship.

Lieutenant Morin set off again on 17 May, accompanied by Guillaume Lebel, William Doyle, and Reuben Pike, to explore northern Banks Island, to find coal seams, and to leave a document that would attest to the annexation of Banks and Victoria islands.[29]

As for Green's expedition[30] he and his party set off on 1 May aiming to reach Mercy Bay on Banks Island and to locate the remains of the ship abandoned by Captain Robert M'Clure in 1853. Covering about 12 miles per day, the group reached their goal on 21 May but found no trace of the *Investigator.*

A little disappointed at finding the earlier explorers' caches empty and not having enough provisions to prolong their stay in this area, Charles Green gave the order to backtrack. His party took 12 days to return to their home base, although not without difficulties, as Green describes in his report.

May 29. [...] All hands were getting played out. Our pemmican was finished and only one tin of biscuits was remaining, with a little Bovril and tea. As our dog[31] was beginning to feel pretty hungry and snapped at anyone going near him, I shot him and cooked the best of him, and all hands made a hearty meal of the meat. [...]

May 30. Weather was thick and foggy and snowdrifts 10 to 12 feet high had to be pulled over. [...]

May 31. [...] We could only afford six biscuits per man daily [...].

June 1. [...] The Boatswain Johnson complained of his knee being badly swollen and stiff. On examining it, I found that he had struck his knee cap against the edge of the ice by falling into a crack. [...]

June 2. [...] We had traveled 20 miles this day, and the men said that they could go no further. Robinson had been blind all day and had to be guided by a drag rope. White's feet were very sore and swollen and gave him much pain. Burke and Johnson complained of pains in their knees, so I gave them the last of the Menard's liniment remaining, to rub themselves with. [...]

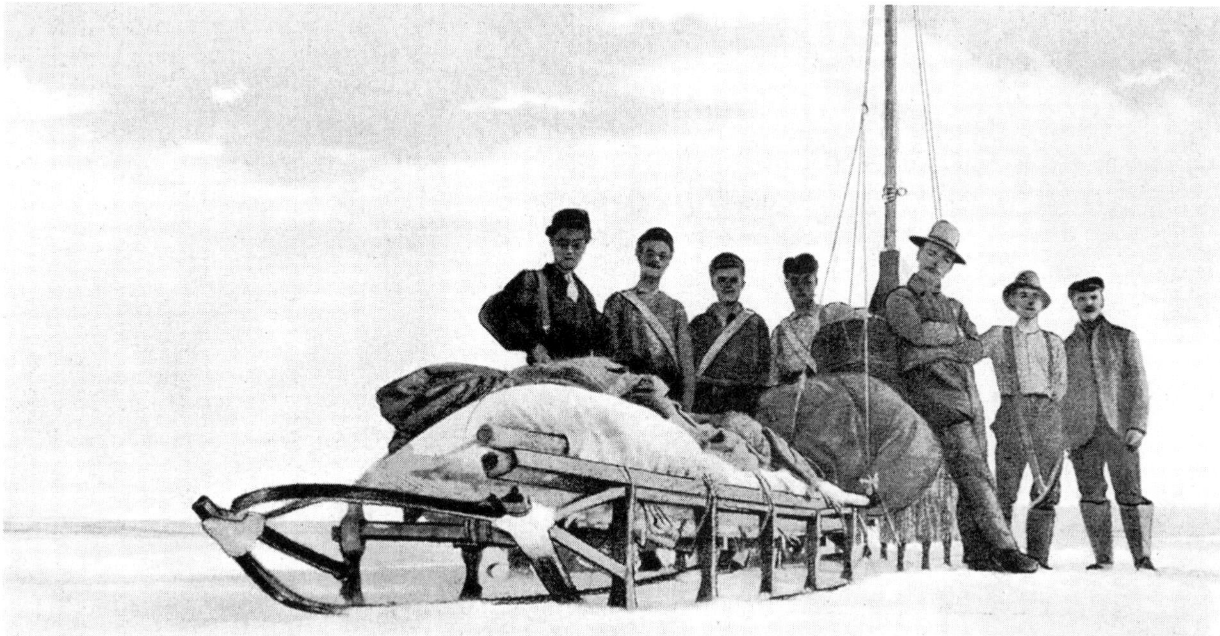

Octave-Jules Morin and his companions on their return from their expedition to Banks Island. [Bernier Collection, *Rapport officiel de l'expédition de 1908-1909*]

June 7. [...] All hands in the morning turned to fixing up sleigh etc., but White being too sick to work, and his feet being badly swollen, I sent him to bed. The boatswain also complained of diarrhea and pains in his leg. Vigneau's eyes were sore, he having broken his glasses. [...]

June 10. Broke camp at seven thirty (7.30) a.m. and travelled till noon. We stopped for dinner and then went on again till we reached Hearne Point, and received help from the ship, which was reached at 4.15 p.m., and we were received by Commander Bernier, and the men were attended to by the ship's surgeon.

⚓

The mechanics of the proclamations of taking possession, as established by Captain Bernier, were essentially the same from one island to another. A fairly high point was chosen, so as to be clearly visible from the sea and here a rock cairn was built to cover and protect the metal box containing the proclamation signed by the captain and some of his men. The Canadian flag was then raised on a mast planted in the cairn, then the event was immortalized in a photograph.

The text of the proclamation of taking possession was always the same.

> [...] This island ...., and all islands adjacent to it, was graciously given to the Dominion of Canada by the Imperial Government, in the year 1880, and being ordered to take possession of the same, in the name of the Dominion of Canada, know all men that on this day the Canadian Government Steamer *Arctic* landed on this point (or island), and planted the Canadian flag and took possession of .... island and all islands adjacent to it in the name of the Dominion of Canada [...].

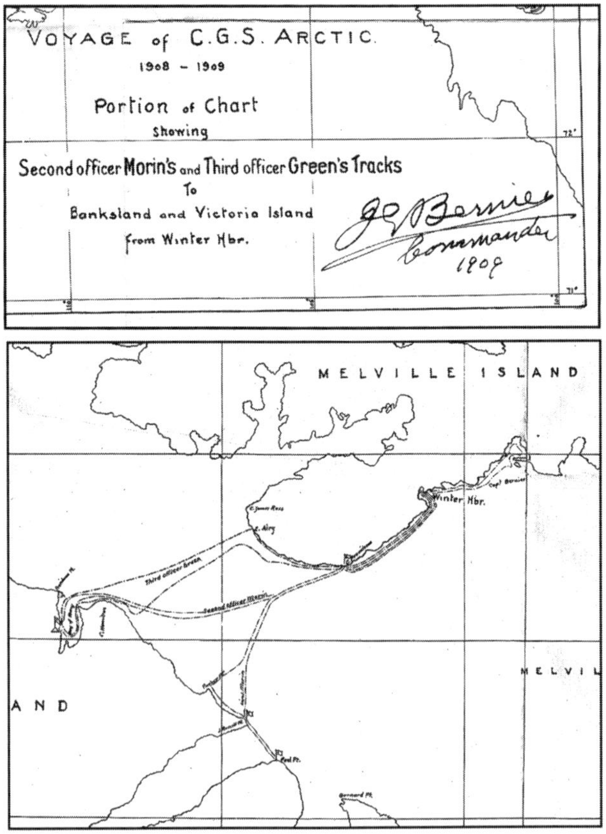

Routes covered by the sledge teams of officers Morin and Green to Banks and Victoria islands, 1908-1909 (Courtesy of Benoît Robitaille).

During the previous expedition Captain Bernier had formally annexed Bylot, Wollaston, Somerset, Griffith, Cornwallis, Bathurst, Byam Martin, Melville, Prince Patrick, Eglinton, Lowther, Russell, Limestone, Young, Davy, Garrett, Prince of Wales, Devon, Beechey, Coburg, Ellesmere, Axel Heiberg, Amund Ringnes, Ellef Ringnes, King Christian, Cornwall, Graham, Buckingham, Kent, Table, Cone, and Baffin islands, as well as a large number of very small neighbouring islands. The man who had been nicknamed "the greatest Canadian annexationist" was determined to complete his task during this second expedition. He chose July 1, Dominion Day, to carry out a ritual that many historians consider to be the most outstanding in the establishing of Canadian sovereignty in the Arctic.

> Dominion Day was celebrated by all on board; all our flags were flying, and the day itself was all that could be desired. At dinner we drank a toast to the Dominion and the Prime Minister of Canada; then all assembled around Parry's Rock to witness the unveiling of a tablet placed at the Rock, commemorating the annexing of the whole of the Arctic archipelago. I briefly referred to the important event in connection with the granting to Canada, by the Imperial Government, on September 1, 1880, all the British territory in the northern waters of the continent of America and the Arctic Ocean, from 60 degrees west longitude to 141 degrees west longitude, and as far north as 90 degrees north latitude. That we had annexed a number of islands one by one, and a large area of territory by landing, that we now claimed all islands and territory within the degrees 141 and 60 west longitude as Canadian territory, and now under Canadian jurisdiction. Three cheers were given in honour of the Prime Minister and Minister of Marine and Fisheries of Canada, and the men dispersed for the balance of the day to enjoy themselves.[32]

Charles Green and his men on their return from their expedition to Banks Island that lasted from 1 May until 10 June 1909. [Bernier Collection, *Rapport officiel de l'expédition de 1908-1909*]

Thus, fully aware of the significance of these proceedings, Joseph-Elzéar Bernier did not hesitate to establish Canadian sovereignty over the entire Arctic Archipelago and even its water bodies, all the way north to the Pole.

> There are those who, even today, continue to discredit Bernier, namely because he overstepped his authority on occasion; they neither understand nor accept that this sea captain, a man of humble origin, could have asserted himself as chief architect of Canadian sovereignty in the Arctic when such initiative was needed.[33]

⚓

At midnight on 12 August the *Arctic* finally left the waters of Winter Harbour, and proceeded cautiously with the tide, following the labyrinth of leads that had formed in the ice. There was a west wind blowing and it was snowing a little.

On Saturday, 14 August she passed Dealy Island, and continued eastward along the coast of Melville Island. The wind frequently changed direction, swinging from west to north, and this contributed to widening the leads.

The captain had decided to push north through Byam Channel in order to reach Byam Martin Channel, separating the northern part of Melville Island from that of Bathurst Island and to push as far north as possible into the Arctic Ocean, in a previously unexplored sector.

> The *Arctic* was in a good seaworthy condition, and her great strength as a ship, induced confidence in her power to reach a high latitude in the polar sea, provided, it came within the bounds of reason, to attempt a passage northwest. I could hardly express my sense of disappointment when [at Key Point] I viewed a vast expanse of heavy, aged ice, presenting an impassable barrier.[34]

Man's efforts were quite puny, compared to this demonstration of the raw power of nature.

> The action of tides and winds, moving this irregular mass, grinds and forces immense bodies upon the shores of the northern islands, and these masses can be compared to nothing less than precipices along many parts of the coast. An icebreaker, of great power might, in time, cut a channel for herself from our mooring point and by drifting and cutting where possible, penetrate to the polar sea.[35]

The *Arctic* turned back south. On 24 August, abeam of Griffith Island, she again found herself surrounded by heavy ice. Since Bernier was determined to find an escape route, he climbed to the crow's nest to look for a feasible route.

The more hostile the environment became, the more vigilant he had to be. He stayed there, day and night, focused on the drifting ice, impotent in the face of the forces that increasingly squeezed the ship. He listened to the wind and the cracking-noises beneath the hull. He watched the slightest changes in the sky and inhaled the scent of the ice. He could detect no sign of shelter nor place of safety. He watched and waited for the right moment.

Five days of hell!

The heavy pack ice yielded slowly and ponderously and on 29 August the *Arctic* managed to forge ahead and to break free and round Cape Hotham on Cornwallis Island.

For the first time in an eternity the sailors could feel their vessel rolling and pitching, and were delighted to be back in open water. Even their commander expressed his happiness at feeling the ship's motion again.

> At noon, on August 30, our latitude was 73° 58' north, longitude 84° 23' west, and at 5 p.m. we passed Cape Crawford, 3 miles distant; near midnight Cape Charles York was passed. The wind was strong from the southeast, but the moon was shining full and clear, and from our ship the sight was unusually grand. Dark clouds were massed behind the Byam Martin Mountains on Bylot Island; the mountain peaks mantled with snow presented a variety of fantastic figures, the sides rugged and black, contrasted with the white peaks, and the dark blue water reflected the sun's rays in a path that reached to the rocky shores.[36]

The ceremony of taking possession of the entire Arctic Archipelago in front of Parry's Rock, Winter Harbour, Melville Island, 1 July 1909. One can recognize Captain Bernier in the front row surrounded by his officers and the crew of the *Arctic*. A muskox calf is licking his hand. Parry's Rock, which is almost the size of a house, still represents an important historic and physical landmark in the Canadian Arctic. [Bernier Collection, *Master Mariner*]

Images to take one's breath away! These were rare moments of rapture that made one forget the wintering, the dull routine, and the constant dangers on the horizon. After all, it was to experience such wonders that they had left home!

On the evening of 1 September as the *Arctic* was carefully negotiating a string of icebergs in Navy Board Inlet the look-out reported two boats manned by Inuit, rowing energetically towards the ship. These were the first humans they had encountered since weighing anchor at Etah, Greenland, on 19 August 1908.

Bernier was happy to have them climb aboard and to transport them to Port Albert, the spot prearranged for picking up mail. It goes without saying that all the men were feverishly anticipating a package, newspapers, or letters with news about their dear ones, or events that had occurred during the year that had just elapsed.

"The news was in all cases of a pleasing and satisfactory nature, with the exception of a letter received by the third officer, which contained the sad information of the death of his mother."[37] This sort of detail perhaps seems too banal and inappropriate in a report full of statistics, lists and scientific observations. It is true that Captain Bernier could have omitted them from his report to his government employer. The fact that he made a point of discussing his companions at every stage in the voyage lets one suppose that, despite his authoritarian character, the "Old Man" had a real affection for the lads who shared his passion and his ambition. He never criticized them. He knew that he would never have succeeded on

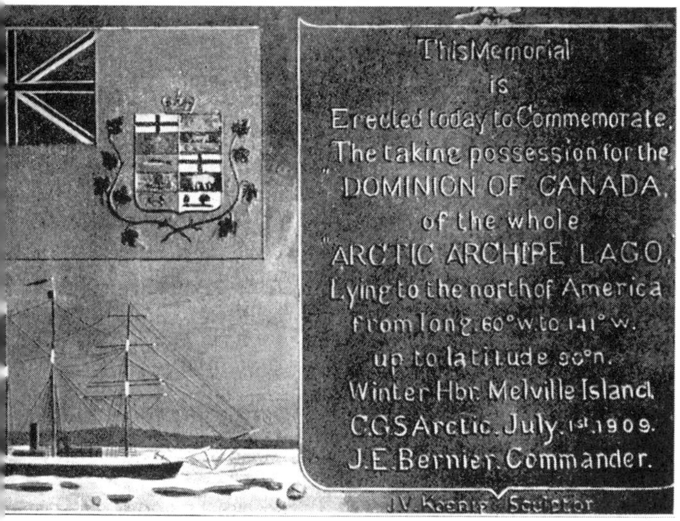

Commemorative plaque on Parry's Rock, 1 July 1909. It was the work of Chief Engineer John Van Koënig. Thus Bernier was being so bold as to cast Canada's arctic frontier in bronze. [Collection Bernier, *Master Mariner*]

this extraordinary foray into the Arctic without their collaboration, their courage, their expertise, and their considerable efforts.

Bernier concluded his report as follows:

> The scientific staff, officers and crew performed their duty faithfully and in some cases heroically; much is due to Dr. Bolduc, for his continual inspection and interest taken in the health of all on board. The heroic conduct of the second and third officers and the men under them, who visited Banks Island and Victoria Island with sledges, for the purpose of raising our flag, entitled them to special reference. The conditions which they met were unexpected, but they overcame obstacles by persistent and dogged determination.[38]

The expedition of 1908-1909 was a triumph!

On the morning of Tuesday, 5 October, the *Arctic* gallantly ended her mission by anchoring off the King's Wharf in Québec. Before unloading the provisions remaining from the voyage, her crew joined in the euphoria displayed by the crowd of journalists and admirers that thronged the decks, carried away by the scale of their exploits. These bold expedition members had just added an area of 500,000 square miles to the arctic frontiers of their country.

The postcard released by Captain Bernier after his glorious expedition of 1908-1909. [Archives of Carol and Louis Terrien]

CHAPTER 13

Mina's hat

"I WAS USED TO A FREE, independent life," wrote explorer Henry Larsen, "and knew that, married or not, I had to return to the North."[1]

The same applied to Joseph-Elzéar Bernier, with an obsessive need for his freedom, the sea, and limitless horizons. The seafarer needed a challenge to live, independently of the love that he felt for his family.

As soon as he had completed a mission, he immediately headed for Ottawa to submit his report to the Minister of Marine and Fisheries. He never dallied at home with Rose, aware, perhaps that they no longer had anything in common. How could he explain the vastness and the miraculous nature of what he had just been experiencing to his home-body of a wife? How could he talk about the dangers without upsetting her? How could he describe the violence of nature without her becoming even more anxious? The captain was like the men coming home from war, who are unable to communicate with those who have continued to live their everyday, normal, peaceful lives. His companions on the voyage were more his family than his real family, having experienced the same emotions, the same fear, the same solitude.

Since he lived in Ottawa while preparing for his expeditions and writing his reports, his ties to Rose, maintained solely by correspondence, became more stretched or weakened. The latter still shared a life with Elmina, widow of Dr. Joseph-Odilon Bourget.[2] It was a less hectic reality than that of the explorer in the limelight, as a few lines from Mina would suggest: "My aunt and I are working very hard at domestic chores and sewing. Life here is a little more monotonous than in Ottawa, but we are working in the hopes of having a short holiday."[3]

A short holiday? Does this mean that they rarely had the opportunity to see anything else but their normal surroundings at Lauzon? A letter from Rose tends to suggest this:

> Dear husband,
>
> I see from the newspapers that you will be setting off again next year. I have still not received anything from you. Time is really dragging for me [...]. If you are going to New York on 1 November, do try to take a week's holiday. There is an excursion to New York from Saturday, 30 October until 8 November. Check the newspaper and if you are going there please take Mina and me with you. This winter you will be even busier than you are now. If you are heading north again next summer. You are so pleased that Sir Wilfrid has given you *carte blanche* that you've given no thought to the pension that you meant to ask him about. Every day I wait for your news. I'm always hoping that you will have a few minutes for us. Everyone is well.
>
> Regards to everyone. With love and kisses.
>
> Your wife who loves you, Rose.[4]

A few minutes in his busy schedule! The triumph of his last expedition was such that the man of the Far

North was in greater demand than ever.[5] He was welcomed enthusiastically in the very prestigious Canadian Clubs of Québec, Ottawa, Toronto, St. Catharine's, and Montréal, where all were keen to hear his lecture on "Our new country, the Arctic Archipelago," accompanied by about a thousand magic lantern "views."

Rose's letter makes allusion to his lecture of 16 October 1909, to the Ottawa Canadian Club where Sir Wilfrid Laurier had given him *carte blanche* to go wherever he wanted on his next expedition: "where he likes, as long as he pleases." Just imagine the feeling of gratification in the mind of the man who had so much wished for the recognition of the Prime Minister of Canada. And especially that the eloquent Sir Wilfrid had expressed "the feeling of pride felt by all my fellow-countrymen."

A few days later Rose dared to mention the monotony of her daily life to her globe-trotting husband:

> I received your yesterday's letter with pleasure. I'm very pleased. I was alone and didn't know how I could pass the time. It is not a matter of lack of work, but of inclination [...]. Here everything is very quiet everywhere. There is rarely anything new. I am really eager to see you. Time really drags [...]. Cécile has come up from L'Islet. She has come to spend some time buying her fall outfit and having it made here. When you go up to New York, please do not forget us. The whole family joins with me in kissing you. Your wife who loves you.[6]

Apart from these two letters from Rose no correspondence between her and her husband has survived. Hence it is impossible to imagine the captain's reaction to his wife's boredom and loneliness. By contrast, a brief expression of apology to Elmina's younger sister, Cécile,[7] lets one suppose that he did reply to letters from his family: "I am really sorry not to have had the pleasure of seeing you, but as you know I am like the bird on a branch, who does not know on which tree it will perch." Despite his busy schedule he involved himself in harmless details that concerned them:

The Berniers around 1915. [Archives of Carol and Louis Terrien]

> I received your letter [...] in which you discussed major things, and I would never have believed that you would be so unassuming as to want to wear a hat that my dear Mina had worn.
>
> I will accede to your wishes and will come to an understanding with Mina with regard to another [hat].
>
> In passing, let me tell you how much young lads would be pleased to know how undemanding you are, in offering to content yourself with so little.
>
> Your devoted uncle.
>
> P.S. Please excuse my writing such a short letter; if you only knew how busy I am.[8]

To another second-cousin, Rose-Marie Bernier, he wrote:

> I am going to New York for a banquet in late November, and since I promised, you can accompany me to New York. In so doing you will get to know your cousin. Ask your parents' permission and make your preparations. That will be for 7 or 8 days [...]. Your affectionate cousin.[9]

This trip was not destined to take place since, in the following month he announced:

CIRCULATION

"LE TEMPS"

Le Temps

AVIS A NOS ANNONCEURS

OTTAWA, LUNDI, 18 OCTOBRE 1909

LE CAPITAINE J. E. BERNIER DEVANT LE CLUB CANADIEN

Il a pousse les limites du Canada jusqu'au Pole. Le Club Canadien lui fait une reception enthousiaste. Details interessants sur son voyage. Sir Wilfrid Laurier le felicite et le remercie au nom du Canada. Le capitaine Bernier propose une delimitation des frontieres internationales dans l'ocean polaire. Ses projets au sujet du Pole.

An article in *Le temps* about Bernier.

> [...] I am annoyed at myself to have missed the opportunity to go to New York for the moment, although it is not my fault. I have turned down a good dinner, but we'll lose nothing by waiting. I'll find you a companion who is prepared to go there.[10]

Captain Bernier gave a lecture to the Arctic Club of America in New York in January 1910. On that occasion Rose, Mina, and the children had the pleasure of abandoning their daily routine and of following him to New York. A grand-daughter of Mina Suzanne Audet-Normandeau[11] relates an episode on this trip that had greatly struck the imagination of her mother, Marie-Marthe, who was then just over 12 years old:

> Aunt Rose was very happy to set off on a trip and wanted a new dress for the occasion. The captain was not keen on buying one for her. Rather he had the intention of having fur hats modelled "for all his women." Rose did not protest and received a magnificent white-fox hat.
>
> My mother thought her little hat was ermine, the fur was so white and soft to the touch. (It was probably the fur of arctic hares that the captain had shot in large numbers on Melville Island).
>
> Before getting aboard the train the captain had handed them packages wrapped in newsprint, tied with a string. It was too late for them to protest. In particular they were not to question him about the contents of the packages which had to be quite valuable since the ladies had to swear to take care of them as if they were utterly priceless! It was a bizarre scene, nonetheless, as the captain led "his women" to the train. They were too elegant to carry their cases but, on the other hand, they were obliged to promenade along with packages in newsprint which dirtied their beautiful, fashionable gloves! What a humiliation.

As soon as she reached New York Aunt Rose declared to her husband that if he did not buy her a new dress she would refuse to sit with him at the banquet being held in his honour. The captain would not yield to her blackmail and she would not back down from her decision. She had to sit elsewhere.

My mother was too young to attend the banquet but she could remember what my grandmother had told her. During the lecture the captain had begun slowly to unwrap the mysterious packages, one by one, for effect. To the general surprise the newsprint had concealed the most beautiful furs that he had brought back from the Arctic. They were his gifts to his friends in New York.

Little Marthe never forgot that exciting adventure with this larger-than-life relative. But, at the bottom of her heart she always bore him a grudge for having made her carry those hateful packages to avoid paying customs dues.

Bernier was not perfect. He liked money and kept a tight hold on the purse strings.

Naturally the friends who received the magnificent furs, originating from the polar regions, were quite enchanted:

> Do you know I am getting to feel so proud at the thought of being the possessor of a real white fox that it is hard to hold me down. Just think, too, they are the very latest thing in furs, and a Paris letter on fashion that I saw the other day, says that you are a mere nobody unless you have them. Now, what do you think of that? You have no idea how much I do appreciate your trapping it for me.[12]

And later:

> My astonishment and joy gave way to veritable ecstasy at the sight of the superb white fox that you were so kind as to bring back for me from your voyage to the arctic regions.[13]

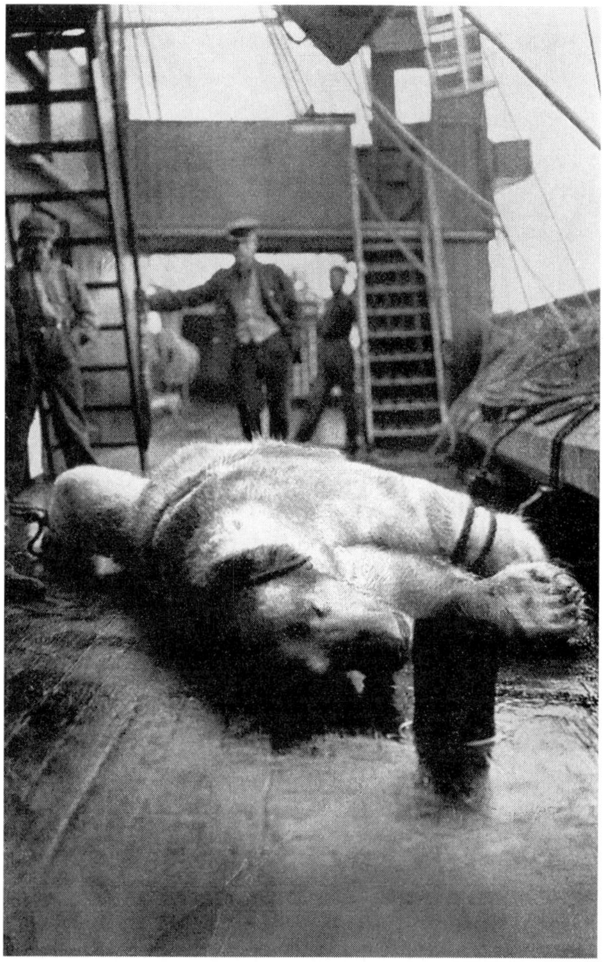

A polar bear killed by Captain Bernier in September 1909. Could this be the same one that he offered to Prime Minister Laurier and that one can still admire in the living-room of his house at Arthabaska, now the Laurier Museum? [Bernier Collection, *Master Mariner*]

CHAPTER 14

The controversial expedition of 1910-1911

On 7 July 1910 the *Arctic*'s sails again swelled as she set off valiantly to conquer the northern seas once again. On board were 35 crew members[1] who had agreed to follow their captain to the ends of the civilized world. Several former companions—Morin, Koënig, Bolduc, Vanasse, Thibault, Chassé, Bouchard, Gosselin, Holden, LeBel, Tremblay, and Doyle—were along on the voyage for a second or third time. The others, young first-timers, possibly seduced by the risks of the unknown, were in for a rude awakening at the realities of the northern wilderness.

Joseph-Elzéar Bernier was still drawn by a desire to explore, despite being over 58 years old, and at the start of his third major government expedition, he was doubly motivated by the idea of traversing the Northwest Passage. The Norwegian Amundsen had already met this challenge between 1903 and 1906 by coasting along the mainland coast. The captain was convinced that he could discover an easier route by the wider and deeper M'Clure Strait.[2] He had had no difficulty in having a special clause to this effect inserted in the departmental instructions, since Prime Minister Laurier had given him *carte blanche* the previous year in the presence of the guests at the Canadian Club in Ottawa.

As well as attempting the Northwest Passage, Bernier also had the mission of patrolling the waters of the Arctic Archipelago, issuing licences to whalers, and fulfilling the functions of game warden and Justice of the Peace.

The *Arctic*'s route was as follows:[3]

On Wednesday, 13 July she ran through the Strait of Belle Isle under sail and steam.

On 15 July she skirted the first iceberg.

At 2 a.m. on the 18th she reached the Arctic Circle.

At noon on the 19th she reached the zone of permanent daylight, while Greenland's enormous peaks stood out majestically in the distance. Visibility was excellent, allowing the crew to spot about 30 whales as they passed by.

On the 22nd she was passing abeam of the island of Disko off the west coast of Greenland.

On the 23rd the weather was foggy and rainy. Bernier had no choice but to swing west to avoid the numerous icebergs blocking his route into Baffin Bay.

By 30 July, passing Bylot Island, the *Arctic* was slowly entering Pond's Inlet.

On 13 August she left Port Albert. Temporarily beset in the ice, she took several days to reach Lancaster Sound.

On 23 August, off Cornwallis Island, the *Arctic* was unable to move freely through the pack, that was becoming steadily closer around her.

On 30 August she finally reached Dealy Island, in south-eastern Melville Island. She then headed for Winter Harbour, to land provisions there before attempting the Northwest Passage via M'Clure Strait.

The ice concentrations in the latter strait were extraordinarily heavy.

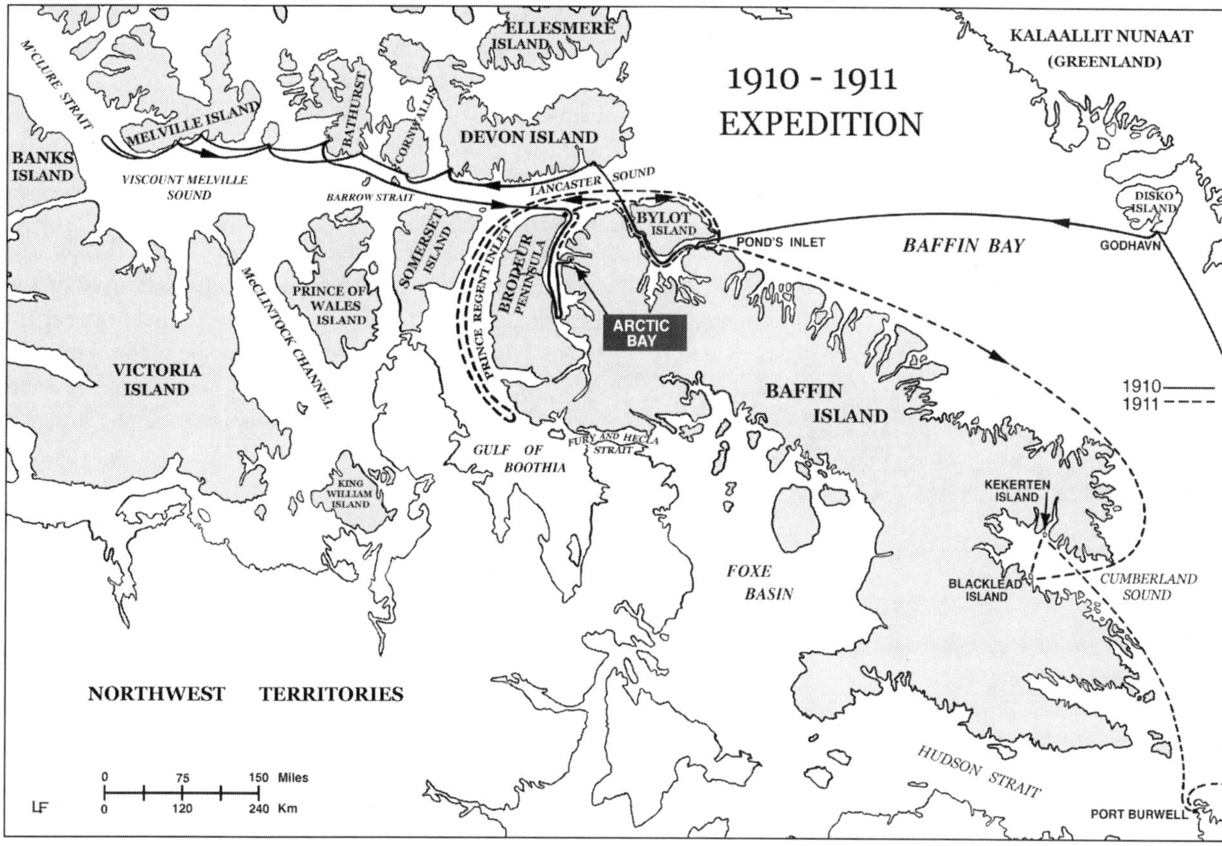

The *Arctic*'s track during the 1910-1911 expedition.

> The voyage was the most difficult I had so far made in Arctic waters. Ice of all kinds from that of the previous winter to ice showing several years growth, was at the time being discharged into the North-West Passage and carried eastward against the progress of the ship.[4]

After repeated attempts the captain had to yield to the wishes of Nature and backtrack to Winter Harbour.

On 2 September Bernier tried his luck again. Having, by dint of great effort, reached about 30 miles to the southwest of Cape Ross at the mouth of Liddon Gulf, he finally had to abandon his plan since the *Arctic*, which was not an icebreaker, could not withstand the enormous pressures of the polar ice. Having studied the history of British expeditions in these waters, he knew only too well that no less than five ships had been abandoned there during the previous century, due to similar conditions.[45] Prudently, Bernier did not want to repeat the errors of his illustrious predecessors. He turned his back on his glorious project and looked for an escape route.

> Our escape from being frozen in near Melville Island I regard as providential. We made all haste eastward. Snow squalls, rain and ice conditions impeded our progress.[6]

The expedition took eight days to reach Admiralty Inlet, and by 15 September was organizing its winter

An iceberg near the Greenland coast, photographed July 1910. [Bernier Collection, *Cruise of the Minnie Maud*, 1921]

quarters at Arctic Bay, off Adams Sound, not far from an Inuit encampment.

During this wintering[7] several trips by boat or by dog sledge were undertaken with a view to surveying the northern part of Baffin Island and the Admiralty Inlet and Brodeur Peninsula areas. One party even managed to reach Fury and Hecla Strait, to observe ice movements there, and to plot the configuration of that strait, which Bernier was contemplating using to reach Hudson Strait, rather than running around Baffin Island. (See map on p. 241).

First Officer Octave-Jules Morin was the first white man to explore the east coast of Admiralty Inlet and Shimik Island, while engineer Émile Lavoie[8] traveled one of the still-unexplored regions of the Canadian Arctic, namely the east shore of Prince Regent Inlet. He drew a map of the west coast of the Brodeur Peninsula, and in particular, discovered the large bay that now bears Bernier's name.

As soon as summer arrived the captain set his men to work with axes and ice-saws to try to cut a channel in the thick ice of Arctic Bay. Despite their considerable efforts the *Arctic* had to wait for a further month before she was completely freed, but on 21 July 1911 she was finally able to leave her winter quarters. She was immediately beset in the drifting ice of Admiralty Inlet and carried southward. It took a week before she could be freed from this dangerous situation, and could make for Bylot Island.

"When Bernier brought the *Arctic* to Pond Inlet […] he was not arriving simply as a representative of the Canadian government. He was now coming home again to his wintering site where he had spent the winter of 1906-07."[9] In fact, by an Order-in-Council dated 9 April 1910, the captain had obtained a grant of 960 acres of land in the Salmon River area, thus becoming the first Canadian landowner in the Arctic. A letter from the Minister of the Interior, dated 1 December 1910, records that a sum of $50 had been received:

> for a strip of land which you have been permitted to purchase in Pond's Inlet, Baffin Land […] to acquire the land in question at $1.00 instead of $50.00 […] upon submitting evidence that there are no conflicting claims and that you have erected a house thereon valued at $200.00.[10]

As well as acquiring this enormous property, which he named "Berniera," Bernier, the businessman, had bought the facilities of shipowner R. Kinnes of Dundee at the station at Pond Inlet, as well as a depot at Button Point on Bylot Island. Hence his return to the Port Albert area was not a disinterested one.

On 15 August Bernier headed back north to Lancaster Sound, bound for Prince Regent Inlet with a view to traversing Fury and Hecla Strait. But all attempts were in vain, since the Gulf of Boothia was a vast field of impenetrable ice.

Hence, all in all this meant the end of a less than eventful expedition. The *Arctic* returned to the Pond Inlet region to issue permits to whalers who had just arrived, then ran south to Cumberland Sound to grant further licences and to collect further customs dues at Blacklead, Kekerten, and Cape Haven—then on south to the Labrador coast and the Atlantic Ocean. This was

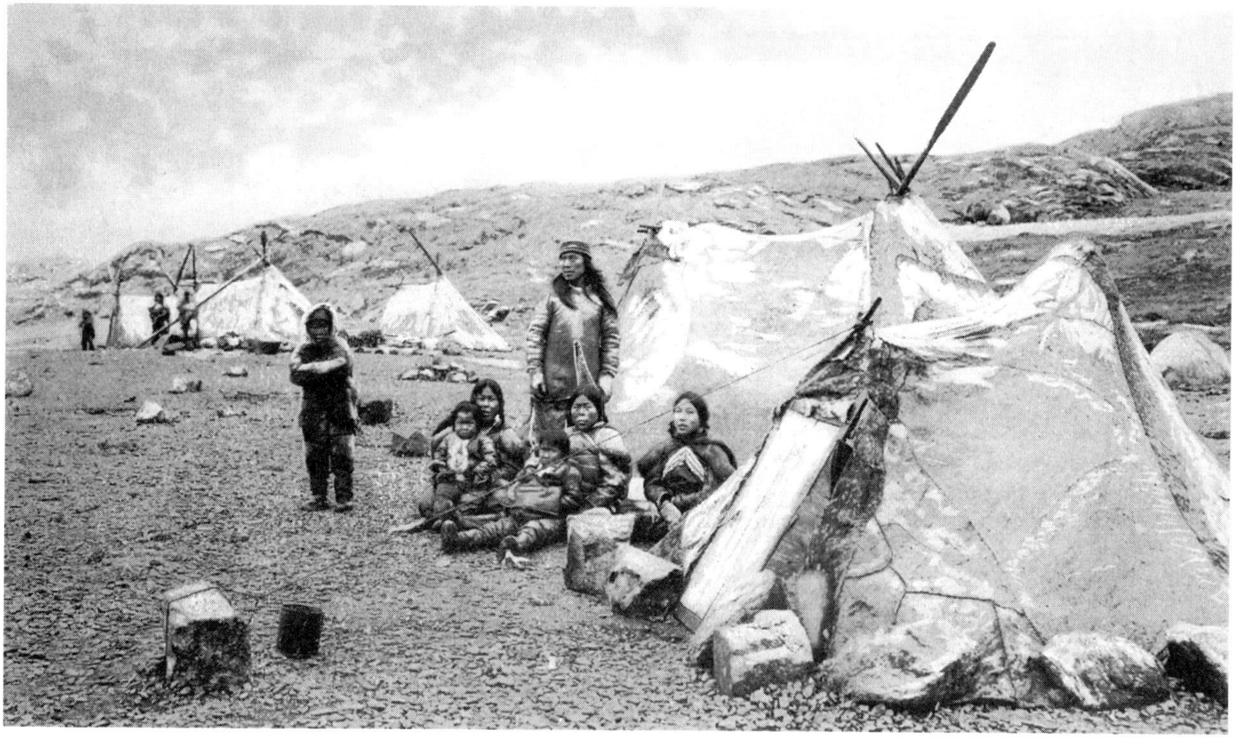

An Inuit encampment near Pond Inlet, 1910-1911. [Bernier Collection, *Cruise of the Minnie Maud,* 1921]

rather a routine activity for these High Arctic adventurers who had walked the tightrope of the unknown, and who had faced the terrible, indomitable environment of the arctic wilderness, never sure how much longer they had to live. These sailors had "earned their spurs" as the "first patrollers" of the Arctic Archipelago. At the end of the voyage some of them perhaps realized that they were no longer ordinary men, and that nothing could ever be as before, among those who had remained behind, safe and warm at home.

On returning to Québec harbour on 25 September 1911 Captain Bernier could tell himself that he was satisfied at having brought his mission to a conclusion. He had fulfilled his role as Fisheries Officer with diligence and adroitness. His ship had travelled 10,000 miles without serious accident and his men had not suffered excessively and had stood the test. He had not had the honour of making the Northwest Passage but he had confirmed Canadian jurisdiction over the Arctic Archipelago, as well as bringing back an impressive amount of rock samples, coal, clay, and minerals for analysis at the Department of Mines.

Unfortunately for him this personal success was overshadowed by two clouds of controversy: the Janes case and the Mathé affair.

Let us first examine the case of Newfoundlander, Robert Janes. In December 1910, while the *Arctic* was wintering at Arctic Bay, Captain Bernier had sent his

Second Officer to Eclipse Basin to carry the mail and to intercept whalers. Janes remained in that area until the *Arctic* passed through the following summer. He discovered coal seams at Canada Point and at the Salmon River as well as shoals of halibut off Cape Weld.

Claude Minotto maintains that Robert Janes had agreed to collaborate in his captain's "commercial program" because he anticipated receiving an equitable share of the profits it realized: "Under the captain's direction he traded, took photos, and shot films. Then he had to threaten Bernier in order to receive his fair half of some $3600 that the accumulated furs were worth."[11] As proof Claude Minotto cites this communication of Janes, dated 15 November 1911:

> I want what is due to me in regard the trading business. You know the balance… Be an honourable, straight man, as you are aware I took you to be. For heaven's sake, think of what I went through in Pond Inlet. Have some consideration for your want of honour…
>
> P.S. I shall not put you to trouble unless I am compelled to do so, you know that.

After lodging a complaint with the Minister of Marine and Fisheries and even with the new Prime Minister, Robert Borden, Robert Janes entrusted his case to the Newfoundland lawyers Furlong and Conroy. Minotto concluded that, faced with a law suit, Bernier replied to the lawyers that he would settle accounts with Janes.

Few people got wind of this conflict between the two men. However it is probable that Janes' recriminations encouraged the assistant steward, Joseph-Eugène Mathé, supported by Octave-Jules Morin and Fabien Vanasse, to issue further accusations against the commander of the recent Canadian expedition to the Arctic. On 1 March 1912 Mathé submitted his denunciations to the Minister of Justice, the Minister of the Interior, and the Minister of Marine and Fisheries, stating that he had proof that Captain Bernier had made use of goods belonging to the government to trade with the Inuit.

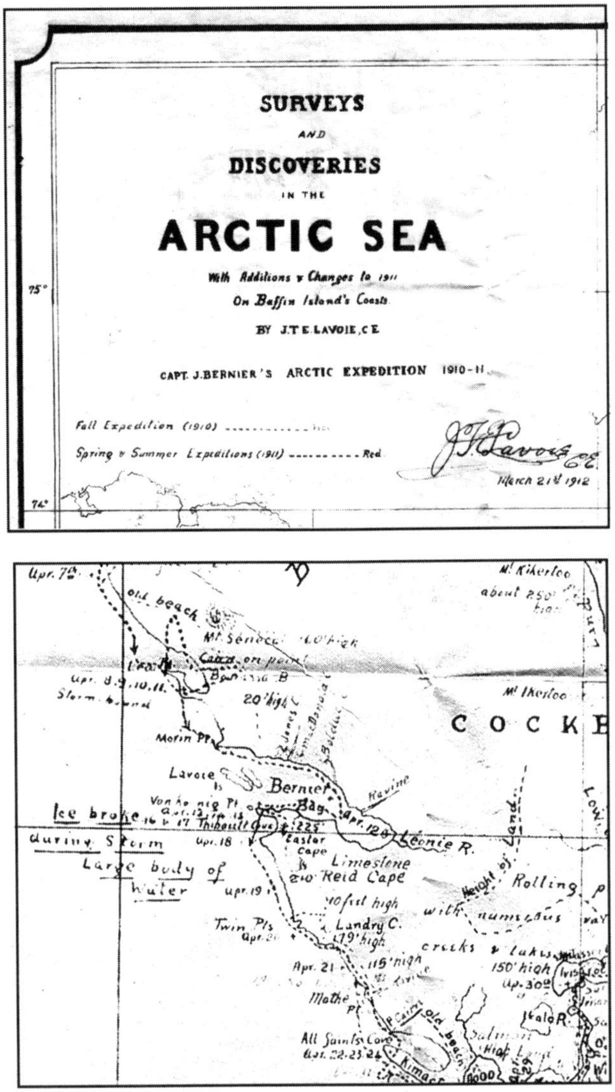

A section of the map prepared by Émile Lavoie, showing the discoveries made by expedition members during the 1910-1911 voyage. Bernier Bay may be seen on the west coast of Brodeur Peninsula. [Courtesy of Benoît Robitaille]

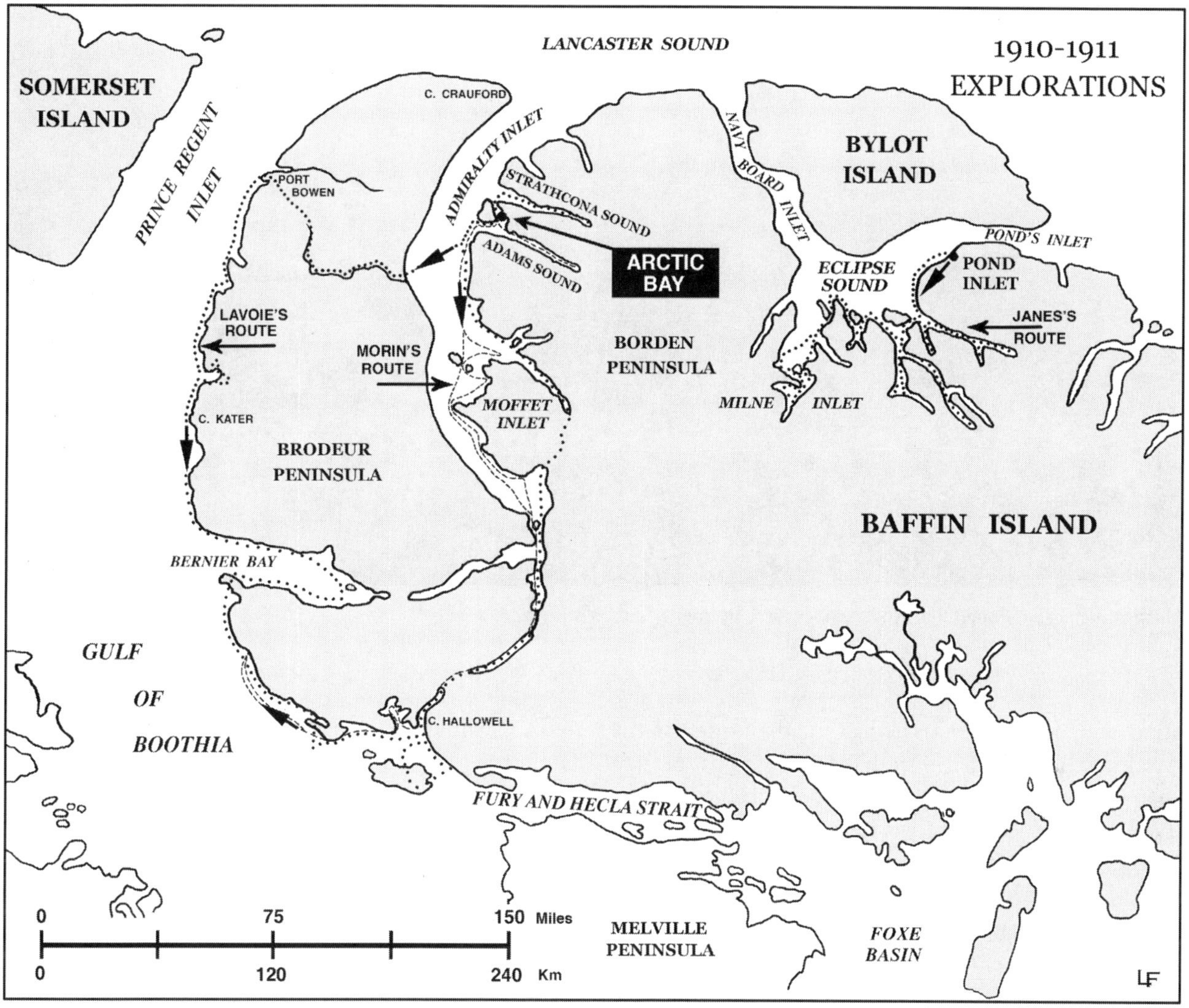

Detailed map of the explorations by Lavoie, Morin and Janes.

> The last cruise to the North was simply and entirely a trading expedition for the personal benefit of Capt. Bernier, and the 2nd Officer, a Newfoundlander named R. Janes, who was the Captain's right bower. All the fur trading and trafficking was carried on through the exchange of goods, provisions, ammunitions, etc., the exclusive property of the Government, and such a traffic should, in all justice, be absolutely stopped […].[12]

Also according to Mathé, Bernier thus obtained furs worth over $25,000.

It is very plausible that Fabien Vanasse, who had long detested the captain, had been the instigator of this controversy.[13] The former Conservative M.P. had become involved with the government expeditions simply to draw a salary and not out of any passion for polar explor-

The trading post at Pond Inlet, 15 September 1906. Bernier renamed it *Berniera* after he had bought it. [Photo: G.R. Lancefield, LAC, PA-139395]

ation, and even less for asserting Canadian rights in the Arctic Archipelago. Right from the start his attitude had been *blasé*, and his tone very scornful. His behaviour was then that of a journalist/lawyer, ousted from political power much against his will, disillusioned, disenchanted, and preferring to take refuge in negativism and to "let off steam" by sarcasm. Moreover he suffered greatly from loneliness among the other members of these expeditions, whom he scrutinized through a magnifying glass and with whom he had little in common. He rarely attended the soirées, isolating himself, and becoming preoccupied with his own person, his poor, frozen nose, his digestive problems, etc. His main target was always the captain, without any real reason and without provocation on Bernier's part, simply because he detested his authoritarian leadership, his ostentatious actions, or because his table manners disgusted him.

When one knows all this, it seems strange that Vanasse should write to the Secretary of the Association de la Casquette: "You have done well to approach Captain Bernier. He has brought back an abundance of souvenirs from the North, and he is very generous."[14]

Suspended from his duties and unpaid, Bernier had to respond to Joseph-Eugène Mathé's grievances. For the members of an enquiry in Ottawa, he listed the furs he had bought from the Inuit with his own money, as well as those he had trapped and given to the Department, strongly denying that he had traded provisions and materials belonging to the Government for furs.

Always on the lookout for a good story *La Presse* wasted no time in informing its readers that Captain Bernier's last expedition was the subject of a public enquiry. "The accusations levelled at present against Captain Bernier are unusually serious, and sensational revelations may well emerge from them."[15] Alongside a photo of Fabien Vanasse the newspaper laid out a series of accusations that had not featured at all in Mathé's letter to the government Ministers. It also added:

The whaling station on Blacklead Island, Cumberland Sound. [Bernier Collection, *Master Mariner*]

> Captain Bernier claimed that he could buy the good will of MP's and Ministers by giving them polar bear skins.
>
> In addition to these dubious dealings M. Mathé accuses the captain of having displayed unfairness and revolting cruelty towards the crew members during the voyage.

The terms and statements used appear to have come directly from the pen of the historiographer: "revolting cruelty," "abuse of power," "on Melville Island he sent everyone ashore with the exception of three or four favourites to kill polar buffalo!"

On the other hand, Martin Caron, a member of the *Amicale des vétérans et marins de L'Islet*, expressed some doubts: "I have read a certain number of accounts of the voyage by seamen from L'Islet who participated in these expeditions; not one mentions any cases of cruelty or of dubious dealings on Bernier's part."[16] He adds, however that relations were often strained between fellow-members of a ship's crew.

Nothing is known about Joseph-Eugène Mathé or as to the reasons that compelled him to act in this fashion and, unfortunately, it is impossible to prove that Fabien Vanasse had dragged him into the affair.

By contrast the fact that Octave-Jules Morin supported these denunciations is quite astonishing. Bernier considered him to be his right-hand man, and in October 1909 he had arranged for the Department of the Marine to make him First Officer. Had there been a quarrel between the two men? Did Morin feel that the captain's personal interests were assuming too great an importance on board the *Arctic*? In reality there was not a single clause in the captain's contract to prevent him from trading furs for his personal profit.

Disappointed at not having succeeded in making a transit of the legendary Northwest Passage, the Third Officer, Edward MacDonald[17] even went so far as to say that the 1910-1911 expedition was more "a fur trading voyage" than a scientific enterprise, and that Bernier had never really had any intention of attempting the Northwest Passage. Nor did this sailor from Prince Edward Island have a very good opinion of the other members of the crew, the majority of whom were French Canadians: "They are a bum lot, and not the kind of men that are required on an expedition like this."[18]

On 24 April Senator Landry wrote to his friend Bernier:

> I see from the newspapers that you have been suspended in anticipation of the outcome of the enquiry that is underway concerning you. Having heard it from your own lips I know that you need not at all fear the result of the enquiry, which is the inevitable consequence of accusations laid by personal enemies in the hope of blackmailing you. With all my heart I hope that you will emerge unscathed and will prove your enemies wrong.[19]

A week later the captain wrote to J.G. Scott, of Québec:

> I feel greatly indebted to you for your kind action on my behalf. I am indeed sorry that three of my men took upon themselves the responsibilities of accusing me so that I could not finish my work North. But I am able to prove what I have done was for the best.[20]

In his memoirs Bernier makes no reference to this intrigue that was mounted against him, nor to the fact that he had to abandon his position with the Department of Marine and Fisheries.

CHAPTER 15

Laurier, the elder statesman

BY 1911 WILFRID LAURIER was coming to the end of his reign. The discontent of the electorate seemed to be general.

> French Canadians screamed that Laurier was going too far while English Canadians screamed that he was not going far enough. Both sides were rejecting his middle-of-the-road policy. As Canada was growing more prosperous and self-confident, compromise solutions became unsatisfactory. Both French and English Canadians wanted bold, new initiatives, something which the old government could no longer offer.[1]

After 15 years in power the man who had always looked for conciliation and compromise was no more than a doddering elder statesman, outshone by a solid, energetic opposition led by the Nova Scotian Robert Laird Borden (1854-1937). On 21 September 1911 the Conservative Party won the election with a strong majority, dethroning the French Canadian Prime Minister who had been able to remain as head of the country by avoiding confrontations with the English Canadian majority.

Laurier had been the defender of an independent Canada in the face of British imperialism and of a Canadian nation under the protection of the British crown, but equal to Great Britain. This nationalist policy that was his own from the very beginning was quite courageous. It ran counter to Chamberlain's plan[2] to form an Imperial Council that would focus the British colonies and would support the British Empire in the event of war. It also ran counter to the strong imperialist current among English Canadians who remained: "true British subjects," more aggressive and more English than the English of England. Even the Governor General Lord Minto took him to task for this dream of Canadian autonomy.

The Victorian-style house that Wilfrid Laurier had built for himself in Arthabaska in 1876. When he was elected Prime Minister of Canada in 1896 he left Arthabaska to live in Ottawa, but he returned to this house during the summers until his death in 1919. [Photo: Lynn Fournier]

Cartoon of Laurier in *La Patrie,* Thursday, 20 January 1920.

By 1911 Laurier was no longer the brilliant Liberal, nor the leader who could sway by his eloquence, his pragmatism, and his charisma. For many French Canadians[3] he had become too Anglicized and had "sold out" to the English, whereas for many English Canadians he remained "the Frenchman at the head of our country," devoid of any British sentiment.

They all forgot that Laurier had once been the most popular politician in Canada.

French Canadians adulated him because he represented the idol to be imitated, the long-awaited saviour, the revenge of the "race," the symbol that anything could be possible in this Canada destined to have the most brilliant future. Admittedly Henri Bourassa and others were disenchanted. But not the majority of Canadians. Those in the West, both oldtimers and newcomers, praised him in turn, because he had given rise to an era of hope and had permitted their region to become deployed on the Canadian political chess-board. Several Ontarians, as well as industrialists and financiers also admired him since they recognized in him the Father of Confederation who finally realized the economic plan of the Act of 1867. Several purely Canadian nationalists exalted him, since he had attempted to diminish the ethnic conflicts in the country, had very often said "no" to the imperialist aims of Britain, and had revived patriotism. And especially because, in the manner of La Fontaine, he had indicated the only means that, if applied moderately and with firmness, might ensure the survival of Canada. And finally the Liberals adored him. A hero with exceptional charisma. A "leader," an incomparable musterer of men and ideas, an enlightened guide, non-doctrinaire, skilful, flexible, and stubborn at the same time, a real master and a giant among them.[4]

Despite his equivocations Laurier had allowed Captain Bernier to establish Canada's northern frontier by annexing all the islands of the Arctic Archipelago. By authorizing concrete gestures such as taking possession, establishing police posts, patrolling, and issuing hunting and fishing licences, Laurier had asserted his country's sovereignty in the Arctic, independently of Great Britain and in the eyes of the world.

Once Borden had come to power Joseph-Elzéar Bernier had lost an ally since the new Prime Minister put an end to Canadian activity in this area.

CHAPTER 16

The schooner *Minnie Maud*

A deep desire to return to the great, icy spaces soon took hold of Captain Bernier. But to get there he needed a ship and a project. He could no longer count on Canada's polar ship, or on the assistance of Borden's Conservatives, who could see no benefit in subsidizing annual patrols in the Arctic Archipelago.

At roughly the same time that Bernier was wondering about his future, the newspapers began circulating a rumour to the effect that during the 1910-1911 expedition Robert Janes had discovered gold veins in the bed of the Salmon River. Enthusiasm drew many prospectors towards Baffin Island and in early summer 1912 two private expeditions had sailed from St. John's, Newfoundland, for the new Eldorado. The ships were the *Algerine* belonging to Henry Toke Munn under the command of Captain John Bartlett and the steamer *Neptune* belonging to Robert Janes commanded by Captain "Lucky" Scott. Neither of these parties found the fortune they had hoped for. Munn's crew experienced the greatest set-backs. On 16 July the *Algerine* was crushed in the pack ice in Pond's Inlet and sank in 20 minutes. The 24 passengers escaped in time and survived thanks to the provisions cached by Captain Bernier in the depot at Button Point on Bylot Island. They were picked up two weeks later by the *Neptune*.

Joseph-Elzéar Bernier decided to try his luck by constituting a third expedition. To put his plans into effect he quickly purchased[1] the *Minnie Maud*, a schooner showing the effects of her more than 20 years. With a length of 85 feet and a beam of 22 feet, and spruce planking more than seven inches thick, this sailing

The schooner *Minnie Maud*, bound for Baffin Island, 1912. [Bernier Collection, *Cruise of the Minnie Maud*, 1921]

Captain Bernier distributing Christie's cookies to the Inuit who, after contact with Whites, had acquired a taste for sugar. [Bernier Collection, *Master Mariner*]

vessel without any power cut a poor figure compared to the three-masted steam barque that he had commanded for the previous eight years. To survive the pack ice the veteran seaman knew that he could not trust the fragile hull, although he had quickly had her dry-docked and sheathed with a thin skin of steel plates.

Limited means, small ship, and small crew! The eight sailors who participated in this commercial operation had undertaken to pay equal shares of the costs of the voyage, against a certain percentage of half the profits. All the remainder of the profits would accrue to Bernier. Napoléon Chassé, William LeBel, Wilfrid Caron, and Alfred Tremblay had already sailed with the captain in arctic waters, while for John LeBel, G. Wilson, G. Lawson, and A.B. Reader, this was their first such experience.

It was not gold so much that attracted Bernier, but rather the wildlife resources of northern Baffin Island. The captain knew a great deal about the local fauna, both through his own experience and through his contacts with the whalers who would normally carry on trade in addition to their regular activities. Along with Bernier's commercial interest in the Arctic was, of course, his desire to establish Canada's rightful claim in the Arctic, a cause that had by now become very dear to him. After having proclaimed so many islands as Canadian territory, Bernier hoped to secure even further his country's sovereignty by actually establishing a settlement in the region around Pond Inlet.[2]

Joseph-Elzéar Bernier had invested too much in this mission to let go of it so easily. Despite the disinterest of the Conservative government his *Minnie Maud* would continue to ensure a Canadian presence in the Arctic![3]

However one should not play down the commercial aspect of the enterprise. Bernier, the businessman, wanted to make a profit from the voyage and the trade with the Inuit remained one of his priorities. Hence the hold of his schooner was full of trade goods: kitchen utensils, files, matches, needles, knives, harpoons, hammers, fox traps, firearms, ammunition, barrels of molasses and sugar, boxes of salt, tea, and sweet biscuits, etc. He had not forgotten to include a large stock of smoking or chewing tobacco to satisfy the needs of these isolated communities.[4]

At 5.00 p.m. on 29 July 1912 a crowd of friends and curious onlookers thronged Québec harbour to salute and encourage the brave men who were setting off on an adventure to "the top of the world." Like the expeditions on board the *Algerine* and the *Neptune*, the one now leaving the Louise Basin on this fine summer's day would not find any gold veins. But unlike the two expeditions that had preceded her, the *Minnie Maud* would winter successfully and return safely, 15 months later with a small fortune in "ivory horns" (narwhal tusks), and bear, arctic fox, and wolf pelts.

During the wintering at Port Albert Captain Bernier organized trips on foot and by sledge to explore little-known areas in northern Baffin Island. Thus Alfred Tremblay, an enthusiastic young fellow of 23 who had learned the rudiments of geology from books published by the federal Government, made one of the most spectacular trips ever made by a white man in the Canadian Arctic. Armed with a Ross 280 rifle and a Colt automatic pistol, this native of Beauport explored regions south of Eclipse Basin and Admiralty Inlet as far as Fury and Hecla Strait and the island of Igloolik, in Foxe Basin. He surveyed and mapped between 3000 and

Alfred Tremblay, one of the great Arctic travellers, in action with his hunting rifle. [A. Tremblay Collection, *Cruise of the Minnie Maud*, 1921]

4000 miles of icy terrain at temperatures of -30° to -60°.

Tremblay recalled: "I also had ten dogs to feed." Several would die during the trip. Accompanied by an Inuit couple, Peewiktoo and Tootillik, his little wife, the three of them were inseparable. Sixty years later Tremblay said of them:

> They never cried; they were like small children in their simplicity. I risked my life many times to save them but I had no fear of dying. They knew this and called me the devil: Too-Pee-Lan. I could speak Eskimo quite well since I had a good memory. For the necessaries of life I could shift for myself.[5]

This great Arctic traveller would end his days in a seniors' hospital in Courville, having had both legs amputated.

Another member of *Minnie Maud*'s crew, A.B. Reader, focused his energies on prospecting for minerals on the shores of Eclipse Sound, on analyzing rock formations on Bylot Island, on studying Inuit customs, and on compiling three of the five dialects spoken by the natives of Baffin Island.

Their captain had always been interested in research and scientific discoveries in the Arctic, not only to draw the government's attention to the importance of the resources to be exploited but because he wanted to advance human knowledge. As early as 1901 Bernier had thought of using kites to photograph arctic land surfaces. He wanted to test the use of the automobile in the Far North. He was interested in raising sheep at Port Albert. He had even been inclined towards using polar bear oil as a medication to counter rheumatism. Here are some testimonials to the success of his remedy.

> That oil is really efficacious against rheumatism. One of our Sisters is completely cured of a knee complaint from which she had been suffering for three years.[6]

And:

> Following your instructions I applied the polar bear oil that you were so kind as to give me. For three years I had been walking painfully and with difficulty. I can now walk feely, without pain and I am truly incapable of thanking you appropriately for the immense benefit that you have thus procured for me.[7]

The captain had also donated a large number of skins of caribou, wolves, muskoxen, and polar bears to the Ottawa Museum. A large proportion of the natural science collection at the Québec Seminary came from his arctic expeditions and from his habit of having the different species of birds and animals peculiar to the regions he had explored, stuffed.

On his return from his expedition of 1912-1913 Captain Bernier informed the Minister of the Interior of the two immense reserves of coal that his men had discovered on Baffin Island.[8] And in 1921 he was involved in financing and publishing the book *Cruise of the Minnie Maud*.

In 1909 Captain Bernier offered this muskox calf to the Experimental Farm in Ottawa, in order to study the possibilities of raising muskoxen. When the Experimental Farm declined, the Holt Renfrew Company accommodated it temporarily in its zoological garden, until it was sold or given to the New York Zoo. [Archives of Carol and Louis Terrien]

> As a guide and reference to all those, whether they be sportsmen, navigators, prospectors, explorers or tourists, who are more especially interested in the remote and comparatively unknown spaces of the frozen Northland.[9]

This book has the advantage of bringing together everything that was known at the time on the fauna, geology, mineralogy, ice movements, currents, tides, seasons, and the history of the Arctic. It describes the materials, techniques, and clothing necessary to survive in this terrestrial zone. It also breaks new ground in that it devotes an entire chapter to the customs, beliefs, superstitions, and dialects of the Inuit, and in daring to raise the question of the future of this people and their lands. It is undoubtedly a very interesting work and very important for evaluating Bernier's knowledge on these subjects.

Let us take a brief look at what he thought of the Inuit. On 6 April 1911, in his cabin on board the *Arctic*, the captain wrote to Alfred Tremblay:

> I hope that you have had good opportunities to learn about the lifestyle of the Eskimos, and to know that we must respect their ideas even if sometimes somewhat banal. When in Rome....[10]

Some of today's Inuit confirm that "[...] to him, they were his equals. He respected them for their capacity to survive in the Arctic, wore Inuit clothing and relied on their expertise as guides."[11]

As one reads the following passages from *Cruise of the Minnie Maud*, one can almost hear Bernier's voice.

The result of a narwhal hunt. This mammal was also called the "sea unicorn." Captain Bernier had narwhal tusks made into lamps or other utilitarian articles. [Bernier Collection, *Cruise of the Minnie Maud*]

> The Eskimos are very much like children and require to be treated with firmness, kindness and justice. They are responsive and grateful for kind treatment and forget neither a kindness nor an injury, nor a broken promise. They are keen observers and have a great sense of humour and mimicry, like children. They have been taught to fear the white man, but in their own hearts, they feel themselves quite as capable and efficient.[12] [...]
>
> The Eskimos are the guardians of the north and are the only hope of salvation for the crews of shipwrecked vessels and exploring parties stranded in those inhospitable regions. They are a peaceable people and most friendly disposed and are deserving of much better treatment than they have hitherto obtained from the scheming traders and white men's scum that have occasionally visited their shores and who have unscrupulously plundered them of their hard-earned produce of the chase.[13] [...]
>
> The suggestions of some well-meaning persons that they be transported to a more hospitable region would, if carried out, cause their extermination in two or three generations. Our variable climate they could not endure as they are keenly susceptible to pulmonary and bronchial affections (sic). Our civilization, too, would only soften and corrupt them, as their racial inheritance is one of physical hardship; [...] but the cardinal graces of faith, hope and charity they seem to have already, for without them they could never survive the six-month night and the many rigours of their home. [...]
>
> There are few things that the Eskimos require to learn from the white man, but there are many Christian qualities inherent in the Eskimos that the white man, on his present plane of civilization, might copy and practice with a resultant benefit to the peace and happiness of the world.[14] [...]
>
> The fundamental point in all my dealings with them has been always to mean just what I say and to have things done exactly as ordered. I have made it to their interest to do what I want done. [...] I have made it a point to be firm with them, but to rule them by love and gratitude rather than by fear and threats [...].
>
> [...] But I want to say again, at the risk of being misunderstood, that I hope no efforts will ever be made to civilize them. Such efforts, if successful, will destroy their primitive communism, which is necessary to preserve their existence. [...] It is this feeling of good fellowship which alone preserves a race. I have taught them some of

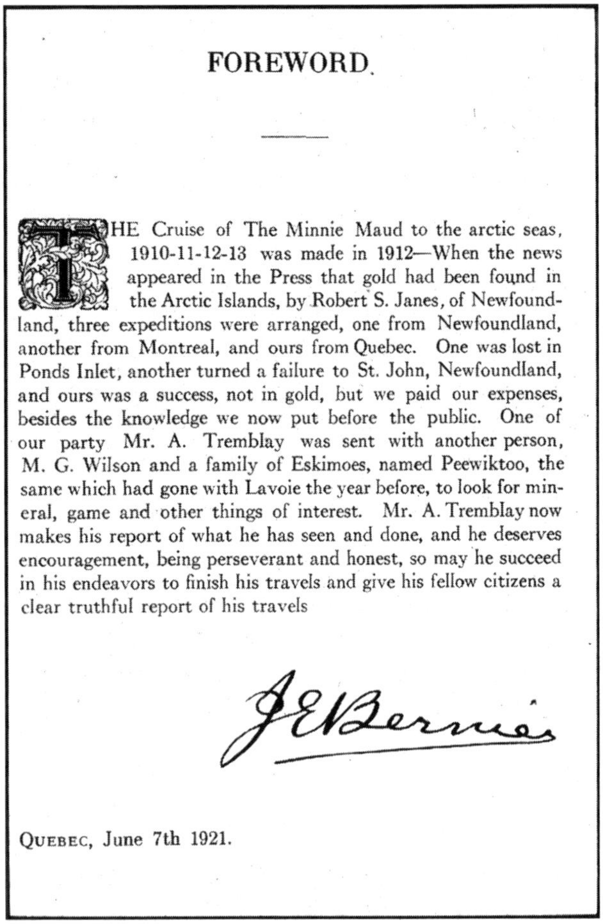

FOREWORD.

THE Cruise of The Minnie Maud to the arctic seas, 1910-11-12-13 was made in 1912—When the news appeared in the Press that gold had been found in the Arctic Islands, by Robert S. Janes, of Newfoundland, three expeditions were arranged, one from Newfoundland, another from Montreal, and ours from Quebec. One was lost in Ponds Inlet, another turned a failure to St. John, Newfoundland, and ours was a success, not in gold, but we paid our expenses, besides the knowledge we now put before the public. One of our party Mr. A. Tremblay was sent with another person, M. G. Wilson and a family of Eskimoes, named Peewiktoo, the same which had gone with Lavoie the year before, to look for mineral, game and other things of interest. Mr. A. Tremblay now makes his report of what he has seen and done, and he deserves encouragement, being perseverant and honest, so may he succeed in his endeavors to finish his travels and give his fellow citizens a clear truthful report of his travels

J E Bernier

QUEBEC, June 7th 1921.

Bernier's introduction to the book, *Cruise of the Minnie Maud.*

the fundamental principles of sanitation, and the care of themselves, the treatment of simple diseases, of wounds and other accidents; but there I think their civilization should stop. This opinion is not based on theory or prejudice, but in eighteen years of intimate study and experience.[15]

Unlike Bernier, authors Alfred Tremblay and A.B. Reader had not accumulated 18 years of experience in the Far North. Hence it is not a great stretch of the imagination if one supposes that they were conveying the impressions and convictions of their captain, the man the Inuit had affectionately nick-named *Kapitaikallak,* "the little fat captain." However writer Shelagh D. Grant[16] considers that since Tremblay never lived with the Inuit more than a few months at a time, his assessment of them was sometimes very negative and even cynical, and contrasted with that of Bernier who appreciated the natives and regularly urged the Canadian government to come to their assistance.

CHAPTER 17

The *Guide*

Early in 1914, when Europe was trapped in a climate of mistrust and hostility, Joseph-Elzéar Bernier travelled to Glasgow to take delivery of a two-masted steamer, the *Guide*, that he had just bought and that was to allow him to pursue his expeditions to the Arctic. He brought it back to Lévis to the G. Davie Company's yards for a refit and to have a steel ice-belt fitted.

Captain Bernier mounted his last two private expeditions on board the *Guide*, from 4 July 1914 until 29 September 1915 and from 1 June 1916 until 20 September 1917. These voyages were commercial enterprises, aimed especially at trading furs with Inuit trappers and at exploiting the seams of soft coal that he had discovered previously, some three miles from the mouth of Salmon River. Since the Federal Government had never showed any interest in these mines Bernier had gone to the trouble of acquiring a permit in due form for coal mining; this undoubtedly represented one of the first such licences issued for the Arctic Archipelago.

Sometimes the captain would use somewhat unorthodox methods for extracting the coal intended for filling the *Guide*'s bunkers, and for heating his trading posts at Pond Inlet and on Bylot Island.

> He brought the *Guide* alongside an island containing one of the finest seams [of coal] and ordered his men to open fire. In a matter of seconds, tons of ready-made fuel came tumbling down the hillside.[1]

Over and above his commercial interests the captain continued to be preoccupied with questions of sovereignty in the Arctic. As soon as he got wind of MacMillan's American expedition, the "Crocker Land Expedition" of 1914-1915, aimed at verifying the existence of Crocker Land which explorers such as Peary believed they had seen to the northwest of Ellesmere Island, "Bernier immediately wrote the deputy minister of Marine and Fisheries in Ottawa, offering to organize an expedition that would attempt to reach the area in question ahead of MacMillan and prevent any possible

Captain Bernier's ship the *Guide* had been built in 1891 by W. Denny Brothers of Dumbarton in Scotland. It was made of iron and its dimensions were: length, 114' 3"; beam, 21'; depth, 11' 4"; tonnage, 156 tonnes. [Collection of Suzanne Audet and André Normandeau]

Inuit and their dogs, a scene that Captain Bernier saw many times during his numerous expeditions in the Far North. [Bernier Collection, *Cruise of the Minnie Maud*]

threat to Canadian claims in that part of the archipelago. His offer, however, was turned down and the MacMillan expedition was sent out as planned."[2]

Bernier was probably greatly disappointed with his government, but this did not discourage him in the slightest from pursuing his own campaign "to promote the Arctic." During the *Guide*'s first voyage he invested $600 in cinematographic equipment and joined forces with two Americans, Rudolph Franke and Arthur Haacks,[3] with the aim of making a film about this "land of the midnight sun." While Charlie Chaplin, Cecil B. De Mille, Douglas Fairbanks, and Mary Pickford were filming their scenes in the great studios in Hollywood, the captain and his partners were trying their luck with their rudimentary equipment in an unpredictable environment and at temperatures below zero that were far from propitious for film-making. Despite its obvious technical imperfections, *Land of the Midnight Sun*[4] was probably the first Canadian documentary made on the arctic frontier.

Bernier wanted to bring back northern images to the people in the South, as he had done so many times during his lectures that he had illustrated with lantern slides. His film brought alive the chaos of the sea ice, Inuit dogs, the Pond Inlet station, the Inuit "in action," majestic icebergs, the *Guide*, and her captain in all his rotundity and with his serious look below his captain's cap. Some people would criticize him for again, as always, hogging the limelight, while others would be delighted to watch exotic scenes that let them escape from their everyday lives.

The personal diary of the *Guide*'s cook, Ludger Lemieux during the 1916-1917 voyage[5] represents an incursion into the thoughts of the young sailors who were accompanying Bernier for the first time. The writings of this seaman from L'Islet-sur-Mer are colourful, sincere, imbued with vivid emotions, and they convey the less-than-romantic realities of Captain Bernier's expeditions.

> *Sunday, 2 July 1916.* [...] First boring day, but not the last. We'll be doing penance for 15 months.
>
> *Sunday, 9.* [...] At 11.00 I told my beads on my fingers, since I've forgotten my rosary.
>
> *Wednesday, 12.* [...] I have to tell you that I made the Capt. tumble on the deck. He was trying to show me how to hoist a jib, but the halyard was twisted around the captain's back, rather than being rove to the bitts.
>
> *Saturday, 15.* Today there is nothing pleasant about the NE wind that is raging; there is a heavy sea and a head-wind. I'm having a miserable time with my pans, which are all trying to fall on the deck. What a pain! The water is pouring into the galley through the open door. The weather is never fine at all; from time to time a mist and a dense fog [...]
>
> *Monday, 17.* [...] The sun set at 11.30, with a completely clear sky. I went up on deck to watch the sunset; I've never seen anything so beautiful.
>
> *Tuesday, 18.* [...] It is very cold; the shrouds and the rigging have half an inch of ice on them. The sea is rough enough to upset my pans; it is quite a laugh to see me swimming in soup and hotch-potch [...]. I would prefer my own bed at my father's place to my bunk here on board [...].

An Inuk in a kayak, watched by a polar bear. [Bernier Collection, *Cruise of the Minnie Maud*].

Wednesday, 19. […] Also I've had an accident: I was carrying the tea and the hotch-potch to the Capt. in the dining saloon when I fell to the deck, spilling everything. The engineer, who arrived just at that moment, said: "What, is somebody having dinner right here?" We had a good laugh. The dog was totally terrified and hid somewhere aft.

Thursday, 20. Today the weather is fine but there is a lot of fog. We moored the ship alongside a large floe and took on fresh water, since we were out of drinking water […] We are moored to a floe half a mile square on which the dog is sporting himself; he was so happy to get off the ship that he did not want to come back aboard […] We've had a sick man on board for the past 9 days. His name is J. Vigneault; he is a sorry sight, poor lad.

Friday, 21. […] There are large floes every 50 feet; but we are still running through between them.

Saturday, 22. Today we are beset in the ice, unable to make any progress […].

Sunday, 23. I can assure you that it has been a very long day; we are still stuck in the ice; we made 10 feet today […] This afternoon the Capt. played a little music for us, but I was unable to listen since I was making some prune jam. This evening I shall be reading; the Capt. gave me a great book […]. Our sick man is not well this evening. It is no fun being sick on board the *Guide*.

Monday, 24. […] Capt. Bernier was firing at seals; according to him he killed them all, but we have not yet seen a single dead one.

Tuesday, 25. […] This morning Capt. Bernier went for a walk on the ice with his dog. The dog was leaping and running about the ice. Around 1 o'clock the ship was nipped in the ice (I was going to say, like Jos. Couillard); dangerous […].

Thursday, 27. Still in the damned ice [...].

Friday, 28. [...] This evening we played on the ice for a spell; we played the fool just as much as we wanted. It is full daylight and the sun is shining day and night. It is really beautiful but it is very difficult to get to sleep early.

Tuesday, 1 August. [...] I then began thinking about the fine evenings I spent at the Trois-Saumons and at Cap St-Ignace, and I could have wept at these memories that troubled me so much. The weather is also very troublesome; we are in the ice and this evening it is snowing very heavily and there is every appearance that it will be a long time before we reach our post.

Wednesday, 2. [...] The ice is squeezing us severely. We were all called on deck to saw and clear the ice to get the ship out of this dangerous situation. After an hour of hard work we got control of the ship, and it escaped from its worrying position [...] As long as the ship can withstand it, in the captain's words. This is not very encouraging. I hope the news is better tomorrow.

Friday, 4. [...] I am bored; I am all alone, especially this evening. It is only 8 o'clock and everyone has gone to bed; it is permanently full daylight.

Saturday, 5. [...] This morning the ice nipped us very severely; the ship was creaking. At 6 a.m. the Capt. called everyone on deck; we worked for 90 minutes at sawing the ice around the ship and used tackles on the ice blocks in order to free the ship from her dangerous situation; it was very cold. We succeeded but we have had to repeat the process every two hours [...].

Sunday, 6. [...]. In the morning everyone was asleep; I was totally alone. I had let my beard grow on my chin and this morning, when I looked in the mirror, I found that I had aged 10 years; that bothered me even more. So then I shaved off this ... paint-brush. In the afternoon I tried to bake a cake. What a disaster! A real plateful of putty! The putty was instantly thrown overboard.[...] This evening there was a big dance on deck. I played the violin and the crew were dancing [...].

Monday, 7. [...] We are still in the ice and still have 600 miles to go. Tomorrow we will be sawing the ice to try to escape. The Capt. is afraid of remaining beset for the winter, which is quite worrying; however we are not discouraged, since we've all decided to make our best efforts to escape from this bad situation [...] I was fishing for cod this afternoon but did not catch any; the water is too deep. Baked another cake this afternoon, and this one, for a change, is first-rate, but I would need four to satisfy the crew. The Capt. told me to keep the recipe this time.

Tuesday, 8. The weather is magnificent and there is no wind. We haven't moved at all. However the ice is not squeezing us too much; fortunately, since we cannot saw it since it is too thick. If, by mischance we have not escaped from the ice in two weeks, we'll be forced to spend an entire year in the ice, with all its hazards. I can assure you there is a lot of talk about it.

Thursday, 10. The Capt. has begun to make us husband the coal; he is like a devil unchained, whereas until now he has been as gentle as kid gloves, he is starting to lose hope. However we can't believe that we must remain here. If that happens I believe that we'll have really white hair by next year [...].

Sunday, 13. A truly miserable day; the weather is fine but we are beset in the ice and a pressure ridge is advancing on us. We've been working like niggers for two hours, sawing the ice to make a passage to escape from the pack ice, and we have succeeded [...].

Monday, 14. [...] Last year they spent only 12 days in the ice where we are now and this year, it has been a month and we've made no more progress than in the first week.

Tuesday, 15. I've never spent such a frustrating day as today: the weather is gloomy, the wind out of the SE and rain all day long. I've been thinking of all those who are dear to me, and that troubled me even more. I tried to banish these dear memories but it was useless: they always come back again. We haven't made a mile of progress today. I don't know what is to become of us at all. If we have to spend the winter here in the ice we'll all go mad. That includes Capt. B. because he is worse than us. He bemoans the situation and is not sleeping. This morning when I took him his coffee, he said to me: "This is a lousy country." I felt like replying "Yes, and anybody who follows you here must be mad." But one has to take courage, since it is no fun anywhere on Earth, and even less fun on the water, especially in the North.

Thursday, 24. What a night we've just spent! The ice began to pack around 9 o'clock. We all worked for part of the night to save the ship. It was trying to settle in jerks, but at times it rose onto the ice to a height of 8 to 9 feet—it was not a laughing matter, I assure you. Around 4 a.m. the ice ceased to pack and the wind dropped. Today the weather is misty but the wind is not very strong. We are out of danger.

Friday, 1 September. We are finally out of the ice and we are steaming towards Baffin Land. We will probably see land tomorrow; that is more encouraging than yesterday.

Saturday 2. This morning, around 5 o'clock I got up and rushed on deck. We are about 20 miles from the bay where we are going to winter, i.e. where we'll anchor the ship for the winter [...]. By 5 p.m. we had reached the place and at 7 o'clock the Capt. gave three whistle blasts to signal our arrival. Two Eskimos were hunting seals. They heard the whistle and came aboard; after supper they headed back to their village at 9 p.m. I can assure you they are a race that evokes pity: they have a suit of sealskin for summer and a deerskin outfit for winter. I am not very eager to wear this myself, since it is a disgusting sight and the smell is foul.

Sunday, 3. A great feast for the Eskimos on board. About twenty of them arrived around 7 o'clock. Men, women, and children. It was quite a big event for them; they are all happy to see us and as they arrived they gave us all names. My name is "Coucoulou" since I am the cook. They spent the day on board and it rained all day. They left at 7 p.m. and the Capt. promised them a dance for tomorrow.

Monday, 4. The Eskimos arrived to work at 7 o'clock. I was obliged to feed them all. After breakfast the boats were washed out and loaded to head for the village. We all left at 2 o'clock for the Eskimo village in question, 3 miles from the ship, and there we transported the goods to the Capt.'s house, measuring almost 14 x 20, divided into four. We finished at 5 o'clock and the dance lasted until 9.30. It was quite a surprise to see the Eskimos dancing; they dance quadrilles and jigs very well. They also danced their dance for us [...].

Ludger Lemieux's diary ended on Saturday, 16 September 1916, dealing with the routine of coaling, hunting ravens and gulls, and a visit from some Inuit.

When he left the Pond's Inlet area in September 1917, Captain Bernier left his First Officer, Wilfrid Caron[6] in charge of his trading posts and his properties on Baffin Island. A few years later he offered his possessions to the Arctic Gold Exploration Syndicate.[7]

Having returned to Québec, Bernier used the *Guide* for carrying freight and mail between the small communities along the St. Lawrence; he parted with it the following year, offering it to the Gulf of St. Lawrence Navigation Company.

The *Guide* was sold again, to a certain Sylvio Guénard in 1921, but in October 1926 it met a tragic end when it sank in the Rivière Godbout. Her 11 crew members died in the shipwreck. As a former owner and specialist in ship design, Bernier had to give testimony before the Commission of Enquiry into Maritime Accidents that was studying the circumstances of the accident. Was it going to end as an unsolved mystery?

In March 1932 when Captain Bernier was thinking of enjoying his well-deserved retirement the shadow of the *Guide* came back to haunt him in the form of an accusation of perjury with respect to the testimony that he had given at the enquiry six years previously. The plaintiff, Raoul Harvey, a member of the 1916-1917 expedition, swore that his commander had made a false declaration before the Dominion Wreck Commission, since he had previously had pieces of the piping and pumps from the *Guide*'s security system removed to sell the lead to the Inuit! In other words Bernier was being blamed for the wreck of the steamer, even though he had not been responsible for it since 1918.

At the hearing on 31 March 1932, when the defence lawyer asked Raoul Harvey why he had waited so long before lodging his complaint, Raoul Harvey equivocated, then replied: "Well, it took us a long time to organize things." Mr. Henri Bernier wanted to know what this meant and Harvey replied: "Well, we had to have money to lodge the complaint." And where did he get the money from? It was Captain Landry, the Québec harbour-master, who had financed him.

Wilfrid "Tit-Loup" Caron was the younger brother of Captain Bernier's adopted daughter, Elmina. [Collection of Suzanne Audet and André Normandeau]

What could have induced two members of the *Guide*'s crew, supported by the Chief Engineer, Harry Arcand, to discredit their former commander?

Captain Bernier never wrote anything on the subject, but since he had maintained the good habit of filing newspaper clippings concerning him, the latter remain the sole source of information that may allow us to understand the motivation behind these accusations. The articles in the *Soleil* and the *Chronicle-Telegraph* of Québec have all the marks of a bad melodrama.

They reveal that Raoul Harvey was an ex-con, known to have been guilty of rum-running. His replies were evasive. His testimony was also rather unconvincing. Harry Arcand rather helped the case for the defence by hesitating frequently and by saying that he could no longer remember clearly having seen the pipes in question in the ship's bilge. Captain Landry unintentionally revealed that he was the instigator of the legal proceedings.

The defence was clearly better prepared. Its main witness was Joseph Samson, inspector of shipping for the Federal government, who had annually inspected the *Guide* between 1915 and 1923. He declared that the system of pipes had always been complete.

On being questioned, Captain Bernier swore that he had never touched the pipes and that, on the contrary, he had improved the system by installing a new safety pump to make his ship even safer.

The last owner, Sylvio Guénard, confirmed that the system of pumps and piping was complete at the time he sold the *Guide*.

> An interesting point was raised by defence attorney Bernier. According to the prosecution the piping and pumps had been removed from the *Guide* by Captain Bernier, in the North, during his last voyage. "But the accused, an experienced seaman, had to see to his own safety," said Mr. Bernier. "How could he have risked returning from the arctic regions to Québec in a ship that had been rendered dangerous?"[8]

The same article reproduced the questioning of one of the seamen on the *Guide*'s first expedition, Claude Vigneault, by the second defence lawyer Mr. Robert Taschereau.

> "Did you have occasion to meet Raoul Harvey, the plaintiff, at Captain Landry's?"
> "Yes."
> "When was that?"
> "Three years ago."
> "What occurred?"
> "They wanted me to sign a paper, but I refused."
> "Did you know what was on it?"
> "No, I did not read it."
> "Why not?"
> "I didn't care too."

Six days later, for lack of conclusive proof, Judge Ferdinand Roy threw out the case:

I find that it is impossible to believe that a man of Captain Bernier's experience and ability would risk his own life, his own ship and the lives of his sailors for what little he would receive for the sake of a few lengths of pipes to the Eskimos. It also appears incredible that supposing Captain Bernier had removed the emergency pump pipes, none of the officers of the ship or the sailors would have taken action to protect their own lives.[9]

This astonishing episode deserves to be publicized because it proves a point: at the age of 80 Captain Bernier was still having to pay for his fame. People were jealous of him and he was thought to be rich.

Harvey was a petty thief who was on the lookout for easy "schemes" to make some money. What better occasion to blackmail the "Old Man?" "Loaded" as he was, he would not hesitate to pay to avoid spoiling his good reputation. But it is impossible to prove these hypotheses, or to explain why Landry financed the affair. However it is clearly apparent that Bernier did not try to bury the scandal, but rather brought it out into the daylight in order to dispel any doubts on the subject.

Alfred Tremblay had said of the formidable captain that he was a hard man, a very hard man, but just, and that he respected anyone who did his duty.

To remain master of his ships the captain had never submitted to aggressors. In 1932, now an old man, he was too familiar with human nature to leave this sort of stain on his eloquent life story.

CHAPTER 18

His war effort

As the *Guide* made fast in Québec harbour in September 1917, Joseph-Elzéar Bernier could not guess that he had lost his true refuge and that henceforth he would be without a point of anchorage. During his absence, time had played a nasty trick on him. Rose had died before him. She had died on 18 April 1917, and he had not been there to hold her hand.

He later wrote:

> She was to live happily with me for forty-seven years, to inspire me in my ambitions, to encourage me in my undertakings, and finally, to my great grief, to pass out of this world when I was thousands of miles away above the Arctic Circle.[1]

On his return from the Arctic Captain Bernier had not only to absorb the enormous shock of the death of his faithful companion, but also what he perceived as betrayal on the part of his adopted daughter, Elmina, who had remarried without his authorization and during his absence.

In the spring of 1916 a doctor friend from Lauzon had introduced the widow Bourget to a prominent flour merchant from the parish of Saint-Sauveur, and a few months later, at the age of 41 she agreed to share his life. Hence, on 24 October 1916, Marie-Clémence Elmina Caron married Cyrille Kirouac in the church of Saint-Joseph in Lauzon.[2]

Even today Mina's grandchildren wonder why she did not wait for her guardian to return before getting married and settling in at Kirouac's house at Saint-Sauveur. Would she have missed the chance of a good marriage and a freer existence if she had postponed things for a year? Could she really count on the generosity of the man who was not her true father in ensuring her future and that of her children, who were already at an age to marry?

Captain Bernier's reaction was astonishing: he turned his back on Mina and her family and definitively cut all affective ties with them because he interpreted her

PRIEZ POUR LE REPOS DE L'AME
DE

Dame ROSE DE LIMA CARON

Epouse de Sieur J. E. Bernier, Capitaine
Décédée à Montréal, le 18 avril 1917
A L'AGE DE 62 ANS

Vierge sainte ! au milieu de vos jours glorieux n'oubliez pas les tristesses de la terre.

Ayez pitié de ceux qui s'aimaient et qui ont été séparés.

J.-A. Kirouac & Cie Québec.

Death notice for Rose-de-Lima Caron. [Archives of Carol and Louis Terrien]

Elmina Caron's family photographed on 3 February 1920. From left to right: Jean-Ernest Caron (seated), Marie-Anna Caron-Nicole-Dionne (standing), Marie-Hélène Caron-Bernier (seated), Marie-Rosalie Caron-Samson (standing), Marie-Elmina Caron-Bourget-Kirouac (seated), Wilfrid-Clément (Tit-Loup) Caron (standing), Marie-Philomène Boucher (mother, seated), Marie-Belzémire Caron-Lemieux (standing), and Marie-Cécile Caron-Bélanger-Samson (seated). [Collection of Suzanne Audet and André Normandeau]

marriage as a betrayal. He probably saw it as proof that she did not appreciate all he had done for her. Moreover it would appear that he blamed her somewhat for Rose's death, since the latter had died in Montréal, only six months after Mina's wedding. The circumstances of her death and of this separation are not known and Mina, like the captain, always refused to talk about this painful subject.

Was this one of the reasons that impelled Bernier to make his war effort? It's possible.

⚓

The First World War, which had begun on 18 July 1914,[3] interrupted Captain Bernier's polar expeditions, but only after September 1917.

> But while the struggle was in progress I was asked to take a ship across the Atlantic as part of a convoy. The old *Percassin [Percesien]* was not sea-worthy, but she was pressed into service and I did my best with her.[4]

The captain took command of the *Percesien* shortly after his birthday, early in 1918. As soon as she left Halifax the old tub began to leak.

> The British men-of-war convoying us ordered me to keep up, but I found that impossible. We gradually dropped behind until we were out of touch with the others. I had no wireless on board and could not communicate with them.[5]

Just imagine the humiliation of this situation for the man who in his youth had beaten every record for Atlantic crossings.

A severe storm rose during the night of 8 February, battering the unfortunate steamer, which held out, however, despite the working of her hull plates. The waves were so violent that the lifeboats and the deck-houses were carried away. The heap of scrap-iron grated and groaned, but stubbornly resisted, just like her captain who, soaked to the skin, scanned the surrounding blackness searching for a point of light. He fired off signal rockets.

The *Lord Erne* "bore down on us. I signalled with a flash light, but evidently on seeing us the Captain thought we were a submarine emerging and made all haste away."[6]

This fear of German submarines was well-founded. During 1917, U-boats waging "total war" in the Atlantic sank an average of 50 ships per week. The resupply convoys were an easy target.

One of the *Lord Erne*'s officers finally deciphered Captain Bernier's signals and convinced his captain to turn back. Unfortunately this merchant vessel was manned by Chinese seamen who had neither the training nor the techniques for handling lifeboats. It was the engineers and the firemen who came rowing to the rescue of Bernier and his crew.

The *Percesien*'s men waited, clinging to the gangway ladder of their poor vessel as she sank lower and lower into the raging sea, aware perhaps that they were not the only victims of this terrible storm.

Once their lives had been saved they expressed their gratitude to their old captain who had been the last to leave the ship.

> [...] That we are preserved at all we owe to your unremitting toil, intelligence, watchfulness and care [...].
>
> When it was seen that our ship was doomed, you went about the work of getting all things in readiness for our embarkation in the life boats in such an orderly, quiet and assuring way, that not a bit of he anxiety you must have felt ever reached us. We were thus cheered and assured that all would be well.
>
> The manner in which the laboring ship was kept in the track of passing ships deserves special praise as also does the matter of making constant use of every method of making our condition and situation known, that was available to us [...].[7]

Bernier was greatly touched by this testimonial.

CHAPTER 19

Women, oh women!

After his war effort Bernier again found himself alone without "his women" and his grandchildren. This was undoubtedly very painful for him, since he was far from lacking in feelings. Mina reported of him that he was severe but always fair, good and kind to her and her children, as well as with all women.

Bernier seemed to be attracted by their presence, by the little pleasant things of their daily life, by the refinement of their surroundings, their beauty, their sensitiveness, and their delicacy, which was such a contrast to his world of seamen, virile, intense, rough, and lacking in finesse.

It is impossible to tell whether he had mistresses, but certain letters from female friends discovered in his personal files leave one a little puzzled: for example one dated 12 January 1912, from Corrine Rosa offering her assistance as a private secretary and signed "Big kisses and pinched cheeks," or one dated 22 January 1912 from Kate Pettit who, on learning that he had forgotten her address, promised that she would tattoo it on his arm!

After the War several single ladies began to prowl around the famous 66-year-old widower, who still represented an excellent catch and who, one would imagine, was rolling in money. To escape from loneliness and from these advances from the female sex, who sometimes seemed to be harassing him, Joseph-Elzéar had the habit of going off to sea or of taking refuge with his Ottawa friends Arthur Farley and Esdras Terrien.[1] It was at the home of one of them that he met his second wife, Marie-Alma.

Marie-Alma Julie Albertine Lemieux was not a very pretty woman. She was quite timid and rarely went out, and refused to live the worldly life of her two sisters. When the man from the Far North was visiting the Farleys, this old maid of 39 preferred to remain in the kitchen rather than mingle with the group. Intrigued, the captain decided one fine day that it was time to go looking for "Alma in the kitchen." She was exactly the kind of woman he needed: gentle, submissive, passive, and without ambition … she really knew her place!

Alma was delighted and a little incredulous at the attentions of this great personage who could have chosen somebody more beautiful, more elegant, more educated, and better provided for than her. Joseph-Elzéar talked of marriage and described the life they would have together in Québec, and she acquiesced, amazed, happy, won over, and perhaps aware that she was soon to become the companion of a legend.

⚓

Where did the captain stay when he was not in Ottawa or at sea? There is only a faint trail in the records of the town of Lévis that indicates that he was "a master mariner living in the town of Lauzon."[2] Nothing more. Some

Three friends in front of Captain Bernier's 1930 Dodge. From left to right: Cécile Terrien, Alma Lemieux, and Marguerite Terrien. [Archives of Carol and Louis Terrien]

seniors from "old Lauzon" claim that he rented a room and an office in the house at number 509, Rue Saint-Joseph, just above l'Anse aux Sauvages. This is probable since some of his letters are headed "Anse aux Sauvages."

From all the evidence Bernier remained attached to this corner of the country. He had even decided to install his future wife in the house of the deceased Captain Julien Chabot, at No. 27, Rue Fraser.

> A site located in the town of Lévis, on the north side of the Rue Fraser, with a house and other buildings, and appurtenances, comprising three lots identified on the official plan of the Quartier Lauzon, numbered 139, 140 and 141.[3]

This was a wooden house built in the Anglo-Norman cottage style in the second half of the 19th century. Its large lot and its location on the Lévis cliff made it a choice property. As soon as he took possession Bernier embellished it with grey-white bricks that he imported from Italy and an enormous gallery-deck that ran around all four sides of the house. It was a building with pleasing proportions, rectangular in plan, topped with a roof with four gentle slopes, with hipped dormer windows, and tall brick chimneys.

One has to rely on the testimony of Simone Dion, a resident of the Rue Fraser, to try to imagine the appearance and certain interior elements of this beautiful three-storey dwelling, since it no longer exists.

She recalls that on entering the house, one was first struck by the height of the rooms, doors and windows on the ground floor, and by the varnished wood floors. The house was always very bright despite the imposing, dark woodwork that adorned all the rooms. After going through the front door, one found oneself in a closed entrance hall that gave onto the central staircase and a corridor that ran right through the house to the sunroom at the back. On the left was a large drawing-room with white sliding doors, a piano, an enormous polar bear skin, paintings of all the captain's sailing ships hanging on the walls, and a suite of furniture in rose wood, made in England. There was even a love-seat

Captain Bernier's house, Rue Fraser, in Lévis. He is standing on the veranda with his second wife, his sisters-in-law, and their children. [Bernier Collection, *Master Mariner*]

covered in a pink, delicate green and blue brocade. "Magnificent, a real museum piece!" Moreover, for the most part the furniture was imported and of quite a luxurious and exquisite style.

The popular Québec actor Marcel Lebœuf corroborated this exotic appearance:

> I remember once going into that house when I was very small and seeing a table that impressed me greatly since I thought at the time that the four legs of this table were elephant tusks. Well, having done some research I discovered the legs of this table that had so impressed me were not elephant tusks, but whale ribs. God knows how many times I have dreamed of everything that that could unlock in my imagination, and of the objects one could see in that home, that had the appearance of Ali-Baba's cave, mixed with pirate treasures or with a story from the thousand-and-one nights.[4]

To the right, as one entered, lay the captain's imposing study. According to Simone Dion:

> It is not true that it resembled a cabin on board a ship, as is often said. There were book-cases filled with books and a beautiful writing desk with several drawers and compartments and a sliding panel to close it. This was his own corner. He kept all the souvenir albums that he had taken the time to assemble, in a large cupboard. There were seven or eight of them, I believe.[5]

The basement had been organized into a modern kitchen and a dining room with enormous windows with a view of the cliff, the St. Lawrence and Québec.

Joseph-Elzéar Bernier married Marie-Alma Lemieux in Ottawa, 1 July 1919. [Archives of Carol and Louis Terrien]

The Berniers liked to spend time there at different periods in the day.

> Upstairs there were three bedrooms lit by dormer windows, a store room for their clothes and their numerous suitcases and the bathroom. They shared the same room and slept in a large brass bed. I remember that in one of the other bedrooms there was an oak bed in the shape of a carriole.
>
> And then, the stairs up to the attic. Oh yes, I explored the attic thoroughly.[6]

Despite being over 87 years old Simone Dion retains intact, precise, vivid memories. She did not know Captain Bernier personally, since she was hired as Alma's lady's companion in March 1934 after his death. But Alma Lemieux talked so much about "her captain" that the young 19-year-old girl felt that she knew him, "to the extent, that I even had the impression that he was following me around the house."

The fact is that Captain Bernier made the decision to buy and furnish this house without consulting Alma. After they were married he took her to Lévis, whereas she thought they would be settling in Québec. It was very distressing for her to find herself far from her family, isolated in this great museum.

Madame Dion added:

> But the captain was the only true love of her life. She was very much in love with him. He was very good to her and he helped her discover the world and the great people of this world.[7]

They had a son, who died at birth. It should be said that Alma had already reached the age of 41, that this was her first pregnancy, and that she was definitely less than careful, since one fine morning a neighbour lady

Simone Dion, Alma Lemieux's lady's companion after Captain Bernier's death. [Photo: Lynn Fournier]

caught her sawing wood behind the house. This loss probably represented the greatest tragedy in Captain Bernier's life. The man who was never in the habit of showing his emotions was unable to hold back the grief and anguish that overwhelmed him as he buried the little body of his only child, his continuity.

In 1999 a granddaughter of Elmina Caron, Michelle Audet, published an autobiography in which she reported that she had met an Inuit woman who identified herself as the granddaughter of Captain Bernier:

> Soon Léa, the first young Eskimo woman whom I had greeted at the start of this experiment, excused herself and blurted out, point-blank: "Captain Bernier is my grandfather!"
>
> […] I made enquiries among people at the Department; they confirmed this fact. It is understandable that the Nouveau-Québec authorities did not mention it at the start of our experiment; they were unaware of the relationship that existed between the captain and my family. In this connection Léa had told me: "It was on his last expedition in 1924, at the Bernier Detachment, that the Captain, at age 72, made a son with my grandmother."[8]

Anthropologist Stéphane Cloutier, who has lived in Iqaluit for a long time and who has followed Captain Bernier's tracks around Nunavut, has written:

> To reply to your letter of 19 June 2002 concerning Bernier's Inuit offspring, the majority of the Pond Inlet elders assert the contrary. They believe that Bernier had no children, although he was twice married to "white" women. The Idlout family, however, claim that they are Captain Bernier's descendants, as Léah Idlout reported. Outside of this family nobody seems to be really acquainted with the situation.[9]

We will never get to the bottom of this story. Unless, of course a DNA test is administered.

CHAPTER 20

The Eastern Arctic Patrol

After his second marriage Joseph-Elzéar Bernier seemed resigned to quitting the sea. Apart from maintaining a voluminous correspondence he was frequently invited to give lectures or to act as an expert consultant on winter navigation and on ice and current conditions in the St. Lawrence River, as well as on various projects such as an air service in winter between Matane and Gaspé.

The captain and his beloved ship had been side-lined since the Conservative government had lost interest in its northern frontier and no longer saw any point in financing this old team.

While Bernier was getting used to the idea of regaining the anonymity of civilian life and was taking the time to test the efficacy of his polar bear oil remedy for his own rheumatism, the *Arctic* was playing a modest role as light-ship[1] at the Lower Traverse in the St. Lawrence estuary, downriver from the Île d'Orléans.

But from his study on the Rue Fraser the retired captain continued to worry about the fate of "his" archipelago and became exasperated at the indifference of the elected officials as to their arctic frontier.

In 1920, however, public opinion began to wake up to the external threats when the Dane Knud Rasmussen announced plans for his fifth scientific expedition that would involve crossing the Canadian Arctic from Greenland to Alaska. At the same time the American newspapers reported that Donald B. Macmillan wanted to explore the territories west of Ellesmere Island with a view to claiming them for the United States. Also in late summer that year a consultative committee[2] recommended to the Canadian Government that it should engage in certain concrete actions that would ensure Canadian sovereignty in the Arctic, such as establishing permanent posts of the Royal Canadian Mounted Police, annual patrols, and the exploitation of the wildlife and mineral resources of the Far North.

In December 1920 Bernier learned that the Minister of the Interior had approved the establishment of two new RCMP posts in the eastern sector of the archipelago, as well as the refitting of the *Arctic* for an expedition that was to head north the following summer under the command of engineer John Davidson Craig. One can easily guess his excitement at the expectation that he might be heading north again, and his great disappointment at the announcement that Craig had engaged Captain H.C. Pickels of Mahone Bay, Nova Scotia, to supervise the repairs to the government ship.

A foreigner on board "his" ship? Nobody knew the *Arctic* like Captain Bernier. Nobody was better qualified to put her back in shape. A cruel disgrace for the man who had bought her and commanded her for more than seven years.

Preparations ceased abruptly in February 1921 when Sir Ernest Henry Shackleton (1874-1922), the British explorer who had tried to reach the South Pole, made an appeal to the Canadian government to subsidize his next initiative in the Arctic. Even though his plans[3] did not meet the particular needs of the Royal Canadian Mounted Police, certain politicians were dazzled by the idea that a Canadian mission might be led by such a great international personage. All the funds allocated for the repairs to the *Arctic* were frozen until the politicians could agree on their choice of commander for the expedition.

Faced by the Federal Government's waffling Captain Bernier decided that it was time to apply a little pressure. On 20 June he declared publicly that he wanted to buy the *Arctic* to go and occupy the arctic frontier as soon as possible. Jealous, and a little concerned hat he might lose his place, Captain Pickels wrote to Craig in a tone that he intended to be both sarcastic and contemptuous.

> I see by the morning paper that Captain Bernier is buying the "Arctic" in his mind and I think he will be in the northern regions in about fifteen minutes. The only thing lacking that will stop him from going will be the Paris models for ladies hats.[4]

Even beyond official circles Bernier represented a certain threat. Clearly, once our retired captain had taken up a cause he rarely relinquished it again, and on 29 July he wrote directly to Arthur Meighen who had replaced Borden as Prime Minister of Canada.

> Honorable Sir,
>
> On the 20th of this month, I went up to Ottawa, and saw Sir James Loughan, Minister of the Interior, on the subject of the events that are developing around Baffin Land.
>
> [...] Mr. MacMillan, an American, has left with the schooner *Beaudoin* [sic] to explore this country of ours, and I fear that with the well known enterprises [sic] of the Americans, they might probably take away from us, what belong [sic] to our Country. Another American has been to my house, and asked me to give him the benefit of my knowledge of Baffin Land, and asked me also to go with him.
>
> I wish to stand on record very strongly in this matter, and advise your Government that although you had taken possession of these northern lands, we run a great risk of losing same, on account of not having held possession and control of same, as possession means occupation.
>
> Alaska was taken away from us, to our everlasting shame and the Americans must not be allowed to get another foot hold on the East, as they have on the West.
>
> Sir Henry Aylesworth stated in one of his judgements that Hudson Bay was a Canadian sea, owing to the fact that we had collected dues from American whalers, and they having paid said dues, they thereby acknowledged our sovereignty.
>
> This same procedure should be put in force immediately for the district of Franklin Land and I am at your disposition to see that this is carried out.
>
> There is a part on Baffin Land around Fox [sic] Channel, which was not properly surveyed, but I hold from the Esquimaux the necessary sketches and information enabling another expedition to finish this survey.
>
> I will hold myself in readiness to discuss this matter further with your Government, as I feel that it is urgent for us to prevent Canada from being despoiled of her very valuable territory.[5]

On 6 December 1921 the Liberals of William Lyon Mackenzie King (1874-1950) won the general election and returned to power in Ottawa.

Wishing to take advantage of this fair wind that was blowing in the national capital and of the enthusiasm of the newly elected members, who seemed less hesitant than their predecessors to protect their arctic frontier, Captain Bernier and his associates[6] in the company, *The Arctic Exchange and Publishing Limited,* lost no time in formulating their own plans for an expedition to the Far North. On 22 February 1922 they presented a detailed program to the Minister of the Interior and claimed the status of official representative in the Arctic, and also command of the steamer *Arctic*.

> Firstly they twisted the knife in the wound, as far as the Minister was concerned, by citing a few concrete examples of the weakness of Canadian governmental authority in the archipelago. Then they offered to occupy the major islands of the archipelago by establishing men and posts there, if the government agreed to grant them, free of

A rare photo of Bernier on board the *Arctic*, but not in his captain's uniform. [Archives of Carol and Louis Terrien]

> charge for the first 15 years, exclusive rights of hunting and stock rearing on the islands north of Lancaster and Viscount Melville sounds, as well as on Prince of Wales and Somerset islands and all of Baffin Island north of the 70th parallel.[7]

While serving their country Bernier and his accomplices had no intention of dying poor, like the majority of sailors of their day.

It is very possible that this request forced the government to act.

The Department of the Interior refused to share its responsibilities and instituted the "Eastern Arctic Patrol," an annual patrol by a Canadian government vessel to the Eastern Arctic, that would continue, with some breaks, until the mid sixties. John D. Craig was reinstated in his position of commander and Joseph-Elzéar's name replaced that of Captain Pickels, who had succumbed to a heart attack in October 1921.

Despite his being 70 years old, Bernier could not be ignored and, of necessity, the governmental authorities had no choice but to recognize his qualities and his vast experience that few Canadians could equal at that time. The retired captain accepted their offer of a salary of $500 per month and on 1 June he received authorization[8] to take immediate charge of the steamer *Arctic* and to look after repairs and final preparations.

⚓

In contrast to the pre-war government expeditions, the departure on 18 July 1922 was not a media event or an occasion to whip up strong patriotic feelings. Only a few members of the families of expedition members had access to the Quai du Roi in Québec harbour. The Liberals did not want publicity before all the police posts were well established and especially did not intend to engage in a public debate on the question of Canadian sovereignty in the Arctic.

As she sailed from Québec the *Arctic* was carrying a considerable weight of supplies: 500 tonnes of coal for her boilers, and a further 25 tonnes to heat the police posts, 225 tonnes of lumber for building the posts[9] and 75 tonnes of equipment and merchandise. On board were 43 men,[10] all trying to find a little privacy and comfort in their extremely cramped accommodations that already smelled of disinfectant, fish, and old vegetables. Apart from the captain and a few crew members they were all about to experience their first adventure in arctic waters, and despite the numerous technical problems that slowed the ship's impetus, the ambiance was rather cordial and enthusiastic.

> The government party and police officers were as enthusiastic as tourists on a cruise ship. Many carried cameras to record images of their fellow travellers and passing icebergs.[11]

Knowing that the professionals, the scientists, and young RCMP officers were not at all prepared for the challenges awaiting them in the North, and concerned about their relations with the Inuit, Captain Bernier chose a quiet moment to inform them about the historical importance of their mission and about the best ways of acting to occupy and organize themselves to survive in an environment as barren and hostile as that of the Arctic Archipelago. He addressed the personnel on the afternoon of 30 July 1922, as his schooner was navigating Davis Strait. This was "Bernier at his best."

The septuagenarian insisted on the fact that the Inuit were full Canadians and that they should be respected and treated fairly, and that one should never make promises to them that one had no intention of keeping "because a native has also a very high sense of honour and he will never deceive you willfully." In sharing his experiences and in offering his good advice on the benefits of physical exercise and social activities or on the importance of keeping control of oneself, of being amicable and pleasant in order to defuse tense situations that might arise between party members, the captain was perhaps hoping to encourage them to reflect on the difficulties ahead and to make them understand that they were solely responsible for their survival and for the success of the mission.

The Eastern Arctic.

On board the *Arctic*, multi-tasking was the order of the day. [Photo: R. Tash, LAC, PA-102293]

> Here one can easily detect the remarkable qualities that made this sailor a leader of men and a captain "for all seasons." Acute powers of observation, matched by an unequalled practical sense, an iron discipline, where breaks for relaxation had their place, a patriotism where ostentation was coupled with a deep sense of Canada's responsibility towards the Eskimos; there was no end to the facets of this fascinating personality. Captain Joseph-Elzéar Bernier played a pivotal role in the history of Arctic Canada; not only was he fully aware of it, but he was anxious to share his convictions with his fellow-citizens.[12]

During her voyage the *Arctic* dropped off two small RCMP detachments, one at Craig Harbour on southern Ellesmere Island on 28 August and the other at Albert Harbour on Baffin Island on 7 September.

As he sailed away Bernier had to admire the courage of these young men left on their own for the first time in these icy wastes. They would have a year to test their determination, their endurance and their sense of humour; a year to erect a police post, to acclimatize themselves to the solitude and the environment, to learn how to build an igloo, to drive a dog team, to trap and hunt like the Inuit; just one year to implant Canadian justice among a people who had their own notion of justice.

As he avoided the ice that was trying to block the entrance to Albert Harbour the "Old Man" must have been wondering how the Mounties would succeed in this latter task, he having earlier written:

> The natives who have been left to themselves, have made no effort to resist the ravages of disease which result from the practices introduced by white men, who make use of them for their own selfish purposes. Murders and other crimes comparatively unknown, previous to the contact of bad white men, occasionally occur amongst the untaught natives who have not the example of exemplary men. In addition to the natural state of the Eskimo, seeds of immorality and crime have been sown, and the natives are in a worse state than before the introduction of our civilization. Since the white man visited the habitations of these people, death among the children is a common occurrence; the best suited race for the cold, inhospitable climes, will disappear if some strenuous efforts are not made to preserve them.[13]

An Inuit couple from the Pond Inlet region. [Bernier Collection, *Master Mariner*]

Despite strong winds driving the ice, Bernier ran quickly into Eclipse Sound and Pond's Inlet, then crossed Baffin Bay to Godhavn in Danish Greenland. Commander Craig was particularly impressed by the cleanliness of the buildings and of the town and by the smiling faces and the beautiful costumes of the local population. This led him to praise the support programs of the Danish government and to urge his own government to assist the Inuit better, especially in terms of education and health services. His requests, like those of Captain Bernier, would fall on deaf ears.

On his return Craig was kind enough to thank the *Arctic*'s captain and to express his appreciation.

> [...] your work is thoroughly appreciated by everyone. It was due largely to your untiring efforts that the ship was able to sail when she did, as was also the early return from what might have easily been a voyage of over a year, this alone saving the Government several thousand dollars [...] through your great knowledge of the north country and the conditions there, and through your willingness to impart the knowledge to others [...].[14]

The retired sailor could be satisfied with his performance. At the age of 70 he had just proved that he could still handle his ship and bring it home safely. His name would remain linked to his country's sovereignty in the Arctic Archipelago.

A photo of the young Queen Victoria accompanied Bernier on his voyages. [Archives of Carol and Louis Terrien]

CHAPTER 21

White justice

WHEN THE *ARCTIC* SAILED FROM QUÉBEC in the late afternoon of 9 July 1923, on board was a special judicial team that was to hold the first trial ever mounted by the administration of the Northwest Territories in the Canadian archipelago. It was presided over by Judge Louis-Alfred-Adhémar Rivet, a former Liberal Member of Parliament for Hochelaga, who had never set foot in the Arctic and had no notion of the customs and habits of the Inuit people. Mr. Léopold Tellier, a young lawyer from Montréal, was to act as counsel for the defence and Mr. Adrien Fallardeau from Québec would be acting for the Crown. Also on board were 28 officers and sailors,[1] Commander John Davidson Craig, his wife Gertrude, cinematographer Georges Valiquette, clerk of the court François Biron, secretary Desmond O'Connell, interpreter Wilfred Duval, and Doctor Leslie Livingstone.

This unusual expedition was to try three Inuit, Aatitaaq, Nuqallaq, and Ululijarnaat, who were accused of the murder of Robert Janes, Bernier's former lieutenant who had opened a trading post at Tulukkaat near the mouth of the Patricia River in Eclipse Sound. In addition to bringing closure to this murder case, that had taken place on 15 March 1920 at a hunting camp near Cape Crawford, and to conclude the official enquiry by Sergeant Alfred Herbert Joy, the Federal administration wanted to set an example so that the Inuit would become familiar with the Canadian judicial system and so that they would learn to respect the laws of the country.

Four hours after the departure from the Quai du Roi, near Grosse Île a tragic accident cost the lives of Third Officer Wilfrid Caron and Commander Craig's secretary Desmond O'Connell. Violent winds were battering the ship and Caron, who was to be the principal witness for the defence in the trial of the Inuit, lost his footing and fell into the sea "while trying to free the mainsail sheet that had caught on the housing for the running light."[2] A lifebelt was immediately thrown in his direction and the lifeboat was launched. O'Connell, who was among those who went to his rescue, thought he vaguely saw his companion in the trough of a breaking wave, and immediately dived in, without realizing that he was diving to his death. A search for them was made, lasting for hours, but in vain. "Tit-Loup" Caron's[3] body was found a few days later on the shoals off Montmagny, while O'Connell's was discovered towards the end of the month, "washed ashore near Pointe-au-Pic, covered in flies, with his nose torn off and one eye missing from its socket."[4] Bernier was appalled by this accident and totally devastated by the death of his second cousin, who was also his protégé, his interpreter, and a loyal officer. Contrary to the popular rumour that he came aboard at Pointe-au-Père[5] the captain was indeed at the helm of his ship when the tragedy struck. A reporter with *L'Événement*, who had interviewed him just before he left Québec, said that Bernier was in a hurry to sail, and that he would not wait any longer for Craig to arrive before putting to sea.[6]

The *Arctic* called at Godhavn in Greenland, then at Craig Harbour and Beechey Island before reaching Pond Inlet on 21 August. The trial began officially on the morning of Saturday 25 August, and over a period of six days about 30 Inuit witnesses presented their testimony in turn to the six officers from the *Arctic* who formed the jury.[7] Rightly or wrongly, and quite independently of the true involvement of Janes in this affair, the jury found Nuqallaq and Ullujarnaat guilty of manslaughter. Aatitaaq was acquitted. In a solemn atmosphere worthy of the Supreme Court, Judge Rivet freed the latter and sentenced Ullujarnaat to two years hard labour at Pond Inlet. As for Nuqallaq he was obliged to serve a sentence of 10 years in Stony Mountain Penitentiary, north of Winnipeg, Manitoba.

Captain Bernier later wrote:

> This was the first court trial in the north and was of interest to the natives. The court took great pains to impress upon their primitive minds a proper notion of white man's justice. But to the Eskimo a punishment that consisted in a cessation of the hard conditions of his life, a free ride to civilization, no work, no worry, good clothing, food and quarters, and people to wait on him, is more in the nature of a translation to heaven. If killing a white man gives a native such unalloyed pleasure why, there is no reason why he should not repeat the offence whenever he wishes to enjoy another holiday at the government expense.
>
> So they reasoned. But quite evidently the white man's logic made some impression on them, for they have not systematically killed for the purpose of being coddled for a year or two.[8]

The man who had been closely associated with the Inuit for over 20 years believed that the Canadian government ought to have taken the time to study and to understand fully their psychology before imposing their laws and ways of doing things upon them.

Shelagh Grant's conclusion is eloquent:

Robert Janes at Canada Point, Bylot Island, 12 June 1911. This is the same individual who gave rise to the story of the gold deposit at Salmon River. [Bernier Collection, LAC, C-010973]

> The trial was not driven by an idealistic quest for justice but motivated by a dual purpose: on the one hand, to teach the Inuit a lesson to ensure *qallunaat* [white men] could live among them without fear, and on the other, to make a statement to the world that Canada was effectively administering its Arctic lands. Some have argued that the trial represented an important step in colonizing the Inuit people. Yet Canada would be a reluctant colonizer, inspired not by a desire to acquire Inuit lands and subjugate the

inhabitants but by the necessity to protect the legacy of British polar explorers.

The 1923 murder trial at Pond Inlet was not a particularly proud moment in the annals of Canadian legal history, but it might have been worse. At some point in the proceedings, common sense prevailed when it was acknowledged that the Inuit of North Baffin were ignorant of Canadian laws. As a result Nuqallaq would not be sentenced to death for killing Robert Janes.[9]

According to Grant a large sum of money had already been invested in the voyage and in the establishment of the police posts and hence Judge Rivet would have had difficulty in justifying a lesser sentence for the accused.

Commander Craig's official report was released to the newspapers well after the *Arctic* had slipped quietly into her berth at Québec on 4 October, when the Inuit prisoner was already en route to Winnipeg.

The majority of the dailies had a tendency to repeat the contents of the press release and, on the same occasion, they did not forget to congratulate the brave captain who, once again, had completed a "sensational" voyage and had completed his mission by steering his faithful ship past icebergs and through pack ice and the arctic seas. Undoubtedly the "good news" and the exploits of this hero of the ice sold more newspapers than the story of a simple Inuk facing "white man's justice."

Commander John Davidson Craig photographed by his wife Gertrude on the deck of the *Arctic*. [J.D. Craig Collection, LAC, PA-210045]

CHAPTER 22

Outmoded

John Davidson Craig, commanding the Canadian expeditions of 1922 and 1923, had always been ashamed of the vessel that had been imposed upon him. Right from the start he had recorded in his personal diary that no other vessel would have been permitted to sail in the pitiful state in which he found the *Arctic* and he had constantly been recommending to those responsible in government that a new polar vessel should be bought, one that would be more impressive and that would encourage the Inuit to recognize the authority of the government. His proposals were ignored, and despite refits, painting, and repairs, the ship was showing signs of wear and cut a wretched figure beside the modern steamers of the Hudson's Bay Company.

Richard Finnie, one of the few expedition members who have recorded their experiences with Captain Bernier, observed that the *Arctic* was outmoded and obsolete. It was a throwback to the era of the great sailing ships of wood and men of iron.[1]

Bernier and his strange schooner had been overtaken by time. Their extraordinary odyssey was drawing to a close. They had only another two voyages to make in the eastern Arctic.[2]

While ensuring a Canadian presence in the Far North, the government expedition of 1924 was to establish two new police posts, re-provision those already operating, relieve the personnel, make scientific observations, and obtain as much information as possible on the natural resources of this vast territory. The Department of the Interior had also agreed to experiment with shortwave radio by installing the first radio transmitter/receiver on a ship in Arctic waters. Antennas allowed the radio operator to receive incoming radio transmissions, but since the system did not include a microphone, he could not transmit.

Richard Finnie, the assistant radio operator, was greatly impressed by the vessel's appearance and fascinated by the abundance of supplies that kept arriving, day after day, in anticipation of a voyage that might last two years. There was so much freight in the hold and on deck that the poor vessel sagged under the load of over 900 tonnes.

In Finnie's words:

> Pacing the bridge, scrutinizing the cargo-handling and gruffly shouting orders in salty French, Captain Bernier dominated the scene. I had met him in Ottawa, but now in his own domain I got to know him well. The wireless room was adjacent to his cabin, and in periods of relaxation he would often invite me in for a chat over a cup of tea.
>
> [...] Bernier was below medium height but massive, with a bull neck and muscular arms and shoulders. Though overweight, he was nimble and sturdy for his age. His head was bald on top, fringed by white hair, and he had a matching walrus moustache. His mouth was large

and contained an array of gold bridgework. His nose was bulbous, his chin heavy, his face broad and florid, and his eyes keen. He wore glasses only for reading.

He could be gracious, but he had been too long exposed to the roughness of life at sea to have acquired much finesse. At mealtimes he tucked his napkin under his chin, grabbed whatever he wanted within reach, slurped his soup, and picked his teeth. [...] He was more at home on the bridge of a ship than in a drawing-room. [...] He was vain and dogmatic. With a gruff, hoarse voice, he was garrulous in both French and English, which he mixed. [...] But despite his foibles he was a colourful, warm-hearted, and likable character.[3]

The government patrols to the northern regions of Canada were not pleasure trips and the expedition members[4] who had signed-on aboard the worn-out, overladen vessel, could expect to experience a good share of adventures, and even to face dangerous situations. The 1924 voyage was not about to disappoint them.

The *Arctic* had sailed from Québec on 5 July, and six days later ran through the Strait of Belle Isle; reaching the open sea she ran north along the Labrador coast and headed for Baffin Island.

Throughout the night of 11 July and the whole of the following day she was battered by gale-force wind gusts, followed by torrential rain. While the ship tried to maintain its course, the heavy deck-cargo of coal absorbed a large amount of water, adding to its weight, dangerously destabilizing the ship as she rolled and pitched exuberantly with her ovoid hull. Nobody aboard could guess how dangerous the situation had become until a giant wave struck the ship with enormous force. The impact was brutal. The *Arctic* heeled violently to port, jarring loose the deck cargo from its moorings. Trapped by this tempest, by the violence of the waves that hammered their ship, by the increasingly critical loss of their coal stocks, and by the fact that the engine room was already under five feet of water, the men on board thought they were already in hell.

Bernier bellowed: "All hands on deck!"

The radio operator, Bill Choat, tried frantically to transmit an S.O.S. under the fixed gaze of his young assistant who realized that this was a pointless activity since they were far too far at sea for any ship to hear them and come to their aid. Ten minutes later it was the turn of the generator to give out. Choat hooked up his wireless transmitter to batteries and continued keying: S.O.S. ...Two hours of desperate effort without a reply!

As Richard Finnie remembered, the night of 12 July "was one of sheer terror and misery." Everyone was soaked to the skin and the water was ice-cold. Désiré Morin was struck broadside by a wave and swept overboard. Another wave immediately picked him up and carried him back aboard. The poor officer was shaken, but emerged unscathed.

The "Old Man" had tears in his eyes, he was so unsure of being able to bring his passengers and crew through this dire experience. But his sense of organization and responsibility quickly took charge of the situation. He smartly ordered a hand-pump set up forward and men to operate it in turn. He organized a bucket brigade to bail out the engine room. His energy was contagious and the bottles of rum that he handed around warmed his sailors' aching muscles.

Despite their considerable efforts the situation seemed to be deteriorating. Bernier therefore decided to lighten his ship by jettisoning part of his deck cargo of coal and lumber. By the morning of 13 July, 200 tonnes of cargo had already been pitched overboard, allowing the ship to right herself. However she had taken such a battering that her crew took several days to restart the engine and get under way again.

Finally, on the evening of 17 July, encouraged by the throbbing of her engines, by the wind in her sails, and the competence of her crew, the *Arctic* picked up the rhythm of her voyage again, and ran towards the calmer waters of Cumberland Sound.

On 22 July Bernier dropped anchor at Pangnirtung in order to resupply the police post and to land geologist J. Dewey Soper, whose task was to study and collect

Captain Bernier with L.-Désiré Morin and Léonidas Lemieux, who were his First Officers on the expeditions from 1922 to 1925. [Photo: J.D. Craig, LAC, PA-102616]

specimens of the flora and fauna of this southern part of Baffin Island. As the captain later recalled:

> We made our usual calls, landing at Godhavn on July 31. [...] The weather was particularly fine and much like that of early spring in more southern latitudes, [...] and the general air of bustle that pervaded the place made it hard to realize that Godhavn lies 200 miles north of the Arctic Circle. To Canadians like ourselves interested in the development of our Arctic territory, Godhavn and its thriving population was an indication of what we may expect at numerous points on the Canadian side in the not distant future.[5]

Between 4 August and mid-September the *Arctic* was discharging freight at Pond Inlet before rebuilding and resupplying the post at Craig Harbour that had been destroyed by fire early in the year. Craig then established a new detachment of the Royal Canadian Mounted Police at Dundas Harbour on Devon Island then tried in vain to reach Bache Peninsula in Kane Basin, 750 miles from the North Pole.[6] The ship was still taking on water, coal stocks were running low, and the ice conditions were such that the *Arctic* was forced to leave part of her freight at Fram Fjord, and the rest at Dundas Harbour.[7] Then, before starting back south they inspected the seams of coal noted earlier by Captain Bernier at Canada Point, then made a stop at Clyde River and Home Bay, south of Cape Henry Kater. Thereafter they got under way again. As Finnie has reported:

Homeward bound, we ran into rough weather and the ship, now being light, bobbed like a cork. So inured were we to discomfort by this time that we almost enjoyed it. Eighty-two days and six thousand miles after our departure we docked at Québec. I had celebrated my eighteenth birthday north of the Arctic Circle and, after all I had been through, I now considered myself both grown-up and a *bona fide* explorer.[8]

Bernier in the bosun's chair in which he was hoisted to the *Arctic*'s crow's-nest so that he could direct her through the pack ice. [Photo: R. Finnie, courtesy of *The Beaver*]

Journalist Harwood E. Steele, who was hired as private secretary to the commander of the 1925 expedition, George Patton Mackenzie, has left some excellent descriptions of Captain Bernier as he captained the *Arctic* on her last patrol voyage in the Canadian archipelago:

> The first thing that struck me about seeing Captain Bernier was that he was "wonderfully well preserved" [...]. He took a very reasonable pride in this physical fitness. His little office was also a rendezvous to Québecois, to whom he was Canada's greatest hero. Every visitor might have to try their strength against the Captain. His favourite stunt was to brace his sturdy body on his short, muscular legs, and challenge you to move him, or to extend an arm like his own bowsprit and defy you to bend it. Cocky young salesmen, husky junior officers, would accept the challenge. But none of those lads could shift Captain Bernier. "I told you so!" His little song of triumph was always the same.
>
> [...] But I did not see the Old Man at his best till we crossed the Arctic Circle. In the ice he was truly in his element
>
> "Rig the bosun's chair!" said he. "I may be too old to climb the rigging but I'm not too old to con the ship!"
>
> This was just as we entered the Baffin Bay pack. And con the ship he did, all day and every day, for nearly three weeks, being regularly hoisted in and out of the crowsnest in that same bosun's chair.[9]

Throughout the voyage young Steele was under the spell of the formidable seafarer and dazzled by his presence of mind, his humour, his knowledge and his composure.

Richard Finnie, who was hired as assistant radio operator, saw things differently. To him the old man and his ship seemed to be coming to the end of their careers, and could no longer serve Canada fittingly. As he relates,[10] as soon as the *Arctic* sailed from the Quai du Roi on 1 July, 1925, the expedition seemed to be doomed to ill-luck. The *Arctic* grazed another vessel moored nearby, smashing one of the lifeboats and tearing it from one of its davits. The engine next broke down and they had to stop at L'Islet to make emergency repairs. It took the vessel a week to reach Anticosti Island in the Gulf of St. Lawrence.

Bad luck was to continue to dog her. The first icebergs they sighted in the Labrador Sea were drifting rapidly in a wild sea. The poor ship creaked and groaned under the pressure of the water that forced its way through every one of her worn seams. Giant waves tormented her complement pitilessly, as if they were in a butter churn. The deck was constantly swept by mountainous seas that broke loose and carried away deck cargo while the men, their nerves frayed, sick, or exhausted by the constant struggle, tried desperately to cling on in order to stay on their feet. Others, down in the hold, were pumping furiously to keep pace with the water that was flooding in through the strained timbers, and was threatening to flood the boilers. They must have been cursing the fate that had brought them on board this slave-ship!

The sea finally calmed down, allowing the seamen to make the necessary repairs in order to continue towards Cumberland Sound. Unfortunately, as she approached southern Baffin Island the *Arctic* became entangled in an exceptionally close field of ice. As Bernier later reported:

> For six days the struggle was continued. But for the fact that I was ordered to make Pangnirtung, I would never have thought of attempting to go in that direction at that time of the season. We no doubt could have got through, but the loss of time would have prevented us from completing the important part of the patrol in the north. The order to retreat was given on the 24th, but even then it was not until 14 days later that the pack was cleared.[11]

Relations between the captain and the commander of the expedition were sometimes strained. According to Richard Finnie, during the previous voyages Bernier's decisions had never been challenged by the government officials who had always bowed to his enormous experience as a navigator and his reputation as an explorer of the polar regions. Things were different with the new commander, George Mackenzie, a well-built man of 52, who took his role seriously. The assistant radio operator appears to have admired this former Gold Commissioner of the Yukon, whom he found tolerant, good-humoured, conscientious and fearless, and who expected straight answers to his questions and could make his own decisions.

One day the captain had miscalculated the ship's position by over 70 miles, and his pride had prevented him from consulting his officers. When questioned by Mackenzie, Bernier was evasive and unable to admit his error of judgment. Mackenzie concluded from this that the "Old Man" was no longer fit to lead such expeditions: "All the captain's predictions have been merely guesses and poor ones at that."[12]

The captain's reaction was that of an old man to his own incompetence. Even the "great Bernier" had to realize that his failings, that were starting to become apparent, were a sign that it was a time to bow out and to leave the stage to those younger than he. This voyage of 1925 was to allow him to cross this difficult threshold and to resign himself to the fact that his active life had ended. At age 73 Joseph-Elzéar Bernier could not deny the inevitable any longer.

After a courtesy visit to Godhavn, the *Arctic* again flirted with disaster, when a giant iceberg drove towards the ship, threatening to crush her. The secretary, Harwood Steele, was full of praise for the captain's skills in succeeding in escaping from this dangerous situation, thanks to his *savoir-faire* and his presence of mind. As far as Richard Finnie was concerned, it was rather Providence and a good wind in the sails that saved them from the clutches of death. These two opposing reactions were symptomatic of the range of attitudes that

PRECIOUS LETTERS RECEIVED

On Board S. S. "C. A. Larsen",
En route, San Pedro, Calif., to
Wellington, New Zealand,
October 31st, 1928.

Captain J. E. Bernier,
27 Fraser St.,
Levis, Quebec.

My dear Captain Bernier,

Many thanks for your kind message transmitted through Mr. Wendt of the Canadian Westinghouse Company.

It is good to carry into the Antarctic the wishes of our friends in Canada for the success of the expedition, and a safe return, especially from the dean of arctic explorers,

Very sincerely yours,

BYRD.

Bernier communicated with Commander Byrd over a long period. [Bernier Collection, *Master Mariner*]

Bernier engendered; he either impressed or upset people by his enormous popularity, his legendary exploits, his longevity, and by everything he represented. One either loved or hated this small French Canadian who had succeeded in an Anglo-Saxon world. One either admired or envied his dreams, his tenacity, his passion, and his courage.

On 19 August the *Arctic* reached Etah where the steamer *Peary* and the schooner *Bowdoin* were lying at anchor; they were part of an American expedition led by Donald B. MacMillan. Between 1913 and 1924 this protégé and successor of the explorer Robert Peary had many times contested Canadian sovereignty in the Arctic Archipelago and had organized extended visits to Ellesmere Island and other areas of the Canadian Arctic. In 1925 he was involved in Lieutenant-Commander Richard Byrd's plan, financed by the US Navy and the National Geographic Society, to explore the Arctic Ocean beyond Alaska. The Byrd-MacMillan expedition was, for the first time, to use three amphibious aircraft to fly over unknown territory, and to use an intermediate base on Canadian territory where supplies and fuel would be available.

This American expedition had started north on 20 June 1925, without obtaining the necessary licences from the Canadian authorities, and when the *Arctic* dropped anchor at Etah, Greenland, it was already homeward bound, having encountered difficulties with the planes during the reconnaissance flights over Ellesmere Island. When Byrd was questioned as to his permits, he stated that MacMillan had advised him that all his papers were in order and that he had received the consent of the Canadian government before leaving. The commander George Mackenzie was skeptical, but he had no means of verifying whether Byrd was telling the truth, since the *Arctic*'s radio transmitter was non-operative.

The British Ambassador raised the matter with the US Secretary of State; in a letter dated 9 December 1925 he informed the Secretary that Byrd and Macmillan had broken three Canadian laws: the Northwest Territories Act, customs laws, and those of the Canadian Council for the Air. No excuse was offered, but subsequently all American expeditions were careful to conform with the wishes of their northern neighbour.

The authors of the book *The True North, the Story of Captain Joseph Bernier* exaggerated the captain's true role when they placed him at the centre of this diplomatic incident. According to Fairley and Israel, it was not the commander, Mackenzie, who led the discussions with the Americans , but rather Bernier who demonstrated his talent as a diplomat by inviting Byrd and MacMillan to dinner, instead of confronting them over the matter of their licence. According to them:

> The dinner was a pleasant affair. Over coffee, Bernier presented his guests with detailed charts of the Arctic, together with copies of Canadian patrol reports. He drew their attention to the location of the R.C.M.P. posts, where travellers could seek aid if needed. He showed them movies in which Canada's administration of the northland was clearly displayed: police, traders, radio operators, customs collectors, game and fisheries officers.
>
> Byrd was amazed. He had not realized the extent of Canadian operations in the North.

After giving this time to sink in, Bernier, ever so gently, suggested that perhaps conditions were not quite right at this time for a flight to the Pole. The mountains of Ellesmere Island were treacherous and could spell disaster for anyone not acquainted with the terrain. It was late in the season. Icing conditions were bad and getting worse. It would be a good idea for the Americans to consider very carefully before going through with their plans.[13]

In his memoirs Captain Bernier stated that he had convinced Byrd not to risk the flight so late in the season, but to make the attempt the following year from Svalbard, Norway, since from there he would not have to fly over high mountains. He was probably correct. Byrd would not have failed to ask the advice of the "dean of Arctic explorers," as he described him in his later writings. At that time the explorers' club was a very select one. All the members knew each other and had an interest in helping each other and sharing their knowledge. Captain Bernier's correspondence provides proof of this exchange of information with the great adventurers, who shared his passion for the icy regions of the world: Nansen, Shackleton, Scott, Byrd, Amundsen, Stefansson, Peary, Cook, MacMillan, Charcot, and Markham.

MASTER MARINER

Gjoa Harbor,
King William's Land,
22 May, 1905,

Capt. J. E. Bernier,
Master of the D. G. S. Arctic,
Fullerton,

Dear Sir,

Your kind letter of the 26th March dispatched by the native "Atangala" — came me in hand — together with a lot of photos and news — the 19th inst. I received it — as you can imagine you — with the outmost pleasure. I did not know any of these news you send. All my comrades here are of course also in high state of delight. I send you my most hearty thanks for your kindness. Your informations about the American Whalers to the westward are very important for me as I did not know it before. The report of R. M. Donaldson of the R.N.W.M.P. was of high interest to me. I am very glad to hear that our news from that time already have reached our relations. The depot at Port Leopold was put in a very good position, but I hope we shall get away without it. Will you please thank Mr. Ben Kuilird of Skien for his good wishes. — Both my comrades and myself send you our best compliments and wishes for your fortune in the Arctic.

I am, Dear Sir, Yours Very Sincerely,
ROALD AMUNDSEN,
Commanding the Norwegian Gjoa Expedition.

398

Captain Bernier was proud of the numerous letters that he received from the great explorers of his day, such as Roald Amundsen. [Bernier Collection, *Master Mariner*]

It was the journalists and writers who turned this amicable dinner into "Bernier's diplomatic mission," eclipsing Commander Mackenzie's participation. This is just another example of the way in which the famous seaman was associated with the affirmation of Canadian sovereignty in the Far North. Even though he was no longer the commander of the government patrols, for his admirers, these still remained "his missions." For a majority of Canadians Bernier remained the champion of the Arctic.

In addition to resupplying the police posts and patrolling in the Canadian archipelago, the 1925 expedition was to take Nuqallaq back home to Pond Inlet. Robert Janes' murderer had served only two years of his sentence at Stony Mountain, but since he was seriously ill with tuberculosis, the Governor General had agreed that he should return to the North.

To prevent him from transmitting this contagious disease to the other passengers he had been confined in a whaleboat on the deck of the ship. At the start of the voyage Dr. Livingstone had observed that Nuqallaq's symptoms of tuberculosis were sufficiently stable that it appeared to be in remission. This impression of well-being was of short duration since from 6 August onwards, when the *Arctic* was a prisoner of the pack ice in Davis Strait, the sick man's condition had deteriorated so rapidly that there were fears that he would die before seeing his family again.

In his isolated corner Nuqallaq had no choice but to make the rounds on board the *Arctic*, calling at Fram Havn, Craig Harbour, and Dundas Harbour. He was laid low by an increasingly high fever. He was taking only liquids and was constantly spitting blood.

Finally, on 3 September, to the great relief of all the passengers the government vessel arrived safely at Eclipse Sound.

Nobody had informed the community of Pond Inlet that Nuqallaq had contracted tuberculosis. Ataguttiaq welcomed home just a shadow of the husband who had left her for his long sojourn in the South, while his friends and relatives believed that the striking physical transformation in a man they had respected for his strength and courage was proof that he had been made to work too hard in the penitentiary. When the *Arctic* got under way again, Nuqallaq was not long for this world. He died on 5 December 1925.

> With Nuqallaq now absent from the scene, one would have hoped that the Inuit could bring closure to this unfortunate episode. Not so. The continued presence of the police and, to a lesser extent, the Hudson's Bay Company would serve as a constant reminder of the settlement's origins. Although government intervention in their lives would have been unavoidable in any circumstances, the death of Robert Janes had accelerated the pace of change, threatening their cultural traditions and individual freedom.[14]

Had the authorities returned the tubercular Nuqallaq to his own people because they were touched by compassion for the poor man, or were they trying to get rid of an embarrassing problem? The decision had grave consequences since Nuqallaq's return led to an epidemic of tuberculosis in the northern part of Baffin Island. Evidently little was known then about the lack of immunity among the natives to infectious diseases, and even less about how to prevent them. All the same, the fact that Nuqallaq was isolated on the deck of the *Arctic* would indicate that there was an awareness that he might spread the disease. It would therefore also have been logical to assume that he might infect the people who had gathered at Pond Inlet to welcome him home.

On 12 October 1925 *L'Événement* of Québec emphasized "the happy return" of the "bold Canadian sailors:"

> The ship's commander, Captain Bernier who, at age 74, is still alert and in good health, was himself on deck, shaking hands with the numerous friends who had come to greet him.
>
> "We have successfully fulfilled the aim of our voyage," Captain Bernier declared to *L'Événement*'s reporter. "As you can see, we've returned safe and sound."
>
> "Will this be your last expedition, Captain?" asked the journalist.
>
> "Oh! I'm always ready to head out again," replied the *Arctic*'s commander "I believe, however, that I've really earned my retirement and that the government will grant me it. But at any event, I am still young and vigorous," the old sea-dog replied with a smile. "And service to my country comes first. If my achievements are not judged sufficient, I'll just keep on going."

Captain Bernier and Nuqallaq en route to Pond Inlet, 1925. [Oswald S. Finnie Collection, LAC, PA-100441]

To his admirers the proud captain still presented the image of the indomitable seafarer. The reality was quite different. Bernier was tired. He came home with several broken ribs, short of breath and with his heart weakened by a terrible blow he had received right in his chest.

The accident had occurred during a course-changing manoeuvre as they were heading for Godhavn. The forward boom had swung so suddenly and forcefully that it caught the captain full in the chest. The impact propelled him aft, and almost hurled him overboard. He was unconscious when he was picked up.

Despite his pain the "Old Man" had retained command of his ship right to the end. This was how he had been brought up. This is how the "men of iron" behaved during the time of the great sailing ships.

But during the last miles as they ran up his beloved St. Lawrence, Bernier was overcome by emotion and, turning to the young journalist, Harwood Steele, who was standing beside him, with his eyes full of tears, he said: "I am going ashore, Mr. Steele. I guess I'll be coiling my ropes." [15]

CHAPTER 23

The *Arctic*'s sad fate

THE *ARCTIC* HAD BEEN INVOLVED in so many arduous battles with the arctic ice that it was no longer seaworthy. And, moreover, times had changed. The annual Canadian patrols demanded larger, more modern ships with grater capabilities. The gallant vessel that had faced so many dangers and overcome so many obstacles during its 21 years of service, was out-dated. The end of its career would draw a curtain over the era of old-style arctic navigation.

Instead of preserving it for future generations Canada decided to get rid of it like a pile of rotten wood. Instead of recognizing its historic value as the Norwegian government had done in the case of Roald Amundsen's *Gjøa* and Fridtjof Nansen's *Fram*, the government officials in charge opted instead to extract profit from its monetary value.

Captain Bernier, who wanted to use his ship as a training ship for young Canadian seamen, was unable to dissuade them. "To be trained aboard the old *Arctic*," he wrote sadly towards the end of his autobiography, *Master Mariner*, "would be an inspiration in itself."

The administrators of course remained indifferent to the old man's wishes.

Bernier and the *Arctic*—their names had always been inseparable. One wonders whether, by relegating the ship to the garbage can, the authorities were not also trying to consign its captain to oblivion, or to diminish the contribution of this French-Canadian to the strengthening of Canadian sovereignty in the Far North? A question that makes a lot of sense when one considers that the Royal Canadian Mounted Police's *St. Roch* has ended up in a choice spot at the Vancouver Maritime Museum.

The *Arctic*'s equipment and gear were transferred to the C.G.S. *Franklin*[1] and the ship itself sold to the Hudson's Bay Company on 20 August 1926 for the modest sum of $9000. The main aim of this transaction was to prevent competitors such as Captain Bernier from acquiring the ship to service their commercial operations in the Arctic.[2]

Instead of returning the ship to a seaworthy condition, which would have cost at least $75,000, the purchaser decided to break the ship up. According to the Hudson's Bay Company's records, the masts and rigging and everything that could be removed were sold off in July 1927 and the hull sold to the Gulf Iron and Wrecking Company of Québec, to be broken up. The annual report of the Company's Fur Trade Commissioner, dated 20 February 1928, confirmed that the *Arctic* had definitely been broken up.

Was this the end of the story? Not entirely. The Department of Transport's Registry of Shipping and the Hudson's Bay Company's documents are at odds with a letter from Captain Bernier, dated 21 July 1926:

L.H. Beer,
Salvage Officer,
Trafalgar Building,
Bank Street,
Ottawa

With further reference to our interview of yesterday, I beg to enclose cheque of $4,000 re sale of *S.S. Arctic* as she now lays at Dep't of Marine and Fisheries Wharf in Québec.

This cheque also covers purchase of whale boat with gear, a 7/8 inch wire hawser with reel and plans of *Arctic* from the Dep't of Interior, and also sails.[3]

Thus, whatever the reasons behind this silence,[4] the fact is that the *Arctic* was not completely dismantled and that Bernier became its owner from the summer of 1926. He took what remained of his poor old ship back to Lévis in the hope that one day he would find a place for it in a Canadian museum.

This dream was never realized, and the gallant ship was never saved from its ruinous state. According to popular rumour the captain could see the hulk of his poor companion from his house on the Rue Fraser. On the other hand some older residents of Lauzon can still recall having played on it in their youth, and claim that it was closer to the Anse aux Sauvages. A Lévis newspaper stated that the *Arctic* was located:

> on the beach, and more precisely a few feet from a house known as "the Jew's house." Another great Francophone Canadian spent several summers in this house. This was our national poet Louis-Honoré Fréchette. That house is now demolished. The Létourneau garage is now located on that lot.[5]

Nowadays, early in the 21st century nobody seems to remember the "Jew's house" or the garage that replaced it.

Radio operator William Choat visited his former captain and, on 10 July 1929, took this photo of the *Arctic*'s empty hull abandoned on the beach at Lévis. Bernier then said to him, pointing to the hulk: "Don't look at it for too long, Bill. That will make you as sad as I am." According to Choat the polar vessel was like a dying animal. [Courtesy of *The Beaver*]

As the years passed local people or simply curious people who made off with the remains of the valuable ship, either as firewood or as relics, were just as responsible for the *Arctic*'s disappearance as the ravages of time, the interests of the Hudson's Bay Company, or the indifference of the politicians.

CHAPTER 24

The book project

OVER THE YEARS THAT FOLLOWED, Joseph-Elzéar Bernier maintained his interest in navigation on the St. Lawrence and in the Arctic.

In 1926 he fitted out the steamer *Beothic,* belonging to Job Brothers, the Newfoundland ship-owners. This merchant ship had been built in the United States especially for working in ice and had been chartered by the Canadian government to replace the *Arctic* in resupplying the Royal Canadian Mounted Police posts and in the Eastern Arctic Patrols.

In 1927 Bernier acted as pilot on board the seagoing tug *Ocean Eagle,* bound from Halifax to Churchill.[1] Strangely, he was thus closing the loop since he was completing his impressive series of voyages to the Canadian North as he had begun, by making a run to Hudson Bay. The Department of Railways and Canals had charged him with escorting a string of barges hauling coal to Churchill to bunker ships in the Hudson Bay area the following summer. This last voyage was undoubtedly one of the most exhausting of his long career.[2]

During this same period he suggested to Prime Minister Mackenzie King that special vessels should be built to ensure winter navigation on the St. Lawrence River and in the Gulf.[3] He also participated actively in the debate on completing the railway to Hudson Bay.

> Since 1907, he had been consulted by various House and Senate commissions for information on ice conditions in Hudson Bay and Strait and the advantages of establishing a railway terminus at either Fort Nelson or Fort Churchill. The Captain considered Fort Churchill the more likely choice, a view held by many others as well, and it was his opinion that finally won out.[4]

At the age of 75, Joseph-Elzéar still believed that he could make his mark on a world that was evolving

Photograph of Bernier and the *Ocean Eagle* reproduced in *Canadian Marine News.* Each new voyage by the intrepid seafarer earned the attention of the Canadian press. [Archives of Carol and Louis Terrien]

rapidly around him. He wrote reports on the radical decrease in the number of whales in the Atlantic and the Arctic, and also on the annual slaughter of baby seals, which in 1926 alone had led to the death of not less than 140,200 suckling seals. He persistently denounced the negative influence of whalers and sailors on the morals of the Inuit and the fact that sexual relations between the two races led to the spread of infectious diseases that threatened the population of the Far North. He insisted on the importance of consolidating Canadian authority in the Arctic and never missed an opportunity of emphasizing it to the politicians and high-ranking federal bureaucrats. As a speaker he was still much sought-after by various clubs, associations, and societies, both in Canada and abroad. And up until the age of 80, he was recruited by the department of Marine as appraiser and specialist in law-suits and enquiries into maritime accidents.[5]

Apart from these activities there was the matter of making arrangements for his retirement. Bernier was hoping that the Liberal government would recognize his services by granting him an annuity. He had had this idea in mind for a long time, but waited until he retired before tackling the matter and appealing to his powerful friends in Ottawa.[6] A special bill in 1927 assured him an annual pension of $2400 from the Department of the Interior.

During this last phase of his life the project to write his memoirs claimed his attention more than anything else. Before drawing a curtain on his extraordinary life Bernier wanted to leave his testimony for posterity. Was this a need to ensure some continuity for a childless man? It is possible. A desire for recognition and immortality? Why not?

> Soon after he retired, in 1926 Bernier announced his intention of writing his memoirs. The publishing company, McClelland and Stewart, approached him almost immediately, but at the first contact with Bernier, George Stewart suggested to the captain that he should entrust the writing of his text to a journalist or a professor.[7]

Bernier in the office of his publisher, Louis Carrier.
[Archives of Carol and Louis Terrien]

On 21 September 1926 the captain signed a contract with the publisher, Louis Carrier & Co. of Montréal. It was then decided to recruit Blodwen Davies to write the texts of two volumes with the titles *Master Mariner* and *Arctic Islands* or *Arctic Canada*.

The retired captain had everything prepared: the chronology of events in his life; a list of elements that he wanted to include; 16 albums filled with photos and private documents; all his reports on his voyages in the Canadian North; a box of letters from fellow-explorers; a brief-case containing his private correspondence; a trunk containing about 60 logbooks; another box on his plans for exploring the Pole, and more.

It is known that the meetings, the dictations, and the writing dragged on for four years since notes in Bernier's handwriting dated 31 May 1930[8] mention that Louis Carrier was claiming that there remained only two or three chapters to complete the first volume. These notes also reveal that Blodwen Davies had already started work on the second volume, but that she had not yet been paid for writing the first text.

One of the many albums assembled by Bernier after his retirement before he wrote his memoirs. [Collection of Carol and Louis Terrien]

The poor captain was really unlucky. The previous month Louis Carrier had gone bankrupt and had sold his interests to a new company, Warwick Brothers and Rutler of Toronto, with Paul Gouin as its president. Bernier was obliged to lodge an appeal with the Bankruptcy Court to redeem his author's rights and to annul his contract.

Another album prepared by Bernier with a view to collecting his letters and photographs. [Collection of Carol and Louis Terrien]

In August 1930 he had not only paid out $3,100 to settle this entire matter, but then the Toronto publisher asked for an additional $750 to pack up and return his photographic plates and documents. He paid $500, and when the boxes arrived some weeks later, they were damaged, allegedly in transit.

Captain Bernier then appealed to the Abbé Élie-J. Auclair of Saint-Polycarpe-de-Soulanges, but he decided "that editing and completing the first volume would be too demanding and arduous a task."[9]

Thus Bernier was left up in the air! He no longer had the health or energy to handle this important project that he had so much at heart, "his life's work," for which his admirers and friends throughout the world were waiting impatiently.[10]

CHAPTER 25

The desire to be recognized

FOR A FEW YEARS BEFORE HIS DEATH IN 1934 Bernier devoted himself in part to pursuing the prestige attached to the political importance of his governmental and private expeditions. This form of megalomania became more pronounced from 1930 onwards. Bernier's correspondence is full of sentences such as: "I will endeavour to live long enough to obtain recognition from the people of Canada and the world at large."

> In May 1931 he had requested the assistance of ex-Prime Minister Meighen, President of the Royal Empire Society, in obtaining a testimonial of recognition from the King of England.
>
> "I beg you to consider my demand for recognition from His Majesty the King, who was personally present when I left Québec, July 28th 1908, to take possession of our Northern archipelago, which I did in 1908-9".
>
> When the Canadian government promised him the Imperial Service Medal, Bernier insisted that it be awarded to him in Ottawa by the Governor General.[1]

The word "megalomania" is an exaggeration. At the end of his life Bernier certainly wanted to be recognized, but not to excess. He had no delusions of grandeur and his private correspondence was not full of requests to that effect. Moreover, did he not have a right to demand that the Imperial Service Medal be awarded him by the official representative of the King of England in Canada? Ought he to accept a less significant gesture because he was French Canadian?

In 1928 Arthur Woollacott had the courage to write:

> If he had been English, the captain would today be Sir Joseph Bernier, ranking with Sir John Franklin, Sir John Ross or Sir Edward Parry, whose services were suitably recognized by the British nation, always anxious to honour the bravery of its heroes with titles.[2]

In other words, the injustice towards the greatest Canadian seafarer was rather startling.

Some of the medals bestowed on Captain Bernier during his remarkable career. [Photo Lynn Fournier, Collection of the Musée maritime du Québec (Musée Bernier)]

THE COUNCIL OF THE
AMERICAN GEOGRAPHICAL SOCIETY
CERTIFIES THAT
Joseph Elzear Bernier
HAS BEEN ELECTED A
FELLOW
OF THE SOCIETY AND IS ENTITLED TO ALL THE RIGHTS AND PRIVILEGES OF FELLOWSHIP
WITNESS THE SEAL OF THE SOCIETY AND THE SIGNATURE OF THE PRESIDENT ATTESTED BY THE RECORDING SECRETARY
NEW YORK, November 23, 1926.
RECORDING SECRETARY
PRESIDENT

Certificate of "fellowship" bestowed on Captain Bernier by the Council of the American Geographical Society on 23 November 1926. [Archives of Carol and Louis Terrien]

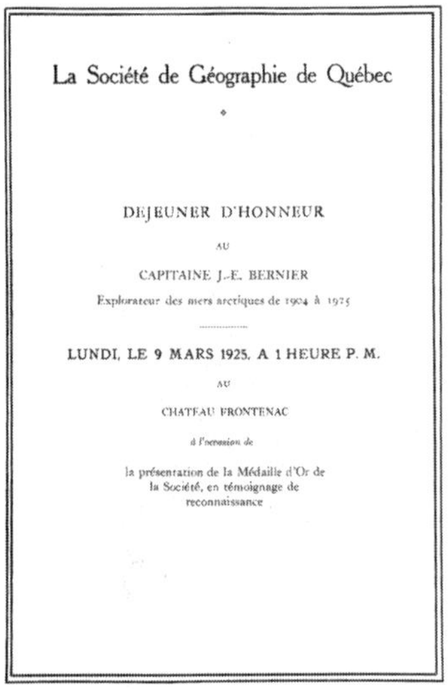

La Société de Géographie de Québec

DEJEUNER D'HONNEUR
AU
CAPITAINE J.-E. BERNIER
Explorateur des mers arctiques de 1904 à 1925

LUNDI, LE 9 MARS 1925, A 1 HEURE P. M.
AU
CHATEAU FRONTENAC
à l'occasion de
la présentation de la Médaille d'Or de la Société, en témoignage de reconnaissance

MENU

Aspic de foie gras de l'Islet
Célery de Lévis — Olives du "Guide"
Consommé Pot au feu "Arctic" en tasse
Dinde rôtie farcie de l'Ile Melville
Petits Pois, Bonne femme esquimaude
Pommes Parisiennes, Passage du Nord-Ouest
Parfait glacé Tricolore du Pole Nord
Mignardise à la "Minnie Maude"
Demi Tasse Sir John Franklin

Invitation from the *Société de géographie de Québec*, on the occasion of the presentation of a gold medal to Captain Bernier, along with the menu for the celebratory lunch on 9 March 1925. [Archives of Carol and Louis Terrien]

In that nowadays it is thought to be entirely normal for popular actors such as Sean Connery, rock singers like Mick Jagger or even businessmen like Conrad Black to buy the title of "Sir," why should one reproach Captain Bernier for seeking the honours that were rightfully his? What always upsets critics as regards Bernier is his lack of humility and the fact that he dared to make himself conspicuous in order to stand out from the crowd.

> Bernier expected to be knighted. It wasn't too unrealistic an expectation either. He had made a significant contribution to securing Canada's islands, and his expeditions were as risky as any previously made by foreign explorers. Men had also been knighted for less.[3]

Captain Bernier was proud of what he had accomplished and he wanted history to remember him. He liked honours and his honours included:

Member of the Explorers' Club of New York and elected its President in 1909, a position bestowed only on merit.
Fellow of the Royal Geographical Society of London;[4] he received their coveted "Sir George Back Award" on 6 April 1925.[5]
Fellow of the Royal Colonial Institute of London.
Member of the Royal Explorers' Society of London.
Fellow of the American Geographical Society.
Vice-President of the Arctic Club of New York.
Member of the Royal Geographical Society of Madrid.
Founding member of the *Société académique d'histoire internationale de Paris*.
Member of the *Société de géographie de Québec*; he received two of its medals including la *Médaille d'or de grand mérite*, on 9 March 1925.
Member of the Royal Empire Society of Québec.
Honorary Member of the Arctic Society of Canada.
Recognized by Leith Nautical College, Edinburgh and by the Royal Scottish Geographical Society, Edinburgh.
Recipient of King George V's Imperial Service Medal, on 25 November 1927.

In 1933 there was some discussion of another honour: in a debate in the Senate on 10 May Joseph-Philippe Baby Casgrain stated:

Diploma as a Founding Member of the *Société académique d'histoire internationale*, presented to Captain Bernier, 2 June 1926. [Archives of Carol and Louis Terrien]

> [...] I sincerely believe that the government of our country ought to do something for him and I request of the Speaker of this House that he recognize by a concrete gesture what this great man, now more than 80 years old, has done for Canada.

Arthur Meighen replied:

> Captain Bernier occupies a unique position in the history of our great northland. His years are now many, but his spirit is strong. He still talks like a youth. It seems to me that Canada owes far more than she has paid him for the wonderful work he has accomplished and the dangers he has faced on behalf of the name and place of this country in the great Arctic sphere. No man has had any experience comparable with his in our northern waters, nor followed a more consistently patriotic course than he.[6]

On 24 August of the following year, Tees Curran, office secretary at the Colonial Institute in Montréal, sent a long letter to the Conservative Prime Minister, Richard Bedford Bennett, concerning Captain Bernier and the possibility that the King of England might recognize his services.

> [...] Our northern islands would very likely be under the flag of the United States today had it not been for Bernier's foresight [...]. Few of us realize fully Captain Bernier's worth or what he has really accomplished for Canada. History no doubt will accord him a worthy place in its pages.
>
> If I might offer an opinion again—I believe if the matter was presented to His Majesty and it was looked upon with favor it would have the approval of Canadians generally and would, no doubt, be a case of "showing honour where honour is due."[7]

He probably had in mind the "Long Service Medal."

The culmination of this period of his life was undoubtedly his meeting with Pope Pius XI. The Holy Father had sent him a special blessing in 1932, followed by the title of Knight of the Equestrian Order of the Holy Sepulchre, the following summer. The captain then decided to go to thank him in person.[8]

When Bernier offered His Holiness a copy of the book on his expedition of 1908-1909, and told him about the cross he had erected on the most northerly land in Canada on Corpus Christi Day, the Pope replied that he knew about it, since he had already read the accounts of his great voyages of exploration with real interest. When the Pope congratulated him on his exploits and gave him his holy blessing, Joseph-Elzéar's eyes filled with tears of emotion.

He was enthroned as Knight of the Equestrian Order of the Holy Sepulchre on 21 January 1934 in Lévis Cathedral. The event was the occasion for a beautiful and warm celebration on the part of his friends and fellow-citizens.

Wearing his magnificent uniform and sword the new knight was a member of the retinue of Cardinal Rodrigue Villeneuve at the inauguration of the Basilica of Sainte-Anne-de-Beaupré on 26 July 1934. And during the major celebrations on the 400th anniversary of Jacques Cartier's arrival in Gaspé, he proudly mounted guard beside the Cardinal as he sang the pontifical mass.

Captain Bernier in the dress uniform of a Knight of the Equestrian Order of the Holy Sepulchre. [Archives of Carol and Louis Terrien]

Medal sent by the Pope to the new Knight of the Equestrian Order of the Holy Sepulchre. [Photo: Lynn Fournier, Musée maritime du Québec (Musée Bernier)]

Esdras Terrien has written:

The celebrations for Jacques Cartier moved him more than any others. He was in a position to appreciate the dangers of the Malouin's voyages of discovery and the value of his great epics of 1534-1541. Jacques Cartier was his ancestor; he had followed in his wake, had matched him in successful audacity and in seagoing experience, and if he was not able to attach his name to some great discovery, it was because, unlike Cartier, he did not have a François I to entrust him with the mission of going to find a part of Adam's heritage. He was at the celebrations in Gaspé; he followed all the ceremonials with attention and interest;

Chevalier Bernier in front of the monument to Jacques Cartier in Gaspé in 1934 during celebrations marking the 400th anniversary of Jacques Cartier's arrival in America. [Archives of Carol and Louis Terrien]

shook hands with the commander of the *Champlain*; spoke to the French, British and American admirals; and returned to Lévis with his heart full of the apotheosis accorded to Cartier after four centuries of waiting. There had been accounts of how Cartier had sailed the waters of the Gulf, ascended the St. Lawrence, and had got to know the natives; was this not what he himself had accomplished over almost a quarter century in the arctic seas? Cartier had not found the route to the Indies, but he had given his king an entire continent. Bernier did not discover the North Pole, but he secured the entire Arctic Basin for his country, stretching north from Canada right to 90° N.[9]

CHAPTER 26

The last great voyage

NO OTHER CANADIAN seafarer has attracted the sympathy and the admiration of the public like Captain Bernier. In his home, on the Lévis cliff, the retired captain continued to fascinate people who wanted to believe that the man familiarly known as the "North Pole man" was immortal, and the press gladly fuelled that interest.

> The captain welcomed the reporter for *Le Droit* cordially and good-naturedly. In his company one immediately feels on intimate terms. He opens to one without ostentation and talks with assurance. His voice is firm and calm. It is confident and assured. He almost always stands while talking; he makes very few gestures; he rarely raises his voice and sometimes he gets excited. He is cheerful, but it is a quiet, peaceful cheerfulness; since his youth he has maintained great confidence in the future and today at age 72 he is vigorous and alert and does not feel the weight of years at all.[1]

> Capt. Bernier is now seventy-five years of age but he looks a good fifteen years less. He is brisk, humorous, alive with energy and has several business propositions in hand and is writing a book of his experience.[2]

The crowds that came to salute him each time that he sailed from the port of Québec on one of his expeditions to the Arctic valued the courage, audacity, and tenacity of this old sea-dog who appeared still to be at the zenith of his strength and courage. It would be no exaggeration to suppose that Bernier enjoyed this popularity and that he was keen on captivating his admirers by continuing to play the role of the invincible hero. Moreover he had always been proud of his physical strength that had helped him to overcome the challenges and dangers of his profession.

But under that fine, florid countenance, the old man was concealing a cardiac weakness which had caused him suffering ever since his last voyage on board the

Captain Bernier on his retirement.
[Archives of Carol and Louis Terrien]

A neighbour, L.N. Huard, who was also the chauffeur, friend, and right-hand man of the famous retiree. [Archives of Carol and Louis Terrien]

Arctic, when he had received that terrible blow full in his chest. In addition to arthritis that attacked his joints in an underhand manner, myocarditis had added a further weakness to his imposing burliness.

The old seafarer's health was no longer robust enough for him to command his ships and crews but this certainly did not prevent him from quenching his thirst for travel as a tourist. Accompanied by his wife he several times crossed the country by train to spend the long winter months in Vancouver, facing the Pacific Ocean. And when the St. Lawrence was no longer enough to silence the call of the open sea, he would pack his suitcases and would invite Alma to embark on a luxury cruise ship that would take them to the warm seas of Bermuda, the Bahamas, or the West Indies.

At his side Alma discovered new landscapes, met new faces, and tasted the charms of travel. In her company Joseph-Elzéar learned to let the time flow by.

In 1931 he had a chalet built on Lac Beaudet, near the Rivière Batiscan, 85 miles north of Québec. In this favourite spot he allowed himself to savour the pleasures of nature in a wild state and of the sport of trout-

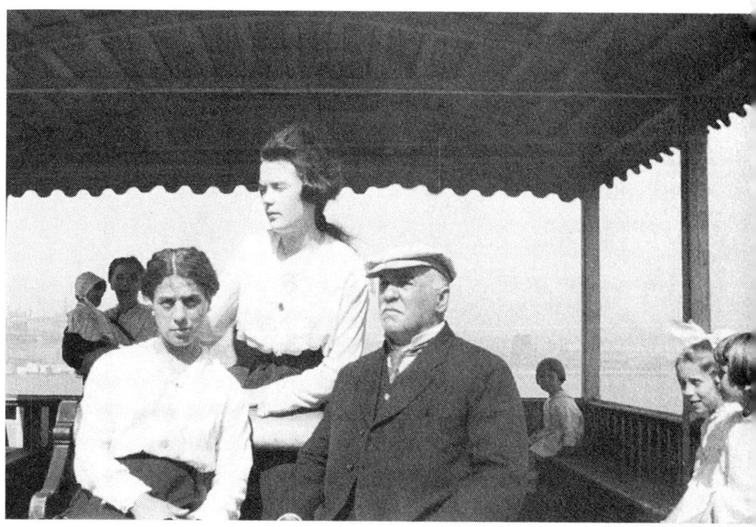

J.-E. Bernier, Alma Lemieux, Marie-Léda Farley, and in the background Marie-Éva Terrien and her children on the rear balcony of the house on Rue Fraser in Lévis. [Archives of Carol and Louis Terrien]

Très Saint Père

Monsieur le Capitaine
J.-E. Bernier
Explorateur au Pôle Nord, humblement prosterné aux pieds de Votre Sainteté, implore pour lui-même et pour les membres de sa famille la Bénédiction Apostolique et l'Indulgence Plénière in articulo mortis, même lorsque, ne pouvant se confesser ni recevoir la Sainte-Communion, repentis, ils invoqueront de bouche ou au moins de coeur le Saint Nom de Jésus

A special benediction from Pope Pius XI addressed to Captain Bernier, January 1933 [Archives of Carol and Louis Terrien]

fishing. There he renewed old friendships and enjoyed the company of his brother Alfred, and memories of their childhood.

Thus Bernier, the proud fighter, was letting go, little by little, as he prepared to accept the inevitable, his last great voyage.

This occurred in early December 1934, while he was participating in the exercises of a parish retreat. One evening he was late and was hurrying to reach the church of Notre-Dame de Lévis, not far from his home, in time. This was too much for his weakened heart. He was obliged to go back home and rest.

On the evening of 16 December, while Alma was doing her Christmas shopping, Joseph-Elzéar suffered a heart attack and collapsed. His wife had a premonition and telephoned home just as attempts were being made to help him up.

As Esdras Terrien has related:

> He took the telephone to answer his wife himself. He told her to come home without delay, but did not explain why.[3]

On returning home Alma found her husband stretched out on a bed in his study. The heart attack had caused a general paralysis. He could no longer speak, but remained fully conscious of what was happening around him. He made himself understood by squeezing his wife's hand. Right from the start, he had the image of Madonna, Star of the Sea, brought to him. It was a gift from his cousin, Sister Marie-Alexis, that had accompanied him on all his voyages and whose aid he had often invoked.

Captain Bernier struggled against his infirmity for 10 days, forcing himself to recite the prayers for the dying. He received a special blessing from the Cardinal, as well as the last sacraments, while prelates, the Lévis priest, curates, and cousins who were priests were constantly in attendance.

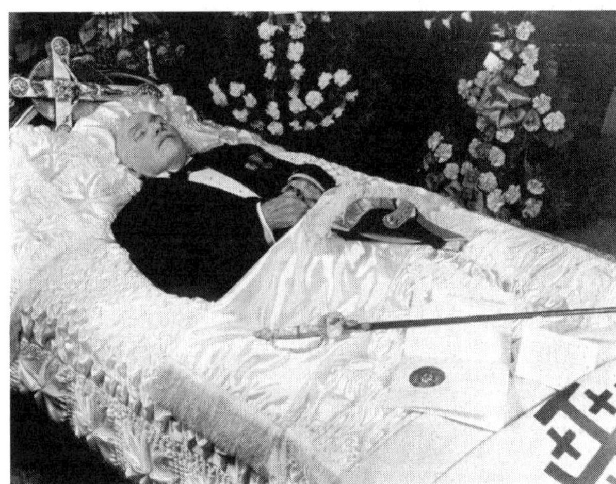

Captain Bernier lying in state in the living room of his home on Rue Fraser in Lévis. [Archives of Carol and Louis Terrien]

The imposing church of Notre-Dame de Lévis is a masterpiece of neo-classical architecture conceived by Thomas Baillargé. When built, in 1850, it was considered to be the second largest church in Canada. [Photo: Lynn Fournier]

His condition became progressively worse and at 4 o'clock on the afternoon of Wednesday 26 December, a little shy of his 83rd birthday "[he] died with a smile having fixed a loving look on his wife."[4]

Right from the start of his paralysis the radio stations had kept the public informed as to his state of health at least three times per day, as they would have done for a Prime Minister, the King, or some very visible public personality.

Many people came to see him, laid out in his white-satin-lined casket. For the curious this was their only chance to visit the house, with its walls adorned with paintings of the ships the famous captain had commanded, with his library, his private office, his charts, the polar bear skin, and all the furniture and objects from exotic countries. Others, young and old, had to see Bernier in his coffin because they were convinced "that he will feature in the history of Québec,"[5] and that one ought to be a witness to this historic moment.

> On the gallery that projected so far over the river that one would have thought it was the deck of a ship, a remarkable cross-section of people was crammed together, elbow-to-elbow: not only relatives and friends but also persons of distinction, officers, associates, and old sailors who were not too proud to cry and were wiping their eyes.
>
> At the summons of the bells, Bernier "got under way" for the last time as the casket crossed the threshold. The door closed behind him. The sound of ships whistles carried from the river and from the quay.
>
> It was snowing heavily. Everywhere—both on the Lévis shore and in the distance over Québec. Nature was wearing a white shroud. One might have thought that all the snows of the Arctic had arranged a rendez-vous to scatter star-shaped flowers on the tomb of a friend, a hero.[6]

The coffin was so heavy, "as heavy as a real bed"[7] that they had great difficulty in carrying it through the front door. The pall-bearers almost dropped it several times as they negotiated the long track trodden in the snow by the visitors, out to the Rue Fraser.

Joseph-Elzéar was leaving this world as he had entered it, during a snowstorm. The atmosphere was wonderfully beautiful, almost unreal, and so appropriate for marking the passage of the man of the Far North to the beyond. The setting was right for the individual.

There was a crowd at the solemn service held at the Notre-Dame de Lévis church on the morning of Saturday 29 December 1934, to honour, one last time, a local man who had been motivated by a love of the sea, by a passion for discovery, and by an extraordinary vision of the scope of Canadian sovereignty in the Arctic.

CHAPTER 27

The mausoleum

In is will Joseph-Elzéar Bernier left his widow $30,000 in cash, as well as assets of $42,000, comprising the property on the Rue Fraser with its furnishings, some lots in Montréal, the cottage at Beaudet, bank deposits, and various shares. He left his brother, Alfred a "life annuity" of $300, "during the life of my said wife. Following the decease of the latter the life annuity will increase to $500, to cover his sustenance, but not to pay his debts." There was no mention of his sister Henriette, nor of his adopted daughter, Elmina. By contrast he added for the benefit of his other relatives the sentence: "I would like to demonstrate by gifts and specific bequests my regard for my nephews and nieces, godsons and goddaughters and other relatives, but my current pecuniary resources do not permit." He also specified his last wishes as was then the custom.

> I wish my body to be buried in my private chapel in the cemetery of Saint-Joseph de Lévis; a first-class service to be held over my body during my funeral and another service, also first-class, on the first anniversary of my death and, in addition, that ten great requiem masses for the repose of my soul be sung as soon as possible after my death.[1]

The death certificate confirmed that the captain was buried by the priest Tanguay, according to his wishes, on 29 December 1934. Those present were: Alfred Bernier, Esdras Terrien, Arthur Farley, J.-E. Martel, Charles L'Italien, Stan Déry, L.N. Huard, J.A. Carrier, Jean-Roland Samson, and Jacques Samson. Alma's name, and those of three of her sisters, Mmes. Martel, Farley and Terrien, as well as that of Henriette Boisjoly, the dead man's sister, were not included on the document, despite the fact that they were present at the religious ceremony in the cemetery. Dr. J.-E. Leblond, who had attended Captain Bernier during his illness, was probably a member of the group.

As he had foreseen, Joseph-Elzéar Bernier was joining the remains of his father, Thomas, his mother Célina, his first wife, Rose and of the son that Alma had lost, in the mausoleum that he had had built in 1888 and in the spot that he had reserved for himself to the right of the entrance. His funerary mausoleum was also a private chapel, since Bernier had obtained permission from Monsigneur Bégin to have the holy mass celebrated there. Workmen had taken a year to build it. The captain had provided the sweat of his brow, the strength of his arms, and a sum of $3000. The sides were of dressed stone, the façade of a pale marble, the high doors were of wrought iron, the high altar of Italian marble, while enormous paintings of religious scenes adorned the interior walls above marble sarcophagi. This structure was worthy of Père Lachaise's most beautiful cemetery monuments that Bernier had perhaps visited in Paris, a rich tomb in the tradition of the country's greatest families.

It was precisely this rich appearance that led to the monument's ruin. Until her death, in July 1961, Alma

Bernier in front of the mausoleum he had built for his immediate family. This photo gives a good idea of the actual dimensions of the structure with reference to Bernier's height, which was 5 feet 4 inches. The arch-shaped frontal stone, on which "Capt. J.E. Bernier" was engraved, was 12 feet long and 2 feet wide and high. [Archives of Carol and Louis Terrien]

had continued to visit and maintain her husband's tomb. Unfortunately after her departure, nobody took over from her and gradually, over the years, the mausoleum became neglected. One day some individuals decided to take advantage of the situation, smashing in the doors, stealing the linen, the sculptures, the decorations and everything that could be removed, including the luxurious Italian marble, the high altar and its contents. This act of vandalism and the decrepit state of the funerary mausoleum was spotted only a few years later by one of the members of the *Société d'histoire régionale de Lévis.*

Jeanne Coudé had been interested in the history of the region for several years when, on 1 August 1983, she read in *Le Soleil* of Québec that Joseph-Elzéar Bernier's memoirs had just been translated. Since she knew that the captain had lived in Lévis, she had the idea of looking for the site of his grave. This was when she discovered the desecration. Indignant at the fate that had been inflicted on the mausoleum of the most "famous French Canadian seafarer" she alerted the Lévis community and exposed the situation in the local press.

The administration of the cemetery undertook to clean up the site, to exhume the bodies, and to preserve the former frontal stone that had been broken into three pieces. As for Jeanne Coudé, she made great efforts to rouse the interest of personalities from the South Shore who might help in finding the funds for erecting a new funerary monument.

> Through the intervention of a committee headed by Mlle Jeanne Coudé, this week the *Sociéte d'histoire régionale de Lévis* is to present plans to the Federal Government which would see the erection of a fine monument, with an approximate value of $25,000, to the memory of Captain J.-E. Bernier.
>
> [...] With the unconditional support of the members of the *Société d'histoire*, Mme Coudé has requested plans and

Jeanne Coudé still watches proudly over Captain Bernier's funerary monument; it is located in plot 533 at the northern edge of the Mont-Marie Cemetery. [Photo: Lynn Fournier]

Sculptor Raoul Hunter was responsible for the design and sculpting of Bernier's funerary monument, while Fernand Chabot enr. of Scott Jonction was responsible for its manufacture and installation. [Photo: Lynn Fournier]

proposals from various sculptors; she has prepared a résumé of the captain's history and of his expeditions, has conceived a plan for a commemorative plaque and has even purchased a strip of land in the cemetery to be absolutely certain that the future monument will have a solid foundation and will not impinge on any graves.[2]

Parks Canada's Committee for Historic Sites and Monuments, whose mission is to honour Canadian personalities, did not support the project because the monument was to be placed in a cemetery.

Mlle Coudé was naturally surprised at this refusal since, in her opinion, if any Canadian merited a mark of recognition from the Federal Government, it was Captain Bernier! She was disappointed but not discouraged.

Finally, thanks to Jeanne Coudé's tenacity, to the efforts of the *Société d'histoire régionale de Lévis* and the support of Jean Garon, member of the Québec National Assembly for Lévis, the Québec Department of Cultural Affairs provided a grant of $20,000 to implement the project.

The monument was inaugurated on 13 June 1984 in the Lauzon section of the Mont-Marie Cemetery.

> Last Thursday, in anticipation of the return of the tall ships, well-deserved homage was paid to Captain Joseph-Elzéar Bernier on the occasion of the unveiling, in the Lauzon cemetery, of a new funerary monument to the memory of the famous explorer of the High Arctic. This event thus commemorated the 50th anniversary of his death and also the 75th anniversary of his taking possession for Canada of the Arctic Archipelago.[3]

CHAPTER 28

The house on the Rue Fraser

When one steps inside the Villa Bernier one breathes the atmosphere of a professional sailor, who dedicated his entire life to the profession that he adored, for which God had specially endowed him, and on the love of which he had spent a goodly fortune.[1]

The octogenarian Simone Dion, who became the widowed Alma's lady's companion when she was only 19 years old, still remembers it as a "ready-made museum." Simone was from the neighbourhood. She was young, cheerful and curious, exactly what was needed to enliven that large house and to fill the void left by the captain's departure.

Alma was a retiring woman. She did nothing with her hands. She preferred to read the newspaper and play cards to pass the time. A truly solitary person. The only times she went out was to visit the cemetery and to go to church to hear Mass on Sundays. These were the only times that people might see her. Monsieur Huard would drive us in the captain's big car. I remember it well; it even had little curtains as protection from the sun [...]. Yes, she was a woman who suffered from insecurity and who was afraid of adventure; quite the opposite of the captain, who never stayed in one place for long [...]. She had lived with a legend and she left the house exactly as he had known it.

[...] It took her some time to digest my marriage to Philip. You understand, after more than nine years, it was like a second bereavement for her.[2]

Louis Terrien also recalls his dear Aunt Alma, having often visited her "in her museum" when he was a child.

She was always humming a tune while she was walking. She was very fond of children and we found her very

Alma Lemieux with her new television set and the precious souvenirs of her dead husband. [Archives of Carol and Louis Terrien]

A rare photo of the interior of the house on Rue Fraser. The three friends are Thérèse Filion (standing), Marguerite Terrien, and Alma Lemieux. [Archives of Carol and Louis Terrien]

pleasant. She would welcome us with open arms, saying "Salut, ô lord." That's what she always said.

[...] After the captain's death, she changed nothing in the house, not even a chair. To her it was holy.[3]

Alma lived for another 17 years in her house on the Rue Fraser, cherishing the memory of her illustrious captain. She would have liked her home to become the Bernier Museum of Lévis, but as in the case of the *Arctic*, no department, association or society was taken with the project. And after her death on 25 July 1961, all the contents of the house were scattered.

> In her will she disinherited the boys in the family because she knew that they could get along on their own. She left everything to the girls, her nieces [...] There were so many things. The cupboards were full of documents. So many papers were thrown out.[4]

There was no auction sale. Her family kept the furniture and the most important items. The rest was sold or given to interested parties.

Captain Bernier's house and land were bought by dentist Georges Lepage in March 1962. The Lepage children inherited everything on the death of their father and, on 17 September 1991, they sold the property to Roger Héroux and his associates of the construction company, Rive Gauche:

Georges Lepage inheritance:

> Guy Lepage & al. to Const. Rive Gauche Inc., sale no. 360191, $280,000 paid
>
> Inher. Georges Lepage to Roger Héroux & al., sale no. 360192, $78,000 paid.[5]

Today there is no longer any trace of Captain Bernier's magnificent home at 27 Rue Fraser. In its place stands a modern structure with a flat roof, looking like a motel from the 60s.[6]

A street in the Desjardins district in Lévis. [Photo: Lynn Fournier]

CHAPTER 29

Bernier's legacy

IN QUÉBEC, at the start of the 21st century, the majority of us do not know who Captain Bernier was; this is because little is said about our maritime history in school texts, and because there is no longer interest in the matter of our arctic frontier needing to be protected. One also has the impression that many Quebecers have a tendency to devalue our countrymen who have accomplished great things outside Québec in the past. For some people, a person like Captain Bernier was a "sell-out" because he had worked for the English and for the strengthening of Canadian sovereignty. Of course they are forgetting to place the work of this seafarer/explorer in its historical context. They are forgetting that in his day Quebecers called themselves "Canadiens français", that the majority of workers were employed by Anglo-Saxon companies, that all business was conducted in English in this colony of the British Empire, and that in the "Dominion of Canada" all important positions were filled by the Federal Government.

If, nevertheless, our collective memory retains some traces of the role of this courageous seaman in our short history, it is because his odyssey has been able to touch and motivate responsive souls, admirers and dreamers.

One such case was that of Gilberte Tremblay who believed that Captain Bernier's courage and determination could inspire her son Michel to surpass himself and to succeed in life. In 1959 she dedicated her book,

This monument was erected in 1962 near the Notre-Dame-de-Bonsecours church. Nowadays it is located alongside the Musée maritime du Québec in L'Islet-sur-Mer, the "sailors' home-port." [Photo: Lynn Fournier]

at heart, was also touched by the mission that the bold seafarer took upon himself. He became not only a collector of significant articles from his career, photographs and mementoes from his polar expeditions, but also a militant, convinced that this son of L'Islet must be restored to his just place in our history books.

> For two years now the Abbé Lionel Mercier, curate of L'Islet has been working to have the public and official circles recognize the merits of Captain Bernier. He has made himself the instigator of plans for a monument to the memory of undoubtedly the most prestigious French-Canadian seaman.[1]

On Sunday, 10 June 1962 Abbé Mercier finally saw the culmination of all his efforts and of his numerous approaches. "Without him," Martin Caron asserted, "there would never have been a monument nor a Maritime Museum in a backwater like L'Islet in the sixties."[2]

One must not overlook the remarkable voyage of the Montréal journalist/sailor Réal Bouvier and his crew in his 35-foot yacht, the *J.E. Bernier II*, the first pleasure craft and the smallest vessel to have circumnavigated North America by way of the Arctic and the Panama Canal. Having left Lachine on 30 June 1976, the expedition wintered at Holsteinsborg in Greenland and at Tuktoyaktuk in the Beaufort Sea, before reaching Vancouver on 15 October 1978, running through the Panama Canal, and returning to the St. Lawrence in August 1979.

Réal Bouvier said that he was born near the river and that somebody who had sailed the St. Lawrence River and Gulf could face any sea in the world. This modern-day adventurer acknowledged right away that Captain Bernier had inspired him more than anybody else, and that he had inculcated in him a passion for the High Arctic and for a life at sea.

> In making the transit of the mythical Northwest Passage on board *J.-E. Bernier II* during the summer of 1977 he [Bouvier] has inscribed his name in the legend of the Arctic alongside those of very illustrious predecessors

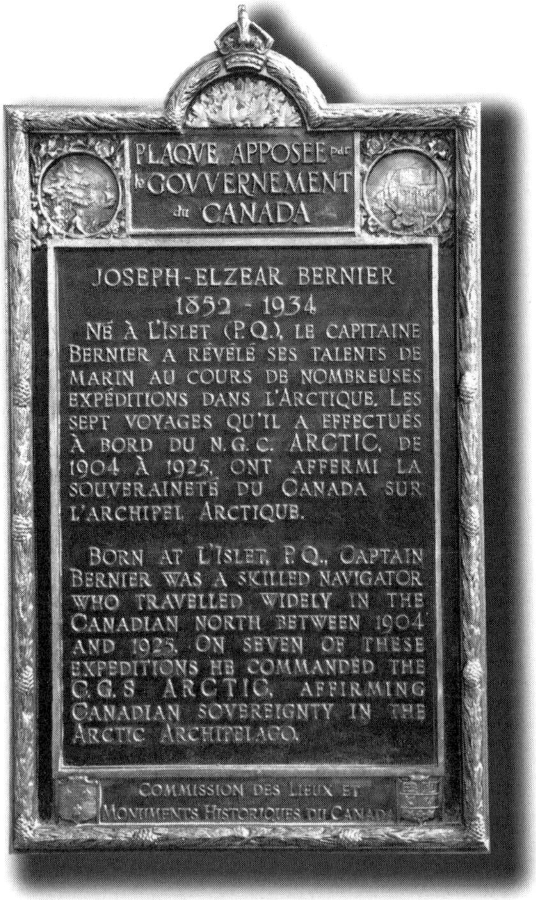

The plaque placed by the Government of Canada on the Bernier monument in L'Islet-sur-Mer. [Photo: Lynn Fournier]

Bernier, capitaine à 17 ans to him as follows: "You asked me for a true story about a captain and ships? Here it is! I'm dedicating it to your father and to you, my little man, who is already dreaming of adventures."

Michel Tremblay has become a famous painter who, even today, acknowledges the hold that Bernier has had on his imagination. "I find it sad," he said, "that we have replaced our real heroes with the latest stars!"

The curate of L'Islet-sur-Mer during the 1960's, Abbé Lionel Mercier, who was the son of a sailor and a sailor

The Musée maritime du Québec (Musée Bernier) in L'Islet-sur-Mer perpetuates the memory of the famous Arctic explorer and preserves the maritime heritage of the St. Lawrence region. [Photo: Lynn Fournier]

> such as Amundsen and Bernier, men to whom he pledged limitless admiration and whose logbooks he had examined minutely before starting.[3]

La Presse also laid stress on the exploit of this small yacht that was following in the wake of the great Bernier.

> We would wager that the fact that the crew of the *J.E. Bernier* had aroused a taste for adventure, and for discoveries in the Arctic in other ordinary young people, would give a helluva lot more pleasure to Joseph [Elzéar] than any honorific title.[4]

Bouvier was probably in agreement with this sentiment since he wanted his yacht to be used as a training-vessel for young people with a passion for the sea, the fate that Bernier had so greatly desired for his valiant *Arctic*, and found it quite natural that the *J.E. Bernier II* ended its days at the *Musée maritime Bernier in L'Islet-sur-Mer*, the birthplace of the man of whom he had dreamed as a child.

Another sailor from L'Islet-sur-Mer, Captain Henri Saint-Pierre, had developed a real fascination for Bernier's stories and exploits. He had sworn to locate the caches and cairns where Bernier had buried messages

Réal Bouvier's yacht, the *J.E. Bernier II*, installed behind the Musée maritime du Québec. [Photo: Lynn Fournier]

during his expeditions to the Arctic. During the course of numerous voyages that he made as captain of the icebreaker *d'Iberville*, Captain Saint-Pierre always took the time to observe and to engrave on his visual memory every contour of the islands, headlands or bays, locked in the arctic ice, so as to recognize the sites indicated in Captain Bernier's reports. Until the day he found his first message buried under rocks at Wakeham Point on Melville Island: "I had noted all the locations described by Bernier. I had located them one by one. I still have some to find; I'll have to search a little more closely."[5]

This extraordinary treasure-hunt allowed him to reenact the deeds of his childhood hero, and to walk in his footsteps within the limits of Canadian territory.

And what does he mean to the rest of the country? Do Canadians of today know the name of the man who gave them their arctic frontier? Are they more interested than Quebecers in maintaining Canada's sovereignty in this vast ice-enshrouded area that is so difficult to deal with. No. The tendency towards forgetfulness and disinformation seem to be a general trend "from coast to coast!"

But Joseph-Elzéar's work has touched several people. The following testimonials are proof of this.

In 1957 T.C. Fairley and C.E. Israel published their account of Bernier's exploits, *The true North. The story of Captain Joseph Bernier*, and justified their being drawn to their subject with a quote from the *Toronto Star* as follows:

Commemorative stamp showing the navigator Bernier observing the *Arctic* beset in the arctic ice, 1977. [Courtesy of Michel Melanson]

The Canadian Coastguard icebreaker CCGS *J.-E. Bernier* as she entered service in November 1967. [Courtesy of Jeanne Coudé]

> It has to be admitted that Bernier is our great arctic pioneer and years ago he kept arctic questions before Canadian statesmen and the Canadian public when our interest was at a low ebb. He, more than any man, kept Canada from tossing away its arctic inheritance.[6]

In October 1964, five scholars met in Toronto with the aim of choosing the 25 Canadians, other than the country's prime ministers, who had most distinguished themselves since Confederation, by their talents and their exceptional achievements. This was quite a formidable jury in its own right. Its chairman was the Honourable Vincent Massey, the first Canadian to be appointed Governor-General (1952-1959), and it included George V. Ferguson, Chief Editor of the *Montreal Star*, Dr. W. Kaye Lamb, historian, President of the Royal Society and Chief Archivist with the Federal Government, Dr. Maurice Lebel, writer, Dean of the Department of Classical Studies at the Université Laval, and Dr. Hilda Neatby, Head of the Department of History at the University of Saskatchewan. The results of this difficult exercise were announced a year later, in the book *Great Canadians. A Century of Achievement.* The captain from L'Islet-sur-Mer was included along with Sir Frederick Banting, Alexander Graham Bell, Henri

These two commemorative stamps were issued simultaneously on 16 September 1977, the one for the French Canadian at L'Islet-sur-Mer and the other at Edmonton for the English Canadian. They are the work of Toronto artist Will Harris. A journalist from the *Peuple-Tribune* commented: "In the absence of a title Captain Bernier is entitled to a stamp!" [Courtesy of Michel Melanson]

Bourassa, Emily Carr, Timothy Eaton, etc. Roger Lemelin's text pays laudatory homage to the valiant seafarer, "Canada's greatest sea explorer,"[7] but the simple fact of having been chosen represented a glorious crowning to his remarkable career. Thus, 30 years after his death, the Canadian intelligentsia assured him a place of choice in the history of the country.

The historian, and the project's editor-in-chief, Pierre Berton ended his introduction as follows:

> Yet I cannot quarrel with the present list since it was the product of reasonable and intelligent thought by highly qualified Canadians who know the story of their country as well as any among us. It is to help others know this story a little better, as we approach our hundredth milestone, that this volume was conceived.[8]

On the basis of this mark of prestige associated with his name, Captain Bernier became an ineluctable feature in Canadian history. The Canadian Government owed it to itself to follow the example of its former Governor-General.

Towards the end of that same year, on 14 December 1965, the Department of Fisheries and Oceans ordered a light icebreaker/heavy buoy-tender from the Davie yards in Lauzon. The CCGS J.*E. Bernier*[9] was launched on 28 April 1967.

Ten years later Canada Post issued two new 12 cent commemorative stamps, in memory of two "men of iron" who had contributed to the development of the country: Captain Joseph-Elzéar Bernier (1852-1934) who had explored Canada's Far North, and engineer Sir Sandford Fleming (1827-1915), who had conceived the steel bridges for the Intercolonial Railway.

And then, on 2 June 1978 the Department of Transport launched the most recent Canadian icebreaking freighter, the M.V. *Arctic*,[10] thus marking the advent of a new generation of arctic freighters. In the wake of Bernier's brigantine, icebreakers transporting limited tonnages of cargo, and merchant vessels escorted by icebreakers, the bulk-carrier M.V. *Arctic* announced the arrival of autonomous "super-powerful" vessels that could tackle the dangerous waters of the Arctic on their own.

The Department of Indian and Northern Affairs contributed to the event celebrating the launch of the M.V. *Arctic* and of Yolande Dorion-Robitaille's book, "*Le capitaine J.-E. Bernier et la souveraineté du Canada dans l'Arctique*." In his address the Minister, Hugh Faulkner praised Bernier fulsomely.

> From 1895 until his death in 1934 that old sea dog, Captain Bernier, either through intervening with politicians, or through publicly taking a position, never ceased to proclaim the importance of Canada consolidating her jurisdiction in the Arctic. There is absolutely no doubt that Bernier possessed quite an extraordinary vision, and almost an innate sense of the great importance of Canadian sovereignty in the Arctic.

The Minister also expressed the wish that Mme. Robitaille's book would remind us of "this man, of

An interpretation by Montreal painter Gilbert Provost of the M.V. *Arctic*, manoeuvring in Canadian arctic waters. This icebreaking freighter was built in 1978 for the shipping company Canarctic Ltd. by Port Weller Dry Docks, an affiliate of Upper Lakes Shipping Ltd. of St. Catharine's, Ontario. [Courtesy Carol and Louis Terrien, who were at the naming ceremony as representing Captain Bernier's family]

ruddy complexion, courageous and determined" and would engrave on the memories of all Canadians, unaware of the northern realities of their country "that Canadian nordicity indeed exists."

More recently the Québec anthropologist, Stéphane Cloutier wrote:

We in turn have followed in the master mariner's wake to northern Baffin Island, to what the Inuit call the "back of the land." We met with elders. They can remember the man they affectionately call Kapitaikallak, Captain Bernier.

[...] They told me: "He is a legend here at Mittimatalik (formerly Pond Inlet)." Mentioning Bernier's name will indeed release a flood of anecdotes and racy stories. Moreover it was the Inuit who put me on Captain Bernier's track, despite the fact that I am myself a native

Captain Bernier's caribou-skin clothing on display at the Musée maritime du Québec in 2001 and 2002 as part of the exhibition *Ilititaa… Bernier, ses hommes et les Inuits.* [Photo: Lynn Fournier]

of the township of L'Islet, Bernier's birthplace, and that I ought to have known all the details of this amazing story even before I arrived in Nunavut in 1994.[11]

The memory of Captain Bernier is perpetuated in the oral traditions of the Inuit of northern Baffin Island. This living memory and the elders' stories revealed to this young researcher from the South, the importance of the inheritance bequeathed to the inhabitants of Nunavut by Kapitaikallak. They inspired him with a taste for digging more deeply, for checking and compiling before it is too late, in order to preserve the accounts of this amazing encounter between two peoples.

> "For the Inuit Kapitaikallak is truly a legend," he stated to a journalist who had become interested in this cultural and anthropological project. "In the south nobody knows him. But it is thanks to him that Nunavut is Canadian today.[12]"

In 2001 and 2002 Stéphane Cloutier collaborated in organizing a travelling exhibition, *Ilititaa… Bernier, ses hommes et les Inuits,* that was inaugurated at the *Musée maritime Bernier,* before being shown at the Nunatta Sunakkutaangit Museum in Iqaluit, the capital of Nunavut.

Initiatives such as these will bring Captain Bernier, seafarer, safely to harbour.

Conclusion

IT WAS STRONGER THAN HE. From childhood Joseph-Elzéar Bernier was searching for something that he could not have found by staying still: his destiny. His driving forces were a taste for exploration, the need for freedom, exciting revelations on a voyage, wonder at the diversity of countries and people, and the pleasure of challenging himself. His foundations were his exceptional vitality, his physical strength and his will power. Bernier was made for adventure. For this inquisitive, independent spirit, raised on the shores of the St. Lawrence and trained by his father, a deep-sea captain, adventure meant the sea. To live out his destiny he became a seafarer.

Few sailors in the world can boast of possessing a résumé as enviable as that of this sailor from L'Islet-sur-Mer. He was a captain at the age of 17. He knocked about every sea in the world. He made over 250 Atlantic crossings. Of these more than 44 were on board wooden vessels newly built in Québec yards, and more than half represented feats of speed, with record speeds of around 22 days. He was responsible for more than 109 vessels of varying tonnages, either by commanding them, or by supervising their construction, repairs or salvage.

It was natural that with the decline of the era of the large sailing vessels Captain Bernier would look for excitement elsewhere, by scanning horizons that were worthy of his talents.

It was logical that as time passed the passion for the sea would extend to the Far North. Both represented an incredible challenge that demanded that one exceed one's limits, and both imposed their rules on the solitary man who dared to face them. To survive in these extreme environments, he used to say, "one must observe nature, obey her as a master, and never try to conquer her."

At the time that he was interested in the arctic regions, he was the only Canadian to publicly reveal a plan for exploring the Arctic. Through his enterprise this man of action could not only claim the merit of being the first to awaken the interest of his fellow-countrymen in the matter of the arctic frontier, but also of being one of the principal supporters of Canadian sovereignty in the Arctic.

> In contrast to the heroes of American history, Canadian national celebrities of the type whose personal image is not dulled by the totally depersonalizing filter of the Canadian government with which they were associated in accomplishing their achievements, are relatively rare.[1]

There can be no doubt that this most illustrious of Canadian explorers caught the popular imagination. His mounting of eight government expeditions on board the *Arctic*, and of three private expeditions, his seven winterings, his piloting the *Ocean Eagle* to Fort Churchill, and all the stories and controversies that surrounded them, provided material for newspaper head-

Captain Bernier's funerary monument in Lévis, located in the Mont-Marie Cemetery in Lauzon-Lévis. Raoul Hunter's stylized work represents a three-masted sailing vessel. There is an aluminum commemorative plaque located on the ground in front of the monument. [Photo: Lynn Fournier]

lines and articles for about 30 years, thereby creating the Bernier phenomenon, the heroic personage, the man of the Pole, the Canadian Viking, the Jacques Cartier of the Arctic, *Nanuk,* the polar bear…

> By contrast, Bernier's achievements offer us something richer and more authentic, precisely qualities that have always been described with least aptitude. This is the profound motivation to go north and to "experience" the North in every way possible: it is the need for remoteness and for discovery that engenders a taste for the cold and the wilderness. It is not just Bernier's personal inclination, but also the inclination that his voyages inspire in others who follow him, whether they admire him or despise him. It is this, perhaps more than any political consideration, that attracted several hundred people to the Quai du Roi each time that Bernier sailed for the Far North. The crowd would gather along the edge of the quay: dozens of caleches would be jammed there, pell-mell. Men in aprons and in stiff collars, women and children, all came to watch. Apart from the dignitaries it was the ship's departure that they had come to see, and not the implementation of a policy. These people had travelled there to witness a gesture that aroused their admiration: the conquest of the arctic frontier.[2]

By watching recent documentaries on modern polar explorers in their sophisticated vessels such as the *Sedna IV,* and on their trips across the arctic pack ice, one can really grasp the enormity of the dangers faced by Captain Bernier and his men in their funny little sailing ship. Despite the support of radar, satellites, computers, helicopters, and their ultra-sophisticated equipment, modern expedition members are still risking their lives when they make their way through the hostile environment of "the roof of the world." Despite the technological facilities placed at their disposal all travellers returning from the polar regions testify to their great vulnerability when facing the difficulties, to their fear, to the complexity of navigation in these treacherous waters, to their loneliness, to the terrifying noises of ice breaking-up, to the petrifying cold, and to the destructive force of ice blocks and of the chaos of ice that exceeds anything they could have imagined. Even today to venture into these cursed zones is to confront the impossible and the unforeseeable and the violence of nature.

Bernier's legendary reputation is not over-rated. Anyone who has walked in his footsteps will tell you so.

It is only by situating him in his period that one can better understand his strength of character and the vast range of his talent. Joseph-Elzéar Bernier was a French Canadian from the South Shore, determined to make a success of his life in an English colony, the Dominion of Canada, and in a world dominated by the British Empire. To establish a reputation in shipping circles controlled by British firms, he had to be doubly talented and competent. For the Canadian government to give him command of its expeditions to the Arctic the captain had to be "the best."

Had he been English, the captain's name would have been written in the pages of our history, prefaced by "Sir."

> Had he been English he would not have been prevented from trying for the Pole.
>
> Had he lived in the United States, great efforts would have been made long ago to perpetuate his memory. Why is this so difficult here?[3]

Unfortunately this pioneer of polar exploration in Canada has been forgotten. Without his perseverance and his extraordinary vision of the scope of Canadian sovereignty in the Arctic, the islands of the archipelago located north of Hudson Bay would perhaps today be foreign possessions, probably American. It is to Bernier that goes the honour of having solidified our northern frontier and of having proclaimed our right to an area of over 500,000 square miles, extending all the way to the Pole.

His exploits and those of his valiant companions represent an important page in our short history. Canadians will recognize him on the day that they become interested in their northern realities.

It's a fair assumption that Joseph-Elzéar would be terribly upset at the dangers that increasingly are threatening the inheritance that he left us … but that's another story.

This aluminum medallion, 36 inches in diameter, is set into the central panel of Bernier's funerary monument. The Saint-Romuald Foundry cast this admirable artistic representation which pays a fine tribute to the legendary seafarer. [Photo: Lynn Fournier]

Notes*

Introduction

1. This great psychoanalyst and modern thinker (1900-1980) wrote several books on the human condition, including *The Art of Loving* (1956), *The Sane Society* (1955), and *The Anatomy of Human Destructiveness* (1973). This quotation is from "Dialogue with Erich Fromm," an interview with Richard I. Evans, 1980.

Part I • Salt water in the veins

Chapter 1 • His ancestors

1. *Master Mariner and Arctic Explorer, a Narrative of Sixty Years at Sea from the Logs and Yarns of Captain J.E. Bernier F.R.G.S., F.R.E.S.*, published posthumously by *Le Droit*, Ottawa in 1939. Henceforth: *Master Mariner.*

2. *Ibid.*, p. 20.

3. The church of Saint-Germain-l'Auxerrois still exists opposite the Louvre in the 1st Arrondissement.

4. It is said that Jean de Lauson was grasping and authoritarian, and that during his six years as Governor, he worked mainly to consolidate his own interests at the expense of the colony.

5. See: Cyril Bernier, *Les Bernier en Nouvelle-France, 1650-1750.* Saint Eustache: Éditions Cyril Bernier, 1996, p. 35. The Jesuit priest, Jérôme Lalemant, who signed this document, was the uncle of the famous martyr, Gabriel Lalemant. The witness was Denis-Joseph Ruette d'Auteuil, royal procurator.

6. More specifically from the parish of Saint-Laurent, now located near the Gare de l'Est in the 10th Arrondissement.

7. *Master Mariner*, p. 21.

8. *Orphelines en France, pionnières au Canada, Les Filles du roi au XVIIe siècle.* Montréal: Leméac, 1992, p. 24.

9. Daughter of Éléonore de Grandmaison and François Chavigny de Berchereau and widow of Charles Amiot, she had received this seigneurie from Intendant Talon on 3 November 1672. Hence Jacques Bernier knew her very well when he put his signature to this transaction.

10. To learn more about this second generation and their descendants, see Cyril Bernier, *Les Bernier en Nouvelle-France.*

11. This information is derived from Captain Bernier's personal documents as well as from genealogist André Bernier.

Chapter • L'Islet-sur-Mer

1. For more on this subject see: *L'Année des Anglais, la Côte-du-sud à l'heure de la conquête*, by Gaston Deschênes. Sillery: Éditions du Septentrion, 1988.

2. "Joseph-Elzéar Bernier, capitaine en toute saison," *North/Nord* 25:3 (May-June), 1978.

3. Gilles Boulet and Yolande Laprise, "L'Islet-sur-Mer, berceau de capitaines et de légendes", *Le Droit*, Ottawa, 6 September 1975.

4. Joseph-Elzéar's grand-uncle, Bénoni, born in 1776, married Luce Koënig (on 20 October 1807), daughter of Baron Edmond-Victor von Koënig who arrived in Canada in 1776, with the German auxiliary troops commanded by Baron Riedesel. All the Koënigs in the Québec area are descended from this Prussian Baron, who remained in Canada in 1783 with the permission of the military authorities (Source: Angèle Gagnon, historian of L'Islet).

5. *Master Mariner*, p. 33.

6. *Ibid.*, p. 35.

7. The name of this female relative was Marie-Émilie Augustine Bernier (1840-1923) and she was the daughter of the captain's uncle, Jean-Baptiste and Émilie Paradis. Throughout his life the captain remained very attached to this cousin, who was one of the founders of the convent at Sillery. Two sisters of Mother Saint-Alexis, Mother Saint-Bernard (Marie-Rose de

* ACL: Archives du Collège de Lévis
ANQ: Archives Nationales du Québec
ASTR: Archives du Séminaire de Trois-Rivières
LAC: Library and Archives of Canada

Lima, 1847-1903) and Mother Sainte-Émilie (Emma, 1844-1893) also joined her in the community of the Sisters of Jésus-Marie.

8. Archives nationales du Québec (ANQ), Benoît Robitaille Fonds.

9. Contract number 1990.

10. Complicating matters somewhat is the fact that the notary identified the deceased father of the future bride as being Joseph LeBourdais, when we know that his Christian name was Jean-Baptiste. The fact that the brother of the future bride, Joseph LeBourdais, alias Lapierre, and his wife Marie-Marthe Couillard acted as witnesses has led certain genealogists to conclude that these latter were the parents of Captain Bernier's grandmother.

11. Contract number 1975, dated 24 December 1810. A *perche* equals 18 feet and an arpent 180 feet.

12. Document 5307, prepared by the notary G.A. Verreau.

13. While preparing to write his memoirs Joseph-Elzéar Bernier drew up a list of 25 members of his immediate family who were practicing the professions of sailor, captain or pilot at this same time.

Chapter 3 • Thomas and Célina

1. *Master Mariner*, p. 44.
2. *Ibid.*, pp. 44-45.
3. *Ibid.*, p. 48.
4. *Ibid.*
5. Jean-Baptiste served for over 30 years as pilot on the St. Lawrence for the Allan Line. He had 11 children by his first wife, who died in 1869. He then married Marie-Elmire-Émélie Lucas who bore him three more children.
6. The details of the Paradis family, as established by genealogist Magdeleine Bourget, can be found as an appendix.
7. Angèle Gagnon has incorporated the results of her years of research into the old houses in the region in her book, *Le village de nos ancêtres, L'Islet*, published in 1994. On p. 19 she makes reference to this dwelling at 276 chemin des Pionniers Est, now the property of Jovette Rousseau and Simon-Pierre Paré.
8. The children who died at an early age were: Thomas-Delphis/or Philippe (1861-63), Augustina (1864 -?), Marie-Léda Justine (1865-1872) and an unnamed child (1870). Célina also lost her dear sister Émilie in 1869. Thomas lost his father in 1868 and his mother in 1873.
9. *Master Mariner*, p. 50.
10. Genealogical research by Magdeleine Bourget in 2002.

Chapter 4 • The house where Bernier was born?

1. P. 148 in *L'Islet, 1677-1977*, privately published by Léon Bélanger in 1977.
2. "L'Islet-sur Mer, pépinière de marins et capitaines célèbres" [L'Islet-sur-Mer, nursery of famous sailors and captains], *Le Soleil*, 9 March 1967.
3. "L'Islet, patrie de marins et du célèbre Capitaine Bernier" [L'Islet, native village of sailors and of the celebrated Captain Bernier], *Le Soleil*, 12 April 1967.
4. *Captain J.E. Bernier's Contribution to Canadian Sovereignty in the Arctic.* Ottawa: Department of Indian and Northern Affairs, 1978, p. 16.
5. *Bernier, capitaine à 17 ans.* Leméac: Montréal, 1972, p. 11. During her research Mrs. Tremblay interviewed Captain Bernier's second wife, Alma Lemieux, as well as Narcisse Paradis, who was the son of Célina's brother, Narcisse Paradis, a spar maker in Québec.
6. Deed No. 835 prepared by notary G.-A. Verreau. This concerned the same piece of land that Jean-Baptiste had acquired from Joseph LeBourdais on 24 December 1810. In the meantime he had built a solid house on it as well as several outbuildings.
7. Deed no. 2028 of notary Verreau.
8. By deed no. 2029 of notary Verreau.

Chapter 5 • The *Zillah*

1. Gilberte Tremblay, *Bernier, capitaine à 17 ans*, p. 13. Joseph-Elzéar was baptized at the church next day, 2 January, by F.A. Oliva, parish priest at Notre-Dame de L'Islet. His godfather was his grandfather Jean-Baptiste Bernier and his godmother Marie-Luce Fabas.
2. *Master Mariner*, p. 52.
3. Rosalie (1833-1924) was the eldest daughter of Marie-Rosalie Bernier and Jean-Baptiste Boucher. She married Étienne-Vincent Couillard in 1857.
4. "Bernier à la conquête de l'Arctique," by Jacques Coulon, in *Sélections du Reader's Digest*, April 1978, p. 57.
5. *Master Mariner*, pp. 54-5.
6. *Ibid.*, p. 55.
7. That medal is part of the permanent collection of the Maritime Museum, Musée Bernier at L'Islet.
8. "Le Capitaine Bernier et sa prochaine excursion au pôle Nord," *La Presse*, Saturday, 4 May 1901.
9. *Master Mariner*, p. 57.
10. *Ibid.*, p. 57.
11. *Ibid.*, p. 58.
12. *Ibid.*, p. 59.

13. *Ibid.*, p. 60.Thomas would wait another year before selling the *Zillah*.

Chapter 6 • Geography to the rescue

1. Gustave Vallat, *À la conquête du Pôle Nord, l'explorateur norvégien Fridtjof Nansen,* Limoges: Maison Eugène Ardant & Cie., 1897, p. 64.

2. He was director of the college from 1858 until 1889.

3. *Master Mariner,* p. 61.

4. *Quand l'Église rhythmait la vie à Notre-Dame-de-Bonsecours de L'Islet,* by André Kirouac. Fabrique Notre-Dame-de-Bonsecours de L'Islet, 1993, p. 11.

5. François-Xavier Chouinard, "Un grand explorateur des mers arctiques," *Bulletin de la Société de géographie de Québec,* Vol. 20, nos. 4 and 5, September-December 1926, p. 272.

Chapter 7 • The *Saint-Joseph*

1. *The Charley-Man, A History of Wooden Shipbuilding at Québec, 1763-1893,* Kingston: Quarry Press , p. 15.

2. Paul Terrien, *Québec, à l'âge de la voile.* Ottawa: Éditions Asticou, 1984, p. 34. On page 46 Terrien states that the "British tended to take the new jobs, whereas the Canadians confined themselves to traditional occupations, including wood-working trades" and that 80% of the joiners and 85% of the carpenters were French Canadians in 1842.

3. See Eileen Reid Marcil's first chapter on "The Timber Trade."

4. *Ibid.*, Appendix B, "Sailing ships built in the Port of Québec, 1765-1893,"and Appendix C, "Outport construction of square-rigged vessels and large schooners and sloops, 1781-1891."

5. Pierre-Vincent Valin was born at Château-Richer in 1827. He is recognized as being one of the major Francophone shipbuilders and ship-owners who employed several hundred workers at Saint-Roch, Saint-Sauveur and Pointe-aux-Lièvres (Hare Point) between 1850 and 1870, and who succeeded in raising an imposing fleet of merchant ships.

6. "Le quai de L'Islet", by Captain Martin Caron, in *Histoire Québec*, Vol. 6, No. 2, November 2000.

7. Eileen Reid Marcil, *The Charley-Man, A History of Wooden Shipbuilding at Quebec, 1763-1893.* Kingston: Quarry Press, 1995, p. 161.

8. *Master Mariner,* pp. 66-67.

9. *Ibid.*, p. 67-68.

10. According to Eileen Reid Marcil.

11. *Master Mariner,* p. 70.

12. This brother of Célina, a spar-maker from Saint-Roch, acquired a great reputation for his skill and the quality of his work. He was mainly attached to Valin's shipyard.

Chapter 8 • The ship's boy comes up to the mark

1. *Histoire du Québec contemporain, de la Conféderation à la crise (1867-1929),* by Linteau, Durocher and Robert. Montréal: Éditions du Boréal Express, 1979, p. 77.

2. For more information on the British North America Act of 1867, see *Canada-Québec, 1534-2000,* by Lacoursière, Provencher and Vaugeois. Sillery: Éditions du Septentrion, 2000, pp. 321-331.

3. Gilberte Tremblay, *Bernier, capitaine à 17 ans*, p. 20.

4. *La Presse,* 4 May 1901.

5. *Master Mariner,* pp. 77-78.

6. *Ibid.*, pp. 81-82.

Chapter 9 • A promotion

1. Guy Bouthillier, "La bataille des langues: la contre-offensive du français", *Dossier Québec,* No. 3. Montréal: Éditions Stock, 1979, p. 76.

2. Yolande Dorion-Robitaille, "Joseph-Elzéar Bernier, capitaine en toute saison," *North/Nord*, Vol. 25, No. 3, May-June 1978, p. 28.

3. *Master Mariner,* pp. 83-84.

4. *Ibid.*, p. 84.

5. *Ibid.*, p. 85.

6. *Ibid.*, p. 86.

7. *Ibid.*, p. 87.

Chapter 10 • The crimps

1. Alain Franck, *Naviguer sur le fleuve au temps passé, 1860-1960.* Sainte-Foy: Les Publications du Québec, 2000, p. 61.

2. Statistics from Paul Terrien, *Québec à l'âge de la voile,* p. 89.

3. Frederick Wallace, *In the Wake of the Wind-Ships.* Toronto: The Musson Book Co., 1927, p. 118. Crimps were agents or procurers who provided captains with crews at inflated prices.

4. Paul Terrien, *Québec à l'âge de la voile*, p. 80.

5. *Ibid.*, p. 92,

6. *Master Mariner,* p. 93.

7. *Ibid.*, p. 94.

8. *Ibid.*, p. 95.

9. *Ibid.*, p. 96.

10. *Ibid.*

Chapter 11 • Accordant with his character

1. *Master Mariner*, pp. 96-97.
2. *Ibid.*, pp. 97-98.
3. *Ibid.*, pp. 98-99.
4. *Ibid.*, p. 100.
5. *Ibid.*, p. 101.
6. *Ibid.*, p. 102.
7. Interview in *La Presse*, 4 May 1901.

Chapter 12 • A confrontation

1. *Master Mariner*, p. 110.
2. *Ibid.*, pp. 110-111.
3. *Ibid.*, p. 111.
4. *Ibid.*, p. 112.
5. *Ibid.*, pp. 112-113.
6. *Ibid.*, p. 113.

Chapter 13 • Captain at 17!

1. *Master Mariner*, p. 116.
2. *In the Wake of the Wind-Ships*, p. 102. Wallace wrote: "The Dominion's "Grand Old Man of the Sea" is a French-Canadian of Québec, Joseph Elzéar Bernier."
3. *The Canadian Polar Expedition*. Ottawa, 1901, p. 15.
4. For example: *The True North, the Story of Captain Joseph Bernier*, by T.C. Fairley and Charles C.E. Israel. Toronto: Macmillan, 1964, p. 29; Pierre Saucier, "Le capitaine Bernier, Jacques Cartier de l'Arctique," in *La Patrie du dimanche*, 6 March 1960; Marie Kronstrom, "Un capitaine au large passé, Joseph Elzéar Bernier," in *La Tribune*, Wednesday 5 March, 1975.
5. *Bulletin de la Société de géographie de Québec*, September-December, 1926.
6. This author is recognized world-wide as the most important writer of stories of the sea.
7. *Master Mariner*, p. 117.
8. *Ibid.*, pp. 117-118.
9. *Ibid.*, pp. 107-108.
10. *Ibid.*, p. 118.
11. *Ibid.*, p. 124-125.

Chapter 14 • A Rose from L'Islet

1. Charles-Joseph-Albert Lozeau was born at Montréal on 23 June 1878 and died there on 24 March 1924. He is recognized as the "poète de l'intérieur" of his generation.
2. See the Caron family genealogy in the appendix. Nothing is known about Rose's only sister, apart from the fact that her name was Marie and that she married Philias Morin on 30 September 1873 at L'Islet.
3. Louis-Stanislas was already a priest at the time of his half-sister's wedding. He died around 1900 in Wisconsin. Eusèbe married Émilie Caron around 1865 at Saint-Jean-Port-Joli. Fifteen children would be born of this marriage. He was over 85 years old when he died, and was buried at L'Islet.
4. Martin Caron, personal communication, June 2002.
5. In her book, *Bernier, capitaine à 17 ans*, p. 26.
6. This was the house at No. 91, chemin des Pionniers Est. One must remember that the Berniers lived there from 1856 until 1873. From 1873 until 1878 they lived at No. 81, Chemin des Pionniers Est, now the "Doctor's lodging." In 1878 Thomas moved his family to Québec, to the Saint-Sauveur district.
7. *Master Mariner*, p. 123.
8. On page 126 of *Master Mariner* he wrote: "We had corresponded regularly." We would like to have found these letters, which have probably disappeared today, with a view to throwing some more light on the captain's sensitive soul.
9. *Bernier, capitaine à 17 ans*, p. 33.
10. *Master Mariner*, p. 126.
11. This uncle had been widowed only shortly before, since his wife, Émilie Paradis, Joseph-Elzéar's mother's sister, had died in 1869.
12. *Master Mariner*, p. 128.
13. See the research of Professor Serge Gagnon on this subject, in his book, *Mariage et familles au temps de Papineau*. Sainte Foy: Presses de l'Université Laval, 1993.

Chapter 15 • The *Saint-Michel*

1. Document registered at Québec, 29 January 1870.
2. *Master Mariner...*, p. 128. This is the only time that Captain Bernier mentions, this sister, who died at an early age. His two other sisters were Marie-Léda Justine, aged seven, and Henriette-Émilie, aged eleven.
3. *Ibid.*, p. 131-2.
4. *Ibid.*, p. 132-3.
5. Azade Harvey, *Auguste LeBourdais, naufragé en 1871 aux Îles-de-la Madeleine*. Montréal: Éditions Intrinsèque, 1979, p. 36.

Chapter 16 • An absinthe-flavoured honeymoon

1. Archives of the Collège de Lévis (ACL). Bernier Collection, series "B", manuscript N-81.
2. *Master Mariner*, p. 139.
3. *Ibid.*, p. 140.
4. *Ibid.*, p. 141. Could this be the negative on a metal plate that represents the only known photo of the young couple from this period? It is likely.

5. *Ibid.*, p. 142.
6. *Ibid.*, pp. 142-143.
7. *Ibid.*, pp. 143-144.
8. *Ibid.*, pp. 144-145.
9. *Ibid.*, pp. 146-147.
10. *Ibid.*, pp. 151-152.
11. *Ibid.*, p. 151.

Chapter 17 • A sought-after ship-deliverer

1. *Histoire de Lévis-Lotbinière*, under the direction of Roch Samson, Institut québécois de recherche sur la culture. Québec: Presses de l'Université Laval, p. 355.
2. Paul Terrien, *Québec à l'âge de la voile*, p. 95.
3. Eileen Reid Marcil, *The Charley-Man*, p. 194.
4. According to Paul Terrien's calculations.
5. Alain Franck, *Naviguer sur le fleuve au temps passé, 1860-1960*, p. 68.
6. *Master Mariner*, p. 184.
7. *Ibid.*, p. 177.
8. *Ibid.*, p. 213.
9. Mario Béland, Curator of Ancient Art at the Musée du Québec, "Portraits of Captain Bernier's ships," *Cap-aux-Diamants*, No. 4, Winter 1997.
10. *Ibid.*
11. List established by Frederick William Wallace, *In the Wake of the Wind-Ships*, p. 105.

Chapter 18 • They sang "Charley-Man".

1. William and Peter Baldwin, originally from Ireland, were among the few shipbuilders in Québec who financed their ships themselves.
2. Jacques Colon, "Bernier conquers the Arctic," *Sélection du Reader's Digest*, April 1978, p. 58.
3. Which means that, from 1870 until 1874, when they were not travelling, the young couple continued to live in L'Islet. But where? Probably with Elzéar's parents, as was then the custom. In 1878 Célina and Thomas came to join their son and his wife at Saint-Sauveur. The Cherrier Almanac of Addresses for the city of Québec and Saint-Sauveur reveals that in 1886 and 1887 Thomas and Célina were still living in that parish and that they were then owners of a boarding house at 8, rue Sainte-Gertrude.
4. *Master Mariner*, p. 231.
5. *Ibid.*, p, 169.
6. *La construction des navires à Québec et ses environs, grèves et naufrages.* Québec: Imprimerie Léger Brousseau, 1897, pp. 7-8.
7. *Master Mariner*, pp. 171-172.
8. *Ibid.*, pp. 189-190.

Chapter 19 • On board the *Quorn*

1. This anecdote about *Quorn*'s race is based on Chapter XIII in *Master Mariner*, "A hunting lady races," pp. 191-198.
2. From: *Master Mariner*, Chapter XIV, "Shipwreck", pp. 199-213.
3. *Ibid.*, pp. 208-209.
4. *Ibid.*, p. 211.

Chapter 20 • A paddle-pump

1. *Ibid.*, p. 215.
2. *Ibid.*, p. 216.
3. *Ibid.*, p. 217.
4. *Ibid.*, pp. 217-219.
5. *Ibid.*, p. 219.
6. *In the Wake of the Wind-Ships*, Frederick William Wallace, p. 108.

Chapter 21 • Sojourn in Southeast Asia

1. *Master Mariner*, p. 222. At that time Lloyds was already the most important insurance company in the world.
2. *Ibid.*, pp. 222-223.
3. *Ibid.*, pp. 223-224.
4. It had no locks and was 162.5 km long, 190 m wide and 20 m deep.
5. *Master Mariner*, p. 224.
6. *Ibid.*, p. 225. It is not known who inherited this ring, or whether it still exists.
7. *Ibid.*
8. *Ibid.*, p. 226.
9. *Ibid.*, p. 227.
10. *Ibid.*
11. *Ibid.*, pp. 227-228.
12. *Ibid.*, p. 229.

Chapter 22 • The ill-fated *Jeannette*

1. *Master Mariner*, p. 232.
2. *Ibid.*, pp. 233-234.
3. *Ibid.*, pp. 236-238.

Chapter 23 • Mina

1. *Master Mariner*, p. 238
2. All the information about Elmina derives from two of her granddaughters, Suzanne Audet-Normandeau, daughter of Marie-Marthe Bourget, and Magdeleine Bourget, daughter of Marie-Albert Bourget. See appendix for further details on this family.

3. *Master Mariner,* p. 240.
4. The *Charley-Man,* Eileen Reid Marcil, p. 361.
5. *Ibid.,* p. 69.
6. *Ibid.*
7. *Le Devoir,* 25 June 1946.
8. In his memoirs Captain Bernier wrote the name as William Charland Jr, whereas the specialists in maritime history, Eileen Reid Marcil and Paul Terrien, who checked the original registrations for the Port of Québec, render the name as William Charland Sr.
9. *Master Mariner,* p. 241.
10. *Ibid.,* pp. 241-242.
11. *Ibid.,* p. 242-243.
12. *Ibid.,* p. 245.
13. Paul Terrien, *Québec à l'âge de la voile,* p. 116.
14. *Ibid.,* p. 118.
15. *Master Mariner,* pp. 247-248.
16. *Ibid.,* pp. 248-249.
17. *Ibid.,* p. 250.

Chapter 24 • Dockmaster at Lauzon

1. Dated 26 October 1886, in the private collection of Carol and Louis Terrien.
2. *Master Mariner,* p. 255.
3. *Histoire de Lévis-Lotbinière,* edited by Roch Samson, Institut québecois de recherche sur la culture. Québec: Presses de l'Université Laval, 1996, p. 345.
4. With regard to the Davie shipyards, one must remember that over time the initial enterprise developed into three distinct enterprises each with its own character and evolution. They were: "Georges T. Davie and Sons", "Davie Shipbuilding" and "Davie Brothers".
5. Article in the *Gazette de Québec* of 29 October 1832, quoted in: *The Charley-Man* by Eileen Reid Marcil, p. 167.
6. Alain Franck, *Naviguer sur le fleuve au temps passé,* p. 165.
7. George T. was the eldest son of Captain Allison Davie and Élizabeth Taylor. Already by 1882 he had purchased new lots and had enlarged the existing shops. He is the founder of the present-day Davie shipyard at Lauzon. George T. had three brothers—Captain William Taylor Davie, Gershom Taylor Davie and Allison Taylor Davie—as well as two sisters. He died in 1907 at the age of 80.
8. Series "B", Archives du Collège de Lévis, Bernier Collection, documents N-43, N-94, N-107 to 110 contain the captain's journal and reports during his years as dockmaster of the graving dock.
9. *Master Mariner,* p. 256.
10. Document No. 28921, Land Titles Office for Lévis.
11. Eileen Reid Marcil, *Au rhythme des marées, l'histoire des chantiers maritimes Davie.* Toronto: McClelland & Stewart Inc., 1997, pp 211-212. George Duncan Davie had paid $3000 for the property. *L'indicateur de Québec, Saint-Sauveur et Lévis,* published by T.L. Bélanger and Éditions Marcotte, would indicate that Davie had perhaps rented the Villa Bernier before buying it.
12. Document No. 29475 at the Lévis Land Titles Office. This property was bounded on the north by that of J.-A Jodoin, on the south by the Rue Saint-Joseph, on the west by Achille Bourget's land and on the east by that of Théophile Guilbault.
13. Document No. 31296, dated 6 May 1890. The annulment of the contract is numbered No. 31423.
14. Document Nos. 29933 and 34848. This land bore the numbers 158 and 159 on the survey map.
15. Document No. 31633, dated 27 November 1890.
16. Documents Nos. 33872 and 33873. Thomas died on 16 November 1893 and the death certificate is dated 27 November 1893.
17. The Saint-Sauveur property was located at 8 Rue Sainte-Gertrude and bore the number 1254 on the survey map. The one in Lauzon bore the number 775 on the survey map and comprised a house and buildings; it had a frontage of 66 feet and a depth of 178 feet. It was bounded on the east by the Rue Saint-Amable, on the west by the property of George Landry, on the south by that of George Pouliot and on the north by the Rue Saint-Honoré. It is unlikely that Thomas and Célina ever lived in this house since the mortgage registration (No. 29108) stipulates that it was bought from Rigobert Bourget then rented to the priest, Édouard Fafard.
18. When she sold it in turn the bill of sale (Document No. 36186, notarized by M. Alphonse Dumoutier of Lévis) records that the property was bought by Louis Paré for $250, and the latter renewed the lease of the parish priest of Saint-Joseph de Lévis. The bill of sale was cosigned by "Célina Paradis, widow of Thomas Bernier, Joseph-Elzéar Bernier, Governor of Québec Prison, Henriette Bernier, estranged wife of George Boisjoly, painter of Schenectady, and Pierre Côté for Alfred Bernier, ice merchant of Sainte-Cunégonde.
19. *Master Mariner,* p. 263.
20. *Ibid.,* p. 267.

Interlude
Governor of Québec prison

1. In the Benoît Robitaille Collection (B.R.) in the ANQ, as well as in the private archives of Carol and Louis Terrien.

2. See the appendix for further information on this subject.

3. The captain said of Joseph (1853-1901) that he was almost a "little brother" since he was the son of his uncle Jean-Baptiste and his aunt Émilie Paradis. This pilot in the making had married Marie-Emma Émilie Turgeon, daughter of Élie Turgeon and Émilie Lemieux in Québec on 17 January 1876.

4. *Master Mariner,* p. 283.

5. *Ibid.,* p. 284. The captain's memory was faulty. Monsieur Casgrain was in the Conservative cabinet of Louis-Olivier Taillon (1892-1896) and Félix-Gabriel Marchand, a Liberal, was Premier from 1897 until 1900.

6. William McClaren was Governor of the Plains of Abraham Prison from February 1892 until February 1895.

7. Damase Potvin, *Les Oubliés.* Québec: Éditions Roch Poulin, 1944, p. 59.

8. For example: Damase Potvin, *op. cit.,* pp. 58-59; Gilberte Tremblay in: *Bernier, capitaine à 17 ans,* p. 52; and François-Xavier Chouinard, "Un grand explorateur des mers arctiques, le capitaine Joseph-Elzéar Bernier," *Bulletin de la Société de géographie de Québec,* Vol. 20, nos. 4 and 5, September-December 1926. Subsequently journalists would repeat this supposition until it became firmly fixed in popular myth.

9. *Master Mariner,* p. 253.

10. The reference is to Charles-Eugène Boucher of Boucherville, Premier of Québec from 1874 to 1878 and from 1891 to 1892.

This personal journal is in the J.-E. Bernier collection, in the Archives du Collège de Lévis. As I have never had access to it, I have had to rely on the research of Claude Minotto for his Master's thesis, *La frontière arctique du Canada: les expéditions de Joseph-Elzéar Bernier (1895-1925).* Montréal: McGill University, 1975, p. 2. Henceforth all references to this manuscript will simply be designated *Minotto.*

11. *Minotto,* p. 2. Minotto quotes a few lines from the captain's personal journal, dated 17 Mach 1892, i.e. three years before he assumed the position, in support of his supposition: "Trip to Québec on personal business. Am working to find positions for some of our good Lévis workers in the Québec Parliament." He thus concludes, that if he had done this for others, he was quite capable of doing so on his own behalf.

12. Letter from Joseph Boivin, Provincial Assistant-Secretary, Carol and Louis Terrien's Archives. This salary would be increased to 1300 dollars by an Order in Council, No. 175, dated 27 May 1896.

13. *Le Monde illustré,* 23 March 1895.

14. *The True North, the Story of Captain Joseph Bernier.* Toronto: MacMillan, 1964, p. 47.

15. Document dated 18 November 1896, ANQ, Québec Prison Collection.

16. There is no information on these two since they were dismissed from their positions before the list was compiled. The two chaplains, Monseigneur Tétu and Reverend M. Richardson, as well as the institution's two doctors, Messrs. Robitaille and LeBel, should also be added to the list.

17. ANQ, Québec Prison Collection. Before Bernier arrived all prison business, even between francophones, was handled in English.

18. *Ibid.*

19. *Ibid.*

20. *Ibid.,* Inspectors' book, report dated 4 December 1895.

21. Letter from L.J. Cannon, dated 14 February 1896. Carol and Louis Terrien's collection.

22. *Master Mariner,* pp. 286-287.

23. *L'Événement,* 6 June 1896.

24. Carol and Louis Terrien's archives.

25. From reading prison documents it would appear that another guard, David Roy, who had been reprimanded several times for his drunkenness and violence, also participated in this campaign of "mud-slinging." His name does not appear on Bernier's list. One can also add Sergeant Jennings, the jailer's assistant, to the list of malcontents since Bernier demoted him because of his age (71), and replaced him with a younger man, the turnkey R.J. Modler.

26. ANQ, Québec Prison Collection. David Roy had perhaps already been dismissed since his name does not appear on the French document.

27. *Le Soleil,* 5 November 1897. The article stressed that the inquiry had finished and that 52 witnesses had been called. It would appear that the employees were accusing Bernier of making the prisoners work for his own benefit and of running the prison like a private hotel.

28. Letter dated 13 November 1909, addressed to J. Caron, Québec Minister of Parliament.

29. Letter from Sheriff Gagnon to Captain Bernier. He ended his letter by congratulating him on the results of the inquiry "the outcome of which was never in doubt." Carol and Louis Terrien's archives.

30. Letter dated 24 March 1898, Carol and Louis Terrien's collection. M. Bernatchez (1838-1906), Liberal Member for the riding of Montmagny, defeated in 1897, was sworn in to his new position on 18 March 1898. He remained in this post until 1906. It is known that he was not as sympathetic as Bernier to the situation of the elderly Jennings, and did not delay in dismissing him.

31. Fairley & Israel, *The True North*, p. 31.

32. *Master Mariner*, p. 289.

33. François-Xavier Chouinard, "Un grand explorateur des mers arctiques, le capitaine Joseph-Elzéar Bernier," *Bulletin de la Société de géographie de Québec*, Vol. 20, nos. 4 & 5, September-December 1926, p. 274.

Part II • "Kapitaikallak," the ice man

Chapter 1 • The plan

1. Yolande Dorion-Robitaille, *Captain J.-E. Bernier's Contribution to Canadian Sovereignty in the Arctic*. Ottawa: Department of Indian and Northern Affairs, 1978, p. 16.

2. Gustave Vallat, *À la conquête du Pôle*. Limoges: Librairie nationale, 1897, p. 118. The *Jeannette* belonged to James Gordon Bennett (1795-1872), owner of the *New York Herald*.

3. Fairley and Israel, *The True North*, p. 11.

4. Full text of Bernier's address as reproduced in Yolande Dorion-Robitaille' s book, pp. 22 and 24.

5. Claude Minotto included the contents of this letter of 12 February 1898 in his Master's thesis, pp. 28-29.

6. *La Patrie*, 9 December 1898.

Chapter 2 • Remuer l'opinion publique

1. One associates the 19th century with the reign of Victoria I (1837-1901), Queen of Great Britain and Ireland and Empress of India. During that period Britain reached the apogee of her development as a world power.

2. René Chopin, *Le cœur en exil*, 1913. René Chopin (1885-1953) was a notary, poet and literary critic for *Le Devoir*.

3. Louis-Edmond Hamelin, *Nordicité canadienne*. Montréal: Hurtubise HMH, 1975, p. 33.

4. ANQ, B.R. Collection.

5. "Psychologie de l'explorateur," by André Leroi-Gourham, in *Les explorateurs célèbres*. Paris: Éditions Lucien Mazenod, 1965, p. 7.

6. *Debates, House of Commons, Canada*. Speech by MP Gourley of Colchester, 30 September 1903.

7. " A Canadian for the Pole" in *Canadian Life and Resources*, 1905, p. 6.

8. Bernier's proposal to the members of the *Société de géographie de Québec*, 27 January 1898.

Chapter 3 • An *idée fixe*

1. *Master Mariner*, p. 298.

2. *Minotto*, pp. 27-28.

3. LAC, Wilfrid Laurier Collection, letter of 5 March 1898.

4. LAC, Laurier Collection.

5. *Ibid.*

6. It was Guy Sylvestre, of the Royal Society of Canada, who gave him this laudatory title in his *Anthologie de la poésie canadienne-française*. Born in Lévis, Fréchette was a barrister, journalist, Member of the House of Commons and Clerk of the Legislative Council. He occupies an important place in Québec poetry since he was one of the first to make French-Canadian literature known abroad.

7. LAC, Laurier Collection, letter of 7 June 1899.

8. Samuel Baillargeon, *Littérature canadienne-française*. Montréal: Fides, 1957, p. 155.

9. Cited in *Wilfrid Laurier, quand la politique devient passion*, by Réal Bélanger. Québec: Presses de l'Université Laval, 1986, p. 67.

10. *Ibid.*, p. 160.

11. "Une gloire des familles Bernier, le capitaine Jos.-Elzéar Bernier", *Le Courrier de Montmagny*, Friday, 29 April, 1960.

12. *Minotto*, p. 32.

13. Yolande Dorion-Robitaille, *Captain J.-E. Bernie's Contribution to Canadian Sovereignty in the Arctic*, p. 29.

14. The Québec National Archives and the collection of Carol and Louis Terrien contain hundreds of letters which he answered systematically. In another private collection we found a handwritten list in which the captain stated that he had written no less than 93,000 letters in promoting his polar project, sometimes using the services of four secretaries. Of these we have found only the names L.A. Morency, Belleau, Brown, F.V. Moffet and the initials I.B. and F.C.M.

15. *Master Mariner*, p. 303.

16. *Minotto*, p. 34.

17. *Ibid.* This diary is preserved as dossier N-33 at the ACL.

18. Carol and Louis Terrien's archives, 1900 correspondence. In her Master's thesis, *Closing the Front Door of the Arctic: Capt. Joseph E. Bernier's role in Canadian Arctic sovereignty* (Ottawa: Carleton University, September 2003), journalist Season Osborne states that in November 1902 Bernier contracted with engineer C. Baillargé to draft plans for a polar ship, *Indestructible*, but that it was never built. Even though the dates do not correspond, perhaps these are the same plans?

19. *Minotto*, p. 40.

20. Carol and Louis Terrien's archives.

21. Letter to Sir Wilfrid Laurier, 4 August 1903. ANQ, Fonds B.R. It is known that he wanted to use this letter in Appendix E of the second volume of his memoirs, that he wanted to devote to the polar question. A list of the 36 points that he was thinking of developing has survived in his personal dossiers at

the ANQ. Unfortunately he died before undertaking this important task.

22. Letter of 22 March 1901. ANQ, Fonds B.R.

Chapter 4 • A subscription

1. *Minotto,* p. 37.

2. LAC, Laurier Fonds.

3. ANQ, B.R. Fonds, dated 23 May 1901.

4. *Ibid.*

5. LAC, Laurier Fonds, letter of 2 July 1901.

6. *Ibid.* Correspondence of 9 July 1901. The reference is to Robert Edwin Peary (1856-1920), American sailor and explorer, who was trying to reach the North Pole from the northwest coast of Greenland. He would not reach his goal until April 1909, using 19 sledges and 133 dogs.

7. Blodwen Davies, "He has added half a million square miles to Canada," *Canadian Magazine,* February 1927, p. 21.

8. Fairley and Israel, *The true North…,* p. 61.

9. LAC, Laurier Fonds, petition dated 12 April 1902. The name of Henri Bourassa (1868-1952) founder of *Le Devoir* appears in it.

10. House of Commons Debates, Ottawa, Thursday, 1 May 1902. Speech by Member John Charlton.

Chapter 5 • Arctic boundaries for Canada

1. *Minotto,* p. xi.

2. This involved exclusive rights to the Indian territories that the "Governor and Company of Adventurers of England trading into Hudson's Bay" or the Hudson's Bay Company, had relinquished to Queen Victoria by the Rupert's Land Act of 1868.

3. "Order of Her Majesty in Council admitting all British Territories and Possessions in North America and all Islands adjacent thereto into the Union, at the Court at Osborne House, Isle of Wight, the 31st day of July 1880", in: *British North America Acts and Selected Statutes, 1867-1962,* prepared by Maurice Ollivier, House of Commons. Ottawa: Queen's Printer, 1962, p. 189-190.

4. According to Ronald St. John Macdonald in *The Arctic Frontier.* Toronto: University of Toronto Press, 1966, p. 203.

5. *Colonial Office Papers,* Series No. 42, Vol. 759, January 29, 1879.

6. The *Hudson's Bay Company* was created by a charter of England's King Charles II on 2 May 1670.

7. The first under the command of A. Gordon in 1884 and the second led by W. Wakeham in 1897.

8. Order in Council No. 2640 of 2 October 1895. The districts of Keewatin and Athabaska were then enlarged.

9. Lacoursière and Bouchard, *Notre histoire Québec-Canada,* Vol. 8, "Vers l'Ouest, 1887-1908." Montréal: Éditions Format, 1972, p. 682. This was a speech given at Somerset, Québec on 2 August 1887 when Laurier took the place of Edward Blake as head of the Liberals.

10. *Minotto,* p. 54.

12. A.P.Low. *The cruise of the Neptune, 1903-04,* Ottawa: Government Printing Bureau, 1906, p. 3.

12. On 20 October 1903.

Chapter 6 • The *Gauss* affair

1. We know only of the Chicago specialist, Dr. W.W. Quinlan because of his medical report dated 1 October 1902. Carol and Louis Terrrien's archives.

2. Marie-Rosalie was the younger sister of Elmina. She was to marry Alfred Samson, who worked at the dock at Saint-Joseph de Lévis. Letter dated 23 June 1903, ANQ, B.R. Fonds. The couple would have 10 children. Some of them can remember their "Captain Capi."

3. Alain Franck, "Joseph-Elzéar Bernier, 1852-1934. Mythe et légende vivante," *L'Escale nautique,* No. 30, summer 2001, p. 5.

4. *Minotto,* p. 143.

5. *Ibid.,* p. 85.

6. Yolande Dorion-Ronitaille, *Captain J.E. Bernier's Contribution to Canadian Sovereignty in the Arctic,* p. 73.

7. *Gauss* bore the name of the famous German scholar and mathematician, Johann Karl Friedrich Gauss (1777-1855). Claude Minotto claims that the Canadian government believed that it could obtain this ship at a lower price by working through Captain Bernier, but that, "impoverished by his campaign for his polar project, Bernier contrived a transaction where his expertise would bring him a supplementary profit" (p. 146). On 4 March 1904 Bernier wrote to a Norwegian agent, B. Nordahl by name: "I have wired you a bid of £12,000 and confirm it now, but it must be well understood that this bid must not be known to any officer of the Canadian Government or other, nor the purchase price. If asked by anyone, say £15,000" (p. 147). One has the feeling that Minotto did not approve of the tactics of this businessman and past-master in the shipping trade. Ultimately the Canadian government bought the ship directly from the German government for £15,000, thereby depriving Bernier of his profit of £3000.

8. Thomas E. Appleton. *Usque ad mare. A history of the Canadian Coast Guard and Marine Services.* Ottawa: Queen's Printer, p. 67.

9. Letter from Captain E. Ménard, 23 March 1904. ANQ, B.R. Fonds

10. Personal diary written between 9 April and 24 May 1904. It was transcribed by his daughter, Carmelle Boucher, 25 years after the sailor's death. Unpublished manuscript in Martin Caron's collection.

11. We've seen how Arthur Boucher's diary raised the matter of the incompetence of the "able seamen" from Montréal. This testimony is important because it acts a counterpoise to the complaints of certain members of the crew.

12. *La Patrie* of Montréal, 14 June 1904.

13. *L'Événement* of Québec, 16 June 1904.

14. Interview, 15 June 1904.

15. Roland Prévost, "La vie aventureuse du capitaine J.E. Bernier," in *La Revue populaire,* February 1932.

16. Quoted in *L'Action nationale,* Vol. XC, No. 9, November 2000, p. 72.

Chapter 7 • Preparations for the voyage

1. D.G.S. = Dominion Government Ship. Subsequently government ships were designated as C.G.S. = Canadian Government Ship.

2. *Minotto,* p. 164.

3. Letter to Minister Préfontaine, dated 8 March 1904 and cited in *Minotto,* p. 165

4. A complete list of the crew in 1904-1905 is included in an appendix.

5. *Master Mariner,* p. 305.

6. He waited until the last minute before resuming his post. In a telegram dated 13 September Deputy Minister Gourdeau asked him to confirm whether he would accept or refuse the post of captain of *Arctic.* An article in the *Toronto Daily Star* of 15 September informed its readers that Bernier was not prepared to play second fiddle on the expedition and that he was still refusing to make a commitment. On the following day the same newspaper reported: "The captain may be sure that he has our sympathy. The whole world is disappointed at a good man being kept down." *Arctic* sailed on the 17th.

7. T.C. Fairley and Charles E. Israel, *The True North. The Story of Captain Joseph Bernier,* p. 69.

8. Esdras Terrien was Captain Bernier's brother-in-law. Even though his article was published on 3 January 1935, shortly after the captain's death, it is not a stretch to suppose that Bernier and Terrien had compared notes on the matter. See the genealogy of Alma Lemieux, in the appendix, to understand how they were related.

9. Laurier's speech in *House of Commons Debates,* 29 July 1904.

Chapter 8 • To Hudson Bay, 1904-1905

1. ANQ, B.R. Fonds

2. The previous year Commander Moodie had been the commanding officer of A.P. Low's expedition. Thus he knew the Hudson Bay region very well. For the full details of that expedition see the *Report on the Dominion Government Expedition to Hudson Bay and the Arctic Islands on board the D.G.S. Neptune 1903-1904,* Ottawa: Government Printing Bureau, 1906.

In *Closing the Front Door of the Arctic, Capt. Joseph E. Bernier's Role in Canadian Arctic sovereignty,* Season Osborne describes Moodie as an authoritarian, difficult man who provoked conflicts with Bernier, just as he had done with Low. For his part Bernier saw him as a usurper, which did not help the situation.

3. *Relation sommaire de voyage de l'*Arctic *à la Baie d'Hudson, en 1904-1905,* edited by Fabien Vanasse on behalf of the Deputy Minister of Marine and Fisheries, Ottawa, 1905, p. 7. For the official report see: "Report of Superintendent J.D.Moodie, Hudson's Bay", in *R.C.M.P. Annual Report,* 1905.

4. The major part of this diary is located in the archives of the Séminaire de Trois-Rivières, Vanasse Fonds, location #0026-B-03. All unidentified citations that follow in this chapter are taken from this diary.

5. Interview with Fabien Vanasse, "Dans la baie d'Hudson et les régions arctiques," *Le Temps,* Ottawa, May 1905.

6. ANQ, B.R. Fonds. Letter to Minister L.P. Brodeur of 17 February 1908. The captain was submitting a résumé of his polar expeditions between 1904 and 1907.

7. Yolande Dorion-Robitaille, *Captain J.-E. Bernier's Contribution to Canadian Sovereignty in the Arctic,* p. 43. Edward had succeeded his mother, Queen Victoria who died in 1901.

8. *Ibid.*

9. To learn more about this region, see Benoît Robitaille, "Évolution cartographique de la rive sud du détroit d'Hudson du XVIIe au XXe siècle: le fjord de Salluit", in: *Hommes et Terres du Nord,* 1989, 3, p. 125 to 130. The geographer writes: "Unaware that Low had explored the fjord the previous year, Bernier, on his first voyage to the North, hoped to really make his mark as its discoverer, while paying homage to his sponsors in Ottawa. [...] Unfortunately, on his return to Québec in October 1905, Bernier learned that Low had forestalled him by a year in Préfontaine Bay!" Benoît Robitaille was an adviser to René Lévesque when he was Québec's Minister of Natural Resources .

10. J.-E. Bernier, *Rapport sur la croisière faite par le trois-mâts mixte "Arctic" de la puissance du Canada dans l'Archipel Arctique et le détroit d'Hudson.* Ottawa, 1910, p. 368.

11. *Ibid.*

12. Fabien Vanasse, *Relation sommaire du voyage de l'*Arctic *à la baie d'Hudson, en 1904-05*, p. 6 and 7. The name White Island recalled that of Colonel White who was then the head of the Royal Northwest Mounted Police.

13. Subsequently Bernier took it upon himself to emphasize the strategic importance of Port Burwell in the numerous memos that he addressed to the Minister of Marine and Fisheries, insisting that aids to navigation be installed and customs dues recovered.

Chapter 9 • The *Arctic* scandal

1. *Minotto*, p. 150-151.

2. Speech by M.P. J.H. Bergeron, *House of Commons Debates*, 1906, Vol. IV, p. 6565.

3. *Ibid.*, Vol. II, p. 3279.

4. *Ibid.*, Vol. III, p. 3287.

5. *Minotto*, p. 153.

6. Anonymous pamphlet discovered by Minotto in the R.L. Borden Fonds, LAC, Vol. 2, No. 67.

7. Fairley and Israel, *The true North*, p. 77.

8. *Minotto*, p. 158-159.

Chapter 10 • And the North Pole?

1. Folio 16970, Department of Agriculture, Ottawa.

2. ANQ, B.R. Fonds.

3. Minotto has explained this decision as follows: "In 1906 Albert Peter Low became, in his turn, Director of the Geological Survey of Canada. Thereafter his time was monopolized by his new functions and he was no longer available for protracted missions in the Arctic Archipelago. It was Joseph Bernier whom the government entrusted with the command of the expeditions to the islands north of Hudson Strait and Bay" (p. 88).

4. Speech by Minister Brodeur, *House of Commons Debates*, 1906, Vol. II, p. 3486.

5. There was a controversy between Peary and Dr. Frederick A. Cook, who, in 1909, both claimed the credit for conquering the Pole. They were both greeted in turn as the discoverers of the North Pole, but without producing definitive proof.

6. "The arctic regions of Canada. An address by Capt. J.E. Bernier before the Empire Club of Canada on December 20, 1909", in: *The Empire Club of Canada Speeches 1909-1910*, edited by Hopkins and J. Castell, Toronto, 1910, p. 67-76.

7. *Master Mariner*, p. 305-306.

Chapter 11 • A frontier to explore, the expedition of 1906-1907

1. List included in an appendix.

2. One recalls the sinking of the largest transatlantic liner in the world that occurred six years later. On the night of 15/16 April 1912, the *Titanic* struck an iceberg south of Newfoundland and sank, causing the deaths of 1500 people. This was therefore a real danger for the small Canadian ship.

3. Bernier, J.-E., *Report on the Dominion Government expedition to Arctic islands and the Hudson Strait on board the C.G.S. "Arctic" 1906-1907*. Ottawa: King's Printer, 1909, p. 332.

4. *Ibid.*

5. Alain Franck, "Joseph-Elzéar Bernier, 1852-1934. Mythe et légende vivante," *L'Escale nautique,* No. 30, summer 2001, p. 5.

6. Jean-Louis Étienne, *Le marcheur du pôle.*Paris: Éditions Robert Laffront, 1986, p. 245.

7. James P. Delgado, *Across the Top of the World.* Vancouver: Douglas and McIntyre, p. 10. Mr. Delgado is director of Vancouver Maritime Museum.

8. Remark by anthropologist Stéphane Cloutier in *Nunatsiaq News*, 2 November 2001, p. 17.

9. Stéphane Cloutier, "Dans le sillage du capitaine Joseph–Elzéar Bernier," *Le Toit du Monde*, Vol. 1, No. 1, spring 2001, p. 18.

10. *Master Mariner*, p. 320.

11. Personal diary of Fabien Vanasse for 19 June 1907, ASTR.

12. LAC, John A. Simpson Fonds, personal diary.

13. Fabien Vanasse de Vertefeuille (1849-1936) had been a barrister, journalist and Editor-in-Chief of the Conservative newspaper *Le Monde*, as well as the Conservative Member for the riding of Yamaska.

14. ASTR, Vanasse Fonds, personal diary, 31 December 1906 and 17 August 1907.

15. *Ibid.*, 23 September 1906.

16. Pond's Inlet is the arm of the sea south of Bylot Island, while Pond Inlet was the whaling station near Port Albert or Albert Harbour.

17. *Minotto*, p. 256.

18. ASTR, Fabien Vanasse Fonds, personal diary, 14 January 1907.

19. *Master Mariner*, p. 322.

20. ASTR, Fabien Vanasse Fonds, personal diary, 13 September 1907.

21. Gilberte Tremblay's semi-fictionalized text, *Bernier, capitaine à 17 ans*, p. 71.

22. J.-E. Bernier, *Report on the Dominion Government Expedition to Arctic Islands and the Hudson Strait on board the C.G.S. "Arctic" 1906-1907* Ottawa: King's Printer, 1909, p. 46.

23. Yolande Dorion Robitaille, Captain *J.E. Bernier's Contribution to Canadian Sovereignty in the Arctic, p. 62.*

24. ANQ, B.R. Fonds, letter of 7 October 1907.

Chapter 12 • The apogee of his career, the expedition of 1908-1909

1. *Atlas historique du Québec, Québec ville et capitale.* Sainte-Foy: Presses de l'Université Laval, 2001, p. 325.

2. See the list in the appendices.

3. ANQ, B.R. Fonds, letter of 18 July 1908. On 23 July Bernier received a "Royal Commission," authorizing him to command the ship and the government expedition, as well as to act as an officer in the Fisheries Service and as Justice of the Peace.

4. *Master Mariner,* p. 325.

5. J.-E. Bernier, *Report on the Dominion of Canada Government Expedition to the Arctic Islands and Hudson Strait on board the D.G.S. "Arctic".* Ottawa: Government Printing Bureau, 1910, p. 16. Hereafter cited as *Official report, 1908-1909.*

6. The *Roosevelt,* the expedition ship of Robert E. Peary, his rival in the race for the Pole, had left the shelter of Foulke Fjord the previous day, heading out to sea.

7. Jacques Coulon, "Bernier à la conquête de l'Arctique", *Sélection du Reader's Digest,* April 1978, p. 60.

8. *Official report, 1908-1909,* p. 22-31.

9. 1 fathom = 6 feet.

10. *Official report, 1908-1909,* p. 31.

11. *Ibid.,* p. 38. Season Osborne (*Closing the Front Door of the Arctic: Capt. Joseph E. Bernier's Role in Canadian Arctic Sovereignty*) does not believe that Bernier would have succeeded in making this transit in his small, wooden vessel. Giant, modern icebreakers, equipped with sophisticated instruments, do not use M'Clure Strait, but opt rather for the southward route between Banks and Victoria islands. This is still an enormous challenge since, up until now, only 114 vessels have traversed the Northwest Passage.

12. *Bernier, Capitaine à 17 ans,* p. 77-79. In their book *The true North, the story of Captain Joseph Bernier,* Fairley and Israel confirm this version of the facts, p. 104-105.

13. *Official report, 1908-1909,* p. 53.

14. *Ibid.,* p. 53.

15. Yolande Dorion-Ronitaille, *Captain J.E. Bernier's Contribution to Canadian Sovereignty in the Arctic,* p. 83. This was also Andrew Taylor's opinion in: *Geographical Discovery: Exploration in the Queen Elizabeth Islands.* Ottawa: Geographical Branch, Department of Mines and Technical Surveys, 1955, p. 117. Bernier revered the memories of polar explorers.

16. *Official report 1908-1909,* p. 68.

17. *Ibid.,* p. 75.

18. *Ibid.,* p. 79.

19. During interviews with descendants of, or persons who knew the expedition members, and with seamen and master mariners who have grown up in the Canadian maritime environment.

20. *Master Mariner,* p. 340.

21. One has only to read three articles that appeared on 6 October 1909 to appreciate this: "Une nuit de trois mois (A night of three months)" in *Le Soleil;* "La fortune sourit aux audacieux (Fortune smiles on the bold)" in *La Presse*; and "Le retour de l'expédition du capt. Bernier—aventure périlleuse de trois hardis marins qui ont souffert de la fatigue et de la faim pour aller prendre possession des terres Banks et Victoria (The return of Capt. Bernier's expedition—perilous adventure of three bold sailors who endured fatigue and hunger to take possession of Banks and Victoria islands)" in *La Patrie.*

22. This is what Napoléon Chassé confided to Fernand Gagon in 1938, during one of their frequent meetings on the quay at Kamouraska. Monsieur Gagnon was then a schooner captain on the St. Lawrence. It was he who built the *Saint-André* that one can admire in the Maritime Museum in Charlevoix.

23. "Voyage au Pôle Nord, le Capitaine Bernier," *Le Trifluvien de Trois-Rivières,* Tuesday 7 July, 1903.

24. *Official report,* 1908-1909, p. 114.

25. "Le mot de l'énigme," *Le Soleil,* Thursday 7 October 1909.

26. Claude Vigneau's personal diary was deposited with the ANQ.

27. "Report of O.J. Morin to Victoria and Banks Island," in: *Official report, 1908-1909,* pp. 126-138. In all the government files his Christian names are Octave-Jules, but in L'Islet-sur-Mer he was also known as Jules-Octave. Born in 1883 he died in 1943.

28. Reuben Pike and Napoléon Chassé. The three men would be hauling a load of 300 lbs. The other five men reached the *Arctic* on 8 May.

29. The details of this second trip that lasted until 24 June 1909, may be found in the *Official report, 1908-1909,* pp. 167—177.

30. "Report of Mr. C.W. Green of trip to Mercy Bay, Banks Island", *Official report, 1908-1909,* pp. 147—161. Although in a more technical and less personal style than that of Morin, this report nonetheless makes fascinating reading.

31. Right at the start of the trip their dog, Tom, had stolen and hidden all their fresh meat.

32. *Official report, 1908-1909,* p. 192.

33. Yolande Dorion-Robitaille, *Captain J.-E. Bernier's Contribution to Canadian Sovereignty in the Arctic,* p. 83.

34. *Official report, 1908-1909*, p. 251-253.

35. *Ibid.*, p. 253.

36. *Ibid.*, p. 260.

37. *Ibid.*, p. 269. This was Charles Green, who had led one of the sledge expeditions to Banks Island.

38. *Ibid.*, p. 323.

Chapter 13 • Mina's hat

1. In his biography, *The Big Ship*, published in 1967, p. 91. This Norwegian (1899-1964) would become the captain of the R.C.M.P. ship, the *St-Roch* and would succeed in making transits of the Northwest Passage in both directions, in 1940-1942 and in 1944.

2. Odilon Bourget had died on 10 November 1904 at the age of 36, following a kidney infection and a heart attack.

3. Letter of 16 December 1909, identified by Claude Minotto in the Collège de Lévis Archives.

4. ANQ, B.R. Fonds, letter of 20 October 1909.

5. He was so much sought-after by eminent associations and various social clubs that he was obliged to hire an agent. According to Claude Minotto this was J.G. Kilt, a paper merchant and seller of fountain pens in Ottawa.

6. ANQ, B.R. Fonds, letter of 26 October 1909.

7. *Ibid.*, letter of 27 October 1909. This was Marie-Cécile Caron (1881-1970) who later married Jean-Philippe Bélanger in 1911, and Jean-Étienne Samson, her second husband, in 1927.

8. *Ibid.*, letter to Marie-Cécile, dated 30 October 1909.

9. *Ibid.*, letter of 18 October 1909.

10. *Ibid.*, letter of 9 November 1909.

11. Interviewed on 15 October 2001 in Québec.

12. ANQ. B.R. Fonds, letter from Kate Pettit of New York, dated 8 November 1911.

13. *Ibid.*, letter from Eugénie Pouliot of Rivière-du-Loup, 23 October 1925.

Chapter 14 • The controversial expedition of 1910-1911

1. See the list in the appendix.

2. One can find a detailed description of what he conceived to be the safest method of making the Passage in *The cruise of the Minnie Maud*, edited by Alfred Tremblay, Québec: The Arctic Exchange and Publishing Ltd., 1921, p. 414-415.

3. See also Bernier's official report: *Report on the Dominion Government Expedition to the Northern Waters and Arctic Archipelago of the D.G.S. "Arctic" in 1910*, Ottawa, 1911.

4. *Master Mariner*, p. 353-354.

5. Robert M'Clure's *Investigator*, Henry Kellett's *Resolute*, Francis L. McClintock's *Intrepid*, Edward Belcher's *Assistance* and Sherard Osborn's *Pioneer*.

6. *Master Mariner*, p. 356.

7. Extracts from Fabien Vanasse's notebooks, in which he describes the meeting of the two worlds during the Christmas festivities in 1910, were published in *Le Toit du Monde*, Vol. 1, No. 3, 2002, p. 10-15.

8. See Gilberte Tremblay's romanticized account, to learn more about the terrible journey of this native of the Baie des Chaleurs. An Eskimo woman saved his life by licking his wounds.

9. *Minotto*, p. 195.

10. ANQ, B.R. Fonds. Another document records that the captain had spent $3,639.15 in developing this concession, when he sold it for £500 in March 1919. Since the value of the British pound has changed over time, one cannot tell if this represented a profit.

11. *Minotto*, p. 197-198.

12. ANQ, B.R. Fonds, letter from J.E. Mathé.

13. Bernier certainly thought so. On 2 March 1912 he wrote to a friend in Ottawa: "It appears that Vanasse has laid complaints with the Minister, and you know what may come of it. What a fellow. We're going to have more trouble with this 'homme céleste'." ANQ, B.R. Fonds.

14. *Ibid.*, letter dated 12 January, 1912 to L. Lapointe.

15. *La Presse*, 12 April 1912.

16. In a letter dated 19 August, 2003.

17. See the article by Alan MacEachern, "Edward MacDonald's arctic diary, 1910-1911," *The Island Magazine*, fall/winter 1999, p. 30-40.

18. *Ibid.*

19. ANQ, B.R. Fonds.

20. *Ibid.*, letter dated 1 May 1912.

Chapter 15 • Laurier, the elder statesman

1. Martin Spigelman, *Wilfrid Laurier*. Don Mills ON: Fitzhenry & Whiteside, 1978, p. 47-48.

2. Sir Joseph Austen Chamberlain (1863-1937) was the British Chancellor of the Exchequer from 1903 until 1905 and from 1919 until 1921, as well as Foreign Secretary under Baldwin from 1924 until 1929. He received the Nobel Peace Prize in 1925.

3. Notably for nationalists such as Henri Bourassa (1868-1952).

4. Réal Bélanger, *Wilfrid Laurier, quand la politique devient passion*. Québec: Les Presses de l'Université Laval, 1986, p. 467.

Chapter 16 • The schooner *Minnie Maud*

1. In *Closing the front door of the Arctic: Capt. Joseph E. Bernier's Role in Canadian Arctic Sovereignty*, Season Osborne claims that Tremblay and Bernier were co owners of the schooner.

Alfred Tremblay never mentioned this fact in the various interviews he granted to journalists after receiving the Order of Canada in 1973. On page 2 of *Cruise of the Minnie Maud*, one finds "the schooner's owner" and not "owners," which would lead one to suppose that there was only one owner. Moreover the Alfred Tremblay Fonds at the ANQ contains no document that might prove his title as owner.

2. Yolande Dorion-Robitaille, *Captain J.E. Bernier's Contribution to Canadian Sovereignty in the Arctic*, p. 92.

3. As he confirmed in *Master Mariner*, p. 408.

4. The reality was that the majority of the Inuit who had had contact with Whites were already addicted to nicotine and counted on the whalers or on resupply ships for their daily dose of tobacco.

5. Claude Tessier, "Un explorateur méconnu de l'Arctique: Alfred Tremblay," *North/Nord*, May-June 1978, p. 46. See also *Le Toit du Monde*, Vol 1, No. 4, spring 2002, p. 28-31.

6. Archives of Carol and Louis Terrien, letter from Soeur Dominique du Rosaire of the Couvent des Soeurs dominicaines de l'Enfant-Jésus, dated 11 October 1926.

7. *Ibid.*, letter dated 11 December 1926 from l'Abbé F. Lemieux of Québec.

8. The stock-taking of the *Minnie Maud* took place on 6 October 1913, as is confirmed in Document No. 116, J.E. Bernier Fonds, ACL. It is not known what became of the schooner.

9. The book was published in 1921 by The Arctic Exchange & Publishing Ltd. of Québec, a company founded in September that year with the aim of financing polar expeditions, making films, and publishing books on the subject. Bernier was one of the five co-founders along with Alfred Tremblay and A.B. Reader, and also the vice-president. The account of the 1912-1913 expedition was their only end-product, since it exhausted their budget and the Federal Government refused to subsidize their other projects in the Arctic.

10. ANQ, Alfred Tremblay Fonds.

11. As mentioned by journalist Jane George in her article "Le patrimoine du Kapitaikallak," *Nunatsiaq News*, 2 November 2001, p. 17.

12. Alfred Tremblay and A.B. Reader, *Cruise of the Minnie Maud*. Québec: The Exchange and Publishing Ltd, 1921, p. 111.

13. *Ibid.*, p. 119.

14. *Ibid.*, p. 137.

15. *Ibid.*, p. 139.

16. *Arctic Justice*. Montréal: McGill-Queen's University Press, 2002, p. 61-62.

Chapitre 17 • The *Guide*

1. Fairley and Israel, *The True North, the Story of Captain Joseph Bernier*, p. 149. This anecdote surfaces in several sources, demonstrating the extent to which the captain's slightest gestures would become a real legend.

2. Yolande Dorion-Robitaille, *Captain J.-E. Bernier's Contribution to Canadian Sovereignty in the Arctic*, p. 105.

3. A. Haacks drowned when he travelled away from the ship to take photographs on some neighbouring islands. After numerous searches his frozen body was found 30 days later, 150 miles from the ship's wintering site.

4. At the National Film Archives, Ottawa.

5. Courtesy of Martin Caron, L'Islet-sur-Mer.

6. To learn more about the great adventure of this second cousin of Bernier's see the article by Magdeleine Bourget, "Un Caron chez les Inuit," in *L'Ancêtre*, Volume 29, summer 2003, p. 305-309. The man they called "Tit-Loup" lived with the Eskimo until 1920 and took a wife, named Panikpak. His descendants in Nunavut perpetuate his memory.

7. Henry Toke Munn, who owned this company, bought all the captain's properties in March 1919, then sold them to the Hudson's Bay Company in 1923.

8. *La Presse*, 14 April 1932.

9. *The Chronicle-Telegraph* of Québec, Wednesday 20 April 1932.

Chapter 18 • His war effort

1. *Master Mariner*, p. 127.

2. It was a happy marriage, even if short, since Cyrille Kirouac died five years later, in 1921. See the appendix for details of how the Kirouac children, including Brother Marie-Victorin, contested their father's will.

3. This conflict would end on 11 November 1918.

4. *Master Mariner*, p. 371.

5. *Ibid.*

6. *Ibid.*

7. ANQ, B.R. Fonds, letter dated 14 February 1918.

Chapter 19 • Women, oh women!

1. These two good friends were also brothers-in-law. Farley, a rich entrepreneur, had married Marie-Léda Lemieux, daughter of Désiré Walenstein Lemieux and Marie-Louise Élisé Arsenau. Esdras Terrien, co-founder of the newspaper *Le Droit*, had married another of the Lemieux sisters, Marie-Eva. See their genealogy in the appendix. All the information on this family comes from Louis, the son of Esdras Terrien.

2. Document No. 57711, before Mr. François-Xavier Couillard, notary of Lauzon, dated 15 October 1918.

3. *Ibid.* The captain agreed to pay "8,500 dollars," $4,000 in cash.

4. "La vie de Joseph-Elzéar Bernier," in *La Tribune* from Sherbrooke, 21 February 2000. As a child Marcel Lebœuf lived on the Rue Fraser, just opposite the captain's house.

5. Interview on 11 June 2002.

6. *Ibid.*

7. *Ibid.*

8. *D'un coup d'aile.* Saint-Romuald: Éditions Sans âge, 1999, p. 183-184. Bernier's last expedition took place in 1925, not 1924.

9. Private correspondence, 9 September 2002.

Chapter 20 • The Eastern Arctic Patrol

1. In 1912 the *Arctic* had returned to Hudson Bay with W.E. Jackson's scientific expedition, under the command of Captain Joseph Couillard of Québec. From 1913 onwards she was converted into Lightship No. 20, with the Transport Section of the Department of Marine. To learn more about the St. Lawrence light-ships see the article by Alain Franck in *L'Escale nautique,* No. 31, fall 2001, p. 5-7.

2. This was the Technical Advisory Board formed by the Department of the Interior.

3. Morris Zaslow presents these plans quite fully in: *The Northward Expansion of Canada, 1914-1967,* p. 21-21.

4. Letter found by Claude Minotto: LAC, RG 85, Vol. 583, files nos. 570-573; letter dated 20 June 1921.

5. Carol and Louis Terrien Archives.

6. Alfred Tremblay, Alexandre Bastien, Joseph-P. Béland and Francis-J. Petitclerc. The Alfred Tremblay Fonds at the ANQ contains a little information on this company, that was founded in 1921.

7. *Minotto,* p. 216.

8. Issued by W.W. Cory, Deputy Minister of the Interior and Commissioner for the Northwest Territories. Carol and Louis Terrien Archives.

9. The Department of Public Works had designed, for the occasion, prefabricated huts that were to be assembled on site.

10. See the list in the appendix.

11. Shelagh Grant, *Arctic Justice.* Montréal: McGill-Queen's University Press, 2002, p. 134.

12. Gordon Smith, "A bit of Bernier", *North/Nord,* Vol. 29, No. 2, summer 1982, p. 52-56.

13. Official report, 1908-1909, p. 317.

14. Letter dated 24 October 1922, Carol and Louis Terrien Archives. The *Arctic* had returned on 2 October, earlier than anticipated.

15. On the topic of the work of Major R.A. Logan, representing the Air Board on this expedition see: Frank. H. Ellis, "Arctic airfield survey," *The Beaver,* September 1945, p. 22-25.

Chapter 21 • White justice

1. Complete list in the appendix.

2. Testimony of Martin Caron of L'Islet-sur-Mer. Accoding to this former sailor, the First Officer was in charge forward, the Second Officer aft, while the Third Officer was amidships with the captain.

3. Magdeleine A. Bourget, "Un Caron chez les Inuit," *L'Ancêtre,* Vol. 29, summer 2003, p.308.

4. *Minotto,* p. 221.

5. Some writers, such as Shelagh Grant (*Arctic justice,* p. 156) claim that he came aboard at Rimouski a few days later, which would have been contrary to his normal pattern.

6. *L'Événement,* 10 July 1923. We are indebted for this source to Magdeleine Bourget, who was pursuing research into the life of her great-uncle, Wilfrid Caron.

7. Léonidas Lemieux, Albert Thériault, William George Earl, Eugène Blouin, Ludger Lemieux and Alfred Lévesque. All the details of the voyage and the travel were covered so well in the recent work by Shelagh Grant, *Arctic Justice,* that it is unnecessary to repeat them.

8. *Master Mariner,* p. 380.

9. *Arctic Justice,* p. 186.

Chapter 22 • Outmoded

1. "Farewell Voyages, Bernier and the Arctic," *The Beaver,* summer 1974, p. 44 to 54. Richard Finnie was so fascinated by the person of Bernier that he wrote articles about him for about 50 years.

2. From 5 July until 24 September 1924 and from 1 July until 10 October 1925.

3. "Farewell voyages…", p. 46-47. Richard (Dick) Finnie was the son of Oswald S. Finnie, Director of the Northwest Territories, who had used his influence to find him a spot on board the *Arctic.*

4. List in the appendix.

5. *Master Mariner,* p. 382-383.

6. It was important to show to the rest of the world that the Canadian administration was well established on Ellesmere Island. As Captain Bernier has explained (*Master Mariner,* p. 388-389), a post was established on Bache Peninsula the following year. As it represented the most northerly post office in Canada, it quickly became Santa Claus's official address. Every year thousands of letters addressed to Father Christmas had to be answered.

7. Initially this post bore the name "RCM Police, Bernier Detachment, North Devon.". When certain officials in Ottawa got wind of this they quickly renamed it "Dundas Harbour." It was close in 1933 and its buildings leased to the Hudson's Bay Company.

8. "Farewell voyages…", p. 49.

9. "The Captain Goes Ashore," *Canadian Magazine*, March 1935, p. 6 and 30. Harwood was the son of Sir Sam Steele, first commander of the Northwest Mounted Police.

10. "Farewell Voyages, Bernier and the Arctic", p. 49.

11. *Master Mariner*, p. 387.

12. LAC, George P. Mackenzie Fonds, diary entry for 15 August 1925.

13. A romanticized biography, published in 1957 and republished in 1964; p. 153-154. For the full story see: D.H. Dinwoodie, "Arctic Controversy: the 1925 Byrd-MacMillan Expedition Example," *The Canadian Historical Review* Vol. 53, No. 1, March 1972, p. 51-65.

14. Shelagh D. Grant, *Arctic Justice*, p. 207.

15. "The Captain goes ashore," p. 32.

Chapter 23 • The Arctic's sad fate.

1. In a letter dated 11 November 1924 (Carol and Louis Terrien Archives) J.D. Craig informed Bernier that the *Arctic* would not be used as headquarters for a scientific expedition, as they had discussed, but would be returned to the Department of Marine and Fisheries. Craig had become the official charged with arctic exploration at the Department of the Interior. He wrote: "there appears to be no further excuse for us retaining the ship and it has been decided to let them have her." It would appear that Bernier was captain of the *Franklin* for a certain time, before heading north with the *Arctic* in 1925.

2. This is confirmed in a letter from Angus Brabant to P.D. Stirling, head clerk with the Hudson's Bay Company in London, dated 9 December 1926 (Hudson's Bay Company Archives, Winnipeg) and in Richard Finnie's article "Farewell voyages, Bernier and the *Arctic*," p. 53-54.

3. ANQ, B.R. Fonds.

4. Of course Captain Bernier's transaction suited everyone: Bernier, who was saving his ship, the Hudson's Bay Company that did not have to disburse the costs of demolition, and the Government of Canada that was getting rid of a problem. One wonders why Bernier did not disclose anything in *Master Mariner*. On p. 389 he wrote: "She was sold to the ship-breakers who, however, found it too expensive to attempt to tear her to pieces, so well had she been put together. She now lies waiting for nobler uses."

5. *Peuple-Tribune*, 14 September 1977.

Chapter 24 • The book project

1. The *Ocean Eagle*, the *Ste. Anne* and the *Kennaquahair* sailed from Halifax on 4 September and completed their mission on 31 November 1927. (ACL, Bernier Fonds, Series "C", N-28).This document consists of an album of 342 photographs on life at Churchill while Series "B", N-125 contains Captain Bernier's journal from this expedition. The captain of the *Ocean Eagle* was William A. Pode. His log can be found at Series "B", N-11 Renamed *Aigle d'océan* in 1961, and owned by the Groupe Desgagnés this ship was wrecked on the Labrador coast in 1975.

2. Benoît Robitaille informed Season Osborne (*op. cit.*, p. 181) that conditions were so terrible off the Labrador coast that Bernier lost several boats and that several of his men narrowly missed losing their lives. There was an enquiry and Bernier was exonerated and congratulated for having led the convoy in a masterly fashion.

3. Carol and Louis Terrien Archives, letter dated 29 October 1928.

4. Yolande Dorion-Robitaille, *Captain J.-E. Bernier's Contribution to Canadian Sovereignty in the Arctic*, p. 107. It is important to note that the collection of her husband, Benoît Robitaille, deposited at the ANQ, includes a large number of documents assembled by Bernier on this subject.

5. For example: the stranding of the British steamer *General Milne* (1923), or of the S.S. *Manchester Civilian* (1926), the collision between the *St. Charles de la Malbaie* and the steamer *Miron-L.* (1926), between the S.S. *Hochelaga* and the S.S. *Leopold L.D.* (1926), or between the *Mariner's Joy* and *La Joshuée* (1932), as well as the accident involving the S.S. *Canadian* in Québec harbour (1932).

6. In a letter dated 20 October 1909 Rose had mentioned that he had forgotten to ask Laurier about it.

7. *Minotto*, p. 270-271.

8. Private archives.

9. ANQ, B.R. Fonds.

10. *Master Mariner and Arctic Explorer. A Narrative of Sixty Years at Sea from the Logs and Yarns of Captain J.E. Bernier* was published by *Le Droit* of Ottawa, five years after the captain's death. Esdras Terrien produced this publication, that combined both volumes that the captain had planned. Alma Lemieux financed it by selling certain lots in Montréal that she had inherited from her dead husband.

Chapter 25 • The desire to be recognized

1. *Minotto*, p. 271-272.

2. Cited by Gilberte Tremblay in *Bernier capitaine à 17 ans*, p. 10, and picked up by several newspapers, e.g. *Le Devoir*,

30 June 1959; *La Presse*, 9 September 1977; and the *Peuple-Tribune*, 14 September 1977.

3. Season Osborne, *Closing the Front Door of the Arctic: Capt. Joseph E. Bernier's Role in Canadian Arctic Sovereignty*, p. 187-188.

4. A title that was also bestowed on such eminent explorers as Parry, McClintock and Shackleton.

5. "In recognition of exploration carried out over a long term of years in Arctic waters." Captain Robert A. Bartlett of Newfoundland had also been awarded this honour in 1918.

6. Carol and Louis Terrien Archives.

7. *Ibid.* Note that R.B. Bennett (1870-1947) was Prime Minister from 1930 until 1935.

8. In a letter to Esdras Terrien, dated 1 July 1939, Alma Lemieux stated that she had made two trips to Europe with her husband, the first during the winter of 1922-23 and the second in September 1933 to go to see the Pope in Rome. ANQ, B.R. Fonds.

9. Article in *Le Droit*, 3 January 1935, reproduced as an appendix to *Les mémoires de J.E. Bernier, le dernier des grands capitaine*, by Paul Terrien. Montré*al:* Quinze, 1983.

Chapter 26 • The last great voyage

1. "Le capitaine Bernier a fait 483,660 milles sur la mer", *Le Droit*, 1925.

2. "He has Added Half a Million Square Miles to Canada," *The Canadian Magazine*, February 1927.

3. Alma contributed to the account of his death in *Master Mariner*, p. 406.

4. Esdras Terrien, "Le Capitaine Bernier", *Le Droit*, 3 January 1935.

5. A youthful memory on the part of the former Federal Member of Parliament for Montmagny-L'Islet, Louis Fortin, that he recalled during his presentation on 2 July 1960 on the occasion of the tricentennial celebrations of the Berniers of America.

6. Gilberte Tremblay, *op. cit.*, p. 120.

7. A remark by Simone Dion.

Chapter 27 • The mausoleum

1. Will signed in the presence of Mr. Joseph G. Couture on 6 May 1930. Carol and Louis Terrien Archives.

2. "Projet de monument à la mémoire de J.-E. Bernier," *Le Soleil*, 23 November 1983.

3. *Peuple-Tribune*, 19 June 1984.

Chapter 28 • The house on the Rue Fraser

1. Testimony of Esdras Terrien, *Le Devoir*, 3 January 1935.

2. Simone moved into the Bernier house three months after the captain died, in March 1935, and remained there until her marriage to Philippe Dion in 1944. These remarks were recorded in June 2002.

3. Louis is the son of Marie-Eva Lemieux and Esdras Terrien. Interviewed on 10 November 2001 in Ottawa.

4. *Ibid.*

5. From the Land Titles Office for the city of Lévis. Captain Bernier's house had already been demolished by the time of this transaction.

6. This is the property that Roger Héroux *et al.* sold to Mohammed Wafa Nazhi Nached on 2 December 1997, registration no. 421989.

Chapter 29 • Bernier's legacy.

1. Newspaper article, early June 1962; source unknown.

2. Letter dated 2 November 2002. Monsieur Caron served as a seaman on board the icebreakers *C.D. Howe* and *d'Iberville*. He was one of the co-founders of l'Association des marins de la Côte-du-Sud which established the Musée maritime Bernier in 1968. He was expressing the wish that the contribution of Curate Mercier, the cooperation of well-wishers from the area and "the long hours of work that had to be put in to build an establishment of this nature" would not be forgotten.

3. Michel Sacco, "Réal Bouvier, navigateur et journaliste," *L'Escale nautique*, No. 24, winter 2000, p. 4. Réal Bouvier died during the summer of 2000.

4. "Gageons que Joseph-Elzéar est bien content," *La Presse*, 9 September 1977.

5. Marcel Pépin, "L'histoire sommeille sous la pierre," *North/Nord*, May/June 1978, p. 17-19. Captain Saint-Pierre found his first message left by Bernier on 28 August 1977 at 14.45.

6. P. 5.

7. Roger Lemelin, "The Master Mariner." In: *Great Canadians. A century of Achievement.* Toronto: McClelland and Stewart, 1965, p. 31-34.

8. Pierre Berton. "Introduction." In : *Great Canadians. A century of Achievement.* Toronto: McClelland and Stewart, 1965, p. 12.

9. The technical details for this ship can be found on the Coast Guard's web-site. The icebreaker made transits of the Northwest Passage in 1976 and 1980. Late in 2000 she was still in service between Halifax, her home port, and Newfoundland.

10. For more detail on this ship see: Ken Webb, "A ship for all seasons," *North/Nord*, Vol. 25, No. 3, May/June 1978, p. 20-27.

11. "Dans le sillage du capitaine Joseph-Elzéar Bernier," *Le Toit du monde*, Vol. 1, No. 1, spring 2001, p. 16-20.

12. Mélanie Saint-Hilaire, "Ilititaa petit navire," *L'Actualité*, 1 May 2002, p. 53-54.

Conclusion

1. *Minotto*, p. 263. Claude Minotto recently admitted to Season Osborne that the person of Bernier had a strong hold on him and that, twenty-eight years after completing his Master's thesis on him, the captain was still in his thoughts.

2. *Ibid.*, p. 293.

3. A remark by Jeanne Coudé. This retired antique dealer, with a passion for local heritage (she has been called the "saviour" of Lévis) and a member of the *Société d'histoire de Lévis*, refuses to be discouraged and continues to knock on the doors of politicians to realize her next dream: a gigantic statue of Captain Bernier, pointing toward the Arctic.

Appendices

1. Robert Rumilly, *Le frère Marie-Victorin et son temps.* Montréal: Les Frères des Écoles chrétiennes, 1949, p. 3.

2. *D'un coup d'aile,* p. 71.

3. Captain Bernier's visitors' book, in the collection of Suzanne Normandeau, at the chalet on the island on Lac Trois-Saumons.

4. Reproduced in the article by Stéphane Cloutier "À la rencontre des deux mondes," *Le Toit du monde,* Vol. 1, No. 2, Autumn 2001, p. 36.

5. Interview with Jean-Pierre Lemieux, 15 July 1971.

APPENDICES

I. Chronology

Locations where Captain Bernier celebrated his birthday

Year	Location
1852	Born 1 January, 18.00, L'Islet-sur-Mer
1853-1854	L'Islet-sur-Mer
1855	Cardenas, Cuba
1856-1867	L'Islet-sur-Mer
1868	At sea, 26° 52'N; 63° 39'W
1869	At sea, within sight of Mount Desert, United States
1870	At sea, 24° 52'N; 89° 26'W
1871	Liverpool, England, on board the *Saint-Michel*
1872	At sea, 24° 27'N; 59° 16'W
1873-1876	L'Islet-sur-Mer
1877	Liverpool, England
1878	Glasgow, Scotland
1879	Liverpool, England
1880	Torbay, English Channel, on board the *Cambria*
1881	Liverpool, England
1882	Deal, Kent, England, on board the *Royal Visitor*
1883	Moulmein, Burma, on board the *Lancashire*
1884	A hotel, Mobile, Alabama
1885	Québec
1886	At sea, 24° 18'S; 85° 10'W
1887	His mother's house, Québec
1888-1890	Saint-Joseph de Lévis (Lauzon)
1891	At sea, 34° 15'S; 71° 26'W
1892	Villa Bernier, Saint-Joseph de Lévis
1893	Baltimore, Maryland
1894	Québec
1895	Montréal
1896-1898	Québec prison, as director
1899	Québec
1900	Newfoundland, on board the *Scottish King*
1901-1902	London, England
1903	Ottawa
1904	Montréal
1905	Fullerton, Hudson Bay
1906	Albert Harbour, Baffin Island
1907	Pond Inlet, Eclipse Sound
1908	Winter Harbour, Melville Island
1909	In the Arctic Archipelago
1910	Arctic Bay, Admiralty Inlet
1911	Albert Harbour, Baffin Island
1912	Ottawa
1913	Pond Inlet, on board the *Minnie Maud*
1914	Saint-Joseph de Lévis
1915	Salmon River, Pond Inlet
1916	Saint-Joseph de Lévis
1917	Pond Inlet, Eclipse Sound
1918	Halifax
1919-1922	Ottawa
1923	At sea, on board the *Minedosa*
1924	Lévis, the house on Rue Fraser
1925	His brother's house, Montréal
1926	Ottawa
1927-1928	At home, Lévis
1929-1931	Ottawa
1932	Bermuda
1933	Ottawa
1934	Lévis

II. Genealogy

Family of Marie-Célina Henriette Paradis, Captain Bernier's mother

Father: Étienne Paradis, carpenter,
born around 1787 died 1870,
son of Jean-Baptiste Paradis and Agathe Côté

*

Mother: Marie-Olivette (or Olivier) Chamberland,
born 9 February 1795 died April 1839,
daughter of Jean-Baptiste Chamberland and Catherine Bittner

*

married 28 January 1817 in Notre-Dame-de-la-Miséricorde church, Beauport

*

Children: Marie-Émilie Marguerite,
born 19 August 1818, Québec,
died 29 April 1869, L'Islet-sur-Mer;
married Jean-Baptiste Bernier, 19 November 1839 in Saint-Roch church, Québec

*

Étienne,
born 2 September 1821, Québec,
died 28 August 1822, Québec

*

Pierre-Édouard,
born 28 June 1823, Québec,
date of death unknown

*

Alexis-Adolphe (or Alexis-Delphis),
born 29 August 1825, Québec,
died 28 January 1830, Québec

*

Narcisse,
born 17 September 1827, Québec,
died 19 July 1906, Québec
married 1) Angèle Delâge, 5 July 1853, Saint-Roch church, and 2) Adéline Lafond, 26 June 1893, Saint-Roch church

*

Napoléon,
born 8 July 1829, Québec,
died 2 January 1830, Québec

*

Étienne-Hector
born 25 November 1830, Québec
died 10 August 1831, Québec

*

Marie-Célina Henriette,
born 12 September 1832, Québec
died 17 April 1906, Hôpital Maisonneuve, Montréal,
buried at Lauzon.
Married **Thomas Bernier**, 19 November 1850, Saint-Roch church

III. Genealogy

Genealogical table for Captain Bernier's first wife Rose-de-Lima Caron

Ancestors: Robert and Marguerite Crenel-Crevet
m. Notre-Dame-de-Québec, 25 October 1637

*

Robert and Marguerite Cloutier
m. Château Richer, 14 November 1674

*

Joseph and Madeleine Bernier
m. Cap-Saint-Ignace, 27 February 1713

*

Joseph and Marie-Élisabeth Lemieux
m. L'Islet-sur-Mer, 15 February 1735

*

Joseph-Hyacinthe and Élisabeth Ursule Boucher
m. L'Islet-sur-Mer, 15 January 1770

*

Louis-Marie (Louison) and Marie-Geneviève Scholastique Couillard des Écores
m. Saint-Jean-Port-Joli, 3 January 1808

*

Father: Louis-Marie (dit Grand Louis) (1812-1900) first married Appolline St-Pierre, L'Islet-sur-Mer, 25 February 1840

*

Half-brothers: Louis-Stanislas (Arthur), born 28 December 1841, died Wisconsin, 1900,
and Joseph-Enselme (Eusèbe) (1843-1930),
m. to Émilie Caron, Saint-Jean-Port-Joli, around 1865

*

Mother: Marie-Priscilla Fournier,
daughter of Joseph and Marie-Victoire Fortin,
m. Saint-Jean-Port-Joli, 30 June 1801

*

Priscilla married Louis-Marie
at Saint-Jean-Port-Joli,
5 July 1850

*

Sister: Marie (birth and death dates unknown),
m. Philias Morin, L'Islet-sur-Mer,
30 September 1873

*

Rose-de-Lima, born 16 January 1855,
died 18 April 1917,
m. **Joseph-Elzéar Bernier**, L'Islet-sur-Mer,
8 November 1870

The grave-stone of Rose's parents, Louis-Marie Caron and Priscilla Fournier, in the old section of the L'Islet-sur-Mer cemetery. [Photo: Lynn Fournier].

IV. Elmina (Mina) Caron, adopted daughter of Rose Caron and Captain Bernier

Family tree (Caron side):

Joseph and Marie Françoise Saucier
m. Saint-Roch-des-Aulnaies, 17 July 1742

*

Jean-Baptiste and Madeleine Pelletier
m. Saint-Roch-des Aulnaies, 5 February 1781

*

Louis and Marceline Dion
m. Saint-Roch-des-Aulnaies, 17 February 1829

*

Louis-Joseph, 1840-1899

Family tree (Boucher side):

Jean-Baptiste and Marie-Josette Cloutier
m. Berthier, 4 August 1755

*

Guillaume and Madeleine Blais
m. Berthier, 10 August 1802

*

Jean-Baptiste and Rosalie Bernier,
daughter of Jean-Baptiste Bernier and Geneviève LeBourdais,
m. L'Islet-sur-Mer, 10 January 1833

The Boucher children:

1. Rosalie (Rose), 1833-1924
   m. Étienne-Vincent Couillard, 1857
2. Jean-Baptiste, 1834-1834
3. Séraphine, 1835-?
   m. Edouard Bernier, 1857
4. anonymous, 1837-1837
5. Achille, 1838-?
   m. Elmire Pelletier, 1859
6. Émilie-Dorothée, 1840-?
   m. Godefroi Létourneau, 1857
7. Philomène, 1844-14 June 1937
   m. François Dion (?-1864), 1862

Parents: Louis-Joseph Caron and Philomène Boucher
m. L'Islet-sur-Mer, 27 December 1866

Siblings:

1. Rosalie, 1867-1867
2. Marie-Zélie, 1868-1871
3. Marie-Hélène, 1870-1952
   m. Joseph Bernier, 1892
4. Gratieuse, 1872-?
   m. Damasse Caron, 1906
5. Jean-Ernest, 1874-1956
   m. Marie-Esther Rousseau, 1903
   m. Alice Parent, 1918 (died 1927)
   m. Eugénie Dion (1890-1963), 1928
6. **Marie-Elmina Clémence**, 1875-1972
   m. J.-Odilon Bourget (1868-1904), 1894
   m. Cyrille Kirouac (1863-1921), 1916
7. Marie-Belzémire, 1877-1950
   m. Félix Lemieux, 1904 (died 1956)
8. Georges, 1878-1879
9. Marie-Rosalie, 1879-1976
   m. J.E. Alfred Samson, 1903 (drowned 1927)
10. Marie-Cécile, 1881-1970
    m. Jean-Philippe Bélanger, 1911
    m. Jean-Étienne Samson, 1927
11. Marie-Anna, 1882-?
    m. Alfred (Freddy) Nicole, 1903
    m. Jean-Albert Dionne, ?
12. Wilfrid Clément, 1887-1923
    m. the Inuk Panikpak, ?
    m. Marie-Anne Rachel Faguy, 1923

First marriage:
Elmina married **Joseph-Odilon Bourget**, son of the late André Bourget and Célina Turgeon on 10 January 1894 at the Saint-Joseph de Lauzon church. Witnesses were Onésime Bourget, civil servant and brother of the groom, and Captain Joseph-Elzéar Bernier "relative and guardian of the bride."

Dr. Bourget was a young man of good family who had studied at the Collège de Lévis from 1882 to 1888 and at the Faculty of Medicine, Université Laval until 1893.

For the first two years of their marriage the couple probably lived with "Aunt" Rose and Captain Bernier until they rented a house on Rue Saint-Joseph, Lauzon, from 1896 till 1904. Odilon replaced Dr. A.A. Marsan as Officer of Health for Lauzon between 1901 and 1903. We know that this work was very demanding and that Elmina liked to accompany him on his extensive travels. "My grandmother Mina was very sociable," Suzanne Normandeau recalled. "She would spend time with people and calmed them while her husband was delivering babies or caring for the sick."

Theirs was quite a short marriage since Dr. Bourget died on 10 November 1904, following a kidney infection and a heart attack. He was buried in the Mont-Marie Cemetery in Lauzon.

Children:

1. Marie-Jeanne (or Rose Elmina)
   born 13 November 1894, at Lauzon,
   godparents: J.E. Bernier and Rose Caron,
   nun at Jésus-Marie de Sillery, for about two years,
   m. Robert Belleau, 25 November 1928, Saint-Sauveur church, Québec,
   died Québec, 18 January 1977
2. Marie-Antoine
   born 2 May 1896, Lauzon,
   godparents: Onésime André Marchand and Rose de Lima Samson,
   died 11 June 1896 and buried in Mont-Marie Cemetery in Lauzon
3. Marie-Marthe
   born 16 May 1897, Lauzon,
   godparents: Joseph Caron and Philomène Boucher,
   m. notary Joseph-Antoine Audet, 25 January 1922, Saint-Sauveur. church, Québec.
   They had eight children.
   died October 1978 and buried in Mont-Marie Cemetery, Lauzon
4. Marie-Albert
   born 27 February 1899, Lauzon
   godparents: L. Caron and Marie-Belzémire Caron,
   studied at Collège de Lévis, 1910-1919,
   Diploma in Forestry Engineering, Université Laval, 1924,
   studied in Sweden and France,
   then joined forestry engineering company, Bélanger, Savard and Bourget,
   Professor of Sylviculture at Laval,
   m. Catherine Lavigueur, 27 April 1927, Québec
   died 19 December 1966, buried in Belmont Cemetery
5. Marie-Reine
   born 16 March 1901, Lauzon
   godparents: Joseph Bernier and Hélène Caron.
   remained single and lived with her mother, Elmina
   died 10 February 1994, Québec, buried in the Audet plot, Mont-Marie Cemetery, Lauzon
6. Marie-Gabriella (or Philomène-Fabienne)
   born 7 February 1903, Lauzon
   godparents: Aimé Bourget and Marie Ruel
   died a month later, 3 March, Lauzon

On her husband's death Elmina became owner of the house on Rue Saint-Joseph and lived there until 1916 when she remarried.

Second marriage:
On 24 October 1916 Elmina married **Cyrille Kirouac** (son of François Kirouac and Marie-Julie Hamel) at the Saint-Joseph de Lauzon church. Witnesses were Alfred Samson and François Kirouac.

Cyrille Kirouac's first wife was Philomène Luneau (daughter of Norbert Luneau, farmer, and Mélodie Audibert); they were married on 29 August 1882. The Kirouac couple established a business at Kingsey Falls in the Eastern Townships, and had numerous children, several of whom died at an early age.

Elmina (Mina) Caron in the autumn of her life. [Courtesy of Michelle Audet]

Cyrille Kirouac left the Eastern Townships to settle in Québec shortly after the birth of Conrad (their only son, born on 3 April 1885). He had a flourishing grain and flour business with a

Cyrille Kirouac, Philomène Luneau, and their six children in 1904. The nun sitting between the married couple is Adelcie, Sister Marie-des-Anges, who became the head of the convent of the Jésus-Marie congregation in Sillery. Conrad, seated at the extreme right, had joined the Brothers of the Christian Schools in 1901. He was Brother Marie-Victorin, botanist, writer and founder of the Botanical Gardens in Montreal (1939).
[R. Rumilly, *Le frère Marie-Victorin et son temps,* 1949]

> warehouse in the Lower Town. He became one of the affluent citizens of Saint-Sauveur. He was respected for his social standing and for his manners, but loved for his good humour and his taste for life. The Kirouacs lived in a large, comfortable house on the Rue Saint-Vallier.[1]

Cyrille Kirouac became a widower in 1915. A year later Elmina came into his life and moved into his fine house in Saint-Sauveur. Theirs was a very happy marriage, despite its shortness. On Cyrille Kirouac's death in 1921 his children contested the will, which left a summer house at L'Ancienne Lorette, as well as other properties and quite a large sum, to his second wife. The Kirouac children won their case. However this family inheritance allowed Conrad, Brother Marie-Victorin, to pay for the major part of his numerous botanical research trips around the world. Brother Marie-Victorin founded the Botanical Gardens of Montréal.

Elmina lost the properties, but she was granted a substantial annuity that allowed her to live at Saint-Sauveur for the rest of her life and to take care of her mother, Philomène, and her sister Marie-Reine.

Her granddaughter, Michelle Audet, has described her as follows:

> My grandmother, Almina, an engaging woman, displayed great wisdom beneath a playful manner; her small, blue, laughing eyes, as round as pearls, flaunted mischievousness. With a mother-of-pearl complexion, short, ash-grey, wavy hair, and fine ankles, my grandmother knew how to present herself elegantly even in the simplest attire. According to others Almina inspired respect and fondness.[2]

Despite the fact that she had a leg amputated at the age of 95 Mina remained energetic, proud and interested in life around her. She expired gently, without regrets on 28 November 1972 while sewing up lace for her little cushions.

The paradise at Lac Trois-Saumons:

In 1902 Captain Bernier negotiated a rental of Île Saint-Pierre on Lac Trois-Saumons for a term of 40 years. Not only was it located near his native village but it was also a paradise for hunting jackrabbits and partridges, and for trout fishing. Around 1906, with the help of friends and relatives from L'Islet, he built a camp which he called "Au Paradis," and settled his adopted daughter, the widow of Dr. Bourget, and her four children there.

The captain continued to visit the spot even after Rose's death. On 22 May 1920 he wrote in the chalet's visitors' book:

> I, the undersigned, declare that the fishing season is open and that the said camp "Au Paradis" is open to all those interested in this camp, on condition that everyone knows its history.
> The first person arrived at 2 p.m., today.
> Second to arrive was J.F. Lemieux of the city of Québec. Since he had to travel a great distance, I declare that he deserves to be considered the true first arrival.
> Signed: Cap. .E. Bernier, from overseas.[3]

Next day, Sunday 23 May, Mina's sister, Marie-Anna, wrote in the same visitors' book:

> It is a new pleasure for me to be able to write a few lines in this book: Having left Montmagny with my guest, Mrs. Capt. J.E. Bernier of Lévis, we spent the night with Mother at L'Islet, and after going to Mass we decided to start for the Lake. Le Paradis is open. The owner of the chalet was here; along with one of our citizens, Mr. J.F. Lemieux. We gave them a surprise; as our guide we have a happy "Eskimo," our "Ti-loup" Wilfrid. Our dear traveller from far away who is spending his last Sunday for 18 months among his own folk here; may he retain good memories of his outing!...
>
> Signed: Mme. (Marie-Anna) Frédy Nicole and Wilfrid C. Caron.[4]

The modern version of Captain Bernier's former chalet on Lac Trois-Saumons. It still bears the name "Au Paradis." [Photo: Lynn Fournier]

This entry reveals that the Captain's second wife, Alma Lemieux had occasion to visit the island on Lac Trois-Saumons and that despite the fact that he had fallen out with Mina Bernier had kept contact with the other members of her family.

When interviewed by a journalist from *Le Peuple*, a year before her death, Elmina, who had become the *doyenne* of the Lac Trois-Saumons residents' club, recalled her visits in summer, accompanied by her adoptive father:

> We arrived at L'Islet by the express train. We got off at Mrs. Édouard Caron's at Trois-Saumons. It was a sort of rest-stop; she invited us to take a rest. We left our city clothes there and in the meantime Mr. Caron was harnessing the carriage. We had to take supplies for three weeks [...]
>
> For me life was wonderful, and it was even more wonderful because I was surrounded by family. What children I had were all around me. I can't say that I was unhappy.[5]

It is impossible to know whether the Captain sold or surrendered his lease and his chalet to Elmina before he died, since his will makes no mention of this property. In 1942 when the lease expired one of Elmina's brothers-in-law, Joseph Bernier, husband of her sister Marie-Hélène, decided to buy the island so that it would remain in the family. Subsequently Antoine Audet, Martha's husband, and Albert Bourget became joint-owners; this explains why down to the present the island, which has acquired the name Audet, remains the property of Elmina's grandchildren and 32 great-grandchildren . Thanks to them the memory of the "man of the Far North" still remains palpable in this paradise, isolated from the rest of the world. The faded photos in the family albums, the worn polar bear skin that has stood guard in front of the fireplace for over 90 years, and the stories inscribed in the visitors' book still recall his life in this, his favourite place.

The descendants of Elmina Caron (Québec) and those of Wilfrid Caron (Nunavut) pose in front of Captain Bernier's former chalet on Lac Trois-Saumons, during a reunion of the "two worlds" in July 2001. [Photo: Stéphane Cloutier, *Nunatsiaq News,* 2 November 2001]

V. Genealogy

Family tree of Marie-Alma Lemieux, Captain Bernier's second wife

Father's side/Lemieux

Pierre (son of Pierre and Marie Lugan, Normandy) &Marie Bénard (daughter of Denis and Marie Michelet, Île-de-France) m. Québec, 10 October 1647

Louis and Marie-Madeleine Côté (daughter of Louis and Élisabeth Langlois) m. Cap-Saint-Ignace, 26 November 1682

Louis and Geneviève Fortin (daughter of Charles and Sainte Cloutier) m. L'Islet-sur-Mer, 11 February 1705

Augustin and Catherine Brisson (daughter of Jean and Catherine Dancosse) m. Saint-Roch-des-Aulnaies, 14 November 1734

Louis-Augustin and Monique Bernier (daughter of Jean-Baptiste and Claire Fortin) m. L'Islet-sur-Mer, 19 January 1761

François-Xavier and Constance Gaudreau (daughter of Jérôme and Élisa Minville) m. L'Islet-sur-Mer, 23 November 1802

Noël and Marie-Julie Pelletier (daughter of Jean-Baptiste and J. Des Trois Maisons) m. Saint-Roch-des-Aulnaies, 14 February 1831

Désiré J. Walenstein (father), married first to Virginie Kyrion, Percé, 26 October 1863

Mother's side/ Gareau dit Arseneau

Mathurin and Julienne Masson, m. Nantes, Brittany

René and Marie-Anne Rivière (daughter of Jean-René and Marie-Françoise Dielle) m. Saint-Anne-de-Bellevue, 21 May 1759

François and Ursule Sabourin (daughter of Louis and J. Dubois) m. Vaudreuil, 11 January 1808

François-Xavier and Adélaïde Bessner (Besener dit Prêt-à-boire) m. Coteau-du-Lac, 16 October 1838

Marie-Louise-Élisé or Élize (mother), 1847-1931

Parents

- Désiré Walenstein, widower of Virginie Kyrion m.Marie-Louise-Élisé, Notre Dame church, Ottawa, 24 November 1872

Lemieux children

- Marie-Léda, m. Arthur H. Farley (son of Richard and S. Gagné), Sacré-Coeur, Ottawa, 8 August 1911
- Marie-Délia, m. Henri Routhier (son of Zotique and M. Proulx) Notre-Dame, Ottawa, 16 November 1897
- Marie-Louise, 1st marriage, Alfred Brûlé (son of Thomas and Emma Loyer), Notre-Dame, Ottawa, 9 May 1895; 2nd marriage, V.E. Martel from Montréal (place and date unknown)
- **Marie-Alma Julie Albertine** (1879-1961) m. Captain Joseph-Elzéar Bernier (son of Thomas and Célina Paradis) Notre-Dame, Ottawa, 1 July 1919
- Marie-Eva, m. Esdras Terrien (son of Hercule and Louise Provencher) Notre-Dame, Ottawa, 29 June 1909
- Marie-Dona, m. Raoul Bélanger (?) (they lived in Vancouver)
- Ludger (no information except that he was killed in a vehicle accident, Miami, 1934)
- Élizé (no information except that he was Ottawa's Fire Chief)

VI. List of ships commanded, built, or refitted by Captain Bernier

Brigantines
1. *Saint-Joseph*
2. *Saint-Michel*
3. *Salinas*

SCHOONERS
4. *Jeannette*
5. *Mary, Queen of the Seas*
6. *Vigie*
7. *Minnie Maud*

Dredges
8. *Hector*
9. *Saint-Joseph*
10. *International*
11. *Hudson Bay*

Lighters

12, 13, 14. government lighters

15. *H.B. Large*

Tugs
16. *Beaver*
17. *Storm King*
18. *Eureka*
19. *Hallenback* (New York)
20. *Petrel*
21. *Ocean Eagle*

Barques
22. *Success*
23. *Yuba*
24. *Octavie*
25. *Neptune*
26. *Tarifa*
27. *Signet*
28. *Queen's Cliff*
29. *Lady Fletcher*
30. *Concordia*
31. *Supreme*
32. *Felicitas*
33. *Roma*
34. *Veritas*
35. *Cambria*
36. *Underwriter*
37. *Romania*
38. *Royal Tar*
39. *Onita*
40. *Tivoli*
41. *Wadina* (twice)
42. *Modern*

Yachts
43. *Célina*
44. *Alma*
45. *Alcido*
46. *Comanche*
47. *Vacuna*
48. *Dona*
49. *Yola*
50. *Vesta*
51. *Esperenza*
52. *Inquirer*
53. *Rapidan*
54. *Wapiti*
55. *Peerless*
56. *Elma*

Boats and auxiliary steamers
57. *Carolina*
58. *Northern*
59. *Southern*
60. *Thames*
61. *Hartford*
62. *Columbia*
63. *Lilac*
64. *Lake Ontario*
65. *Scottish King*
66. *Gauss*
67. *Arctic*
68. *Titania*
69. *Polynesian*
70. *Norse King*
71. *Deddington*
72. *Lake Huron*
73. *Canopus*
74. *Panama*
75. *Bratsburg*
76. *Thornholm*
77. *Alcides*
78. *Fr. Bouvet*
79. *Percesien*
80. *Guide*
81. *Labrador*
82. *Lady Evelyn*
83. *Champlain*
84. *Cerro Gardo*
85. *Cragsmore*
86. *Cathoon*
87. *Canonsburg*
88. *Ellerslie*
89. *Fansdale*
90. *Fighart*
91. *Gebhard*
92. *Saguenay*
93. *Canada*
94. *Québec*
95. *Montréal*
96. *Trois-Rivières*
97. *Berthier*
98. *Algerian*
99. *Passport*
100. *Corinthian*
101. *Corsican*
102. *Spartan*
103. *Finbar*
104. *Franklin*
105. *Saritonio*
106. *Okuchobee*

Square-rigged ships
107. *Quorn*
108. *Germanic*
109. *Dominion*
110. *Lanarkshire*
111. *Royal Visitor*
112. *Scottish Hill*

VII. Crew members

***Arctic's* Hudson Bay Expedition, 1904-1905**
J.-E. BERNIER, Captain
Alfred BERNIER, First Officer, as far as Sydney
George BERG, First Officer
Octave-Jules MORIN, Second Officer
M.S. FLOOD, Doctor
Fabien VANASSE, chronicler
Frank D. McKEAN, artist and photographer
W.H. WEEKS, purser
J.D. MOODIE, Commander, NWMP
Alex MOODIE, secretary
Geraldine MOODIE
Albert PELTIER, Captain, NWMP
H.E. HAYE, Sergeant, NWMP
D. McARTHUR, Corporal, NWMP
J.D. NICHOLSON, Corporal, NWMP
F.E. HEYES, Constable, NWMP
C. McMILLAN, Constable, NWMP
J. BUNCH*, Constable, NWMP
H. VERITY, Constable, NWMP
A. STATHERT, Constable, NWMP
L.E. SELLES, Constable, NWMP
Joseph LEMIEUX, Chief Engineer
John Van KOËNIG, Second Engineer
E. CRAGLE, electrician
J.-U. LEMIEUX, oiler
Achille RACINE, oiler
Paul MERCIER, stoker
Frederick PECK stoker
Joseph THIBAULT, cook
J. ALBERT, cook's assistant
C.L. MURRAY, steward
Paul LEVASSEUR, assistant steward
George NORMAND, waiter
John WARD, waiter
Joseph FRANCOEUR, cabin-boy
George KENNEDY, carpenter
M. MURPHY, boatswain
Joseph-George LESSARD, seaman
B. PERRINE, seaman
John CONWAY, seaman
Luke EVAN, seaman
Sylvester CAIN, seaman
Thomas WALSH, seaman
John CONNERS, seaman
Styvens SMALLCOMBE, seaman
James HEARN, seaman
Beny KELLERID, seaman
Gandoire FORTIN, seaman

* Drowned at Fullerton, 5 July 1905.

***Arctic's* expedition, 1906-1907**
J.-E. BERNIER, Captain
Georges HAYES, First Officer
Octave-Jules MORIN, Second Officer
Charles W. GREEN, Third Officer
Joseph-R. PÉPIN, Doctor
Fabien VANASSE, chronicler
James DUNCAN, Customs Officer
J.A. SIMPSON, Customs clerk
George R. LANCEFIELD, photographer
W.H. WEEKS, purser
John Van KOËNIG, Chief Engineer
Émile BOLDUC, Second Engineer
Ernest CROTEAU, electrician

Paul MERCIER, oiler
Frederick BROCKENHENSER*, oiler
Ulric BÉGIN, stoker
Ernest LAHAYE, stoker
Louis BERNIER, stoker
Joseph THIBAULT, cook
Louis BEAULIEU, cook's assistant
Paul LEVASSEUR, steward
Napoléon STREMENSKI, assistant steward
Harry CHARRON, waiter
Alexandre PATENAUDE, waiter
Hervé PERRON, waiter
Louis JEFFREY, cabin boy
Michael RYAN, carpenter
William ROSS, boatswain
Benjamin TAVERNER, boatswain
Joseph-Georges LESSARD, quartermaster
Napoléon CHASSÉ, assistant quartermaster
Thomas DOYLE, seaman
William COADY, seaman
Sylvester CAIN, seaman,
Ruben PIKE, seaman
Thomas FRAIZE, seaman
James HEARN, seaman
Richard BARRON, seaman
James RYAN, seaman
George A.BÖDEKER, seaman
Joseph GOULET, laundryman

***Arctic's* expedition 1908-1909**
J.-E. BERNIER, Captain
Georges BRAITHWAITE, First Officer
Octave-Jules MORIN, Second Officer
Charles W. GREEN, Third Officer
Joseph-Étienne BOLDUC, Doctor
Fabien VANASSE, chronicler
W.E. JACKSON, meteorologist
J.G. McMILLAN, geologist
Franck HENNESSEY, naturalist
W.H. WEEKS, purser
John Van KOËNIG, Chief Engineer
Émile BOLDUC, Second Engineer
Ernest LAHAYE, oiler
Alfred BOURGET, oiler
Georges GOSSELIN, stoker

* Died of a heart attack and buried at Albert Harbour.

D. ROBINSON, stoker
Joseph (Johnny) LECLERC, stoker
I. BÉGIN, cook
Wilfrid VAILLANCOURT, cook's assistant
Joseph THIBAULT, purser and steward
O. ROBITAILLE, assistant steward
Reuben PIKE, waiter
Joseph-R. GOULET, waiter
Gédéon GAGNÉ, carpenter
William JOHNSON, boatswain
Joseph-Georges LESSARD, quartermaster
Napoléon CHASSÉ, quartermaster
Arthur DESJARDINS, quartermaster
Claude VIGNEAU, quartermaster
Thomas HOLDEN, seaman
Thomas WHITE, seaman
Daniel LANE, seaman
Sven ANDERSON, seaman
William LeBEL, seaman
Alphé BOUCHARD, seaman
T.W. BURK, seaman
John SIMMS, seaman
William Dan DOYLE, seaman
Henry WAKEHAM, seaman
George A. BÖDEKER, seaman
James BRACE, seaman
Louis WISTLE, seaman
Paul TREMBLAY, seaman

***Arctic's* expedition 1910-1911**
J.-E. BERNIER, Captain
Octave-Jules MORIN, First Officer
Robert S. JANES, Second Officer
Edouard MacDONALD, Third Officer
Joseph-Étienne BOLDUC, Doctor
Fabien VANASSE, chronicler
J.T.E. LAVOIE, meteorologist
Arthur ENGLISH, prospector and taxidermist
John VAN KOËNIG, Chief Engineer
Émile BOLDUC, Second Engineer
Paul MERCIER, oiler
Aurélien LEGENDRE, oiler
Albert NOLET, oiler
Auguste VÉZINA, oiler
Johnny LECLERC, stoker
Napoléon GARANT, stoker
Philip C.F. REYNOLDS, cook

Louis BEAULIEU, assistant cook
Joseph THIBAULT, purser and steward
Joseph-Eugène MATHÉ, assistant steward
Benoît CHARTRAND, waiter
Paul TREMBLAY, waiter
Napoléon NORMAND, carpenter
Napoléon CHASSÉ, boatswain
Thomas HOLDEN, boatswain
Joseph-George LESSARD, quartermaster
Alphé BOUCHARD, quartermaster
William LeBEL, quartermaster
Wilfrid C. CARON, seaman
Louis BERNIER, seaman
William MORIN, seaman
Eugène MONFORT, seaman
William DOYLE, seaman
Auguste ST-MICHEL, seaman
Alfred TREMBLAY, seaman
James BRACE, seaman
Eugène NADEAU, seaman
George GOSSELIN, laundryman

Expedition on board the schooner *Minnie Maud*, 1912-1913
J.-E. BERNIER, Captain
Napoléon CHASSÉ
John LeBEL
William LeBEL
Wilfrid C. CARON
G. WILSON
G. LAWSON
Alfred TREMBLAY
A.B. READER

Expedition on board the *Guide*, 1914-1915
J.-E. BERNIER, Captain
Wilfrid C. CARON, First Officer
Claude VIGNEAU
Joseph-Robert LESSARD
LECOURT
Louis BERNIER
V. PICARD
Rudolph FRANKE
Arthur HAACKS

Expedition on board the *Guide*, 1916-1917
J.-E. BERNIER, Captain
Wilfrid C. CARON, First Officer
Raoul HARVEY, Second Officer
Harry ARCAND, Chief Engineer
Johnny VIGNEAULT
Joseph-Robert LESSARD
M. GAGNON
V. PICARD
Ludger LEMIEUX
LANDRY

***Arctic's* expedition, 1922**
John Davidson CRAIG, expedition leader
J.-E. BERNIER, Captain
Lazare-Désiré MORIN, First Officer
Léonidas LEMIEUX, Second Officer
Leslie D. LIVINGSTONE, Doctor
W.H. GRANT, secretary
Major R.A. LOGAN, surveyor
L.O. BROWN, surveyor and meteorologist
T.P. REILLY, assistant surveyor
G.H. VALIQUETTE, cinematographer
C.J. BLAIR, radio operator
C.E. WILCOX, Inspector, RCMP
F. McINNES, Corporal, RCMP
B.C. JAKEMAN, Corporal RCMP
H.P. FRIEL Constable, RCMP
C.G. FAIRMAN, Constable, RCMP
F.L. FIELDER, Constable, RCMP
H.J. MUST, Constable, RCMP
E. ANSTEAD, Constable, RCMP
H.P. LEE, Constable, RCMP
W.B. MacGREGOR, Constable, RCMP
Albert ThÉRIAULT Chief Engineer
Philippe LAPERRIÈRE, Second Engineer
Gaston BARRAS, oiler
Lucien DENDRON, oiler
Albert LECLERC, stoker
Henri LEGRAND, stoker
Josaphat BOULANGER, stoker
Donat BERTRAND, stoker
Honoré MORIN, cook
Émile DESCHÊNES, cook's assistant
George-J. VINET, steward
Gérard DUBOIS, assistant steward
J.-E. VAILLANCOURT, waiter
Samuel FLEURY, waiter
Adjutor LECLERC, boatswain
Napoléon NORMAND, quartermaster

Claude VIGNEAU, quartermaster
Napoléon CHASSÉ, quartermaster
Joseph-W. POITRAS seaman
Walter PETERS, seaman
Hypolite ARSENAULT, seaman
Alfred LÉVESQUE, seaman

***Arctic's* expedition, 1923**
J.D. CRAIG, expedition leader
J.E. BERNIER, Captain
Lazare-Désiré MORIN, First Officer (41*)
Léonidas LEMIEUX, Second Officer (49)
Wifrid C. CARON**, Third Officer (35)
Leslie D. LIVINGSTONE, doctor
Desmond O'CONNELL***, secretary
Hon. Louis-Alfred-Adhémar RIVET, judge
Wilfred DUVAL, interpreter
François BIRON, counsel, clerk
Adrien FALARDEAU, counsel for the crown
Léopold TELLIER, counsel for the defence
Georges VALIQUETTE, cinematographer
Franck D. HENDERSON, surveyor
William-George EARL, radio operator
Albert ThÉRIAULT, Chief Engineer (42)
Philippe LAPERRIÈRE, Second Engineer (54)
Xavier LEMELIN, oiler (23)
Arthur GOUPIL, oiler (18)
Louis VOYER, stoker
J.-B. POTVIN, stoker
Charles FRÉDÉRICK, stoker
Adélard CARON, stoker
Adjutor CARON, cook
Edgar RUEL, cook's assistant
Eugène BLOUIN, steward
Jules GOSSELIN, assistant steward

* Captain Bernier indicated the ages of some of his men who were on the 1923 expedition in a private document. Carol and Louis Terrien Archives.

** Wilfrid Caron drowned in the St. Lawrence on the way to the Arctic.

*** Claude Vigneau was a member of the group who tried to save Caron. His journal (ANQ) describes how O'Connell thought he saw his companion in the water, and how he drowned when he jumped out of the lifeboat to look for him. He mentions five others who were with him in the lifeboat, but who are not included in the crew list: Messrs. Shotwell, Michelson, Semple, Tredgold and Soper.

J.-A. ST-PIERRE, waiter
O. OUELLET, waiter
Claude VIGNEAU boatswain
Joseph-M.POITRAS, carpenter and quartermaster (43)
Ludger LEMIEUX carpenter and quartermaster (37)
Napoléon CHASSÉ, quartermaster (39)
J. BARRETTE, quartermaster (on crew list, but never appeared)
Alfred LÉVESQUE, seaman
Hypolite ARSENAULT, seaman
Émile LEBLANC, seaman

***Arctic's* expedition, 1924**
Franck D. HENDERSON, expedition leader
J.-E. BERNIER, Captain
Lazare-Désiré MORIN, First Officer
Léonidas LEMIEUX, Second Officer
Napoléon CHASSÉ, Third Officer
Leslie D. Livingstone, Doctor
J. Dewey SOPER, naturalist
Ludlow J. WEEKS, geologist
Dr. Alfred Sidney JOHNSON, optometrist and geographer
Roy TASH, cinematographer
William (Bill) F. CHOAT, radio operator
Richard FINNIE, assistant radio operator and photographer
Albert ThÉRIAULT, Chief Engineer
Philippe LAPERRIÈRE Second Engineer
Xavier LEMELIN, oiler
Louis OUELLET, oiler
Léon GAGNON stoker
Albert LECLERC, stoker
Louis VOYER, stoker
Viateur BOURGET, stoker
Télesphore LACHANCE, cook
Adolphe GAMACHE, cook's assistant
J.-A. CLOUTIER, steward
Jules GOSSELIN, assistant steward
Charles-Auguste CHOUINARD, waiter
Antoine POIRIER, waiter
Claude VIGNEAU, boatswain
Joseph-M. POITRAS, carpenter and quartermaster
Hypolite ARSENAULT, quartermaster
Alfred LÉVESQUE, quartermaster
Lionel ST-PIERRE, seaman
Émile LEBLANC, seaman
Alphonse CYR, seaman
Fabien ARSENAULT, seaman
and six members of the RCMP

Captain Bernier's last expedition on board the *Arctic*, 1925

George Patton MacKENZIE, expedition leader
J.-E. BERNIER, Captain
L.-Désiré MORIN, First Officer
Léonidas LEMIEUX, Second Officer
Napoléon CHASSÉ, Third Officer,
Harwood E. STEELE, journalist, and expedition leader's secretary
Leslie D. LIVINGSTONE, doctor
Ludlow J. WEEKS, geologist
George H. VALIQUETTE, cinematographer
Inspector WILCOX, RCMP
Sergeant A.H. JOY, RCMP
and three RCMP officers
NUQALLAQ, prisoner
Robert FOSTER, radio operator
Richard FINNIE, radio operator and photographer
Albert THÉRIAULT, Chief Engineer
Eudore ROY, Second Engineer
L.J.L. CHALIFOUR, Third Engineer and electrician
Edouard PLANTE, oiler
Antoine HAMELIN, oiler
Josephat BOULANGER, oiler
Gérard HAMELIN stoker
Sylvio DESCHÊNES, stoker
Wilfrid GRANCHER, stoker
Joseph LEMIEUX stoker
Joseph THIBAULT, cook
Émile DESCHÊNES, cook's assistant
J.-A. CLOUTIER, steward
Jules GOSSELIN, assistant steward
Freddy NICOLE, carpenter and waiter
Charles-A. CHOUINARD, waiter
Paul LALIBERTÉ, waiter
Joseph MERCIER, boatswain
Joseph-M. POITRAS, carpenter and quartermaster
Lionel ST-PIERRE, quartermaster
Alcide GAGNÉ , quartermaster
Florian SIMARD, seaman
Maurine CÔTÉ, seaman
Thomas MARCOUX, seaman

VIII. Letter from Fridtjof Nansen

Lysaker
10 September 1904

Dear Captain Bernier,

I have not been able to obtain any reliable information with regard to the plan of your forthcoming expedition, but as far as I can gather from occasional notes in the papers, I understand that you have bought the "Gauss," and intend with her to sail through Behring Strait, and to make a drift across the North Polar Basin. This is the one expedition which I have advocated, and which I have been looking forward for, because in my opinion such an expedition would give us a material of scientific observations, compared with which those of other arctic expeditions in the future would be of little importance. But the most important part of the scientific work of the expedition would certainly be the oceanographical observations, as with the modern instruments and the drift ice to work from, it would be possible to do work which would be of fundamental importance for our knowledge of oceanography in general and to make the North Polar Sea in several respects the best known part of the ocean. It is certainly unnecessary for me to tell you this, but as I have perhaps more experience than anybody else in arctic oceanography, I write to say that if I can help you in any way with your oceanographical equipment, I shall be pleased to do so. I think that such a unique opportunity for oceanographical research should be made use of as well as possible, and with the best and most modern instruments and methods that we now dispose of. I hope that you are going to take with you a man who is specially trained for oceanographical research and that this man will have no other scientific department to take care of, for he will certainly get his hands full with the oceanography alone, if it shall be well done. I can say so much from my own sad experience. I only wish that I had nothing else to do on board the *Fram*. If you would send the man over to the Central Laboratory for the International Study of the Sea in Christiana of which I am the director, we would certainly do our best to teach him all our modern methods of oceanography, which I feel justified to say are great improvements from all older methods. I believe also that through the aid of the Central Laboratory, you would be able to get a better and more complete outfit of oceanographical instruments than you can otherwise obtain, and in the name of the Central Laboratory I can assure you of our readiness to assist you. We have now succeeded in constructing current-meters, deep-sea thermometers, water-bottles, etc., which are satisfactory according to modern requirements, and we have tested them by numerous experiments and expeditions. I now only long to see them used in the North Polar Basin, and were it not that life is so short, and there are also other things to be done, I would certainly not hesitate to make another drift with the *Fram* from the sea north of Behring Strait.

Having had sad experience of how much time and how many unique opportunities for making important discoveries are lost through not having had the necessary training in the special scientific work before one starts on the expedition, I think it to be my duty to trespass on your valuable time in this way.
Wishing you success in your great undertaking,

I remain,
Yours very sincerely,

Fridtjof Nansen*

* *Master Mariner*, p. 392-394. Captain Bernier had added, at the bottom of this letter: "Needless to say, with such encouragement from the greatest authority on polar work, I felt justified in pushing my plans vigorously."

IX. Proceedings

The ceremony accompanying the erection of a cross on Melville Island, 13 June 1909*

In the year of our Lord, nineteen-hundred-and-nine, Sunday, the thirteenth day of the month of June, at three o'clock in the afternoon, there took place, on the summit of the mountain, located northeast of Winter Harbour on Melville Island (Sir W. Edward Parry's (1819-1820) North-East Hill at Winter Harbour), the solemn inauguration of the "Commemorative Cross" from the 1908-1909 cruise of the Canadian Government Ship, the steamer *Arctic*.

The ceremony was presided over by Joseph-Elzéar Bernier Esq., Captain of the steamer *Arctic*, in command of the present cruise, and Special Royal Commissioner charged with taking possession, in the name of the Dominion of Canada, of the arctic islands located between the meridians of 60° and 141° West, as far as the latitude of 90° North, transferred to Canada, in North America, by the Imperial Government in 1880.

On this occasion the Catholic choir of the steamer *Arctic*, under the direction of Mr. Georges Gosselin, of the Engineering Department, gave a sacred concert, specially prepared for the occasion, and with the following order of service:

The commander opened the ceremony with the sign of the cross and with the recital, in concert and in a loud voice, of the first ten of the rosary; then Mr. Georges Gosselin, supported by the choir, sang the verse:

"O Crux Ave, Spes Unica."

After the recital of the second ten of the rosary, which followed the singing of the "Crux Ave," Mr. George Gosselin gave the canticle "Long live Jesus! Long live his Cross!" which was followed by the third ten of the rosary.

Mr. Émile Bolduc, Second Engineer then intoned the psalm "Laudate Dominum omnes gentes."

This was followed by the fourth ten of the rosary, then Mr. Georges Gosselin intoned the canticle "Te Deum Laudamus." After which the fifth and last ten of the rosary was recited.

The ceremony ended with the "Benedicamus Domino," intoned by Mr. Georges Gosselin, while the congregation replied with "Deo Gratias," in powerful and sincere tones of faith and enthusiasm.

The captain then thanked those present for this act of Christian faith and patriotism that they had performed in the midst of the cold solitude of the northern wastes.

The cross erected on Melville Island, June 1909. [Bernier Collection, *Rapport officiel de l'expédition de 1908-1909*]

* ASTR. Original text by chronicler Fabien Vanasse.

The following gentlemen, all from the complement of the steamer *Arctic*, were present, and they signed their names to this act of taking possession of Canada's arctic regions, by the cross and in the name of Christ the Redeemer.
"Adveniat regnum Tuum."

Winter Harbour, Melville Island, Arctic Canada, Sunday 13 June 1909.

	J. E. Bernier	
Arthur Desjardins	Émile Bolduc	Georges Gosselin
Alfred Bourget	Johnny Leclerc	Ernest Lahaye
Paul Tremblay	Wilfrid Vaillancourt	J. Thibault
Jos. R. Goulet	Franck Hennessey	Thomas Holden
O. Robitaille	James Brace	Alphé Bouchard
Gédéon Gagné	Napoléon Chassé	
Dr. Joseph E. Bolduc	Fabien Vanasse, chronicler	

All the Catholic members of the *Arctic*'s crew were there, with the exception of the Chief Engineer, John von Koenig and quartermaster Jos. Lessard, who were on an expedition to Cape Providence, and Lieutenant Jules Morin, Dan Doyle and M. Bégin, who were on an expedition to Banks Island.

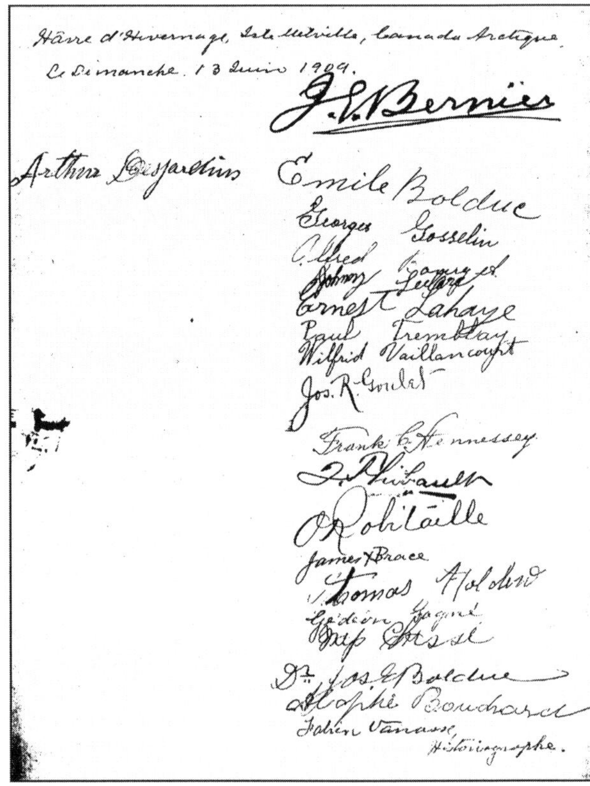

The signatories to the report on the ceremony accompanying the erection of a cross at Winter Harbour on Melville Island. [Vanasse Fonds, ASTR]

X. The J.-E. Bernier Fonds

The contents of the Joseph-Elzéar Fonds in the Archives of the Museum of the Collège de Lévis*

Series A: Printed works.
Inventory of the volumes preserved in Captain Bernier's private library. These volumes deal particularly with navigation and exploration, but also with subjects as varied as religion, politics and literature. This series contains 60 titles catalogued alphabetically by author's name.

Series B: Manuscripts.
Group I: Journals and log books, kept by the captains or engineers who worked on various vessels such as the *Ocean Eagle, Arctic,* S.S. *Franklin,* S.S. *Guide, St. Finbare,* C.G.S. *Champlain, Jeannette.*
17 files, arranged chronologically.

Group II: Journals and log books, kept by Captain Bernier. These documents refer to his voyages on board the numerous vessels that he commanded, describe techniques of marine navigation and pilotage on the St. Lawrence and describe his activities when he was director of the Lévis dry-dock and of the Québec prison. They also contain his activities in Ottawa towards an expedition to the North Pole as well as numerous details on all his voyages to the Arctic.
71 files, arranged chronologically.

* Research carried out in January 1974 by Guy Dinel, now head of the Archives Division, Université Laval. As I was refused access to this collection I cannot confirm whether it is still complete, nor the state of the documents and objects that it contains.

Series C: Photographs.
Photos taken during the *Arctic's* numerous expeditions to the arctic regions; landscapes, establishments, natives, hunting, fishing and navigation. There are also family photos and of ship building, views of Québec, L'Islet, Lauzon and Lévis during last century.

There are 23 albums in their original condition. They contain around 5,600 photos, of which in some cases there are several prints.

There are also 13 boxes filled with dozens of negatives of varying sizes and materials (glass plates, acetate etc.) as well as 170 slides (3½ x 3½) showing northern landscapes, and 3 films shot in the Far North.

Series D: Miscellaneous.
Albums containing newspaper clippings and reviews, copies of letters and files relating to marine and aerial navigation and to arctic exploration. It includes files on the Peary/Cook controversy, on Amundsen, Byrd, Macmillan, etc. There is also the correspondence between Captain Bernier and explorers and politicians between 1877 and 1934.
28 albums in their original condition.

Series E: Maps.
An impressive number of navigational charts.

In addition to these series of documents there are about 30 assorted objects: a sextant, a wooden bust, ink-well, clock, a carved bamboo cane, etc.

Bibliography

ALMOLKY, Bill. "Captain Bernier, a Forgotten Canadian Hero," *Star Weekly Magazine*, 22 August 1964.

APRIL, Jaqueline. "Les laboureurs de la mer: la garde côtière canadienne en mission dans l'Arctique chaque été," *North/Nord Vol.* 25, No 3, May/June 1978.

APPLETON, Thomas E. *Usque ad Mare. A History of the Canadian Coast Guard and Marine Services.* Ottawa: Queen's Printer.

Atlas historique du Québec, Québec ville et capital. Sainte-Foy: Presses de l'Université Laval, 2001.

AUDET, Michelle. *D'un coup d'aile.* Saint-Romuald: Éditions Sans âge, 1999.

BAILLARGEON, Samuel. *Littérature canadienne-française.* Montréal: Fides, 1957.

BÉLAND, Mario. "Portraits of Captain Bernier's Ships," *Cap-aux-Diamants,* No. 4, Winter 1997.

BÉLANGER, Léon. *L'Islet, 1677-1977.* Privately printed, 1977.

BÉLANGER, Réal. *Wilfrid Laurier, quand la politique devient passion.* Québec: Presses de l'Université Laval, 1986.

BERGER, Carl. "The True North Strong and Free." In: *Interpreting Canada's Past,* Vol. II, *After Confederation,* edited by J.M. Bumsted. Toronto: Oxford University Press, 1986, p. 157-174.

BERNIER, Cyril. *Tricentenaire des Bernier au Canada.* Association des familles Bernier d'Amérique, Inc., 1968.

—. *Les Bernier en Nouvelle-France, 1650-1750.* Éditions Cyril Bernier, 1996.

BERNIER, Joseph-Elzéar. *Master Mariner and Arctic Explorer. A Narrative of Sixty Years at Sea from the Logs and Yarns of Captain J.E. Bernier, FRGS, FRES.* Ottawa: Le Droit, 1939.

—. *Report on the Dominion of Canada Government Expedition to the Arctic Islands and the Hudson Strait on Board the C.G.S. "Arctic" 1906-1907.* Ottawa: King's Printer, 1909.

—. *Report on the Dominion of Canada Government Expedition to the Arctic Islands and Hudson Strait on board the D.G.S. Arctic.*" Ottawa: Government Printing Bureau, 1910.

—. *Rapport sur la croisière faite par le trois-mats mixte "Arctic" de la puissance du Canada dans l'Archipel arctique et le détroit d'Hudson.* Ottawa: Imprimerie nationale, 1910.

—. *Report on the Dominion Government Expedition to the Northern Waters and Arctic Archipelago on the D.G.S. "Arctic" in 1910.* Ottawa: King's Printer, 1911.

—. "The Arctic Regions of Canada. An Address by Captain J.E. Bernier before the Empire Club of Canada, on December 20,1909." In *The Empire Club of Canada Speeches, 1909-1910.* Toronto: Hopkins, J. Castell, 1910, p. 67-76.

—. "Our Northern Heritage. An Address by Captain J.E. Bernier, F.R.G.S. before the Empire Club of Canada, Toronto, Thursday, October 7, 1926." In *The Empire Club of Canada Speeches, 1926.* Toronto: Empire Club, 1927, p. 222-228.

BERTON, Pierre. "Introduction." In *Great Canadians. A Century of Achievement.* Toronto: McClelland and Stewart, 1965, p. 12.

BOURGET, Magdeleine. "Un Caron chez les Inuit," *L'Ancêtre,* Vol. 29, summer 2003, p. 305-309.

BROWN, R.H.C. *The Canadian Polar Expedition or Will Canada Claim her Own?* Ottawa, 1901.

Chopin, René. *Le cœur en exil.* Montréal: G. Crès, 1913.

Chouinard, F.-Xavier. "Un grand explorateur des mers arctiques, le capitaine Joseph-Elzéar Bernier," *Bulletin de la Société de géographie du Québec*, Vol. 20, Nos. 4&5, September/December 1926.

Cloutier, Stéphane. "Dans le sillage du capitaine Joseph-Elzéar Bernier," *Le Toit du monde,* Vol. 1, No. 1, spring 2002, p. 16-25.

—. "À la rencontre des deux mondes," *Le Toit du monde,* Vol. 1, No. 2, fall 2002, p. 34-39.

—. "Alfred Tremblay, véteran du désert blanc," *Le Toit du monde*, Vol. 1, No. 4, spring 2002, p. 28-30.

—. "Noël à bord du C.G.S. *Arctic,*" *Le Toit du Monde,* Vol. 1, No. 3, winter 2002, p. 10-15.

—. "Le capitaine Bernier, explorateur et conférencier du Grand Nord," *Le Toit du monde,* Vol. 2, No. 1, summer 2002, p. 24-27.

Coulon, Jacques. "Bernier à la conquête de l'Arctique." In *Sélection du Reader's Digest,* April 1978, p. 56-61.

Craig, J.D. *Canada's Arctic Islands. Log of Canadian Expedition 1922.* Ottawa: F.A. Acland, 1923.

Davies, Blodwen. "He has Added Half a Million Square Miles to Canada," *Canadian Magazine,* February 1927.

—. "Heroes of the White Frontier," *Onward,* 14 August 1955, p. 522-523.

Delgado, James P. *Across the Top of the World.* Vancouver: Douglas and McIntyre, 1999.

Deschênes, Gaston. *L'année des Anglais, la Côte-du-Sud à l'heure de la conquête.* Sillery: Éditions Septentrion, 1988.

Dexter, Grant. "Who Owns the Arctic?" *Canadian Magazine,* March 1930.

Dinwoodie, D.H. "Arctic Controversy: the Byrd-Macmillan Expedition Example," *The Canadian Historical Review,* Vol. 53, No. 1, Mach 1972, p. 51-65.

Ellis, Frank H. "Arctic Airfield Survey," *The Beaver,* September 1945, p. 22-25.

Étienne, Jean-Louis. *Le marcheur du Pôle.* Paris: Éditions Robert Laffront, 1986.

Fairley, T.C. and Charles E. Israel. *The True North, the Story of Captain Joseph Bernier.* Toronto: Macmillan, 1957; 1964.

Finnie, Richard S. "Farewell Voyages, Bernier and the Arctic," *The Beaver,* summer 1974, p. 44-54.

—. *Canada Moves North.* New York: Macmillan, 1942.

—. "Joseph-Elzéar Bernier (1852-1934)," *Arctic*, Vol. 39, September 1986, p. 278-279.

—. "Bernier and the Arctic," *Explorers' Journal*, September 1975, p. 130-139.

Franck, Alain. *Naviguer sur le fleuve au temps passé, 1860-1960.* Sainte-Foy: Les Publications du Québec, 2000.

—. "Joseph-Elzéar Bernier, 1852-1934. Mythe et légende vivante," *L'Escale nautique,* No. 30, summer 2001, p. 5-8.

Frazer, Robin. "Captain Joseph-Elzéar Bernier, Dean of Arctic Explorers and Architect of Canadian Sovereignty in the Arctic," *Inuit today*, Vol. 9, April 1981, p. 36-40.

Gagnon, Angèle. *Le village de nos ancêtres, L'Islet.* Éditions Angèle Gagnon, 1994.

Gagnon, Serge. *Mariage et familles au temps de Papineau.* Sainte Foy: Presses de l'Université Laval, 1993.

Green, C.W. "Report of Mr. C.W. Green on Trip to Mercy Bay, Banks Island." In Bernier, J.-E., *Report on the Dominion of Canada Government Expedition to the Arctic Islands and Hudson Strait on Board the D.G.S. "Arctic."* Ottawa: Government Printing Bureau, 1910 p. 147-161.

Grant, Shelagh D. *Arctic Justice. On Trial for Murder, Pond Inlet, 1923.* Montréal: McGill-Queen's University Press, 2002.

Hamelin, Louis-Edmond. *Nordicité canadienne.* Montréal: Hurtubise HMH, 1975.

Harvey, Azade. *Auguste LeBourdais, naufragé en 1871 aux Îles-de-la-Madeleine.* Montréal: Éditions Intrinsèque, 1979.

Johnston, Kenneth. "Canada's Title to the Arctic Islands," *Canadian Historical Review,* Vol. 14, March 1933, p. 24-41.

Ketchum, W.Q. "Last of the Great Master Mariners," *Canadian Geographical Journal*, Vol. 15, No. 3, September 1937, p. 150-153.

Kirouac, André. *Quand l'Église rhythmait la vie à Notre-Dame-de-Bonsecours de L'Islet.* L'Islet: Fabrique Notre-Dame-de-Bonsecours, 1993.

Lacoursière, Jacques. *Canada-Québec: synthèse historique, 1534-2000.* Sillery: Éditions du Septentrion, 2000.

Lacoursière, Jacques and Bouchard, Claude. "Vers l'Ouest, 1887-1908," *Notre histoire Québec-Canada*, Vol. 8. Montréal" Éditions Format, 1972

Larsen, Henry, with Frank R. Shaw and Edward Omholt-Jensen. *The Big Ship.* Toronto/Montreal: McClelland and Stewart, 1967.

Landry, Yves. *Orphelines en France, pionnières au Canada. Les Filles du roi au XVIIe siècle.* Montréal: Leméac, 1992.

Lemelin, Roger. "Joseph Elzéar Bernier, the Master Mariner." In: *Great Canadians, a Century of Achievement.* Toronto: McClelland and Stewart, 1965, p. 31-34.

Leroi-Gourham, André. "Psychologie de l'explorateur," In *Les explorateurs célèbres.* Paris: Éditions Lucien Mazenod, 1965.

Linteau, Paul-André. *Histoire du Québec contemporain, de la Conféderation à la crise (1867-1929).* Montréal: Éditions du Boréal Express, 1979.

Low, Albert Peter. *Report on the Dominion Government Expedition to Hudson Bay and the Arctic Islands on Board the D.G.S. Neptune 1903-1904.* Ottawa: Government Printing Bureau, 1906.

MacDonald, Robert St. John. *The Arctic Frontier.* Toronto: University of Toronto Press, 1966.

MacEAchern, Alan. "Edward MacDonald's Arctic Diary, 1910-1911," *The Island Magazine,* fall/winter 1999, p. 30-40.

Marcil, Eileen Reid. *The Charley-Man. A History of Wooden Shipbuilding at Québec, 1763-1893.* Kingston: Quarry Press, 1995.

—. *On chantait "Charley-Man." La construction de grands voiliers à Québec de 1763 à 1893.* Sainte-Foy: Les éditions GID and Eileen Reid Marcil, 2000.

—. *Au rhythme des marées; l'histoire des chantiers maritimes Davie.* Toronto: McClelland and Stewart, 1997.

Mastin, Howard. "The Arctic in the National Interest." In: *Fireproof House to Third Option, Studies in the Theory and Practice of Canadian Foreign Policy,* edited by Peter St. John. Winnipeg: University of Manitoba, Department of Political Science, 1977, p. 103-134.

McClymont, Ian. "Laurier et l'Arctique," *L'Archiviste,* September/October 1988, p. 10-12.

Minotto, Claude. *La frontière arctique du Canada: les expéditions de Joseph-Elzéar Bernier (1895-1925).* Montreal: Master's thesis in history. McGill University, 1975.

Morin, O.-J. "Report of O.J. Morin to Victoria and Banks Island." In Bernier, J.-E. *Report on the Dominion of Canada Government Expedition to the Arctic Islands and Hudson Strait on Board the D.G.S. "Arctic."* Ottawa: Government Printing Bureau, 1910, p. 126-138.

Ollivier, Maurice, editor. *British North America Acts and Selected Statutes, 1867-1962.* Ottawa: Queen's Printer, 1962.

Osborne, Season L. *Closing the Front door of the Arctic: Capt. Joseph E. Bernier's Role in Canadian Arctic Sovereignty.* Ottawa: Master's thesis in journalism, Carleton University, 2003.

Pépin, Marcel. "L'histoire sommeille sous la pierre," *North/Nord,* Vol. 25, No. 3, May/June 1978, p. 16-19.

Potvin, Damase. "Capitaine Joseph-Elzéar Bernier." In *Les oubliés.* Québec: Roch Poulin, 1944, p. 51-62.

Prévost, Roland. "La vie aventureuse du capitaine J.E. Bernier," *La Revue populaire,* February 1932.

Proulx, G.-E. "Le capitaine J.-E. Bernier (1852-1934) aura son monument au cimetière de Lauzon," *Bulletin de la Société d'histoire régionale de Lévis,* No. 14, summer 1984, p. 25-27.

—. "Le monument Bernier," *Bulletin de la Société d'histoire régionale de Lévis,* No. 15, fall 1984, p. 22-23.

—. "Le rôle du capitaine J.E. Bernier dans l'Arctique," *Bulletin de la Société d'histoire regionale de Lévis,* Nos. 18 and 19, summer/fall 1985, p. 32-36.

Robitaille, Benoît. "Évolution cartographique de la rive sud du détroit d'Hudson du XVIIe au XXe siècle: le fjord de Salluit," *Hommes et Terres du Nord,* 3, p. 125-130.

Robitaille, Yolande Dorion. *Captain J.E. Bernier's Contribution to Canadian Sovereignty in the Arctic.* Ottawa: Department of Indian and Northern Affairs, 1978.

—. "Joseph-Elzéar Bernier, capitaine en toute saison," *North/Nord,* Vol. 25, No. 3, May/June 1978, p. 28-35.

Rosa, Narcisse. *La construction des navires à Québec et ses environs, grèves et naufrages.* Québec: Léger Brousseau, 1897.

RUMILLY, Robert. *Le frère Marie-Victorin et son temps.* Montréal: Les Frères des Écoles chrétiennes, 1949.

SACCO, Michel. "Réal Bouvier, navigateur et journaliste," *L'Escale nautique*, No. 24, winter 2000, p. 4.

SAINT-HILAIRE, Mélanie, "Ilitataa petit navire," *L'Actualité,* 1 May 2002, p. 53-54.

SAMSON, Roch, coordinator. *Histoire de Lévis-Lotbinière.* Québec: Institut québecois de recherche sur la culture, Presses de l'Université Laval, 1996.

SMITH, Gordon W. "Canada's Arctic Archipelago: 100 Years of Canadian Jurisdiction, Part I: The Transfer," *North/Nord,* spring 1980; "Part II: Making the North Canadian," *North/Nord,* summer 1980.

—. "A Bit of Bernier," *North/Nord,* Vol. 29, No. 2, summer 1982, p. 52-57.

SPIGELMAN, Martin. *Wilfrid Laurier.* Don Mills Ontario: Fitzhenry & Whiteside, 1978.

STEELE, Harwood. "The Captain Goes Ashore," *Canadian Magazine,* March 1935.

TAYLOR, Andrew. *Geographical Discovery: Exploration in the Queen Elizabeth Islands.* Ottawa: Geographical Branch, Department of Mines and Technical Surveys, 1955.

TERRIEN, Paul. *Les mémoires de J.E. Bernier, le dernier des grands capitaines.* Montréal: Les Quinze, 1983.

—. *Québec à l'âge de la voile.* Hull: Éditions Asticou, 1985.

TESSIER, Claude. "Un explorateur méconnu de l'Arctique: Alfred Tremblay," *North/Nord,* May-June, 1978, p. 46.

TREMBLAY, Alfred. *Cruise of the "Minnie Maud". Arctic seas and Hudson Bay 1910-1911 and 1912-1913.* Québec: The Arctic Exchange and Publishing Ltd., 1921.

TREMBLAY, Gilberte. *Bernier, capitaine à 17 ans.* Montréal: Leméac, 1959 and 1972.

TREMBLAY, Jack. *Captain White Bear, the Story of Captain Joseph Bernier, Explorer.* Fredericton: Brunswick Press, 1967.

VALLAT, Gustave. *À la conquête du Pôle Nord, l'explorateur norvégien Fridtjof Nansen.* Limoges: Maison Eugène Ardant & Cie., 1897.

WALLACE, Frederick William. *Wooden Ships and Iron Men.* Toronto: Hodder and Stoughton, 1924.

—. *In the Wake of the Wind-Ships.* Toronto: Musson Book Co., 1927.

WATT, F.W. "The Theme of Canada's Century," *Dalhousie Review,* summer 1958, p. 151-166.

WEBB, Ken. "A Ship for All Seasons," *North/Nord*, Vol. 25, No. 3, 1978, p. 20-27.

WOOLLACOTT, Arthur P. "He Saved the Arctic for Canada," *MacLean's Magazine,* 1 January 1929.

ZASLOW, Morris. *The Opening of the Canadian North: 1870-1914.* Toronto: McClelland and Stewart, 1971.

—. The *Northern Expansion of Canada: 1914-1967.* Toronto: McClelland and Stewart, 1988.

Index